Art and Architecture

From the middle of the eighteenth century, with the growth of travel at home and abroad and the increase in leisure for the wealthier classes, the arts became the subject of more widespread appreciation and discussion. The rapid expansion of book and periodical publishing in this area both reflected and encouraged interest in art and art history among the wider reading public. This series throws light on the development of visual culture and aesthetics. It covers topics from the Grand Tour to the great exhibitions of the nineteenth century, and includes art criticism and biography.

Some Account of Gothic Architecture in Spain

An architect and architectural theorist, George Edmund Street (1824–81) was one of the key proponents of the 'High Victorian' Gothic style in nineteenth-century Britain. He is best known as the mind behind London's Royal Courts of Justice. Elected an associate of the Royal Academy in 1866, Street became its professor of architecture in 1880. In 1874 he received the gold medal of the Royal Institute of British Architects, and he served as the Institute's president in 1881. This two-volume work was first published in 1865, and is reissued here in its 1914 version, edited by the American art historian Georgiana Goddard King (1871–1939), who reminds her readers that Street's guide was pioneering in its time, and remains indispensable to the understanding of the Gothic era in Europe. The work takes the reader on a tour of Spain's most ancient and architecturally important towns and cities.

Cambridge University Press has long been a pioneer in the reissuing of out-of-print titles from its own backlist, producing digital reprints of books that are still sought after by scholars and students but could not be reprinted economically using traditional technology. The Cambridge Library Collection extends this activity to a wider range of books which are still of importance to researchers and professionals, either for the source material they contain, or as landmarks in the history of their academic discipline.

Drawing from the world-renowned collections in the Cambridge University Library and other partner libraries, and guided by the advice of experts in each subject area, Cambridge University Press is using state-of-the-art scanning machines in its own Printing House to capture the content of each book selected for inclusion. The files are processed to give a consistently clear, crisp image, and the books finished to the high quality standard for which the Press is recognised around the world. The latest print-on-demand technology ensures that the books will remain available indefinitely, and that orders for single or multiple copies can quickly be supplied.

The Cambridge Library Collection brings back to life books of enduring scholarly value (including out-of-copyright works originally issued by other publishers) across a wide range of disciplines in the humanities and social sciences and in science and technology.

Some Account of Gothic Architecture in Spain

VOLUME 2

GEORGE EDMUND STREET

EDITED BY GEORGIANA GODDARD KING

CAMBRIDGE
UNIVERSITY PRESS

CAMBRIDGE
UNIVERSITY PRESS

University Printing House, Cambridge, CB2 8BS, United Kingdom

Cambridge University Press is part of the University of Cambridge.

It furthers the University's mission by disseminating knowledge in the pursuit of
education, learning and research at the highest international levels of excellence.

www.cambridge.org
Information on this title: www.cambridge.org/9781108071178

© in this compilation Cambridge University Press 2015

This edition first published 1914
This digitally printed version 2015

ISBN 978-1-108-07117-8 Paperback

This book reproduces the text of the original edition. The content and language reflect
the beliefs, practices and terminology of their time, and have not been updated.

Cambridge University Press wishes to make clear that the book, unless originally published
by Cambridge, is not being republished by, in association or collaboration with,
or with the endorsement or approval of, the original publisher or its successors in title.

GOTHIC ARCHITECTURE IN SPAIN

SOME ACCOUNT

OF

GOTHIC ARCHITECTURE IN SPAIN

BY

GEORGE EDMUND STREET, F.S.A.

EDITED BY

GEORGIANA GODDARD KING

SEGOVIA FROM THE ALCAZAR

VOL. II

LONDON AND TORONTO

J. M. DENT & SONS LTD.
NEW YORK: E. P. DUTTON & CO. 1914

CONTENTS

APPENDIX

LIST OF ILLUSTRATIONS

GROUND PLANS

GOTHIC ARCHITECTURE
IN SPAIN

CHAPTER XII

VALENCIA

FROM Toledo I took the railway to Valencia. But as the junction of the Toledo branch with the main line is a small station of the meanest description, and as there were three or four hours to dispose of before the mail train passed, I went back as far as Aranjuez, intending to dine there. The station is close to the palace, a large, bald, and uninteresting pile. The principal inn is kept by an Englishman with a French wife, and as it was not the right season for Aranjuez we had great difficulty in getting anything. In truth the French wife was a tartar, and advised us to go back again; but finally, the husband having interceded, she relented so far as to produce some eggs and bacon.

Aranjuez seemed to consist mainly of the palace and its stables, and to be afflicted with even more than the usual plague of dust: but in the spring no doubt it is in a more pleasant state, and may, I hope, justify the landlord's assertion that there is nothing in the world to compare with it!

Late in the evening we started for Valencia: it was a bright moonlight night, so that I was able, when I woke and looked out, to see that the country we traversed was an endless plain of extremely uninteresting character and that we lost little by not seeing it. I should have preferred leaving the railway altogether, and going by Cuença on my way to Valencia; but time was altogether wanting for this détour, though I have no doubt that Cuença would well repay a visit.

At Almanza, where the lines for Alicante and Valencia separate, there is a very picturesque castle perched upon a rock above the town, and here the dreary, uninteresting country, which extends with but short intervals all the way from Vitoria, is changed for the somewhat mountainous Valencian district, which everywhere shows signs of the highest luxuriance and

II   A cultivation, resulting almost entirely from the extreme care and industry with which the artificial irrigation is managed. The villages are numerous, and around them are beautiful vineyards, groves of orange-trees, and rice-fields; whilst here and there clumps of tall palm-trees give a very Eastern aspect to the landscape. The churches seemed, as far as I could judge, to be all modern and most uninteresting. After passing the hilly country, a broad plain is crossed to Valencia. Here the system of irrigation, said to be an inheritance from the Moors, is evidently most complete. Every field has its stream of water running rapidly along, and the main drawback to such a system, so completely carried out, is that the beds of the rivers are generally all but dry, their water being all diverted into other and more useful channels. The Valencian farm-labourers' dress is quite worth looking at. They wear short, loose, white linen trousers and jackets, brilliantly coloured *mantas*—generally scarlet—thrown over their shoulders, coloured handkerchiefs over their heads, and violet scarfs round their waists. They have a quaint way of sitting at work in the fields, with their knees up to their ears, like so many grasshoppers; and their skin is so well bronzed that one can hardly believe them to be of European blood. They are said to be vindictive and passionate, but they are also, so far as I saw them, very lively, merry, and talkative. The farms appear to be very large, and when I passed the farmers were hard at work threshing their rice. This is all done by horses and mules on circular threshing-floors. In many of the farms eight or ten pairs of horse may be seen at work at the same time on as many threshing-floors, and the effect of such a scene is striking and novel.

As we went into Valencia we passed on the right the enormous new Plaza de Toros, said to be the finest in Spain. Railroads will, I suppose, rather tend to develop the national love for this institution, and this theatre must have been built with some such impression, for otherwise it is difficult to believe that a city of a hundred and twenty thousand inhabitants could build a theatre capable of containing about a tenth of the whole population!

The national vehicle of Valencia is the *tartana*, a covered cart on two wheels, with a slight attempt only at springs, and rendered gay by the crimson curtains which are hung across the front. Jumping into one of these, we soon found ourselves at the excellent Fonda del Cid, whose title reminds us that we are on classic ground in this city of Valencia del Cid.

The Cid took the city from the Moors after a siege of twenty months, in A.D. 1094, established himself here, and ruled till his death, in A.D. 1099. The Moors then regained possession for a short time, but in A.D. 1238 or 1239 it was finally re-taken from them by the Spaniards.

It is hardly to be expected that anything would remain of Christian work earlier than A.D. 1095, or, more probably, than A.D. 1239, and this I found to be the case. The cathedral, dedicated to the Blessed Virgin, is a church of only moderate interest, its interior having been overlaid everywhere with columns, pilasters, and cornices of plaster, and the greater part of the exterior being surrounded so completely with houses that no good view can be obtained of it.

The ground-plan is, however, still so far untouched as to be perfectly intelligible (1). It has a nave and aisles of four bays, transepts projecting one bay beyond the aisles, and a lofty lantern or Cimborio over the Crossing. The choir is one bay only in length, and has a three-sided apse. An aisle of the same width as that of the nave is continued round the choir, and has the rare arrangement of two polygonal chapels opening in each of its bays. The vaulting compartments in the aisle are therefore cincopartite, those throughout the rest of the church being quadripartite. A grand Chapter-house stands detached to the south of the west bay of the nave, and an octagonal steeple, called " El Micalete," abuts against the north-west angle of the west front.

The ritual arrangements are all modern, and on the usual plan. The western bay of the church is open;- the stalls of the Coro occupy the second and third bays; and metal rails across the fourth bay of the nave and the Crossing connect the Coro with the Capilla mayor.

The evidence as to the age of the various portions of the building is sufficient to enable us to date most of the work rather accurately. The foundation of the church is recorded by an inscription over the south transept door to have been laid in 1262:[1] and some portion of the exterior is, I have no doubt, of this date. The whole south transept front, a portion of the sacristy on the east side, and the exterior of the apse, are all of fine early-pointed style, and, in the absence of any specific

---

[1] Anno Domini m.cc.lxii. x. Kal. Jul. fuit
Positus Primus lapis in Ecclesia Beatæ
Mariæ sedis Valentinæ per venerabilem
Patrem Dominum Fratem Andream Tertium
Valentinæ civitatis Episcopum.

statement of their date, might well have been thought to belong to quite the commencement of the century. But I think a careful examination of the detail will show that the work is possibly not so early as it looks: and it has so much in common with Italian work of the same age, that we need not be surprised to find in it features which would nevertheless be inconsistent with its execution in the middle of the thirteenth century in any work of the north of Europe. The south transept façade consists of a round-arched doorway, with a horizontal cornice over it, and a large and fine lancet-window above. The door and window have respectively six and three jamb-shafts, and the abaci throughout are square in plan. The archivolt of the doorway is very rich: it includes five orders of enriched dog-tooth moulding, one order of seraphs in niches, one of chevron, one of scalloping, and two of foliage: good thirteenth-century mouldings are also freely used. The shafts are de-tached, and there is foliage on the jamb between them. The abaci are very richly carved with animals and foliage, and the capitals are all sculptured with subjects under canopies (2). The detail of the whole of the work is certainly very exquisite. Undoubtedly in the north of France such work would be assumed to have belonged to the twelfth rather than the thirteenth century; but the quatrefoil diapering on the capitals, the canopy work over the subjects in them, and the pronounced character of the mouldings and dog-tooth enrichment, make it pretty clear that the recorded date applies to this work. Indeed I do not know how we can assume any other date for it without altogether throwing over the extremely definite old inscription: for as it is evident that the south transept and choir are of the same date, it is difficult to see how it could have been possible to speak of the first stone, if all this important part of the fabric were already in existence.[1] Close to the transept on the east, in the wall of what is now a sacristy, is another lancet window, of equally good, though simpler detail. Enough, too, remains of the original work in the exterior of the apse to show that it is of the same age as the south transept. The clerestory windows seem to have been simple broad lancets; there are corbel-tables under the eaves; and the buttresses are very solid and simple. On the interior nothing but the groining has been left untouched by the pagan plasterers of a later day.

[1] This doorway ought to be compared with the south door of the nave of Lérida cathedral, the detail of which is so extremely similar to it that it is impossible, I think, to doubt that they were the work of the same men (3).

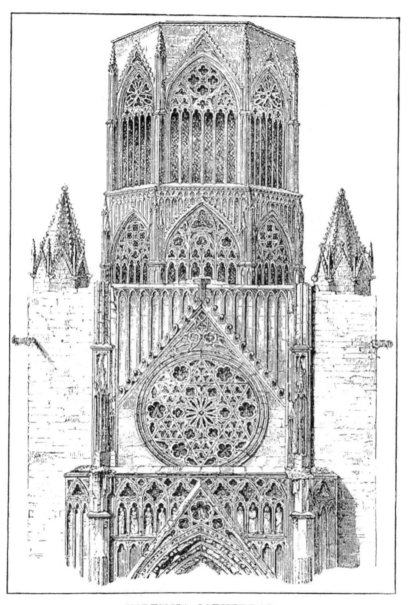

VALENCIA CATHEDRAL
NORTH TRANSEPT AND CIMBORIO

I have found no evidence as to the date of the next portion of the fabric, which is the more to be regretted as it is altogether very important and interesting in its character. It includes the whole façade of the north transept, a noble lantern at the Crossing, and a small pulpit, and the whole of this is a good example of probably the latter half of the fourteenth century. The north transept elevation is extremely rich in detail. The great doorway in the centre of the lowest stage—*de los Apósteles* —has figures under canopies in its jambs, and corresponding figures on either side beyond the jambs. The arch is moulded, and sculptured with four rows of figures and canopies, divided by orders of mouldings. The tympanum of the door is adorned with sculptures of the Blessed Virgin with our Lord and angels. Over the arch is a gabled canopy, the spandrels of which are filled with tracery and figures. Above, and set back rather from the face of the doorway, is a rose window, the very rich traceries of which are arranged in intersecting equilateral triangles; over it is a crocketed pediment, with tracery in the spandrels and on either side, and flanked by pinnacles. Every portion of the wall is panelled or carved. This front affords an admirable example of that class of middle-pointed work which was common in Germany and France at the end of the thirteenth and beginning of the fourteenth centuries. The style prevailed for some time, and it was probably about the middle of the fourteenth century that this building was executed.

The pulpit is placed against the north-east pier of the Crossing; it has evidently been taken to pieces and reconstructed, and it is not certain, I think, that it was originally a pulpit. Many of the members of the base and capital of its stem, and the angles of the octagonal upper stage, are modern, and of bronze; the rest is mainly of marble. The stem is slender, and the upper part is pierced with richly-moulded geometrical traceries, behind which the panels are filled in with boards, gilt and diapered with extremely good effect. A curious feature in this pulpit is that there is now no entrance to it, and if it is ever used for preaching, the preacher must get into it by climbing over the sides!

The lantern or Cimborio, though in some respects similar to, is no doubt later than the transept; it is one of the finest examples of its class in Spain. Mr. Ford says that it was built in A.D. 1404, but I have been unable to find his authority for the statement,[1] and though he may be right, I should have been inclined to date

Madoz gives the same date.—*Dicc. Geo. Esp. Histórico.*

it somewhat earlier. It is an octagon of two rather similar stages in height above the roof. Crocketed pinnacles are arranged at each angle, and large six-light windows with very rich and varied geometrical tracery fill the whole of each of the sides. The lower windows have crocketed labels, and the upper crocketed canopies, and the string-courses are enriched with foliage. From the very transparent character of this lantern, it is clear that it was never intended to be carried higher. It is a lantern and nothing more, and really very noble, in spite of its somewhat too ornate and frittered character.[1]

The portion of the work next in date to this seems to have been the tower. This, like the lantern, is octagonal in plan, and it is placed at the north-west corner of the aisle, against which one of its angles is set. A more Gothic contempt for regularity it would be impossible to imagine, yet the effect is certainly good. The circumference of this steeple is said to be equal to its height, but I had not an opportunity of testing this. Each side is 20 ft. 8 in. from angle to angle of the buttresses, so that the height, if the statement is true, would be about 165 feet. It is of four stages in height; the three lower stages quite plain, and the belfry rather rich, with a window in each face, panelling all over the wall above, and crocketed pediments over the win-

THE MICALETE

dows. The buttresses or pilasters—for they are of similar projection throughout their height—are finished at the top with crocketed pinnacles. The parapet has been destroyed, and there is a modern structure on the roof at the top. The evidence as to the age of this work is ample. It is called " El Micalete " or " Miguelete," its bells having been first hung on the feast of S. Michael.

---

[1] The illustration which I give of this lantern is borrowed from Mr. Fergusson's *Handbook of Architecture*.

Some documents referring to it are given by Cean Bermudez,[1] and are as follows:—

I. A deed executed in Valencia before Jayme Rovira, notary, on the 20th June, 1380, by which it appears that Michael Palomar, citizen, Bernardo Boix and Bartolomé Valent, master masons, estimated what they considered necessary for the fabric of the tower or campanile at 853 scudi.

II. From the MS. diary of the chaplain of King D. Alonso V. of Aragon, it appears that on the 1st January, A.D. 1381, there was a solemn procession of the bishop, clergy, and *regidors* of the city to the church, to lay the first stone of the Micalete.[2]

III. By a deed made in Valencia, May 18th, A.D. 1414, before Jayme Pastor, notary or clerk of the chapter, it is settled that Pedro Balaguer, an " able architect," shall receive 50 florins from the fabric fund of the new campanile or Micalete, " in payment of his expenses on the journey which he made to Lérida, Narbonne, and other cities, in order to see and examine their towers and campaniles, so as to imitate from them the most elegant and fit form for the cathedral of Valencia."

IV. By another deed, made before the same Jayme Pastor, September 18th, A.D. 1424, it is agreed that Martin Llobet, stone-cutter, agrees to do the work which is wanting and ought to be done in the Micalete, to wit, to finish the last course with its gurgoyles, to make the " *barbacano*," and bench round about, for the sum of 2000 florins of common money of Aragon,[3] the administration of the fabric finding the wheels, ropes, baskets, etc.

An inscription on the tower itself, referred to by Mr. Ford (but which I did not see), states that it was raised between A.D. 1381 and A.D. 1418, by Juan Franck, and it is said to have been intended to be 350 feet high.[4]

It is evident, therefore, that several architects were employed upon the work, and I know few facts in the history of mediæval art more interesting than the account we have here of the payment of an architect whilst he travelled to find some good work

---

[1] *Noticias de los Arquitectos*, etc., i. 256.

[2] *Viage Lit. á las Iglesias de España*, i. 31.

[3] L'an 1238, lorsque Jaques I. Roi d'Arragon assiégoit Valence, qui était au pouvoir des Mores, il déclara que les premiers qui l'emporteroient auroient l'honneur de donner les poids, les mesures, et la monnaye de leur ville à ceux de Valence; là dessus ceux de Lérida s'y jettèrent les premiers, et prirent la ville. C'est pourquoi, lorsqu'on repeupla Valence, ils y envoyèrent une colonie, leurs mesures, et leur monnaye, dont on s'y sert encore aujourd'hui; et la ville de Valence reconnoit celle de Lérida pour sa mère.—*Les Délices de l'Espagne*, iv. 613. Leyden, A.D. 1715.

[4] Ponz, *Viage de España*, iv. 21, 22.

to copy for the city of Valencia. The steeple of Lérida cathedral will be mentioned in its place, and it is sufficient now to say that it is also octagonal, of great height, and dates from the commencement of the fourteenth century. I know nothing at Narbonne which could have been suggestive to Pedro Balaguer, but the city was Spanish in those days, and is probably only mentioned as one of the most important places to which he went.

When the Micalete was built the nave of the church seems to have been still unfinished, the choir and transepts and part of the nave only having been built. In 1459, under the direction of an architect named Valdomar, a native of Valencia, the work was continued, and the church was joined to the tower. The authority for this statement is a MS. in the library of the convent of San Domingo, Valencia, which says: "In the year of our Lord 1459, on Monday, the 10th of September, they commenced digging to make the doorway and arcade of the cathedral; Master Valdomar was the master of the works, a native of the said city of Valencia." [1] Of Valdomar's work in this part of the church nothing remains, the whole has been altered in the most cruel way, and the most contemptible work erected in its place. Valdomar appears to have died whilst his work was in progress, and to have been succeeded by Pedro Compte, who concluded the work in 1482. The manuscript already quoted from the library of San Domingo is the authority for this statement, and describes Pedro Compte as " Molt sabut en l'art de la pedra." [2]

On the south side of the nave there is a Chapter-house, which is said by Ponz [3] to be the work of Pedro Compte, and to have been built at the cost of Bishop D. Vidal Blanes, in A.D. 1358. If this statement is correct, it follows that there were two architects of this name, the second having erected the Lonja de la Sedia, to which I shall have presently to refer, in A.D. 1482. The tracery of the windows, and the details generally of the Chapter-house, is so geometrical and good, that it is probable that the date given by Ponz may be depended upon. It is a square room nearly sixty feet in diameter, and groined in stone. The vault is similar to those which I first saw at Burgos, having arches

---

[1] Valdomar also built the chapel " de los Reyes," in the convent of San Domingo, commenced 18th June 1439, and completed 24th June 1476 This convent is now desecrated, and I did not see it, but it is said still to contain a good Gothic cloister.

[2] Pedro Compte is mentioned as having been invited by the Archbishop of Zaragoza to a conference with four other architects as to the rebuilding of the Cimborio of his cathedral, which had fallen down in 1520.

[3] *Viage de Esp.* iv. 29, 30.

thrown across the angles to bring it to an octagon, and the triangular compartments in the angles having their vaults below
the main vault.   It is lighted by small windows very high up
in the walls on the cardinal sides, and these are circular and
spherical triangles in outline, filled with geometrical tracery.   On
the south side is a very elaborate arcaded reredos and altar, and
on the west a pulpit corbelled out from the wall.   The design
and detail of the whole are extremely fine, and I regret that I
was able to make but a very hurried examination of it, and no
sketches; meeting here, almost for the first time in Spain, with a
sacristan who refused to allow me to do more than look, the fact
being that it was his time for dinner and siesta! (4)

    In the old sacristy to the east of this room are still preserved
two embroidered altar frontals, said to have been brought from
our own old S. Paul's by two merchants, Andres and Pedro de
Medina, just about the time of the Reformation.[1]   They are
therefore of especial interest to an Englishman.   They are very
large works, strained on frames, and were, I believe, hangings
rather than altar frontals, as they are evidently continuations
one of the other.   The field is of gold, diapered, and upon this
a succession of subjects is embroidered.   On one cloth are
(beginning at the left) (1) our Lord bearing his Cross; (2) being
nailed to the Cross; (3) crucified, with the thieves on either side;
(4) descending from the Cross; (5) entombed.   The next cloth
has (1) the descent into Hell; (2) the Maries going to the
sepulchre; (3) the Maries at the tomb, the angel, and (4) the
Resurrection.   The effect of the whole work is like that of a
brilliant German painting, and the figures are full of action and
spirit, and have a great deal of expression in their faces.   The
diapered ground is made with gold thread, laid down in vertical
lines, and then diapered with diagonal lines of fine bullion
stitched down over it to form the diaper.   The gold is generally
manufactured in a double twist, and borders and edgings are all
done with a very bold twisted gold cord.   The faces are all
wrought in silk, and some of the dresses are of silk, lined all over
with gold.   The old border at the edge exists on one only of the
frontals.   The size of each is 3 ft. 1 in. by 10 ft. 2 in., and the
date, as nearly as I can judge, must be about A.D. 1450.   There
is also preserved here a missal which once belonged to Westminster Abbey.

----

[1] Spain boasts other like treasures, *e.g.* a figure still preserved at Mon-
doñedo, and which is still called "la Ynglesa," because brought from
S. Paul's.—*See* Ponz, *Viage de España*, iv. 43.

I could find no other church of any interest. There are several which have some old remains, but they are generally so damaged and decayed, that it is impossible to make anything of them. One I saw desecrated and occupied by the military, and was unable to enter; and there is another in a street leading out of the Calle de Caballeros, which has a very fine round-arched door-

PUERTA DE SERRANOS, VALENCIA

way, with three shafts in the jambs, and good thirteenth-century mouldings in the arch, and which is evidently of the same age as the south door of the cathedral. The capitals have each two wyverns fighting, and the abaci are well carved. The church, however, was desecrated, and no one knew how I could gain admission to it (5).

The walls and gates are of more interest. They are lofty, and generally well preserved. The two finest gates are the Puerta de Serranos, and that del Cuarte. The former, said by

Ford [1] to have been built in A.D. 1349, is a noble erection. Two grand polygonal towers flank the entrance archway, which is recessed in the centre. Above this the wall is covered with tracery panelling, and then a great projecting gallery or platform, supported on enormous corbels, is carried all round the three exposed sides of the gateway. The towers are carried up a considerable height above this gallery, and it is probable that there was originally a wooden construction over it, of the kind which M. Viollet le Duc, in his treatise on military architecture, has shown to have been commonly adopted in fortifications of this age. The Puerta del Cuarte is of the same description, and has two circular flanking towers, but is less imposing, and is said to have been built in A.D. 1444. Both gateways are completely open at the back, enormous open arches, one above the other, rendering them useless for attack against the city; and the corbelled-out passages at the top are not continued across the back (6).

The domestic remains here are of some importance. One feature of rather frequent occurrence is the window of two or three lights, divided by detached shafts. The earlier examples have simple trefoil heads, and sculptured capitals to the columns. In the later examples there are mouldings round the cusped head, and the abaci and capitals are carved; but it is a very curious fact that whenever I saw any old towns on the coast of the Mediterranean, there I always saw some specimens of this later kind of window, with detail and carving so identical in character that I was almost driven to the conclusion that they were all executed in the same place, and sent about the country to be fixed! Nevertheless, they are always very pretty, so that one ought not to grumble if they do occur a little too often. The shafts are generally of marble, and often coupled one behind the other.

The Arabs had a name for this class of windows, and as we have not, and want one, it may be as well to mention it. They are called *ajimez*, literally windows by which the sun enters. The Arabs seem to have supplied many of the architectural terms in use in Spain, and probably we owe them in this case not only the name, but the design also. Among other Arab words still in common use, I may mention Alcazar, Alcalá, Tapia, and many more are given in vocabularies.

One of the earliest of these *ajimez* windows is in a house on the east side of the cathedral; and a fine example of later date

[1] *Handbook of Spain*, i. 367.

VALENCIA

THE CASA LONJA

is in an old house in the Calle de Caballeros, the internal court and staircase of which are also picturesque, though hardly mediæval. All the houses here seem to be built on the same plan, with the stables and offices on the ground floor, arranged round an internal court, an open stone staircase to the first floor, and the living - rooms above. The fronts towards the streets are usually rather gloomy and forbidding-looking, but the courts are always picturesque. The finest domestic building in the city is the Casa Lonja, or Exchange, which was commenced on the 7th November, 1482, the year in which the works at the cathedral were completed by Pedro Compte. There is no doubt, I believe, that he was the architect; and on March 19th, 1498, he was appointed perpetual Alcaide of the Lonja, with a salary of thirty pounds (" libras ") a year. He was also *Maestro Mayor* of the city, and was employed in several works of engineering on the rivers and streams of the district.[1] The main front of the Lonja is still very nearly as he left it, a fine specimen of late Spanish pointed work. The detail is of the same kind as, but simpler than, the contemporary works at Valladolid and Burgos, and there is a less determined display of heraldic achievements; though the great doorway, and the window on either side of it which open into the great hall, and which are so curiously grouped together by means of labels and string-courses, have some coats-of-arms and supporters rather irregularly placed in their side panels. The great parapet of the end, and the singular finish of the battlements, are very worthy of note, and give great richness to the whole building. The principal doorway leads into a fine groined hall, 130 feet long by 75 feet wide, divided into a quasi-nave and aisles of five bays by eight columns, sculptured and spirally twisted. The portion of the building to the left of the centre is divided into three chambers in height, the upper and lower rooms being low, the central room lofty and well proportioned. The lower rooms have plain square windows; the next stage, windows of much loftier proportions, and with

AJIMEZ WINDOW, VALENCIA

---

[1] Cean Bermudez, *Arqua. y Aquos. de España*, i. 139.

their square heads ornamented with a rich fringe of cusping. There are pointed discharging arches over them. The upper stage of this wing is extremely rich, the window-openings being pierced in a sort of continuous arcading, the pinnacles of which run up to and finish in the parapet. This parapet is enriched with circular medallions enclosing heads, a common Italian device, betokening here the hand of a man whose work was verging upon that of the Renaissance school. At the back is a garden, the windows and archways opening on which are of the same age as the front (7).

Valencia, though not containing any building of remarkable interest, is nevertheless well worth a visit: it is a busy city, full of picturesque colour and people. The *manta* or rug worn by the peasants throughout Spain is here seen in perfection: it is of rich and very oriental colour, and charms the eye at every turn. I went into a shop and looked at a number of them, and there were none which were not thoroughly good in their colour; and, worn as they are by the sunburnt peasants, hanging loosely on one shoulder, they contrast splendidly with their white linen jackets and trousers and swarthy skins. The river is, at any rate in the autumn, the broad dry bed only of a river, with here and there a puddle just deep enough for washerwomen. The water is all carried off to irrigate the fertile country around, and troops of cavalry and artillery, with their guns all drawn by fine mules, were hard at work exercising where it ought to have been. On the side of the river opposite to the city are some rather nice public gardens, with fine walks and drives planted with noble trees. A drive which begins here extends all the way to Grao, the port of Valencia, some two or three miles off. In the afternoon it seems to be always thronged with *tartanas*, carriages, and equestrians on their way to and from the sea: and each *tartana* is full generally of a lively cargo of priests and peasants, men, women, and children, all laughing, cheerful, and picturesque. I went to Grao to embark on the steamer for Barcelona. There is nothing to see there save the usual accompaniments of a seaport, and the provision for a large and fashionable population of bathers from Madrid during the summer months. For their convenience small and very rude huts are put up on the beach, and left there to be destroyed by the winter storms. Not much is sacrificed, as they are of the very rudest description, and evidently devised for the use of people who go to Grao to be amused and to bathe, and not merely to show themselves off as fine ladies and gentlemen.

At Valencia the national love for the *mantilla*, which in courtly Madrid seems to be now half out of fashion, finds vent in the positive prohibition at one of the churches for any woman to enter who wears a bonnet in place of it! (8)

NOTES

(1) Valencia Cathedral belongs to the Limousin or " hall " type of great churches, in which the aisle is almost as high as the nave and the division between them diminished as much as possible. Even the lantern is only the Catalan model subtilised.

(2) Capitals consecutively storied are so rare in Spain that I transcribe the subjects of these from my note book. For the precise references to Scripture and the Creed I am indebted to D. Roque Chabas.[1]

I. (*a*) The Holy Ghost on the Waters (Gen. i. 2). (*b*) Creation of the Angels—" and of all things visible and invisible."

II. (*a*) Creation of the Stars and the Universe—" maker of Heaven and earth," (*b*) and of Adam.

III. (*a*) Creation of Eve. (*b*) Temptation (Gen. iii. 6). Eve receives the apple and Adam eats.

IV. (*a*) God calling to the hidden pair (Gen iii. 8), (*b*) and giving them coats of skins (Gen. iii. 21), or perhaps the fig leaf (Gen. iii. 7).

V. (*a*) Expulsion, with the flaming sword and seraph. (*b*) Adam and Eve go out in their coats of skins, he with a spade.

VI. (*a*) Abel's Sacrifice (Gen. iv. 4). (*b*) Abel's death (Gen. iv. 8).

The door comes here, then the series continues:

VII. (*a*) Three sons of Noah go out to people the earth (Gen. ix. 19). (*b*) Drunkenness of Noah (Gen. ix. 21).

VIII. (*a*) God speaks to Abraham (Gen. xii. 7). (*b*) Abraham goes on a camel to Bethel (Gen. xii. 8).

IX. and X. are out of order, both the columns and the halves. The series continues with:

X. (*b*) Abraham comes back from killing the kings, with spoil in a waggon, Melchizedec offers a cup, the King of Sodom, crowned, lies prostrate (Gen. xiv. 16-18). (*a*) The angels in Mamre (Gen. xviii. 1-2).

IX. (*a*) Isaac cutting wood (Gen. xxii. 3). (*b*) Isaac on the Altar (Gen. xxii. 9).

XI. (*a*) The burning bush (Exod. iii. 2-5). (*b*) Moses at the battle (Exod. xvii. 12-13).

XII. (*a*) Moses installs judges (Exod. xviii. 25-26), (*b*) and receives the tables of the law.

(3) The door of Agramunt is 1283, the door of Lérida 1204-74, the door of Valencia may well be 1262-78.

[1] *Boletin de la Sociedad Española de Excursiones*, 1899.

(4) Traditions persist in Spain and Valencia has still an unkind sacristan, who would rather blow out his candle than answer questions about what he is showing off. The alabaster reredos has a central painted scene about the relief of the Crucified, SS. Mary and John in a well-developed landscape. The cathedral is rich in pictures of the fifteenth and sixteenth centuries; the Chapel of the Purissima shelters four scenes from the life of S. Maur in the manner of Pinturicchio, that of S. Thomas of Vilanova four quattrocento saints—a Franciscan, a doctor in green, S. Benedict, and S. Michael. The angel's shield is a mere frame for a great crystal *cabochon*, nor is this example the only one besides that in England attributed to Vermejo. The *Virgen del Puig* in an eastern chapel looks rather charming if one could see her. Though the high altar-piece by Ferrando de Almedina, 1506, is nearly insupportable, copied from the Italian of the High Renaissance, the two doors below on either side the altar are sincere in colour and facial types, with rich brocades and backgrounds of Spanish landscape, mountains, rocks, and castles. In the inner sacristy hang, among a collection nowhere bad, at least ten good pieces, and Juanes' half figures of two saintly bishops, S. Thomas of Vilanova and S. John of Ribera, if they are really his, show him to better advantage than usual, with infinite urbanity and suavity in the dim tones of greyish or ivory flesh.

(5) This I could not identify, and I am afraid the doorway may have been pulled down. The other church may have been S. Nicholas, in which the wide sanctuary and eastern choir is adorned with the spoils of two retables that Baedeker gives to Juan de Juanes— Italianate pictures, bland and fair. Here you may notice two peculiarities of Spanish use: one that the alb is very short, but the sleeves of it are very long and worn wound around the arms; the other, that a server carries a silver wand dangling from his wrist, with which he points the places in the great choir-books on the central lectern.

(6) The walls are gone, the gates are restored.

(7) The *Audiencia* near the cathedral can hardly be neglected. Fine enough is the lower hall, its rich gilded ceiling touched with red and green, and five magnificent windows framed in stone, but I know nothing more grandiose than the upper hall of nearly twice its size, built in 1599. The ceiling and gallery are of warm carved wood, the dado is of fine tiles, blue predominating, and the whole of the wall space peopled with stately regents, very much alive, without the least vulgar insistence on either themselves or you. Such a one was Haywood's figure of the Noble Spaniard.

(8) This was probably the Jesuit church of Corpus Christi, for Baedeker mentions a similar prohibition there. In the adjoining college, which sustains *clausura* against women, is kept, among other pictures, the Virgin of the three Borgias, which M. Bertaux believes to be a votive offering from the widow of the Duke of Gandia and to contain his portrait with that of Jaufrey and Cæsar Borgia. At the church of S. Thomas delightful *azulejos* line the court and the passage to it.

The Museum, besides a great deal of representative trash, contains two drawings and four portraits by Goya and a portrait of himself by Velasquez, and two rooms full of characteristic, often beautiful, primitive pictures. Among the retables collected in the earliest room are three from the Charterhouse of Porta Coeli (now a hotel). The earliest, offered by Bonifazio Ferrer, who was S. Vincent's brother and was professed in 1396, is mainly Sienese in quality, but inserts seven little scenes of the sacraments, around the Crucifixion, on the panel. The Flemings were quick to catch the trick, but I am afraid the Valencian instance is the earliest. The wings represent the Baptism of Christ and the Conversion of S. Paul, among entirely Sienese mountains. There was a thriving school in Valencia, deriving from Siena, by the end of the trecento. Lorenzo Zarazoga, " very subtile and apt in his office," who had left the town during the wars between Aragon and Castile, was recalled by the council in 1374, and offered a hundred and fifty gold florins if he would stay permanently. There is not, however, I believe, a single picture certainly by his hand. To about 1420-40 belongs a predella of S. Dominic, of infinite charm in such scenes as where the baby saint has rolled out of the cradle and lies on the floor asleep. A little portable triptych, rather Germanic within, carries on the shutters S. Paul the Hermit and a young Spaniard of a bishop. A polyptych labelled *Escuela Italiana XV. Siglo* is certainly not that. The dark brownish flesh tints, like some north Italian masters, suggest the school of Navarre; absolutely Spanish are the brocades of the Madonna and S. Laurence the deacon; SS. Agatha and Agnes stand on a tiled floor. In the retable of Holy Cross, from Porta Coeli, ascribed at the museum to Pedro Nicolau, who was working in Valencia, 1400-1409, the compositions are still Italian, but the work is not. It shows French and Burgundian ascendency. The thirst for blood, monsters, and horrors comes from the north, and the long noses recall the painters of Charles V. and the Duke of Berry: the ample cloaks and singular head-dresses recall the designs of André Beauneveu. The Crucifixion occupies the centre, Christ in Judgment sits above, and in the wings, on the left, Seth receives the tree from an angel at the gates of Paradise and plants it on Adam's grave; Constantine fights a good fight. S. Helena and a Jew raise a dead woman by the virtue of the Cross. Heraclius on the right fights with the son of Chosroes single-handed on a bridge over the Danube, other folk looking on; faces Chosroes enthroned in his blasphemous trinity between the Cross and the Cock; and carries the Cross into Jerusalem, stripped to his shirt. Some time after this, perhaps about 1425, comes another altar-piece from the same church, of S. Martin between SS. Ursula and Anthony Abbot. The elder saints are plainly portraits, the old man magnificently painted, especially about the eyes, and perhaps the young man is a portrait too, of a king's minion. He is like a young lover from an ivory mirror-case, depicted by a court painter; his white horse a fairy steed; if there is a trifle too much of conscious feeling, there is not a trace of *minauderie*. The delicate stamped patterns that run up the side of the panels and cross just behind the haloes are much the same in a big Annunciation I thought very fine indeed. An adolescent curled angel with a jewel on his brow, vested in cope and stole, very Spanish about the face, makes the pendant to a fair Madonna, bare-headed, in red frock trimmed with ermine at throat and wrists. The flesh tones incline to the ivory, and the same subdued whiteness in the angel's robe, with red and something dark (once blue or green), are all the colours in the piece. The floor is tiled; I felt a touch of Burgundian in the Spanish of it, nothing Italian, no exaltation in line or face, but immense seriousness of composition and expression. A Florentine named Girardo had been in Valencia in 1402; in 1426 Alfonso the Magnanimous gave to Anton Gueran the title of King's Chamber-Painter. Meanwhile in 1396 Master Andrés Marçal of Sax, "pintor alemany," received the commission to paint a Last Judgment, Heaven and Hell, in the Great Council Hall. Nicholas Marçal, probably a relative, worked at Palma in Mallorca between 1407 and 1418. The big retable in the opposite room, dated 1450-70 and labelled, "German influence," looked to me much more French; the treatment of the Coronation with the Dove outspread, proceeding from the mouths of the Father and the Son, recalled the greater Coronation of Enguerrand Charenton, though the style did not. The sea gives up its dead, devils hook up souls from the waters under the earth. The Borgia Pinturicchio in this room, more charming and sober than usual, has remarkably brown flesh tints. Jacomart Baço is represented only by a pupil's work, 1460-70, of real beauty and distinction—SS. James and Giles, the types very Spanish, restrained and comely. Baço himself I had hoped to see at Jativa in the great Borgia triptych (*circa* 1450), but I was prevented from going there and to Gandia; I did, however, meet him unexpectedly at Segorbe. A Christ before Pilate (*circa* 1500) is attributed to Master Rodrigo of Osuna, hitherto known only by the South Kensington Epiphany, which was painted by "*lo fill del Mestre Rodrigo.*" There is said to be a Crucifixion painted by him in the last years of the fifteenth century, in the church of San Nicholas. Valencian art had a more suave and formal beauty than Catalan, but it was to decline upon sugared trivialities in the full sixteenth century.

Segorbe is said to possess paintings by Juan de Juanes, and six great fifteenth-century retables, of which the greatest is that kept in the sacristy of S. Martin de las Monjas—the retable of S. Martin, fetched from Val de Cristo, and painted by Jacomart in 1457. The panels contain in the centre, S. Martin enthroned, the Madonna and angels, the Crucifixion; and six scenes from the legend in the sides. There must have been more once. A retable in the sacristy of the cathedral is nearly related—a Madonna enthroned among music-making angels forms the central panel, below an Annunciation and above a Coronation; at the sides six scenes, the Nativity, Epiphany, and Resurrection of our Lord, the Ascension, Pentecost, and Dormition of the Blessed Virgin. It represents a great tradition rather than a great genius. The cathedral has been rebuilt; the present high altar-piece is worthless, but fragments of an earlier one are scattered through the lateral chapels: SS. Apollonia, Christopher, Vincent, Paul, and Roch, a Dominican friar, a female saint with a palm and an exquisite profile, a bishop, an abbot, and an apostle. The painting, on a gold ground, is as large and rich as some of the early Venetian work in oils. I saw no signs of the central panel to

such a retable. A number of heads in the sacristy—SS. Joachim
and Anna meeting, the Visitation, the Annunciation—may, despite
the difference of scale, belong to the same composition; they have
the same excellence of a bland and ample and golden beauty. Ponz
saw Juanes' receipt for this retable, ordered by Bishop Gilaberto
Marti, dated 1530. In one of the fourteenth-century cloister chapels,
before the place was locked up for the day, I found in a quattrocento retable of S. Clare, sensitive types, a touch of delicate affecta-
tion, but great beauty of silhouette and feature. Other paintings
were in other chapels, but the chapter was in a hurry to get home,
and the kindness of one canon could only avail for this much and
for the pleasure of the cloister itself, irregular in shape, with an upper
gallery, very much like English perpendicular, orange and medlar
trees in heavy fruit, lilac and box, and a mossy fountain. Eleven
in the morning in the rain ended ecclesiastic Segorbe for the day.
The ruins of Val de Cristo I could not see for the weather; they are
Carthusian, i.e. late, but looked picturesque. I had wished to push
on to Darocca and Teruel—to see in the former, amongst other
things, in the church of Santo Domingo de Silos the retable of S.
Martin, Aragonese of the late quattrocento, and an earlier retable
of S. Michael in the Collegiata; in Teruel, the Mudejar architecture
of the cathedral and the high altar-piece, which was delivered
by Jacobo Mateo in 1418. The weather interfered. At Sagunto
the Roman ruins are worth seeing even in the rain, and they and the
castle must be an untiring delight on long, fine days; but the church
will not repay much exertion. The centuries have been merciless to
destroy and the present architect has outstripped them. The sculptures about the south portal are provincial and the bronze doors
themselves wretched papery stuff beaten up in the eighteenth
century.

It was my ill luck to have put off visiting a number of the smaller
towns on the east coast until spring, with the idea of having then
more light and warmth for work, but last spring was remarkably
rainy, and successive trips were broken up by bad weather. For as
certainly as you cannot see retables, dark at best, in a dark Spanish
church, even when helped by candle-ends and a pocket electric light,
just so surely you cannot photograph the outside of a building in a
streaming rain. At some places it was the first rain in two years, at
some the first in five, but it was always rain. I have never yet taken
a photograph in Zaragoza, neither in January, May, nor yet July.
Twice for the same reason I could not get to San Juan de la Peña, or
even so far as Jaca, which will soon be open to France by railway
direct. The normal Spanish weather is wonderfully lovely, but it
is a necessity, not a luxury—the only condition in which normal
existence is possible.

CHAPTER XIII

No one should go from Valencia to Barcelona without paying a visit to Tarragona. It is even now easy of access, and before long will be still more accessible by means of the railway which is being made between the two towns. I travelled from Barcelona to Tarragona and back again by diligence, and both journeys, unfortunately, were made for the most part by night, so that I am unable to speak very positively about the scenery upon the road. But both on leaving Barcelona and again before I reached Tarragona the road was very beautiful, and I have no doubt it would reward any one who could contrive to give up more time and daylight to it than I could. There is but one town of any importance on the road—Villafranca de Panades, —and here I caught a glimpse of an old church, which seemed to be of the fourteenth-century Catalan type, and fully to deserve examination (1).

The approach to Tarragona is very lovely. The old city stands on the steep slope of a hill, crowned by the stately mediæval cathedral, and surrounded on all sides by walls, which are still very perfect and in some parts unusually lofty and imposing. Below and beyond the walls to the left, as you approach, is the mean and modern town which covers a low promontory, and is now the centre of all the trade and business of the city. A broad street, in which are the principal inns, divides the two halves of the city, on the upper side of which the whole architectural interest is centred. The views on all sides are beautiful. Looking back to the east one sees hill after hill, ending in point after point, which jut out into the sea one beyond the other, and, combining with the deep blue waters of the Mediterranean, produce the most charming picture. To the south, looking over the modern town, mole, and harbour, is the sea; whilst to the west the eye wanders, well content, over a rich green expanse of level land, studded all along its breadth with rich growth of trees, till the view is bounded by the hills which rise beyond the old town of Reus, now an active and enterprising centre of manufacturing industry.

I ought, no doubt, to fill many pages here with an account of the Roman antiquities, which are numerous and important, Tarragona having been one of the most important Roman stations in Spain. But they have been often described, and the time at my disposal allowed only of a hurried glance at them, unless I chose to neglect in their favour the—to me—much more interesting Christian remains, which I need hardly say I was not prepared to do. The city walls are, I believe, to a considerable extent Roman. There are remains—though but slight—of an amphitheatre; the magnificent aqueduct, some little distance from the city, is one of the finest in Europe; and, finally, there is a museum full of Roman antiquities, which seem well to deserve due examination (2). But I was obliged to neglect all these, giving them the most cursory inspection, as I found in the cathedral ample occupation for every minute of my time.

This is certainly one of the most noble and interesting churches I have seen in Spain. It is one of a class of which I have seen others upon a somewhat smaller scale (as *e.g.* the cathedrals at Lérida and Tudela), and which appears to me, after much study of old buildings in most parts of Europe, to afford one of the finest types, from every point of view, that it is possible to find. It produces in a very marked degree an extremely impressive internal effect, without being on an exaggerated scale, and combines in the happiest fashion the greatest solidity of construction with a lavish display of ornament in some parts, to which it is hard to find a parallel. Unfortunately the documentary evidence that I have been able to find as to the age of the various portions of this church is not so complete as I could wish. A very elaborate and painstaking history of the city is in course of publication; but when I was there [1] the first volume only of this had been published, and this was confined entirely to the Roman antiquities contained in the Museum and other collections. The volume of *España Sagrada* which relates to Tarragona contains but few documents of any value, and I have been unable to put my hands upon any other which contains any at all. Yet there cannot be much doubt that a see whose history is so important, and whose rank is so high,[2] must have in

---

[1] In May 1862.

[2] Tarragona is the see of an archbishop, who claims to be equal, if not superior, to the Archbishop of Toledo. Practically, of course, he is nothing of the kind, yet he carries the assertion of his dignity so far that I noticed a Mandamos of the Cardinal Archbishop of Toledo hung up in the Coro, in which his title, " Primada de les Españas," and the same word in " Santa Iglesia Primada," were carefully scratched through in ink.

its archives a vast store of information, out of which might be gathered all the material facts as to the foundation of, and additions to, the church.

A few notices of the building of the cathedral have, however, come under my eye, and of these the most important are the following:—In A.D. 1089 [1] Pope Urban II. addressed an epistle to the faithful, recommending them to aid in every way in the restoration of the church, which had then just been recovered from the hands of the Moors. Not long after this, in A.D. 1131, Pope Innocent II. issued a Bull, wherein he recommended the suffragan churches to contribute to the cost of rebuilding the cathedral.[2] More than a century after this, works were again in progress, for in the necrology of the cathedral, on 11th March, 1256, mention is made of " Frater Bernardus, magister operis hujus ecclesiæ; " whilst again, in 1298, Maestro Bartolomé is mentioned as the sculptor who wrought nine statues of the apostles for the western façade, the remainder having been executed by Maestro Jayme Castayls in 1375.

Comparing this cathedral with that of Lérida, of which the date is tolerably well ascertained, it is difficult to pronounce decidedly which is the oldest, except that the eastern apse here, which is very peculiar in its character, has every appearance of being a work of the middle of the twelfth century, at the latest, and earlier by far, therefore, than the foundation of the church of Lérida, which was not commenced until A.D. 1203, and which was finished and consecrated in A.D. 1278. I believe, indeed, that the eastern part of this cathedral may most probably have been commenced about A.D. 1131, in consequence of the Bull of Innocent II., though the greater portion of the fabric (including the nave and its aisles and the cloister) seems to me to have been executed at the end of the twelfth and during the first half of the thirteenth century; and it is very possible, therefore, that the Brother Bernardus, who died in 1256, may have been the architect of the larger part of the existing fabric, both of the church and its cloister (3).

The original plan of the cathedral was very simple. It had a nave and aisles, transepts, with apsidal chapels to the east of them, a raised lantern or Cimborio over the Crossing, and three parallel apses east of it. On the north-east side of the church— an unusual position, selected probably in obedience to some local necessity—is a large cloister of the same age as the church,

---

[1] *España Sagrada*, xxv. 214.
[2] *Historia de los Condes de Barcelona*, p. 183.

with a Chapter-house on its southern side. The piers throughout are clustered in a very fine and massive style, and of a
section which is often repeated in early Spanish Gothic; each
arch being carried on two coupled half-columns, and the groining-shafts being placed in a nook in the angle between each of
these pairs of columns. The nave piers are no less than 11 ft. 9 in.
in diameter, the clear width of the nave being about 40 ft. 8 in.,
and the span of the arches east and west about 20 ft. The
bases are finely moulded, and have foliage carved on the angle
between their circular and square members. The capitals and
abaci are carved generally with a most luxuriant exuberance
of conventional foliage, whilst the broad solid unmoulded and
unchamfered sections of the arches which rise above them seem
to protest gravely against any forgetfulness of solidity and
massiveness as the greatest elements at the disposal of the
architect. The groining of the nave and its aisles is all quadripartite, as also is that of the transepts, save at the extreme end
of the northern transept, which is covered with a pointed waggon-
roof. The choir has two bays of cross-vaulting on its western
portion and a semi-dome over the apse—a form of roofing which
is repeated over the other early apses; that of the north transept
having been rebuilt in the fourteenth century, and vaulted in
the usual manner. It is probable that the cross-vaults in the
choir were not originally contemplated, as they are carried on
small shafts raised on the capitals of the main groining-shafts,
which may perhaps have been intended to carry a waggon-vault.
The roof of the apse is considerably lower than that of the choir,
and a small rose window is pierced in the spandrel between the
two. The arch in front of the semi-dome of the apse is—like all
the other main arches—pointed, though those which open into
the smaller apses are semi-circular. The latter, being in the
lower part of the wall, were, no doubt, completed at an early
date; whilst the former, being on the level of the groining, would
not be finished until much later. The apse is lighted with three
windows in the lower part of the wall, which are richly shafted
inside, and by seven small and perfectly plain round-arched
windows, pierced in the lower part of the semi-dome with very
singular effect. On the exterior all these windows are remarkable for a very wide splay from the face of the wall to the glass
—a feature of early work in England, and usually preceding
the common use of glass. The walls are carried up a considerable
height above the springing of the dome, in order to resist its
thrust, and are finished at the top with a rich projecting corbel-

table, from which, at regular intervals, five divisions are brought still further forward, looking much like machicoulis, and yet evidently introduced only for the sake of effect, as there is no access to them. These projections are square in plan, carried on very large corbels, and the cornice under the eaves has a course of square stones set diagonally—a kind of enrichment very common in brickwork, and which I saw in the early church of

APSE OF CHOIR

San Pedro at Gerona. The great depth of this cornice is very imposing. The stone roof above it abuts against a gable-wall, carried by the arch on its western side; but owing to the destruction of the original finish of the staircase turrets, and the erection of a steeple in the angle between the choir and the transept, the general view has to some extent lost its original stern Romanesque character.

The exterior of the other apses on the south has the same appearance of age. The wall of one of them has been raised several feet at a later date, but the other is still altogether in its original state. Both are, of course, very low and insignificant as compared with the choir. The whole detail of the great eastern apse appeared to me to have much more the air of having been the work of an Italian than of a French architect (4). The masonry is in extremely large square blocks, many of the window-heads being cut out of one block of stone, and in this part of the church I found a large number of masons' marks on the face of the stones. These tally, like most of those I have seen in Spain, very closely with those which are found in our own buildings, and indeed with those which are used by our own masons at the present day: it is, however, comparatively rare to find them on

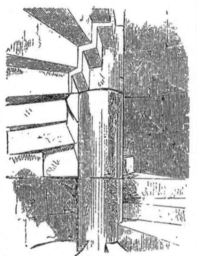

NEWEL STAIRCASE

the outer face of the stones.[1] The stones marked in this way are tooled on the face, and I observed that stones worked by the same man were marked indifferently with perpendicular and diagonal tooling lines. On the south side of the choir, just at its junction with the principal apse, is a staircase which leads to the roof: this is carried up in a large square turret, and is of remarkable construction. The newel is 1 ft. 6 in. in diameter, and worked in stones, each of about 2 ft. 3 in. in height. Each of these has three corbels, with sockets for the steps, which are thus supported by the newel and yet independent of it. The

aisles on either side of the choir seem to have been intended to form the lower stage of steeples. On the south side the Romanesque tower seems to have been built no higher than the height of the side walls of the church; but subsequently—*circa* A.D. 1300–50—it was carried up as an octagonal steeple, with buttresses against the canted sides of the lower stage over the angles of the square base, finished with crocketed pinnacles. This tower occupies the angle between the choir and transept, and I suppose that traces would be found of a corresponding tower

[1] The Chapter-house at Fountains Abbey has one of the largest collections of masons' marks I have ever seen, and in this case they are of much value, as proving how large was the number of skilled masons employed on this one small building at the same time. At Tarragona I saw nothing like the same variety of marks.

on the opposite side, somewhat in the way so commonly met with in all the German Romanesque churches. Unfortunately the north choir aisle was altered if not rebuilt in the fourteenth century, and I was unable to examine the walls above it, where the evidence of the existence of a second tower would have to be sought. The roof of the apse on the east side of the south transept presents an admirable example of a semi-dome, with the masonry arranged in the usual fashion in regular horizontal courses, and the moulding of the abacus of the arch in front of it carried round it as a string-course at its springing.

The rest of the church is of rather later date than the east end. It is all just of that transitional period in which, whilst the pointed arch was used where great strength was required, the round arch was nevertheless retained for the smaller openings in the walls. But the capitals throughout the church are sculptured so magnificently, and in so well developed a style, that it is impossible to regard the work anywhere, except at the extreme eastern end, as one in which a Romanesque influence was paramount. We have, indeed, here one of those cases in which almost all the character of the work has been stamped on it by the hands of the sculptor rather than of the architect; for I believe that, had it presented us with a series of plain Romanesque capitals, we should have felt no difficulty about classing the whole work as essentially Romanesque in style, whereas now the effect is rather that of a glorious Pointed church, the exuberance of whose sculpture is kept in subordination by the stern simplicity of the bold unmoulded arches, the massive section of the piers, and the regularity of the outline and firmness of shadow which the deep square abacus everywhere enforces. Here, then, I thought I saw one of those openings which are now and then almost accidentally given us for the infusion of new vigour and greater spirit into our own works. It is no copying of a Spanish work that I should wish to see attempted, but only a deliberate determination on the part of the builder of some one building in England to emulate the grand solidity of this old Spanish church; and if he feels that this is by itself too rude and unpolished for an over-civilised age like ours, then let him take a lesson from the same old Spanish work, and show the extent of his refinement in the subtle delicacy of the sculpture with which he adorns it. We have few if any such churches in England. Our transitional examples are neither very numerous nor very fine; and it is in Germany and in Spain—so far as my experience goes— that we find the finest examples of this noble period. In neither

of these countries was the progress of architectural development so rapid as it was in England and in the north of France,
and consequently such churches as the cathedrals of Tarragona,
Lérida, and Tudela were rising in Spain at the same time as
the more advanced and scientific, but perhaps less forcible
and solemnly grand cathedrals of Salisbury, Lincoln, and Wells
were being built in England.

I hardly know when I have been much more struck than I
was with the view of the interior of the transept, of which I give
an engraving. For though the picturesque furniture of later
times, the screens and pulpits, the organs and other furniture,
are in great contrast with the glorious solidity of the old work,
the combination of this with them makes a singularly beautiful
picture.

The nave of the cathedral at Tarragona has been a good deal
altered by the introduction of large fourteenth-century clerestory
windows of three lights. There is not and there never was a
triforium, and the clerestory throughout was, I have no doubt,
the same in design that it still is in the transepts, lighted by a
simple round-headed window in each bay. The groining has
transverse arches or ribs of very large size, diagonal ribs formed
with a bold roll moulding only, and no wall ribs.

The lantern over the Crossing still remains to be described.
It is octagonal in plan, segmental arches being thrown across
the angles of the square base to support its diagonal sides. The
groining springs from immediately above the apex of the main
arches, and the light is admitted by windows alternately of three
and four lights. Its interior is very fine. The ribs of its eight-
celled vault are very bold, and the dog-tooth enrichment is
freely used round all the arches and along the string-courses.
The diagonal or canted sides of the lantern are carried on pointed
arches, the space below which is filled in with pendentives, with
the stones arranged in courses radiating from the centre. Such
a form of pendentive is rarely seen in works of this age. The
details of this lantern are all rather rude, and its height is not
great, as it rises only some twenty-five feet above the roofs.
The outside has at each angle a buttress, with an engaged shaft
in front of it, and the windows are all set within simple enclosing
arches. Their tracery is that of ordinary first-pointed windows,
the three-light windows having lancet lights, with the centre
light longer than the others, and the four-light windows having
the two centre lights longest. The old outside roof is destroyed;
but the finish of the lanterns of Lérida and of the old cathedral

TARRAGONA CATHEDRAL
VIEW ACROSS TRANSEPTS

of Salamanca seems to make it pretty certain that it was intended
to have a pyramidal or domical stone roof. Access is now gained
to the top of the lantern by means of a passage boldly carried
on an arch which is thrown from the belfry window of the south-
east steeple to the side of the lantern. I ought to have mentioned that the upper stage of this steeple is groined, and that
the bells are hung in the window openings; but this is not their
original place, the jambs having been cut away to make room for
them. Its upper stage seems to have been finished with a
pinnacle at each angle, and a gable over each window rising
through the parapet—a somewhat similar design to that of the
great tower at Lérida, and to that of the Micalete at Valencia,
both of which ought, therefore, to be compared with this, and
with which it is probably contemporary.

The roofs are covered throughout with pantiles; but these are
evidently not the old covering, being put on very carelessly and
interfering with the design of the stonework. The position of
the windows in the central lantern proves that in the beginning
of the thirteenth century the roofs must have been very flat, and
the probability is, therefore, that they were all covered with
flat-pitched stone roofs, similar to those of Toledo and Avila.

Few of the original windows remain save those already noticed
in the eastern apses. At the west end of the aisles there are
circular windows, without tracery and with very bold mouldings
enriched with two or three orders of dog-tooth ornament. The
windows in the aisles of the nave have all been destroyed by
the addition of chapels against the side-walls, whilst the clerestory has been filled for the most part with early geometrical
tracery windows in place of the lancets, with which it was, no
doubt, originally lighted.

The doorways are numerous and somewhat remarkable for
their position. There are three at the west end, whereof those
to the aisles are of the date of the earliest part of the fabric,
whilst the great central western doorway, being an addition of
the fourteenth century, will be described further on. The tympanum of the western door of the north aisle is sculptured with
the Adoration of the Magi, the figures all in niches and carved
in small and very delicate style. The door of the south aisle is
similar in style, but simpler and without sculpture. The other
doors are, as will be seen on reference to the plan, placed in a
most unusual position in the north and south choir aisles. It
is rare in churches of this plan to find any doorway east of the
transept, and where the aisles or chapels are so short this seems

TARRAGONA
INTERIOR OF CLOISTER

to be a very good rule.   Here the access to the church is so near
the altars of these aisles as to produce a bad effect.   The north
door was evidently so placed because it was necessary to put the
cloisters in a most unusual position, to the north-east of the
church, and I suppose we must assume that the south door was
put in a corresponding position for no better reason than that it
might match the other.

The door from the cloister into the church is the finest in the
church.   It is a round-arched doorway, with four engaged shafts
in each jamb, and a central shaft, which is remarkable for the
grand depth and size of its sculptured capital and base.   All the
capitals are very delicately wrought, and with an evident knowledge of Byzantine art; and that of the centre shaft has a subject sculptured on each face, of which the three which are visible
are: (1) The Procession of the Kings; (2) their Worship of our
Lord; and (3) the Nativity.   The fourth side is concealed by
the modern door-frame, the doorway not having had a door at
all originally.   A deep plain lintel forms the head of the door,
and above this the tympanum is filled with that often-repeated
scheme, our Lord in a vesica-shaped aureole, surrounded by the
emblems of the Evangelists, each of which has a book, as also
has our Lord, who holds His in the left hand, whilst He gives
His blessing with the right hand.   The small spandrel between
the round arch of this door and the pointed arch of the vault
above, is filled with a circle containing the monogram,
supported by two angels.   On the same (south) side of
the cloister is the entrance to the Chapter-house, which
follows the invariable type of Chapter doorways, having a
central doorway with a window on either side of it.   One of the
groining-ribs is brought boldly down between the doorway and
one of the window openings, a peculiarity which should be
compared with the similar arrangement of the Chapter-house at
Veruela.[1]   The detail is precisely the same as that of the rest
of the cloister, the arches all being semi-circular, and the side
openings being of two lights, with coupled shafts in place of
monials.   In the east wall of the cloister, and close to the
Chapter-house, is another fine doorway of the same early style.
Its door was painted very richly with angels holding coats-of-
arms; but this delicate work is now almost all defaced.   This
spacious cloister is one of the most conspicuous of the earlier
portions of the cathedral.   A public thoroughfare does now, and
probably did always, bound the cathedral close to its southern

[1] See p. 388.

wall, so that there was no room for the cloister in the usual position to the south of the church. But it is very rare, I think, to find the Chapter-house built as it is here, opening out of the southern alley of the cloister, in place of the eastern. Its character is unusually good, even in this country of fine cloisters. Each bay has three round-arched openings divided by coupled shafts, and above these two large circles pierced in the wall. The arches and circular windows are richly moulded, and adorned largely with delicate dog-tooth enrichments. Some of the circular windows above the arcades still retain—what all, I suppose, once had—their filling in, which was of very delicate interlacing work, pierced in a thin slab of stone, and evidently Moorish in its origin, though, at the same time, the work probably of Christian hands, as in some of them the figure of the Cross is very beautifully introduced.[1]

It is so rare to find any such influence as this exerted, that these traceries have an artificial interest. Yet they are in themselves very charmingly designed, and serve admirably to break the too-powerful rays of the sun. Indeed, nothing in its way can be much prettier than the effect of the shadows of these delicate piercings thrown sharply on the pavement by the brilliant sunlight. The groining is carried by triple engaged shafts, and its thrust resisted by buttresses, with an engaged shaft on their outer face. The groining is simple quadripartite, and the ribs are well moulded; many of the capitals are carved with great vigour, and some of their abaci are covered also with stories admirably rendered. Take, for instance, this story of the Cat and the Rats, which I sketched on one of the abaci of the southern walk of the cloister. It is full of a spirit and humour which are thoroughly foreign to the conventional traditions of our present school of workmen. Give one, nowadays, such a story to illustrate, and the result would probably be simply absurd, whilst in the hands of this natural Tarragonese artist the whole thing is instinct with life and humour, to as great an extent now as it was when his brother workmen first gathered round him and laughed their approval of the speedy retribution which met the silly rats when they forgot to tie the limbs of their enemy. I ought to have sketched the capitals which were under this abacus, for they were sculptured with cocks fighting, with their wings and heads so ingeniously arranged as to conform to the ordinary outlines of the early

[1] *See* illustrations of these on the ground-plan of Tarragona Cathedral, Plate XV., p. 40.

II   C

thirteenth-century foliage capital. It is rarely that so much
fine and original sculpture of various kinds is to be found in
one such church as this; and I recommend those who follow my
footsteps here to go prepared to devote some little time to the
accurate delineation and careful study of it.

Much of the flooring of the cloister appears to be coeval with
it;[1] and though composed of the very simplest materials, it is
most effective. Most of the patterns are formed with red tiles
of different sizes, fitted together so as to make very simple
diapers, and with the addition here and there of small squares

SCULPTURED ABACUS IN CLOISTER

of white marble, which are used with the tiles. Some of these
have an incised pattern on their face, sunk about a quarter of
an inch; and in one case I found that this pattern had been
filled in with red marble. The pattern is arranged with a broad
stripe down the centre of the cloister, and on either side of this
a succession of varying arrangements of tiles is contrived, each
pattern being continued but for a short distance. Here, with
the simplest materials, very great variety of effect is obtained,
whilst, with the much smarter and very elaborate materials of
the present day, we seem to run every day more risk than before
of sinking into the tamest monotony.

In the west wall of this cloister there is a monumental recess
of completely Moorish character, very delicately adorned; and

[1] *See* detail of this pavement on Plate XV., p. 41.

on one of the doors I noticed that the wood had been covered with thin iron plates, stamped with a pattern, gilded, and fastened down with copper nails. The Chapter-house, of whose entrance archways I have spoken, is a square room, roofed with a stone waggon-vault of pointed section; and at the south end of this is a seven-sided apse, which seems to have been added to the original fabric *circa* A.D. 1350. On the eastern side of it are some large sacristies, but they did not appear to be old.

So far the work I have had to describe has been all, with the exception of part of the steeple and Cimborio, not later than the end of the thirteenth century. It is evident, however, that considerable works were undertaken in various parts of the fabric at a later date. Most of the nave windows were taken out, in order to insert others with very fair geometrical traceries; the upper part of the steeple was, as we have seen, erected; and finally the west front was, in great part, reconstructed. The original west front of the aisles still remains, with a simple doorway, and richly moulded and carved circular windows, without tracery. Pilaster buttresses are placed at their north-west and south-west angles, and these have shafts at their angles, but have lost their old finish at the top. Probably another door and circular window of large size occupied the end of the nave in the original design; but these have been entirely removed, to make way for a work which, though it seems to have been commenced in A.D. 1278,[1] has all the air of complete middle-pointed work, and was evidently not completed until late in the fourteenth century. The existing central doorway is of grand dimensions, with figures under canopies on either side, and round the buttresses which flank it. In the centre is a statue of the Blessed Virgin with our Lord, and above, on the lintel, the Resurrection; and the tympanum is pierced with rich geometrical tracery. The pedestal under the statue of the Blessed Virgin has sculptured on its several sides—(1) the Creation of Adam; (2) of Eve; (3) the Fall; (4) Adam and Eve hiding themselves; and (5) the Expulsion from Paradise. These subjects are very fitly placed here, the Fall in the centre coming just under the feet of her who bears our Lord in her arms, and thus restores the balance to the world. The arch is lofty, but only moulded; and

[1] In 1278 M. Bartolomé wrought nine figures of the Apostles for the façade; and in 1375 M. Jayme Castayls agreed to execute the remainder. His contract is made under the direction of Bernardo de Vallfogona, acting as architect to the Chapter, and father probably of the man of the same name who was consulted about Gerona cathedral, and who executed the reredos of the high altar at Tarragona in A.D. 1426, and died in A.D. 1436.

above it is a pediment of extremely flat pitch.   Above this, again, is a large and finely-traceried circular window.   The lower part only of the gable remains, and this is of very steep pitch, and must always have been intended to be a mere sham.   Whenever this sort of thing is done, there is always some ground for suspicion that the architect may have been a foreigner, unused to the requirements of a southern climate; and, at any rate, most of the work in this façade might very well have been executed by a German architect, for its character is all that of German, rather than of Spanish art.   It recalls, to some extent, the façade of the north transept of Valencia Cathedral, though scarcely so much as to appear to be the work of the same hands. It is to be regretted that the great western gable is incomplete, for, unreal as it is, its outline must have been fine; and even now, seen as it is in its small Plaza from the steep, narrow, dark and shady street, surmounting the flights of steps which lead up to it, the effect is very striking.   The traceries, both of the tympanum of the doorway, and of the circular window above, are sharp geometrical works, very delicately executed.   The upper part of the western gable above the circular window seems to have had three windows, but these are now partially destroyed. The hinges and knockers of the western doorway are elaborately designed, covered with pierced traceries, made with several thicknesses of metal.   The doors are diapered all over with iron plates, nailed on with copper nails, and with copper ornaments in the centre of each plate.   The buttresses are bold, but rather clumsily designed.   The statues of the door-jamb are carried round their lower parts, and the stage above is occupied with traceried panels.   A great crocketed pinnacle conceals the set-off, and forms, with the flat pediment of the doorway, a group in advance of the real face of the western wall.   Other crocketed pinnacles probably finished the angle buttresses on each side of the main gable, but they are now destroyed.

The north side of the nave is not easily seen, being enclosed within walls and behind houses; but the south side is fairly open to view.   Here, however, much of the original design is now completely concealed by modern additions.   The two western bays have chapels, added in the fifteenth century; the third bay a domed chapel of the seventeenth century; and there are two other late Gothic chapels in the two bays nearest the south transept.   On the north, side chapels have been added in the same fashion, those in the two western bays alone being mediæval. From the west side of the south transept a fair view is obtained of the best portion of the old exterior. The transept gable is extremely flat in pitch; the buttresses are all carried up straight to the eaves, and the trefoiled eaves-arcading, which recalls the favourite brick eaves-cornices of the Italian churches, is returned round them at the top, and a deep moulding, covered with billets, is carried along over the eaves-arcading. The original semi-Romanesque window, with its very broad external splay, still remains in the bay of the transept next to the Crossing; but the other windows have been altered; and there is a rich traceried rose window in the southern façade. The exterior of the lantern is certainly not very attractive. The entire absence from view of its roof is a fault of the most grievous kind; though, otherwise, its windows, recalling as they do the traceries of our own first-pointed, are not at all to be condemned. I doubt very much whether this lantern was ever a fine work on the exterior; but we may well be content to have anything so fine as the interior, and may fairly pardon its architect for his failure to achieve a more complete success.

The internal arrangements here do not present much subject for notice. The Coro is in the nave, and in the screen on its western side the entrance-doorway still remains. It is of marble, of two well-moulded orders, and the outer order of the arch has voussoirs of grey and white marble counterchanged. The steps are of dark marble, with three shields in low relief on the riser of each, and the bearings which occur here are seen also in the keystone of the tower vaulting—both being works of the fourteenth century. The choir stalls and the panelling behind them are of the very richest and most delicate fifteenth-century work; and the great desk for books, in the centre of the Coro, is of the same age.[1] The stall-ends are covered with delicate tracery, put on in a separate piece against the end, and not carved out of the solid. The divisions between the panelling at the back of the stalls are wrought with foliage and animals of really marvellous execution, and a band of inlaid work with coats-of-arms goes all round just above the stalls. There is a throne on the right hand of the entrance to the choir, and another at the east end of the south side; but both of these are of Renaissance character.

Many of the choir books are mediæval, with large knops at their angles, and a piece of fringed leather under each knop. At the east end of the Coro, and in a line with the west wall of

[1] The stalls of the Coro were executed between A.D. 1479 and 1493, by Francisco Gomar of Zaragoza.

the transepts, is the iron Reja, and on each side of it a pulpit facing east. These have all the appearance of having been rebuilt. They have the same armorial bearings as the doorway to the Coro; and as the screen in which the latter is now built is not old, it is probable that they all form part of the same old choir screen, and that the two pulpits were the ambons. I saw nothing to prove decidedly whether the Coro was in its original place, or whether it has been moved down into the nave as at Burgos.

The great organ is on the north side of the Coro; it is not very old, but its pipes are picturesquely arranged, and it has enormous painted wings or shutters.

Much of the pavement is old; that in the choir proper—the Capilla mayor—is of marble in various stripes of patterns extending across the church.[1] The nave is also paved with marble, arranged in lines and patterns divided to suit the position of the columns. The Coro alone is paved with tiles, and this seems to some extent to prove that this part of the floor has been altered, which would be the case if the stalls were moved down from their original position. The high altar has a very rich reredos executed for the most part in marble, and rich in sculptured subjects (5). There is a doorway on each side of the altar, opening into the part of the apse shut off by this Retablo. Here the pavement has a large oblong compartment, which seemed to me to suggest the original position of the altar to have been much nearer the east wall than it now is. This space is indicated in my ground-plan, and though it is more than usually set back towards the wall, it was no doubt a more convenient position in so short a choir than that which the present altar occupies (6).

There is a richly-sculptured monument of a bishop on the southern side of the sacrarium.

It will be seen that here, as is the case with so many other Spanish cathedrals, though the scale is not very great, the dignity and grandeur of the whole conception is extreme. The cloister, indeed, yields the palm to few that I have seen, and it is in scale only, and not in real dignity and nobility, that the interior of the church does so.

I did not discover any other old church in Tarragona, yet I should suppose there must be some in so large a city (7). There is a four-light *ajimez* window, of the type so common on this coast, in the Plaza in front of the cathedral; and in the Plaza

[1] *See* the illustration of this marble pavement on Plate XV., p. 41.

della Pallot is an early round-arched gateway, with a coeval two-light opening above.

In the wall of a chapel to the east of the cathedral (8) I found a fairly good example of an early headstone, perfectly plain in outline, and finished with a flat gable, in which is incised a cross under an arch, the inscription being carried across the stone in the common mode, just below the pediment.

I had not time to make excursions to any of the other churches in this district, but there are some which appear, from what I have learnt, to be so fine, that it is to be hoped others will contrive to inspect them. The monasteries of Vallbona (9) and Poblet, and the church of Sta. Creus,[1] not far from Poblet, seem to be all of great interest. Poblet and Sta. Creus seem both to have cloisters with projecting chapels somewhat similar to that shown on my ground-plan of the monastery at Veruela.

The church at Reus, too, is interesting, from the fact that the contract for its erection is preserved, and has been published by Cean Bermudez. It dates from A.D. 1510. This town is a few miles only from Tarragona, and after seeing Poblet and Vallbona, the ecclesiologist would do well, I think, to make his way across to Lérida, instead of returning to Barcelona, as I did. But I wished much to examine the Collegiata at Manresa on my way to Lérida, and for this purpose the line I took was on the whole the best.

I bade farewell to Tarragona with a heavy heart, and with a determination to avail myself of the first chance I may have of returning to look once more at its noble and too little known cathedral.[2]

---

[1] Vallbona has a very fine Romanesque cruciform church with eastern apses and a low central octagonal lantern; Poblet was an early cross church with a fourteenth-century central lantern, and a cloister of the same age; and Sta. Creus is an early church with a fourteenth-century cloister, which has a projecting chapel with a fountain in it on one side similar to that at Veruela.—Parcerisa, *Recuerdos*, etc.

[2] There is a good inn here, the Fonda del Europa (10). But beware of the Fonda de los Cuatro Naciones, which is dirty and bad. Tarragona may be reached easily by steamboats from Barcelona. They go twice a week in five or six hours, I believe.

Detail of Moresque Tracery in Cloister.

Nave

Coro

Modern Chapel

Modern Chapel

Modern Chapel

Pulpit.

Pulpit.

Before 1200.
13th Century.
14th Century.
15 & 16th Cent?.
Modern.

PLATE

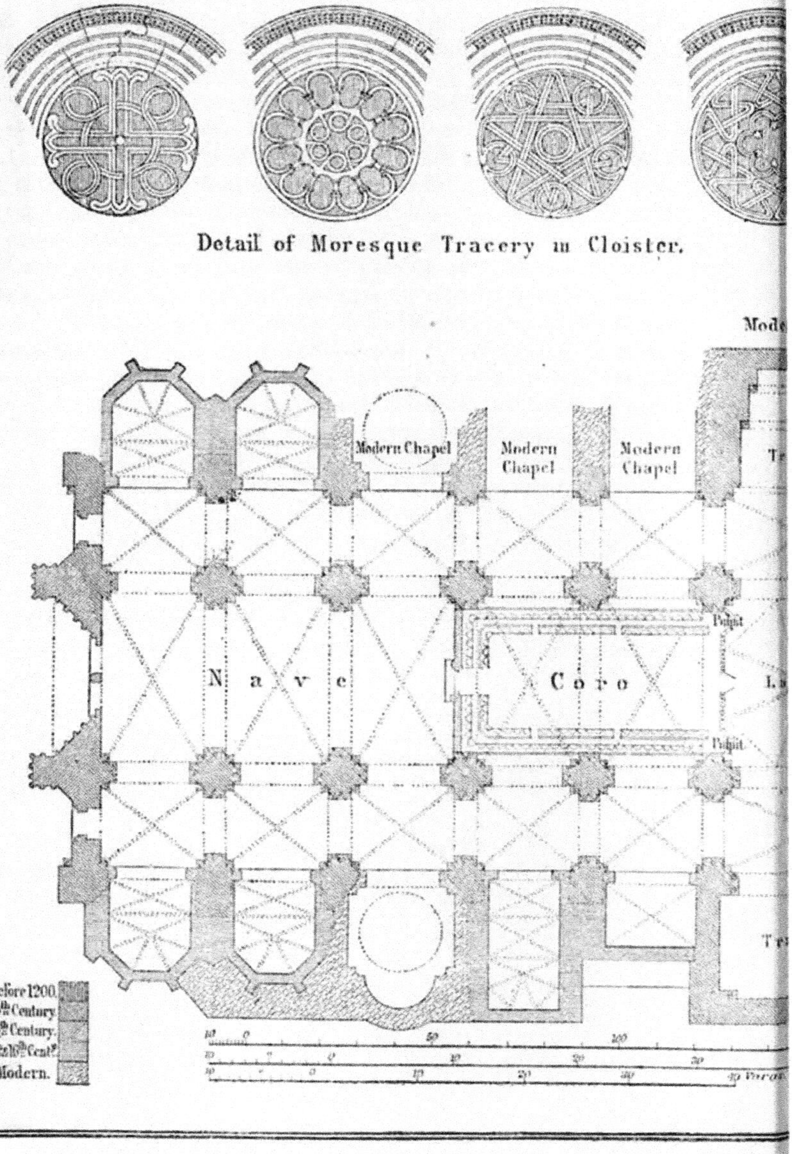

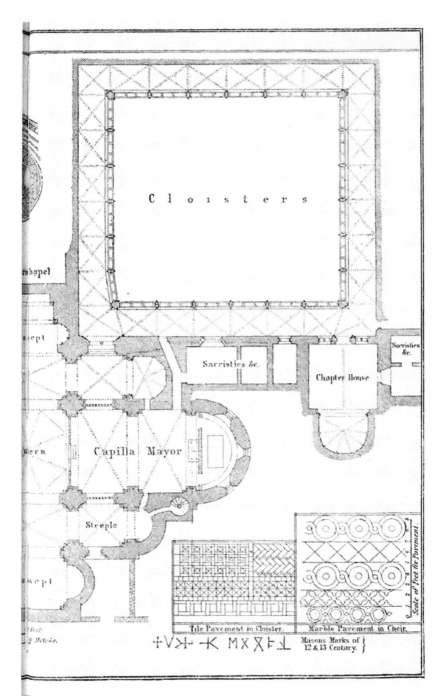

Cloisters

Chapel

sept

Sacristies &c.

Chapter House

Sacristies &c.

ern

Capilla Mayor

Steeple

sept

Feet.
Metres.

Tile Pavement in Cloister.

Marble Pavement in Choir.

Scale of Feet for Pavement.

✝ V ⊁ ⊬ ✶ ⊀ M X ⊠ Ⴀ ⊥   Masons Marks of }
12 & 13 Century. }

XV.

NOTES

(1) At Vilafranca de Peñades the church (restored) is of late Gothic, passing into Renaissance, with a single very wide nave and a crypt like that at Barcelona. Here is, or lately was, a retable of S. George, painted some time after 1424 by a close follower of Luis Borrassá; at the chapel of Peñafiel (or Penafel), three-quarters of an hour to the south of the town, a retable of S. Michael, that, dimmed as it is, keeps a hint of fairy grace, and one of S. Lucy, a trifle later, by the same master. At San Martin Sarroca, seven miles to the north-west, the great retable is from the same hand as the S. George, and even nearer to the forms and composition of Luis Borrassá himself. The church of S. Martin counts as one of the greater Romanesque churches of Catalonia: of the eleventh century, cruciform, barrel-vaulted, with a famous side portal and a superb arcade around the apse, both without and within.

(2) It also contains the best of the sculptures from the ruins of Poblet, and in particular two alabaster groups of statuettes from a tomb that can challenge contemporary French work. The heads of three monks in copes are exquisite and completely Spanish; so is the somewhat acrid humour of the other group. Behind both are remains of the deep blue glass that once filled in the background.

(3) S. Bernard Tort is said to have begun it, but the fineness of detail and vaulting looks like the early thirteenth century. More probably Bishop Hugh (died 1193) began the works and got the walls to a certain height, the central apse and the two lateral apses, the pillars up to the capitals of the aisles. Rocabert (1199-1214) finished the transepts and began the crossing. Aspargo finished this and consecrated it in 1230. In 1231-51, the aisles were vaulted and in 1272 the nave by Bishop Olivella, who also made the façade. The crossing must have had a wooden roof, for the lantern is later than this. In 1287, Archbishop Rodrigo Tello, we are told, finished the west front, in 1331 the Patriarch of Alexandria dedicated it afresh, and in 1375 they were still about the statues.

(4) On the other hand, we know that in 1128 Robert of Normandy came back to Tarragona, bringing both soldiers and workmen, so that there is a presumption for French builders in the town long before Fray Bernardo.

(5) The Retablo Mayor was made (circa 1426-50) by Pedro Juan de Vallfogona and Guillem de la Mota. The former was the son of the master-overseer of the cathedral, D. Bernardo; he collected money due to him on the work 1425, and again on December 15, 1436; he was working January 2, 1445, on the retable of the See of Zaragoza; in April of that year he came to Tarragona, presumably to watch operations there, went back May 28, and on the 16th of August was ill. After that we hear no more. He died well along in middle life, for as early as 1416 he had been called by the chapter of Gerona to confer about the vault, along with his associate, Guillem de la Mota. This alabaster retable is planned precisely like earlier painted ones,

only with a juster subordination of size and disposition of scenes. The Madonna reigns, standing under a great canopy, flanked by SS. Tekla and Paul, under canopies hardly less; and twelve smaller reliefs tell her history through the Infancy and Passion to Pentecost and the Coronation. Six reliefs of the same proportions, but a rarer art, ranged in a sort of lower story, relate the long martyrdom of the virgin patroness on either side. In the centre, directly behind the altar gradine, five niches enshrine a Pietà: the dead Christ, naked, upheld by an angel, between SS. Mary and John, Nicodemus, with the three nails pouched up, and Joseph of Arimathea with the lance—now broken. The last two, as belonging to the Older Dispensation, wear their haloes octagonal. The story of S. Tekla's conversion by S. Paul, which opens the series, with the two that close it, of wild bulls in a crowd and a bishop discovering the saint's arm in a mountain cave, are merely admirable, but the other three, which present her in the flames, among the lions, and in the swamp full of toads and vipers, are astounding creations. I am not the only one to see unaccountable parallels to the bronze reliefs of the Far East in the low relief of a background held in clear, successive planes, and treated with vivid multitudinous detail, and in the extraordinary quality of the curling and elastic line, that swirls like a lasso and licks like a fire. The edges of drapery, the waves of flame, the beard of Joseph of Arimathea, the eddies of the slimy pool, the modelling of the heads and of the nude, belong not to marble, but to metal-work.

(6) The Chapel of the Tailors, in the richest style of the fourteenth century, is good in line everywhere, the statues lovely, the corbels not aggressively secular. In the retable, which presents in the predella the Ten Virgins, and above, the whole sacred story from the Annunciation to the Coronation, the iconography is that of northern France. The work is local, that of some one a better carver than artist; a craftsman safe in detail or in familiar scenes, but puzzled to manage fresh inventions. Yet, though the dramatic episodes are neither composed nor plastic, the rows of figures have a pleasant ripple, like horsemen in Greek reliefs.

The tomb of the Infant, D. John of Aragon, who died, aged thirty-three, in 1334 (a son of John the Just and Blanche of Anjou), was carved by an Italian of the school of Giovanni Pisano, sent probably from Naples, who adorned it, amongst other saintly figures, with the two SS. Louis—his uncle, the Bishop of Toulouse, and his great great-uncle, the King of France.

A few early pictures linger on. Behind the gilded temple that blocks an eighteenth-century chapel in the transept, on a Catalan retable of S. Bartholomew, I deciphered, amongst other things, the diverting history of a child who wouldn't grow up. In twenty-five years he wore out four nurses, who lie dead about the floor. At last the saint drove the devil out of him. In the cloister an exquisite retable of S. Mary Magdalen is full of romantic feeling. In one scene outside a castle she turns to smile at her lover, much as in Rossetti's drawing; in another, a king rows ashore from a ship in the offing, and finds a queen lying dead upon the beach, with her baby at her breast—the motive is familiar in romances of the south of

France. In another chapel of the cloister Nuestra Señora de la Esperanza is cloaked like a Madonna of Mercy.

(7) S. Pablo, in the court of the Seminary, is of the twelfth or thirteenth century, with possibly a Visigothic door and certainly Mudejar arches to the cornice—but the whole is restored out of all consideration.

(8) The little detached chapel of S. Tekla, which stands within the cathedral enclosure, is not older than the fourteenth century.

(9) *Cistercian Foundations in Catalonia.* Vallbona de las Monjas is in the form of a Latin cross; the three apses and transepts Romanesque, with the main portal in the west wall of the northern; the nave of four bays without aisles, a lofty Gothic; a low lantern tower over the crossing and a tall one, surprisingly, over the next to last bay of the nave. In 1157 a noble gentleman, Ramon de Argensola y Vallbona, founded two cloisters, one for men and one for women, at Colobres and Vallbona respectively; in 1176, by repeated request of Doña Berenguela de Cervera, the two were united under the Abbess Doña Oria de Ramon, and placed under the Cistercian rule. Two other early foundations I did not see: Santa Maria de Savany, which was Benedictine originally, refounded by the Cistercians in 1223, lies up near the borders of the province of Huesca, three kilometres from Pont de Suert. The ruins are said to be fine. Santa Maria de Escarpe has been rebuilt in the Greco-Roman style: it was founded by Don Pedro the Catholic, and his son Jaime I. Of the remaining two, Santas Creus should be seen before Poblet, both because it is less ruinous now, and because it was less magnificent always. It may be most easily visited from Valls, where I am told there is a good inn, and I saw that there was a good Catalan church, but the little hostelry just outside of the monastery gate would do well enough. There I found a sufficient dinner, a quiet bedroom to wash up and rest, and an outlook over the rustling tops of trees that should harbour nightingales.

Like Fountains Abbey and San Galgano, Pontigny and Fossanuova, Veruela and its own elder sister of Poblet, Santas Creus lies in a river valley, visible for a long time, as the road approaches across the flanks of the hills opposite, yellow against the yellow hillside. It is not prepossessing, lifting Renaissance towers and domes out of the midst of battlements. Even from that distance the church looks like nothing but a fortress, and close at hand proves itself to be square-topped and battlemented—nave, aisles, and transept—in strong horizontal lines; the square east end juts out beyond the transepts, the square west end stands up above the aisles; a long curtain wall, battlemented and loopholed, masks the west walk of the cloister, and ends at another round-arched, low portal, strongly defended, the Puerta Real. Through a baroque gate-house and a shabby rococo square, where entertainment was once provided for guests of less than princely rank, one comes to the low, round-arched west door (the Romanesque work of Gothic builders) without a tympanum, without statues, dwarfed by the huge pointed window broken through above, and one passes into a church, high, austere, and dark. Beyond the nave and aisles of six bays and the lantern, which should have been early Gothic and is actually bad Renaissance, stretch transepts of two bays and five square chapels on the eastern side, all of the earliest transitional style, with quadripartite vaults. The slightly pointed transverse arches, wide and unmoulded, come down upon a wide pier, very slightly cruciform, with a high base. The clerestory windows are round-headed and deeply splayed; the east end has three such, now blocked, below the great rose, and one apiece in the chapels. In the face of the north transept, two fine windows open above a door reached by seven steps. Out of the south transept the stairs go up to the dormitory, and above that room still remains for a little window in the gable. Below the stairs a door opens on a passage which turns and reaches the cloister just north of the chapter house; doors to the cloister are set in the sixth and the second bay of the south aisle. The Coro now fills the nave from aisle to aisle and from the crossing to the third bay; to the original choir probably the monks came in from the cloister by the eastern door and the lay brothers to their own part by that further west.

Founded in the twelfth century by the Moncadas and endowed by them and other great Catalan houses, the monastery never wanted money for building and re-building, which went on steadily and soberly. The progress of the work is recorded on a manuscript formerly in the convent library, by a note of the fourteenth century. As early as December 4, 1150, Ramon Dapifer de Moncada had made over entirely to the abbot of the Cistercian monastery of the *Gran Selva* some land in Valdaura, with mill and water rights. With twelve monks and three lay brothers, William, the first abbot, founded and then abandoned a monastery. He tried again at Anchosa in 1153 with a fresh foundation from Ramon Berenguer IV., but it proved too sterile and too near to towns and people. When they finally began work on the banks of the little river Gaya they were held up by a dispute between neighbouring bishops as to jurisdiction. The community was moved in 1169, Pedro de Puigvert being abbot. In September 1174, the church was begun; July 29, 1191, was laid the first stone of the foundations of the dormitory of the young monks. June 21, 1211 (being the day of Pentecost), the convent of this monastery moved into a new church, with forty-five monks. March 22, 1225, the convent was exchanged for the greater room of the church for matins (" *vigilias matutinas.*"). June 24, 1302 (the Decollation of S. John Baptist), the work of the refectory was begun. September 13, 1303, was laid the first stone of the cloister, finished in 1346. " The things above said were taken from various very old books of the convent, which were falling to pieces, and written by me, Fray Bartolome de la Darnosa, in this book in the month of June, year of the Lord, 1367." Finished in 1378, the walls around the church, dormitory, and cloister were begun on the first of January, 1375, " on account of great scarcity of food," but relief works had to be dropped when the convent felt the pinch, and no more was done. The cloister was paid for in large part by Jaime II. and Blanche of Anjou, whose arms adorn the Puerta Real at the end of the south walk with the Catalan bars and the French lilies; it was consecrated in November of 1341, presumably in their presence, as it had been finished in January. The lavabo and chapter house are probably preserved from an earlier cloister, as at Veruela, La Oliva, and Fitero. The so-called Old Cloister, which lies in the maze of buildings to the eastward, is dated 1163. The palace in that same quarter (now under exhaustive restoration) was built chiefly by Peter III. the Great (1276-95), and Jaime II. of Aragon (1291) whose tombs stand in the church under the richest stone tabernacles. That over the tomb of Pedro was ordered by Jaime II. and probably made by Beltram Riquer of Barcelona, architect of the royal palace there, who in 1314 made Jaime's monument. The carved shrine of Don Pedro rests upon a huge porphyry bath, sustained by two lions, which was fetched from Sicily by Lauria, the High Admiral. He is buried near where his master thus lies literally like an emperor—like Frederick II. in Palermo and Constance of Aragon, his spouse. Other tombs also survive, one of the fourteenth century, in the north transept, of a mitred abbot, his face humorous without loss of dignity. The cloister is full of tombs, some older than itself—arks laid up in pointed niches bearing the arms of the Monteliu; or, between twisted shafts, the counters of the Moncada; in quatrefoils the eagle of Bernardo de Selva, who lies with the long sleeves of his alb wrapped over his hands; or, above saints in cusped arcades, the stag of the armed knight, D. Ramon de Alemany de Cervello. The vault is sexpartite, ten bays along the church, nine the other way; the tracery, much of it, broken. The serried foliage or elaborate grotesques of the capitals are the luxuriant fourteenth-century stuff that Spain carries off better than France; but the hexagonal fountain-house, which shelters on the south side a hexagonal basin, dripping, overgrown with moss and maidenhair, is as strict as S. Bernard's rule. On each side, a pointed arch of two square orders enclose a pair of round arches and a lozenge or a circle in the tympanum. Three pairs of coupled shafts receive the inner arches, and the corners of the structure are strengthened by a buttress, square as far as the string course which marks the level of the capitals and receives the outer arch, thence up a half-column with a plain capital. Under the low roof the entrance to the chapter house is of the same pattern, except that the enclosing arches are round and the edges moulded, the orders and the shafts doubled. Two windows flank a door over which the double arches meet on a pendent corbel. Within, the nine bays of quadripartite vault are carried on four columns and pyramidal corbels against the wall; the capitals are of interlaced withes, or of the same delicate overlapping leaves, like a larger laurel, as those at the entrance. Beyond this on the south a barrel-vaulted passage leads eastward to the Great Cloister, of low, pointed arches without tracery or vaulting, the sloping timber roof carried on great arches thrown across the corners. The refectory is of 1733—but the stables are vaulted with stone. Between the two cloisters, over the chapter house, lay the dormitory of the novices, roofed with timber and plaster; the immense pointed stone arches rest on corbels, wrought in a Romanesque low-relief of *entrelacs*. To the south of this they show the library, with stucco cornice and artesonado ceiling. The *Torre de las Horas*, opposite, is of 1344. The palace, which lies to the south-east, is an exquisite toy. In the first court a stairway, carried on a single porphyry pillar, leads up to a gallery of pointed arches on slender columns, quatrefoil in section, with delicate Catalan capitals and painted timber roof. The next court has a third story—a low loggia of delicate stucco reliefs; elsewhere a loggia of fine brick-work arches hangs over the wall and looks abroad. The ceilings are artesonado, or timbered, coffered, or worked in fine plaster reliefs. The rooms are almost as curiously small as at the Alhambra—an adorable palace, built for the little ivory ladies and lovers of the fourteenth century.

Poblet, older and more royal, was sacked in 1835: the birds that fly around the desecrated altar and flash through the high southern windows, shake the trails of pale ivy hanging there. Mossén Barraguer gives an astonishing account of the mingled excitement and sullen hate, terror and curiosity, with which the townspeople hurried down the road to ransack and destroy. There may have been pilfering on the spot, but cupidity was not a motive. They knew the monks for decent folk and easy-going; yet they expected to find dungeons, bones, prisoners white-haired or maniac. They destroyed for the sheer excitement, like stoning a cat, or Jew-baiting. It gives one pause—and I have paused here for two only out of many considerations: one that it seemed to throw some light on possible incidents in the Dissolution of the Monasteries at home, which was managed on the whole better. Though the church saved no more, the destruction of property was less. Furthermore, it is not yet over, at any rate in Spain, and the sentimental argument that retables should be left in churches where nobody can see them now, may as well face the practical assurance that if they are so left they will be burned with the churches, and nobody can see them ever.

In 1149, when D. Ramon Berenguer had taken Lérida, married Doña Petronella, the heiress of Aragon, and gone to Provence to settle some sporadic rebellions, he made Cistercian friends there, and on the 19th of the following January he yielded to the Abbot of Fontefroide in the diocese of Narbonne his "Huerta de Poblet" for a monastery, in return for which certain religious, indicated by S. Bernard, from the said Fontefroide, were to settle there. The monks came some time between August 18, 1150, when he repeated the donation, and May 6, 1151, when he made one to "S. Mary of Poblet, Stephen its Abbot, and the monks who there serve God," confirmed by Eugenius III., himself a Cistercian, in a bull of November 30, 1152. The date of the monks' final settlement is given as September 7, 1153, though it is hard to see how the east end could have been ready for them. The church and the adjoining wing of the cloister (here on the north side) were probably the work of Alfonso II. (1162-96), the Gothic walks of the cloister, the refectory, library, chapter house, and some other parts may belong to Jaime I. (1214-76). The seven chapels of the south aisle and the lantern were built by Abbot Ponce de Capons, 1330. Peter IV. (1336-87) gave the great wall with ten towers that straitly encloses the monastery proper, 1367-77. Martin the Humane (1395-1410) raised a lovely and a kingly palace at the west that he did not live to occupy. The cloister of S. Stephen was rebuilt in 1415. Great lords and great benefactors were the houses of Cardona, Cervera, and Angle-sola; in the seventeenth century they overlaid kings' tombs with their own in the transepts, as from the thirteenth they had filled up the Galilee, the cloister, and the monks' burial ground. Jaime Castayls of Tarragona in the last quarter of the fourteenth century contracted with the abbot for some of the tombs under the crossing. The great marble retable, of six stories with wings returned for a whole bay, is ruined now; its date is 1625. Despite all the Renais-sance marbles, and the eighteenth-century adornments on the façade at the west, Poblet conveys a far greater feeling of the Romanesque elements than Santa Creus, chiefly because these persisted in the plan, the vaulting and the sculpture of the capitals. From the Galilee, crowded with lovely tombs, that stretches across three bays a ribbed quadripartite vault on corbels, a round-arched door with painted mouldings opens into the nave; the aisles had once small windows, and the nave a rose above the roof of this. The church has seven bays and transepts of pointed barrel-vault, with one bay of the same east of the crossing and a chevet of five compartments. Two apsidal chapels with barrel-vault and semi-dome open east of the transepts and five more out of the ambulatory. This, after barrel-vaults in the bays parallel to the lateral chapels, has five bays of irregular quadripartite. The vault of the crossing is domical with an opening to the lantern above, and all the apsidal and transept chapels have a like incongruous lantern. The vaulting of the aisles (quadripartite) was raised in the fourteenth century; the piers are cruciform in plan, with an engaged shaft. The trans-verse arches are pointed and so are (very slightly) those of the nave arcade, of two orders, but the great longitudinal arches that run from the floor to the string courses just below the vault are round, and so are the deeply splayed windows of the clerestory. They are mostly plain, a few carved with a cross or strapwork, two on the west end of the south aisle, when the work was almost finished, with timid suggestions of leaves. The empty church, ruined, but not ruinous, filled with sunlight, scented with the roses and grass of the cloister, is like a natural force, a mountain valley or a great river, with the freshness of bright dew, and the stillness of early light. The cloister, though it is the glory of Poblet, is only one treasure among many. The south walk may be of the twelfth century, with seven bays, not all alike in width, of round arches on coupled shafts under a deeper arch; and the rest, six bays, of two, three, or four lights, of thirteenth-century Gothic, with Romanesque reminiscences. The whole has quadripartite vaulting, many shafts and capitals in one style, which, whether covered with *entrelacs*, or with a network pattern, or with leaf motives, betray the presence of Arab workmen; the bases have beautiful *griffes*. The chapter house stands on the east side with the usual nine bays, and the usual two double windows and a door between, this time a single round arch carrying many orders of serried shafts; but it opens also to eastward by three similar windows into another cloister, with incomparable effect. The hexagonal fountain-house looks severe and Romanesque, two round arches and a lozenge set under a round arch; but that is moulded and carried on three pairs of columns delicately wrought, and the capitals of the central shaft are developed Gothic. The superb refectory opposite it, with a barrel-vault, and a fountain in the midst, with stairs going up behind an arcade to the lector's pulpit, and tall windows on three sides, is of the late twelfth or early thirteenth century, like the kitchen adjoining on the west. To the east, beyond a square room used for a passage, the thirteenth-century library is now divided into two rooms, of four and five bays respectively, and vaulted upon a row of pillars down the centre. The floors here have been raised, which dwarfs the proportions of the fine windows and vaulting-ribs. This runs due north, and opens, not out of the cloister, but out of the barrel-vaulted passage, which runs eastward from the north-east corner of the cloister and flanks the chapter house; above this entire range, from the farther end of the library to the transept wall of the church, lies the dormitory of the novices, thirteenth century also, with an upper and a lower range of windows, and nine bays of superb pointed transverse arches on capitals richly and fantastically wrought in low relief. This, of course, had a stairway down into the north transept; the day stairs which go down beside the chapter house into the cloister yawn in the middle of the floor. In the dormitory of the elder monks, less lofty and less splendid, built above the "*bodega*," or stores, at the north-west, the arches of nine bays strike the floor at the centre and rebound in a second aisle. The novices have a seventeenth-century cloister, along the west wall of the library, reached by a flight of steps from their dormitory ; besides the cloister of S. Stephen, east of the chapter house and archives, another lies further south-east behind the apse, attached to the infirmary and the sinister *Torre de Locos;* and in the north-east yet another cloister arcade flanks a great stack of seventeenth and eighteenth century buildings used for the entertainment of great lords. At the north-west are the sunken vats and pipes for wine, and the store-house vaulted strongly on three great pillars; from this angle of the cloisters, a passage led to the Puerta Real, in the encircling wall, plain, round-arched, flanked by two immense octagonal towers, and to the king's rooms. The abbot's quarters, perhaps for convenience in entertaining, seem to have lain, during the latter centuries, southward of the church, and therefore outside the enclosure; they were reached by a bridge that gave access to the west of the church high up. Of the palace of Don Martin the Humanist, its keen, yet ample beauty, I despair to speak. The windows, some square-headed, some pointed, filled with circles, or sharp pinnacles, or flame-shaped curves, recall most the development that late Gothic reached in Venice. All the carving has that same delicate, luxurious realism of people who feel themselves more alive amid vivid impressions, but these must be also precious and costly by the quality of the marble and the carver's dexterity. Most of all you feel that here, for a single happy hour, on which converged all the influences of sun and season and soil, an art suddenly and supremely flowered.

Outside these walls, but within the wider enclosure of the monastery, lie other buildings not wholly fallen to decay; the chapel of S. George, with a graceful, flamboyant door, the ruinous chapel of

S. Catharine, a gatehouse, and then, set off from the rest by a walled avenue in which fine trees mask the defensive value, the *Puerta Dorada*, crowned by a once gilded Virgin. The hamlet receives guests still in summer time; the railway station of Espluga has an inn and good people; the road between the two, excellent for carriages, not too long for unambitious walkers, is musical a good part of the way with running water and silver poplars (*pobos blancos*), from which the original hermitage took its name, Populetum.

(10) I feel regret but duty in testifying that at present the Fonda de Europa, in Tarragona, is the most cynically dirty in Spain, and that the landlord may misrepresent the inns in other places when he thinks thereby to profit himself.

CHAPTER XIV

BARCELONA

THE architectural history of Barcelona is much more complete, whilst its buildings are more numerous, than those of any of our own old cities, of which it is in some sort the rival. The power which the Barcelonese wielded in the middle ages was very great. They carried on the greater part of the trade of Spain with Italy, France, and the East; they were singularly free, powerful, and warlike; and, finally, they seem to have devoted no small portion of the wealth they earned in trade to the erection of buildings, which even now testify alike to the prosperity of their city, and to the noble acknowledgment they made for it.

· The architecture of Cataluña had many peculiarities, and in the fourteenth and fifteenth centuries, when most of the great buildings of Barcelona were being erected, they were so marked as to justify me, I think, in calling the style as completely and exclusively national or provincial, as, to take a contemporary English example, was our own Norfolk middle-pointed. The examination of them will, therefore, have much more value and interest than that of even grander buildings erected in a style transplanted from another country, such as we see at Burgos and Toledo; and beside this, there was one great problem which I may venture to say that the Catalan architects satisfactorily solved—the erection of churches of enormous and almost un· equalled internal width—which is just that which seems to be looming before us as the work which we English architects must ere long grapple with, if we wish to serve the cause of the Church thoroughly in our great towns.

For a manufacturing town, this, the Manchester of Spain, is singularly agreeable and unlike its prototype. The mills are for the most part scattered all over the surrounding country, which rises in pleasant undulations to the foot of the hills some four or five miles inland from the sea, and beyond which the country is always beautiful and wild, and sometimes—as in the savage and world-renowned rocks of Montserrat—quite sublime in its character. On my first journey I arrived at Barcelona by a steamer from Valencia. The views of the coast were generally extremely beautiful, until shortly before our arrival, as we passed the low level land through which the Llobregat finds its way to the sea; beyond this the great rock and fortress of Monjuic rise boldly in front, and rounding its base into the harbour, the tall octagonal towers and turrets of the cathedral and other churches came in sight. Little, however, is seen of the sea from the city, the fortifications of Monjuic on the one side, and the harbour and new colony of Barcelonette which occupies a point jutting out beyond it seaward on the other, completely shutting it out. One result of this is that, whilst nothing is seen of the sea, so, too, the seafaring people seem to confine themselves to Barcelonette, and not to show themselves in the thronged streets of the city. Another fortress, a little inland on the east, places Barcelona under a cross fire, and prevents its growth in that direction; but wherever possible it seems to be spreading rapidly, and every external sign of extreme prosperity is to be seen. The streets are generally narrow, tortuous, and picturesque, with the one noble exception of the Rambla, a very broad promenade running from the sea quite across the city, which has a road on either side, and a broad promenade planted with trees down the centre. Here in the early morning one goes to buy smart nosegays of the Catalan flower-girls from the country, and in the evening to stroll in a dense mob of loungers enjoying the cold air which sweeps down from the hills, and atones for all the sufferings inflicted by the torrid midday sun.

It will be best, in describing the buildings here, to begin with those of the earliest date, though they are of comparatively unimportant character, and in part fragments only of old buildings preserved in the midst of great works undertaken at a later date. The Benedictine convent of San Pablo del Campo, said to have been founded in the tenth century by Wilfred II., Count of Barcelona,[1] was restored by Guiberto Guitardo and his wife about 1117, and in 1127 was incorporated with the convent of San Cucufate del Vallés.[2] The church is very interesting. It is small and cruciform, with three parallel apses,

---

[1] He was buried here, and this inscription was formerly in the church: " Sub hac tribuna jacet corpus condam Wilfredi comitis filius Wilfredi, simili modo condam comitis bonæ memoriæ. Dimittat ei Dñs. Amen. Qui obiit, vj. Kal. Madii sub era DCCCCLII." (A.D. 914).

[2] San Cucufate del Vallés is not far from Barcelona; it has a fine early cloister somewhat like that of Gerona Cathedral, an early church with parallel triapsidal east end, octagonal lantern and tower on south side (1). *See* illustrations in Parcerisa, *Recuerdos, etc., de Esp. Cataluña*, ii. 23, etc.

an octagonal vault on pendentives over the Crossing, and a short nave, which, as well as the transepts, is covered with a waggon-vault. The apses are vaulted with semi-domes. The west end is the only perfect part of the exterior, and deserves illustration. The work is all of a very solid and rude description, though I am almost afraid to give it credit for being so old as is said. The circular window is, however, an interpolation; and if this were removed, and another small window like the others inserted in its place, the whole design would no doubt have an air of

WEST FRONT OF SAN PABLO

extreme antiquity. The ground-plan is a typal one here, and prevails more or less in all the early churches from Cataluña to Galicia. One or two others of the same description seem to have a fair amount of evidence of the date of their consecration, and it is at any rate unlikely that a church built in A.D. 914 would require rebuilding in about a hundred years, which must have been the case here, if we assume that we have not still before us the original church. On the south side of the nave there was a cloister added, probably in the course of the eleventh century, and there is some difference in the character of its design and workmanship, and that of the church and its west front. This cloister is very small, having on each side four arches, divided by a buttress in the centre of each side. The openings are cusped some with three and some with five heavy foliations, plain on the outside, but both moulded and carved on the inside face. The cusping is not at all Gothic in its character, being stilted in a very Eastern fashion, nor is it constructed like Gothic work, the stones being laid over each other, and cut out in the form of cusps, but not constructed anywhere with stones radiating on the principle of an arch. The shafts between the openings are coupled one behind the other, and have well-carved capitals. A fourteenth-century doorway, with a cross for the finial of its label, opens from the north wall of the cloister into the nave; and in the east wall is an extremely good entrance to the Chapter-house of the same date, and showing the usual arrangement of a doorway with a two-light traceried opening on either side. There are also some old monumental arches in the walls.

This church, which forms so important a feature in the early architectural history of Cataluña, is near the western end of the city, and its west front and cloister are enclosed within the walls of a small barrack; but as Spanish officers and soldiers are always glad to lionise a stranger, there is no difficulty in the way of seeing them. A simple early-pointed doorway, under a very flat tympanum, has been added to the north transept, and there is some evidence of the small apse near it having been arcaded on the outside. The pendentive under the dome is similar in its construction to those under the dome of the curious church of Ainay, at Lyons. Above them there is a string-course, and then the vault, which rises to a point in the centre, and is not a complete octagon, the cardinal sides being much wider than the others. The west doorway has in its tympanum our Lord, S. Peter, and S. Paul; over the arch are the angel of S. Matthew and eagle of S. John, and above, a hand with a cruciform nimbus, giving the benediction (2).

San Pedro de las Puellas, on the other side of the city, was rebuilt in A.D. 980, by Suniario Count of Barcelona, and his wife Richeldi, and was consecrated with great pomp in A.D. 983.[1] This church has been wofully treated, but it is still possible to make out the original scheme. It was a cruciform church of the same general plan as San Pablo, with a circular dome at the Crossing, and a waggon-vault to the south transept, the nave, and the western part of the chancel. The other parts were altered at a later date. Very bold detached columns with rich capitals

[1] Cean Bermudez, *Arq. de España*, i. 12.

carry the arches under the dome, and another remaining against the south wall of the nave suggests that there were probably cross arches or ribs below its waggon-vault. The sculpture of the capitals is very peculiar; it is quite unlike the ordinary Romanesque or Byzantine sculpture, and is very much more like the work sometimes seen in Eastern buildings. It is a type of capital first seen here, but reproduced constantly afterwards all along the southern coast, and not, so far as I know, seen at all in the interior of Spain.

There is no mark of a chapel on the east side of the south transept, and, as the apse has been rebuilt, it is impossible to say what the original plan of the head of the church was (3).

In the Collegiata of Sta. Ana, we have the next stage in the development of Catalan architecture. This is said to have been built in A.D. 1146,[1] and is also a cruciform church, with a central raised lantern, barrel-vaults in the transepts, and two bays of quadripartite vaulting in the nave. The nave probably dates from about the end of the twelfth or beginning of the thirteenth century, being lighted with simple lancet-windows, and having bold buttresses. When I visited this church the chancel was boarded up for repairs, and I am unable to say certainly whether the east end is old, but it appeared to me to have been modernised (4). The exterior of the lantern is very peculiar; above the roof it is square in plan, but with eight buttresses around it, radiating from the centre, and evidently intended to be carried up so as to form the angles of an octagonal central lantern, of which, however, only the lowest stage remains. The present finish of the lantern is a steep tiled roof, which springs from just above the point at which the angles of the square base are cut off; and on the western slope of this roof a steep flight of stone steps leads to the very summit. The object of this arrangement is quite unintelligible. At the west end of the church, and set curiously askew to it, is a cloister of the fourteenth century, with a Chapter-room on its east side, opening to the cloister with a round-arched doorway, on either side of which is a good early middle-pointed two-light window, making the group so

[1] According to Ford it was built by Guillermo II., Patriarch of Jerusalem, in imitation of the church of the Holy Sepulchre.—*Handbook for Travellers in Spain*, p. 416. It was one of the churches founded by the Order of the Holy Sepulchre in Jerusalem after the year 1141, in which they sent emissaries to Spain for the purpose.—*Viage Literario á las Iglesias de España*, xviii. 139. The necrology of the monastery contained the obit of a canon who came from Jerusalem, called Carfilio, as follows: " Obiit Caifilius frater Sancti Sepulchri, qui edificavit ecclesiam sanctæ Annæ."—*Viage Lit.* xvii. 144. *See* ground-plan of this church on Plate XVII., p. 79.

invariably found in old Chapter-house entrances. The west doorway of the church is severely simple, with a square opening and plain tympanum under a pointed arch. Along the north side of the cloister is a fine ruin of a hall of the thirteenth century, the construction of which is very characteristic and peculiar. It is of two stages in height. Segmental arches across the lower rooms carry the floor beams, which are placed longitudinally, and over them in the upper room bold pointed arches are thrown to carry the roof. The roof was of very flat pitch, and consisted of a series of purlines resting on corbels built into the wall over the stone arches, upon which were laid the common rafters. I shall have to illustrate a similar roof which still remains in the church of Sta. Agata, so that I need not say more on the subject now than that this type is an exceedingly effective one, and occurs repeatedly in the Barcelonese buildings. The cloister of Sta. Ana is of two stages in height, and very light, graceful, and Spanish in its character. The columns are quatrefoil in section, and the capitals are later works of the same eastern character as those already described in San Pedro, and have square abaci. There is, perhaps, scarcely sufficient appearance of solidity and permanence in such extremely light shafts, seeing that they have to support a double tier of arcades all round the cloister; but nevertheless the whole effect of the work is very beautiful. The old well with its stone lintel remains, and some fine orange-trees still adorn the cloister court.

The other early works here are doorways and fragments now incorporated in other and later works, so that we need no longer delay our inspection of the cathedral, which is, as it ought to be, the pride of the city. The ground-plan which I give [1] will best explain the general arrangements of this remarkable church. Its scale is by no means great, yet the arrangement of the various parts is so good, the skill in the admission of light so subtle, and the height and width of the nave so noble, that an impression is always conveyed to the mind that its size is far greater than it really is. Of course such praise is not intelligible to those who believe with some enthusiasts that the greatest triumph of architectural skill is to make a building look smaller than it really is—a triumph which the admirers of S. Peter's, at Rome, always claim loudly for it—but most unsophisticated men will probably prefer with me the opposite achievement, often, indeed, met with in Gothic buildings, but seldom more successfully than here.

The history of this church is in part given in two inscrip-

[1] Plate XVI., p. 72.

tions on the wall on either side of the north transept door-way,[1] from which it appears that the cathedral was commenced in A.D. 1298, and was still in progress in A.D. 1329. The latter date no doubt refers to the transept façade. But this was not the first church, for one was consecrated here in A.D. 1058, and the doorway from the cloister into the south transept, and another into the chapel of Sta. Lucia, at the south-west angle of the cloister, are probably not very much later than this date. But the bulk of the work is evidently not earlier than the beginning of the fourteenth century, and its design appears to be owing to one Jayme Fabra or Fabre,[2] an architect of whom we first hear at Palma in Mallorca. In the deed which I give in the Appendix, he describes himself as " lapiscida," citizen of Mallorca, and says that he is about to go to Barcelona, to undertake a certain work there at the request of the King of Aragon and the bishop. This was in A.D. 1318, and it is clear, I think, from the terms of his contract,[3] that Fabre was something more than architect, and really also the builder of this church in Palma. The term used might indeed lead us to suppose that he was a mere mason, but the request of the king and the bishop proves

[1] The inscription on the right hand of this door is as follows:—

+ In : noïe : Dñi : nri : Ihu : Xri : ad . honorë . + Sce : Trinitatis Patš . et . Filii . et . Sps . Sci . ac . Beate . Virginis : Marie . et Sce crucis . Sce . q . Eulalie . Virginis . et . Martiris . Xri . ac . civis Barchn cujus . sõm . corpus . in ista . requiescit . sede . opus . istius . eccë . fuit inceptum . Kl . Madii año . Dñi . m.ccxcviii . regñate . illustrissimo . Dño Jacobo . rege . Aragonü . Valñ . Sardinie . Corsice . + comite . Q . Barchinone.

The other inscription is on the left side of the same door:—

In . noïe . Dñi . nri . Ihu . Xri . Kds . Novëbr . anno . Dñi . m.ccc.xxix regnante . Dño . Alfôso . rege . Aragonü . Valëcie . Sardinie . Corsice . ac comite . Barchn . opus . hujus . sedis . operabatur . ad . laudë . Dei . ac Bte . M Sce + Sceq . Eulaïe.

[2] The inscription which records the depositing of the body of Sta. Eulalia in the crypt below the choir in A.D. 1339 says that " el Maestro " Jayme Fabra and the masons and workmen of the church, Juan Berguera, Juan de Puigmolton, Bononato Peregrin, Guillen Ballester, and Salvador Bertran, covered the urn with a tomb and canopy of stone.—Cean Bermudez, *Arq. de España*, i. 63. Diego, *Historia de los Condes de Barcelona*, pp. 298-301.

[3] " The directors of the work of the new temple," says S. Furio (*Diccionario historico de los Professores de las Bellas Artes en Mallorca*, p. 55), " agreed to give to the architect, Master Jayme, eighteen sueldos a week for the whole of his life, as well when he was ill as well; and during the work, in case he should have to go on matters of business to Mallorca—his country—the Chapter bound themselves to pay him his travelling expenses and maintenance as well going as returning. They promised also to give a house rent free for him and his family, and two hundred sueldos annually for clothing for him and his children."

that he was much more than this, and is useful as showing that these titles literally translated are very apt to mislead.[1] The crypt of Sta. Eulalia under the choir was completed in A.D. 1339. Jayme Fabre is said to have been master of the works until A.D. 1388, in which year he was succeeded by el Maestro Roque, who had an assistant, Pedro Viader. He received three " sueldos " and four " dineros " a day, and a hundred sueldos each year for clothing, and in course of time his salary was raised to " two florins or twenty-two sueldos " a week. His assistant received fifty sueldos a year for clothes and three sueldos and six dineros a day for his double office of substitute for the principal architect and workman. Roque no doubt was able to work elsewhere, whilst his assistant, or clerk of the works, was confined to one work; in this way the apparent strangeness of the similar pay to the two men is explained.[2] Roque, who is said to have commenced the cloister, was succeeded by Bartolomé Gual, who was one of the architects summoned to advise about the cathedral of Gerona in 1416, and then described himself as master of the works at Barcelona cathedral; and, finally, Andres Escuder placed the last stone of the vault on September 26, A.D. 1448 (5).

Having thus shortly stated the history of the building, let me now attempt to describe its architecture and construction. It will be seen that the plan is cruciform. The transepts do not, however, show much on the exterior, as they form the base of the towers which are erected, as at Exeter cathedral, above them. The plan of the chevet is very good; it presents the French arrangement of an aisle and chapels round the apse in place of the common Spanish triapsidal plan; but the detail is all completely Catalan (6). The arches of the apse are very narrow and stilted, and the columns throughout are composed of a rather

[1] Mr. Wyatt Papworth's very learned and complete dissertation on this subject in the *Transactions of the Royal Institute of British Architects* may be referred to as the best paper that has been published on the architects of our buildings. I shall reserve what I have to say on this subject for the last chapter of this volume.

[2] It is rather difficult to ascertain the exact value of the sums mentioned in these documents—a sueldo and a dinero being both disused. The former is said to have been a piece of eight maravedis, the latter a small copper coin. This at the present day would be only a little over threepence a day. In A.D. 1350 we find William de Hoton, the master-mason at York Minster, receiving 2s. 6d. a week—as nearly as may be the same wages that Roque received. Hoton had also a premium of £10 a year and a house, and liberty to undertake other works.—*Fabric Rolls of York*, Surtees Soc., p. 166. At Exeter, in the year 1300, Master Roger, the master-mason, received 30s. a quarter, or about 2s. 4d. a week.—*Fabric Rolls of Exeter*, in Dr. Oliver's *Lives of the Bishops of Exeter*, pp. 392-407.

BARCELONA

EAST END OF THE CATHEDRAL

confused jumble of thin mouldings awkwardly arranged. Above
the main arches is a very small arcaded triforium, and above
this a range of circular windows, one in each bay. The groining
springs from the capitals of the main columns, so that the
triforium and clerestory are both enclosed within its arched
wall-rib; they are consequently very disproportioned in height
as compared with those of northern churches. But here the
architect evidently intended to grapple with the difficulties of
the climate, and, designing his whole church with the one
great object of minimising the light and heat, he was compelled
to make his windows small. The clerestory windows were
traceried, and filled with rich stained glass, which was well
set back from the face of the wall. The result is a perfect success
as far as light and shade and the ordinary purposes of a Spanish
congregation are concerned, but the difficulty of taking notes,
sketches, or measurements, in most parts of the church, even
at mid-day, can hardly be imagined. The dark stone of which
the whole church is built increases not a little the sombre magnificence of the effect. There is nothing peculiar about the
chapels of the chevet; but under the centre of the choir, and
approached by a broad flight of steps between two narrower
flights which lead to the high altar, is the small crypt or chapel
already mentioned as that in which the remains of Sta. Eulalia
are enshrined. An inscription[1] records the date of the translation of her remains to this spot in A.D. 1339, but the present
state of the chapel is not suggestive of the possession of any
architectural treasures, being remarkable only for the ugliness
of its altar, and the number of its candlesticks. Behind the
altar, however, there still remains the shrine of the saint. This
is a steep-roofed ark of alabaster carried upon eight detached
columns. The ark is sculptured at the sides and ends with
subjects from the life of Sta. Eulalia, whilst the roof has her
soul borne aloft by angels. The columns are of marble, spiral,
fluted, and chevroned, with capitals of foliage, and one or two
of the bases are carved with figures in the mediæval Italian
fashion. A long inscription is carried round the base of the ark,
which again records the death of the saint, her burial in Sta.
Maria del Mar, and her translation to the cathedral in A.D. 878,
and afterwards to the spot where she now rests. The detail of
this shrine looks very like that of Italian Gothic of the same age;
and as it is particularly described in the contemporary memorial

---

[1] Given in *España Sagrada*, xxix. 314, in facsimile. In the edition of
1859 engravings both of the shrine and of the crypt are given.

of the translation, it is no doubt part of the work on which
Jayme Fabre had been engaged.

The transepts are groined at the level of the side chapels, and
again with an octagonal vault just above the aisle roof, and
below where the square base gives place to the octagon on
which the upper part of the steeples is planned. It is therefore
only on the ground-plan that the transepts show themselves, and
here they form porches, that on the south side opening into
the cloister. The planning of the nave is very peculiar. It
seems as though the main requirement of the founders of this
church was a plentiful number of altars; for, as will be seen on
reference to the plan, there are no less than twenty-seven distinct
chapels inside the church, and twenty-two more round the
cloister. The chapels in the south aisle have a row of other
chapels, which open into the cloister, placed back to back with
them, and the windows which light the former open into the
latter, showing when seen from the nave chapels their glass, and
when seen from the cloister chapels the dark piercings of their
openings. The arrangement is not only extremely picturesque,
but also another evidence of the care with which the sun was kept
out of the building. On the north side the chapels are uniform
throughout, and their windows are pierced in the long unbroken
north wall. The Coro here is in its old position in the two eastern
bays of the nave, with the old screens around it and all its old
fittings. It is to be observed, however, that here, where the late
Spanish arrangement was from the first adopted, the western
entrance to the choir was preserved, and so the awkward blank
which the wall of the Coro generally presents on entering is
not felt. There are no signs of any parclose screens across the
transept, and the position of the chapel of Sta. Eulalia makes it
improbable that there ever were any. It seems, indeed, that
such a church as this must from the very first have been built
for precisely the kind of worship still used in it. There was
never any proper provision for a crowd of worshippers joining in
any one common act of prayer or worship. The capitular body
filled the Coro and sang the services of the day unnoticed by the
people; whilst, as they separated to the chapels to which each
was attached, the people followed them by twos and threes to
the altar services in which only they wished to join. At present
not more than about half the altars are commonly used; yet
still each morning mass was generally being said at three, or
four, or five of them at the same time, and each altar every day
seemed to have a considerable group of worshippers, among

whom I noticed a considerable number of men of the upper class. The high altar seems always to have had curtains on either side of it, their rods being supported on columns of jasper in front. These curtains were drawn at the *Sanctus*, and remained so until the consecration was completed (7). One sung mass only is celebrated at this altar each day, and an old treatise on the Customs of the Church cites in defence or explanation of this rule the words of a very early council, *una missa et unum altare*.[1] West of the Coro are two bays of nave, over the western of which rises the lower part of a rich octangular lantern. This is carried on bold piers of square outline, which, from the very simple arrangement of the shafts of which they are composed, have the grandeur of effect so characteristic of Romanesque work. The cross arches under the lantern are lower than the groining, and on the east face the spandrel between the two is filled in with rich tracery and arcading. Arches are thrown across the angles to carry the octagonal lantern, of which the lowest stage only—which is well arcaded—is built. The whole of this work is so good of its kind that it is much to be lamented it was never completed; the design of the octagonal lantern at the west, and the two more slender octagonal steeples at the Crossing, would have been as striking in its effect, doubtless, as it would have been novel in its plan, though it may be doubted whether, in so short a church, it would not have been overpowering (8). Above the side chapels, on each side of the nave and at the west end, another floor is carried all round. The only difference is that the rooms above the chapels are square-ended, not apsidal, and there seems to be no evidence of their having been intended for altars. I saw no piscinæ and no Retablos in them, and was tempted to imagine that the present use may, perhaps, have been the old one—that of a grand receptacle for all the machinery in fêtes, functions, and the like, of which a Spanish church generally requires no small store.[2] There are arches in the wall, affording means of communication all round this upper floor, and the chambers all open to the church with arches, and have traceried windows in their outer walls. The transverse section of the nave is therefore novel, and unlike any other with which I am acquainted, and interested me not a little.

The exterior is, perhaps, less interesting than the interior. The chevet is fine, but with nothing in any way unusual in its

---

[1] Villanueva, *Viage á las Iglesias de España*, xviii. 157.
[2] The account of the building of Segovia Cathedral, given in the Appendix, mentions the provision of rooms for this purpose.

BARCELONA CATHEDRAL
INTERIOR OF WEST END OF NAVE

design; the upper part of the buttresses is destroyed, and the walls finish without parapet or roof, so as to make the church look somewhat like a roofless ruin.   The steeples are quite plain below their belfry stage, under which are arcaded string-courses; the belfry stages themselves are richly panelled and pierced, and surmounted by pierced parapets.   They are not perfectly octagonal in plan, the cardinal sides being the widest, and their height from the floor of the church is as nearly as I could measure 179 ft. 6 in., whilst their external diameter is about 30 feet.   It is on ascending these towers that one of the greatest peculiarities of the Barcelonese churches is seen; they are all roofless, and you look down on to the top of their vaulting, which is all covered with tiles or stone neatly and evenly laid on the vault, in such a way as effectually to keep out the weather.   The water all finds its way out by the pockets of the vaults, and by pipes through the buttresses with gurgoyles in front of them.   Everything seemed to prove that this was *not* the old arrangement, for it is pretty clear that the walls had parapets throughout, and that there were timber roofs, though I saw no evidence as to what their pitch had been.   The present scheme, ugly and ruinous as it looks—giving the impression that all the church roofs have been destroyed by the fire of the fortresses above and at the side of the city—seems nevertheless to have solved one of those problems which so often puzzle us—the erection of buildings which as far as possible shall be indestructible.   There is now absolutely no timber in any part of the work; but it is of course questionable whether a roof which endures the test of a Spanish climate, with its occasional deluge of rain succeeded by a warm drying sun, would endure the constant damp of a climate like ours.   But at any rate the makeshift arrangement which is universal here is very suggestive.   The flying buttresses are insignificant, owing to the small height of the clerestory.

Descending from the roof, the only other old portion of the church to be mentioned is the north transept.   It is here that the two inscriptions given at p. 57 are built into the wall on either side of the lofty doorway.   The doorway is finely moulded, and has a single figure under a canopy in its tympanum; above it the whole face of the wall is covered with very rich arrangement of niches, making an arcade over its whole surface, but there are no figures left in them (9).   Over this again is a rose window under an arch, and then the octagonal tower.   To the east of the transept are some round-headed windows, but my impression is that they are not of earlier date than the rest of the work. The outer wall of the north aisle of the nave has a row of very richly moulded windows lighting the chapels, and other windows over them which light the galleries over the aisle chapels. The eaves here have a simple round-arched corbel-tabling.

The west front is all modern and squalid; the original design for its completion is said to exist among the archives of the cathedral, and ought to be examined; I was not aware of this until long after I had been at Barcelona. Don F. J. Parcerisa[1] gives a view of this proposed front—an extremely florid Gothic work—but the drawing is so obviously not the least like an old one, that I hardly know how far to trust the statements about it which he makes. He describes it as being on parchment, sixteen palms long, and much defaced. The print is drawn in perspective, and elaborately shaded. It is a double door, with a steep gable above filled with extremely rich flamboyant tracery, and there are large pinnacles on either side and a great number of statues.

The cloisters are not good in their detail, but yet are very pleasant; they are full of orange-trees, flowers, and fountains. One of these is in a projecting bay at the north-east internal angle, and is old; another by its side has a little S. George and the Dragon, with the horse's tail formed by a jet of water; and a third, and more modern, plays in the centre among the flowers. In addition, there are some geese cooped up in one corner, who look as if their lives were being sacrificed in order to provide *patés* for the canons; and finally a troop of hungry, melancholy cats, who are always howling and prowling about the cloisters and church, and who often contrive to get into the choir-stalls just before service, whence they are forthwith chased about by the choristers and such of the clergy as are in their places in good time! These cloisters are said to have been completed in A.D. 1448,[2] and I have no doubt this date is correct. On the exterior they are bounded on three sides by streets, and the apsidal ends of the chapels do not show, the wall being straight and unbroken. The cloister is lofty and has panelled buttresses between the windows, of which latter the arches only remain, the traceries having been entirely destroyed (10). The view from hence of the church is one of the best that can be obtained, the octagonal transept towers being the most marked features. The floor is full of gravestones, on which the calling of the person

---

[1] Parcerisa, *Recuerdos, etc., de España, Cataluña,* i. 57.
[2] *Viage Lit.* xviii. 145.

commemorated is indicated by a slight carving in relief of the implements of his trade.

The chapel of Sta. Lucia, at the south-west angle of the cloister, is probably a relic of the first church; it has a very fine round-headed doorway with its arch-mouldings covered with delicate architectural carving, and a lancet window under its very flat-pitched gable. The roof inside is a pointed waggon-vault. The door from the cloister into the south transept is of about the same date; it has three shafts in the jamb (one of them fluted), very deep capitals and abaci covered with carving of foliage, and an archivolt covered with chevron patterns of a flat and very unusual character. The label is large and carved with very stiff foliage. The foliage here is to a slight extent copied from the acanthus, but much of it is derived from some other leaf—I believe from the prickly pear.

When the fabric has been passed in review much still remains to be seen within its walls. A large number of the altars, particularly those of the cloister chapels, were furnished in the fifteenth century with Retablos of wood richly carved, and then painted with subjects: these are always placed across the apse, leaving a space behind the altar, to which access was obtained by doors on either side of it. Perhaps then as now the priest attached to the altar kept his vestments in the chapel in which he ministered, and these spaces may thus have been utilised. Usually, nowadays, in Spanish churches, for some ten or twenty minutes before the offices are sung in the choir, priests may be seen unlocking the gates of their chapels, vesting themselves, and then going one by one to their stalls in the choir, and there waiting till, on the clock striking the hour, the service commences. The paintings in the old Retablos are sadly defaced and damaged; but many of them have evidently had much value and interest. They are usually rather of Flemish than of Italian character, generally well and quaintly drawn, and with those striking contrasts of colour on gold grounds, of which this early school was so fond (10). The doors on either side of the altar have generally a whole-length figure of a saint painted on them.

Across the outer archway of all these chapels is an iron *grille*; very many of these are mediæval; and in the cloister in particular there is a very considerable variety in their treatment, and often great delicacy of execution. I have before noticed the excellence of the smiths' work in the Spanish churches. Yet though their work is of the latest age of Gothic, it is never marked by that nauseous redundance of ornament in which so

BARCELONA CATHEDRAL

VIEW OF THE STEEPLES FROM THE CLOISTER

many of the most active metal-workers of the present day seem to revel. Hence it is always worthy of study. The doors in these screens are generally double, and shut behind some sort of ogee-arched crocketed head, and sometimes there are crocketed pinnacles and buttresses on either side. The locks are often,

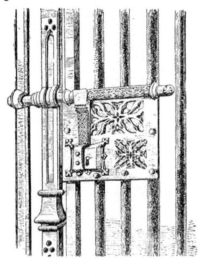

LOCK ON SCREEN IN CLOISTER

of course, specially elaborate; and the illustration which I give of one of them will serve to show their general character. In all the screens here the lower part is very simple, consisting generally of nothing but vertical bars, through which one can see without difficulty to the altars which they guard. The ornament is reserved for open traceried crestings, with bent and sharply-cut crockets, for traceried rails, and for the locks and fastenings.

The woodwork of the choir-fittings is of very late date,[1] but good of its kind. The stall-divisions are richly traceried under the elbow, and the misereres carved with foliage. Behind the stalls, and under the old canopies, is a series of Renaissance panels, covered with paintings of the arms of the Knights of the Golden Fleece.[2] The canopies above are very delicate, and of the same character as the stalls. The carved oak pulpit is corbelled out at the east end of the north range of stalls, and is approached by a staircase outside the arcaded stone parclose, which still remains north and south of the choir. This staircase, with its arched doorway between pinnacles at the bottom, its traceried handrail fringed at the top with fantastic ironwork, and

---

[1] The lower range of stalls was made in 1457, by Matias Bonife, for fifteen florins for labour for each. In his contract with the Chapter he agrees to carve all the seats, but " in no wise any beasts or subjects." In 1483 Miguel Loquer made the pinnacles of the upper stalls. The Chapter disputed the goodness of his work, and he died—partly of disgust, apparently—during the lengthy dispute. The Chapter then named arbiters, who, after a formal examination, pronounced them to contain grave defects.—Parcerisa, *Recuerdos, etc., Cataluña,* i. 59.

[2] Here, in 1519, Charles V. celebrated an installation of the Golden Fleece—the only one ever held in Spain.—Ford's *Handbook,* p. 413.

its door cunningly and beautifully made of open ironwork, is quite worth notice.

The Bishop's throne, second only in height and elaboration to that of Exeter, occupies its proper place at the east end of the southern side of the choir, with one stall for a chaplain beyond it. It will be remembered that in most Spanish cathedrals it is placed where the door from the nave into the choir ought to be: here, however, the old arrangement has never been altered.

The principal altar has a very Gothic Retablo, covered with gilding till it looks like gingerbread. I imagine it to be modern. It has curtains on either side, with angels standing on the columns which carry the rods. The iron screen across, in front of the altar, and round the apse, is none of it old.

Near the door to the sacristies a hexagonal box for the wheel of bells is fixed against the wall; and just below it a fine large square box arcaded at the sides, and painted, appears to contain a couple of larger bells (11).

The sculpture here is not very remarkable. Over the east door of the cloister is a Pietà in the tympanum, whilst the finial of the canopy is a crucifix. The bosses at the intersection of the ribs in the nave are of enormous size, and each has a figure or subject. The boss in the chapel over the font in the north side of the west door has the Baptism of our Lord, and another in the large chapel in the north-west of the cloister has the Descent of the Holy Ghost, and the eight bosses around it the Evangelists and Doctors. Some of the monuments are peculiar. The effigy is generally laid on a sloping stone, so as to suggest the greatest possible insecurity. There are sculptures on the tombs and inside the enclosing arch; a favourite and odious device in this last feature is to make the radius of the label much longer than that of the arch below it; and the space between the two is then filled with tracery. The nave groining was once painted. There seems to have been cinquecento foliage extending from the centre, about half-way across each vaulting cell; and the ribs were painted to the same extent. In the aisles there seems to have been no painting anywhere but on the ribs.

The old organ occupies the north tower, and is corbelled out boldly from the wall. Below it is a pendant, the finish of which is a Saracen's head, which, for some reason unknown to me, is held by Catalans to be appropriate to the position. There are enormous painted shutters, and a projecting row of trumpet-pipes. The organ was first of all built in the fourteenth century; Martin Ferrandis, organ-builder of Toledo, having bound himself, by a contract dated July 25, 1345, to construct it for 80 libras [1] (pounds).

The sacristies are old and vaulted. The sacristan knew of no old vestments or vessels to be seen there; and as they were always occupied by clergy I had to satisfy myself with his ignorance.

The bishop's palace is on the south side of the cloister: its quadrangle still retains some remains of good late Romanesque arcading, ornamented with dog-tooth, nail-head, and billet mould; and probably there is more to be seen if access were gained to the inside. On the opposite side of the cathedral is a vast barrack, dating from the fifteenth century, and which, first of all a palace, was given in A.D. 1487 by Ferdinand to the Inquisition. It seems now to be a mixture of school, convent, and prison, and is apparently without any architectural interest.

The grandest church, after the cathedral, is that of Sta. Maria del Mar, a vast building, of very simple plan, and exceedingly characteristic of the work of Catalan architects.[2] An inscription written in Limosin (Catalan) on one side, and in Latin on the other,[3] gives the date of the commencement of the work as A.D. 1328; and it is said by Cean Bermudez not to have been finished until A.D. 1483;[4] but Parcerisa[5] says that the last stone was placed on November 9, 1383, and the first mass said on August 15, 1384; and I am inclined to think that the latter dates are the more likely to be correct. I have found no evidence as to the architect of this church: he was one of a school who built many and exceedingly similar churches throughout this district. My impression is that he was most probably Jayme Fabre, the first architect of the cathedral. Fabre had constructed a church for the Dominicans at Palma, in Mallorca, between the years 1296 and 1339. Of this church I can only learn the dimensions; but these point to a church of the same class as those in Barcelona. It had no aisles, and was 280 palms long by 138 broad. The cathedral in the same city is figured in Parcerisa, and is similar in plan to Sta. Maria del Mar, but of far larger dimensions, the width from centre to centre of the nave columns being 71 feet, and the whole church 140 feet wide in the

[1] *Viage Lit.* xviii. 142.
[2] Plate XVII., p. 78.
[3] In nomine Dñi nostri Jesu Christi ad honorem sanctæ Mariæ fuit inceptum opus fabricæ ecclesiæ Beatæ Mariæ de Mari die Annuntiationis ejusdem, viii. Kal. Aprilis Anno Domini MCCCXXVIII.
[4] Cean Bermudez, *Arq. de España*, i. 61.
[5] *Recuerdos, etc., Cataluña*, i. p. 66.

clear, and with the chapels 190 feet. There are north and south
doors, and octagonal pinnacles at the west end, and, as will be
noticed, its dimensions are proportioned just as at Sta. Maria del
Mar (12). I do not think that Fabre's name occurs in connection
with the cathedral at Palma; but his fame must have been
great, as he was specially summoned to Barcelona by the king
and bishop; and nothing is more likely than that he would then
have been consulted about this other great work going on at the
same time, and in which, though the general design is different,
there are so many points of similarity. The church at Manresa
is said to have been commenced in the same year, 1328; and it
is extremely similar in all respects to Sta. Maria del Mar, as I
shall have further on to show when I have to describe it.

But whether these churches are to be attributed to the influence of one man suddenly inventing an innovation, or of a
school of architects working on the same old traditions—and I
have been unable to find any kind of evidence of this—it is
certain that they are very similar. They are marked by extreme
simplicity, great width, and great height. Usually they have
no arcades and consist of broad unbroken naves, always groined
in stone, and sparely lighted from small windows high up in the
walls. The two examples, so far as I know, which surpass all
others, are the single nave of Gerona, seventy-three feet wide in
the clear, and the nave and aisles of the Collegiata at Manresa,
sixty feet wide from centre to centre of the columns and a hundred and ten between the walls of the aisles. The Barcelonese
examples do not equal the extraordinary dimensions of these
two churches, but they are still on a fine scale. Sta. Maria del
Mar is the only Barcelonese example with aisles. It has—as will
be seen by the plan [1]—an aisle round the apse, and small chapels
between the buttresses. These apses are all internal only, so
that the side elevation of the church shows a plain straight wall
pierced with windows. This is a very favourite device of this
school, and has been already noticed in the north wall of the
cathedral, and in the wall all round the cloisters. The interior
of Sta. Maria del Mar is very simple. Enormous octagonal
columns carry the main arches and the groining ribs, which all
spring from their capitals. The wall rib towards the nave is
carried up higher than the main arches so as to allow space
between them for a small circular and traceried clerestory
window in each bay. The arches of the apse are very narrow,
and enormously stilted. There are small windows above them,

[1] Plate XVII., p. 78.

Reference to Plan.

a . Nave.
b . Lantern.
c . Choir.
d . Old Screen.
e . Modern Screen.
f . Pulpit.
g . Bishops Throne.
h . Aisles.
i . Chapels.
j . Transepts.
k . Sacristies.
l . Screen (Reja).
m . Steps down to Chap. of S.Eulalia.
n . Steps up to Altar.
o . High Altar.
p . Altars.
q . Cloisters.
r . Fountain.
s . Fountain of S.George.
t . Chapel of S.Lucia.
u . Chapter Room.
v . Treasury.
w . Cloister doors.
x . Not examined.
y . Garden.
z . Organ Over this Transept.

Capilla

Mayor

Before 1200
13th Century.
14th Century.
15th & 16th Cent?
Modern.

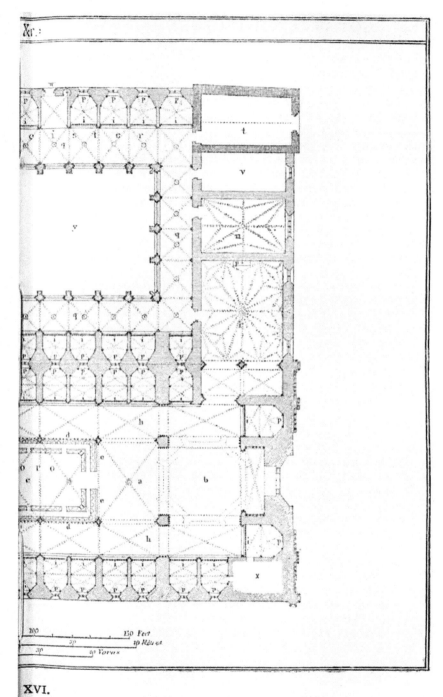

XVI.

but they are modernised. The aisles are groined on the same level as the main arches, a few feet, therefore, below the vault of the nave, and they are lighted by a four-light traceried window in each bay, the sill of which is above a string-course formed by continuing the abacus of the capitals of the groining shafts. Below this there are three arches in each bay, opening into side chapels between the main buttresses. Each of these chapels is lighted by a traceried window of two lights; and the outer wall presents, as will be seen, a long unbroken line, until above the chapels, when the buttresses rise boldly up to support the great vaults of the nave and aisles. The Barcelonese architects of this period were extremely fond of these long unbroken lines of wall; and there is a simplicity and dignity about their work which is especially commendable. Long rows of little sheds for shops which have managed to gain a footing all along the base of the walls rather disturb the effect, though they and their occupants, and the busy dealers in fruit who ply their trade all about Sta. Maria del Mar, make it a good spot for the study of the people(13).

The altar is a horrible erection of about A.D. 1730 (14), and all the internal fittings are modern and in the worst possible taste.

The view which I give of the west front will explain the whole design of the exterior. Unquestionably it is a grand work of its kind, with good detail throughout. The great octagonal pinnacles at the angles are, however, awkwardly designed, and quite insufficient in scale for the vast mass of building to which they are attached. They are reproduced in all the churches of the same class in Barcelona; and indeed most of the features of one of these churches are common to the others. The tracery in the circular window at the west end certainly looks later in date than that of the others in this church, and than that in the west front of Sta. Maria del Pi, which was commenced in A.D. 1329, but not completed until much later. It is worth mention that the western doors of this church are covered with iron, cut out into the form of cusped circles, with rather good effect.

The church of SS. Just y Pastor is of the same class as Sta. Maria del Mar, but its foundation is slightly later, as it seems to have been commenced *circa* A.D. 1345. It consists of a nave without aisles, but with chapels between the buttresses—one chapel in each bay. There are five bays, and an apse of five sides. The altar stands forward from the wall, and stalls are ranged round the apse. The nave is 43 feet 6 inches in width in the clear by about 130 feet in length. The vaulting is quadripartite throughout, with large bosses at the intersection of

STA. MARIA DEL MAR, BARCELONA
SOUTH-WEST VIEW

the ribs, on which are carved—1, the Annunciation; 2, the Nativity; 3, the Presentation; 4, the Adoration of the Magi; 5, the Resurrection; 6, the Coronation of the B.V.M. The whole church has lately been covered with painting and gilding, in the most approved French style, and to the destruction of all appearance of age. The light is admitted by three-light windows with good geometrical traceries, very high up above the arches, into the side chapels, and by two-light windows in the chapels themselves. At the west end are remains of the usual octagonal flanking turrets; but the whole front is modernised. The side elevation is a repetition of those already described, presenting a long unbroken wall below, out of which the buttresses for the clerestory rise.

Santa Maria del Pino is a still grander church, but on the same plan, with the addition of a lofty octagonal tower detached at the north-east of the church.[1] This is four stages in height, and the belfry-stage has windows on each face. The traceried corbel-table under the parapet remains, but the parapet and roof are destroyed. The nave here consists of seven bays, is fifty-four feet wide in the clear, and has an eastern apse of seven sides. The chapels between the buttresses are not carried round the apse, but an overhanging passage-way is formed all round outside, upon arches between, and corresponding openings through, the buttresses just below the windows. The north door here is a very fine early work of just the same character as those already described in the earliest portions of the cathedral. It appears to be a work of the end of the twelfth century, and much older than any other portion of the church. The west front has a doorway with a figure in a niche in the tympanum, and a system of niches round and above it, enclosing it within a sort of square projecting from the face of the wall. The whole scheme is so exceedingly similar both in design and detail to that of the north transept door of the cathedral, that we may fairly conclude them to be the works of the same man. Above the door is a large circular window filled with good and very rich geometrical tracery. A church existed here as early as 1070;[2] and Cean Bermudez says that the first stone of the present church was laid in 1380, and that it was concluded in 1414.[3] Parcerisa,[4] on the other hand, says that materials were

---

[1] Plate XVII., p. 79.
[2] *Viage Literario á las Iglesias de España*, xviii. 161.
[3] *Arq. de España.*
[4] *Recuerdos, etc., de España, Cataluña*, vol. i.

granted for the work in 1329, that it was nearly finished in 1413, and consecrated in 1453;[1] whilst in A.D. 1416 we have Guillermo Abiell describing himself as master of the works of Sta. Maria del Pi, and of S. Jayme, in Barcelona, when he was called as one of the Junta of architects to advise about the building of the nave of Gerona cathedral.[2]

S. Jayme, of which Abiell was the architect, is a small church in the principal street of the city, with an ogee-headed door with a crocketed label between two pinnacles. Above are some small windows; and the whole detail is poor in character, and exactly consistent with what might be expected from an architect at Abiell's time. I believe, therefore, that either Abiell was only the surveyor to an already existing fabric, who wished to make the most of his official position among his brethren at Gerona, or that if he really executed any works at Sta. Maria del Pi they were confined to the steeple, which is of later character than the church. I believe that the real meaning of the dates given by the authorities just quoted is as follows:—In A.D. 1329 stone was granted for the work which was then no doubt just commenced at the same time as the similar work in the transept of the cathedral; and the consecration probably took place in A.D. 1353, a date which occurs in an inscription in the church, and has been, I suspect, read by Parcerisa by mistake, 1453; and the work commenced in A.D. 1380 was probably the steeple, which was completed in A.D. 1414. To decide otherwise would be to ignore altogether all the information to be derived from the character of the architectural detail, which, after all, is to a practised eye a safer guide than any documentary evidence. I should assume, too, from the identity of the character of the two works, that Jayme Fabre was the architect who designed the church, and that Guillermo Abiell probably built the tower some time after his death.

I must now take my readers back somewhat to an earlier church, which is full of interest, but very different from those which I have been describing, and of different style. This is the church of Sta. Agata, situated just to the north of the cathedral. I have been unable to learn anything as to its history (15). It has a nave of four bays, spanned by pointed arches, which carry the wooden roof, and a groined apse of five sides. East of

---

[1] An inscription is given by Villanueva, *Viage Literario*, xviii. 162, said to be cut on the jamb of the side doorway, which records the consecration of this church on June 17th, 1453.

[2] *See* Appendix.

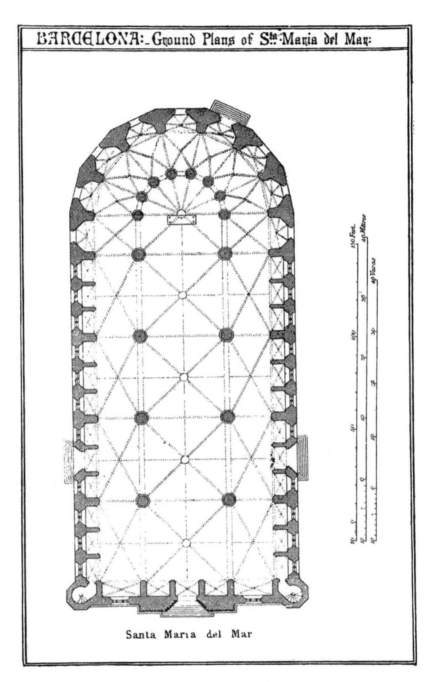

BARCELONA: Ground Plans of Sta Maria del Mar.

Santa Maria del Mar

PLATE XVII.

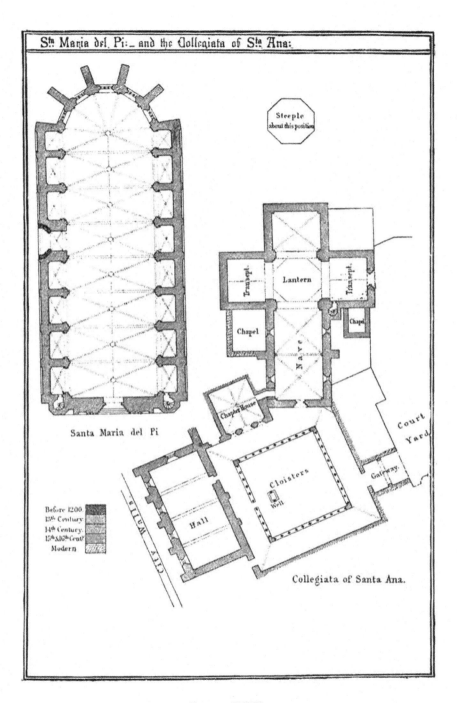

Santa Maria del Pi

Collegiata of Santa Ana.

Steeple
about this position

Transept. Lantern Transept.

Chapel Chapel

Nave

Chapter House

Cloisters

Well

Court Yard

Gateway.

Hall

Before 1200
13ᵗʰ Century.
14ᵗʰ Century.
15ᵗʰ & 16ᵗʰ Cent?
Modern

CITY WALLS

Stᵃ Maria del. Pi: _ and the Collegiata of Sᵗᵃ Ana:

PLATE XVII.

the apse is a waggon-vaulted chamber, whose axis is at right angles to that of the church, and out of it rises a delicate octagonal steeple, the belfry-stage of which has two-light windows on four sides, and gables on each face.   These gables run back till they intersect the base of a low stone spire, which is now nearly destroyed, but the lower part of which can be clearly

INTERIOR OF SANTA AGATA

made out from the neighbouring steeple of the cathedral.   A staircase, ingeniously constructed in the thickness of the south wall (16), leads up from the nave to the pulpit (now destroyed), and thence on again to a western gallery.   Some of the windows are like domestic windows in design, having a slender shaft-monial with the capital of foliage so often repeated in all the towns from Perpiñan to Valencia.   The great height of the windows from the floor—about twenty-six feet—secures an admirable effect of light, and their detail is thoroughly good early middle-pointed. The southern façade has a great deal of that picturesque irregularity which is always so charming when it is natural. The door is in the western angle of the south front, partly built under a great overhanging arch, which carries the wall of a building which abuts on the west end of Sta. Agata. The lower half of the walls has small windows irregularly placed, lighting the eastern chapel, the pulpit, and the passage to the gallery; and then above them the wall is set back a couple of feet between buttresses, and each bay has an extremely well designed and moulded window of two lights, with geometrical tracery. The finish of the walls at the top is modernised. The construction of the roof is very effective, and at the same time of a most unusual character; it consists of a series of purlines resting on corbels in the walls over the arches across the nave; and though it is of flat pitch, this is but little noticed, owing to the good proportions of these arches, which are so marked a feature in the design.

The same kind of roof exists still in the great hall of the Casa Consistorial, and evidently once existed also in the church which I shall presently mention in the Calle del Carmen. In England we have somewhat parallel examples at Mayfield and the Mote House, Ightham; but these Barcelonese examples are useful, as showing how, when a flat-pitched roof is of necessity adopted, a very good internal effect may nevertheless be secured. This church is now desecrated, and used as a sculptor's workshop.

Another church, of which only the ruins now remain, in the Calle del Carmen, must, I presume, be Nuestra Señora del Carmen, founded in 1287.[1] This building was evidently greatly altered in the fourteenth century. It was first of all roofed with a flat roof, carried on arches across the nave, as at Sta. Agata, and subsequently the walls were raised and the church was groined. The groining is now destroyed, and behind it are seen the corbels in the cross wall marking the rake of the first roof. The aisles had roofs gabled north and south, and their windows good fourteenth-century tracery. This church of seven bays in length is 43 feet wide between the columns of the nave, and nearly 80 feet wide from north to south. Compared with Sta. Agata, it seems to prove that this class of timber-roofed church was introduced here between the early waggon-

---

[1] Cean Bermudez, *Arq. de España,* i. 55. But Diego, *Historia de los Condes de Barcelona,* p. 316, puts the foundation in A.D. 1293.

vaulting of the chapel of Sta. Lucia and of Sta. Ana, and the great quadripartite vaults of the cathedral and the other churches of its class (17).

The other churches here are not of much interest. The front of San Jayme has already been incidentally mentioned: its interior is modernised. San Miguel is probably a very early church,

CASA CONSISTORIAL, BARCELONA

having a Roman mosaic pavement preserved in the floor. It has a pointed waggon-vault, and a sixteenth-century stone gallery at the west end. The western front has a rich west door, half Gothic and half Renaissance, with S. Michael and the dragon in the tympanum, and the Annunciation in the jambs. The flat gable has its old crocketed coping and cross, and two very small windows. The best feature is the tower, a simple structure, square in plan, from within the parapet of which, over the centre, rises a small square turret, open at the sides and roofed with four intersecting gables. It is a pretty arrangement for carrying a fifth bell, the other bells hanging in the belfry windows in the Italian fashion. The church of San Anton has a groined narthex or porch all across the west front, with three open arches in front. The nave cannot be wide, and has chapels between the buttresses, but I did not see the interior (18). Another church, that of San Gerónimo, is on the same plan, but of later date.[1] The churches of the Renaissance class are numerous and ugly; but Berruguete and his followers hardly perpetrated so many freaks in art here as they did in the centre of Spain; had they been more popular, there had been much less for me to describe. But in truth, rich as this old city still is, it was much richer, two or three noble churches having disappeared at a comparatively late period, either during the war or in subsequent popular disturbances.

The civic buildings are quite worthy of the ancient dignity of the city. The Casa Consistorial, and the Casa de la Disputacion, face each other on opposite sides of the principal square, not far from the cathedral. The former has a modern Pagan front, but on the north side the old work remains. This building is said to have been commenced in A.D. 1369, and finished in A.D. 1378;[2] and inside the great hall I noticed an inscription (which unfortunately I neglected to copy) with the date of 1373. The old front to the north of this building seems worthy of illustration. The enormous arch-stones of the principal doorway are very common throughout Cataluña, and are seen indeed as far east even as Perpiñan. The figure of S. Michael (19) has metal wings; and as the little church dedicated in honour of the same archangel is just on the other side of the Casa, it seems as if there was some special connection between the two buildings. The *patio* or quadrangle is oblong in plan, and on the first floor the passage is open to the air, with delicate arches all round. On the east side of this passage a door opens into a noble hall, with a dais for the throne at the upper end, and doorways on each side of the dais. This hall is spanned by four moulded semi-circular arches rising from corbels formed of a cluster of shafts. These arches support a flat ceiling of rafters, with boarding between them, resting on corbels in the cross walls. The light is admitted by large cusped circles high up in the side walls, and by good *ajimez* windows of three lights at the dais end. The rafters of the roof

---

[1] Villanueva, *Viage Literario*, xviii. 165, mentions the convent of San Francisco as still existing (in 1851).

[2] Parcerisa, *Recuerdos, etc., Cataluña*, i. 107.

are all painted with coats-of-arms enclosed within quatrefoils, with a very rich effect.   The dimensions of this room are about 40 feet wide by 90 feet long, and 45 feet in height.   In a passage near it is an admirable *ajimez* window, which, as it illustrates this common type very well, is worth preserving a record of.   The marble shafts here are only three inches in diameter.

The Casa de la Disputacion *was* still more interesting; but on

AJIMEZ WINDOW

my last visit the delicate arcades of its beautiful *patio* were all being walled up with common brick, leaving narrow slits of windows, which I suppose are to be glazed, to save the degenerate lawyers for the future from any of the chance squalls of wind or rain which their predecessors have endured since the fifteenth century, when Master Pedro Blay, the architect, superintended its erection.   This *patio* is of three stages in height, with a picturesque external staircase to the first floor.   The lofty corridor round the first floor leads to the various courts and offices, and in one angle of it is the entrance to the chapel, consisting of three small arches, forming a door and two windows, with the wall above them covered with an elaborate reticulation of tracery. The arches have ogee crocketed canopies, and the side arches iron *grilles*. This chapel is dedicated to S. George, the tutelar saint of Cataluña, and a figure of the saint rivals that of S. Michael in the Sala Consistorial (20). There are here some extremely well-managed overhanging passage-ways corbelled out from the walls, and various excellent features of detail. The parapets generally to the various passages are of plain stone slabs, pierced here and there only with a richly traceried circle.

Another old building—the Lonja or Exchange (21)—was built near the sea in A.D. 1383.[1] But everything old has been completely destroyed, with the one exception of its grand hall, which still does service as of old. This consists of three naves, divided by lofty and slender columns, which carry stilted semi-circular arches. The ceiling is flat, of the same description as that of the Sala Consistorial. The dimensions are about 100 feet in length by 75 feet in width.

Another great building, founded soon after, *circa* 1444, was intended for a cloth-hall:[2] in 1514 it was converted into an armoury, and subsequently into a residence for the Captains-General of Cataluña; it has been completely modernised throughout the exterior, and I did not see the interior.

Cean Bermudez mentions an interesting fact about the construction of the old Mole. It was built, he says, by Estacio, a famous hydraulic architect of Alexandria, in A.D. 1477; and the city authorities took counsel about it with the most learned professors of Syracuse, Rhodes, and Candia (22).

NOTES

(1) See note 22, at the close of the chapter, on San Cugat and Pedralbes.

(2) San Pablo has been freed from surrounding buildings, and the barrack has disappeared. On the west front the other two evangelical beasts, the lion and the ox, flank the outer arch of the doorway and may be recognised in the drawing.

(3) San Pedro was burned in the popular rising three years ago, at the same time with S. Anthony Abbot, and the restoration since has been pretty complete rebuilding.

(4) It is now so blocked up with the altar and dossal as to be invisible. Santa Aña is said to possess a Pentecost by Luis Borrassá, but I never could find it in the dark.

[1] Cean Bermudez, *Arq. de Esp.* i. 70.　　　　　[2] *Hala de paños.*

(5) A little more detail has come to light. Jaime II. and Bishop Bernard Peregri founded it, May 7, 1298. In 1329 the apse and transepts were done, in 1338 the crypt and Capilla Mayor, and the relics were translated; at that time they were carving the keys for the vault of the nave, *i.e.* over the choir. In 1388 were raised the pillars of the trascoro, near which was the chapel of the shoemakers, that they built in 1345. In 1420 the nave was finished and west wall put up. The bays of the trascoro belong to Master Riquer, 1388. At that time Master Francesch Franch was working on the cloister; Andres Escuder finished it in 1451, and under Bishop Sapora finished the cathedral. In the last third of the nineteenth century the west front was constructed in the most approved imitation of French Gothic. In 1912 was finished the French Gothic lantern at the west. Men are already complaining that it does not compose well with the octagonal Catalan towers eastward, and that the dead stone work of the façade is wrong anyway.

(6) The plan is almost copied from that of Narbonne, and the style is a compromise between that of Languedoc and that of the north of France. But the effect is like none of these: the cathedral of Barcelona is a perfect thing, a whole not to be accounted for by the sum of its parts. If French, yet it is not imitative; if late, yet it is not decadent; and it cannot be measured against a church of its own size, but stands comparison with the greatest. The grace of Amiens is lighter and brighter, the beauty of Chartres is darker and more austere, but the charm of Barcelona is unparalleled in its warmth and intimacy. In it found expression, at a moment of immense economic expansion, a great and a free people, immensely conscious of life, and of a life of their own.

(7) The curtains are no longer there. On the other hand, a bit of ritual is observed that I have seen elsewhere only in Toledo. At the moment before the Elevation a square of velvet at the back of the altar is raised (red velvet embroidered about the edge with gold, for every day), against which the Host is discernible from any distance, pale and luminous.

(8) The finished lantern floods with pale light the western half of the church, which is a doubtful advantage.

(9) On the door of S. Ives (San Ibo) in the north transept they were still working in 1329: this one, called after San Severo, belongs to an older church, but not that of Ramon Berenguer *el Viejo*. It is of the first third of the thirteenth century in the Byzantine-Limousin style (*i.e.* Romanesque of the south of France), altered for this place by cutting the lintel, suppressing the mid-post, and damaging the archivolt, as may be seen by looking carefully, then giving it afterwards a tympanum and an extra high outer archivolt, both of Gothic traceries.

(10) They have been restored, and the early Catalan paintings sometimes referred to as in the cloisters are most of them now in the chapter-room and the ante-room through which this is approached. The canons are always there, doing business of their own, from nine to eleven, and any one is at liberty to enter and stay the two hours. In the inner room are the choicest, and first of them is the Pietà of B. Vermejo, which is painted in oils and not by a Catalan. Whether

Bartolomeus Rubeus is not Maître Roux, or Meister Roth, or Maestro Rosso, is still disputed, but Sr. Sanpere fairly nailed the country, if not the province, when he noted that the R in the signature belongs to Spanish palæography. Here also are the best panels of a retable of the Transfiguration, painted perhaps by Benito Martorell, and ordered certainly by Bishop Simon Salvador, who died in 1445, for the chapel under that invocation. In the Transfiguration, Elias is habited quaintly as a Carmelite monk, after the Spanish use; in the Way to Emmaus, and the scene where the Risen Christ visits His Mother and S. John in a garden, the sudden bit of intimate life is unexpected and keen; in the Feeding of the Multitude the entire panel is patterned over with figures like some Japanese pieces, and the haloes spotted up and down it complete the composition of an immense decorative genius. The pictures in the other room are more various and more battered: a predella of hermits in the Thebaid by a pupil of a pupil of the Lorenzetti; a retable of SS. Cosmo and Damian, full of anecdote; another retable, very ruined, showing only a delicate Madonna's head and a squatting fat-faced angel like an Outamaro. An exquisite pale panel of SS. Clare and Catharine, in the Cabrera altarpiece, is flanked by six little saints and six little scenes, with a Crucifixion above, a predella below, and the ancient doors that led behind the altar. The composition of the retable, in Spain, explains on reflection the composition of the panels: inevitably there is no centralisation, simply difference of scale, and everything is as important in its turn as everything else. The whole is *not* a whole, that is to say simultaneous, but in sequence: this is a narrative, and not a monumental, art. The Madonna which the King Don Martin sent from Valencia is not kept here, and I have never had sight of it, but from photographs I am disposed to venture that it came from Sano di Pietro. In the cloister is a fine retable of SS. Tekla and Sebastian, the latter, as usually in Catalan art, a grave bearded man. It is very possibly by Pedro Alemany, who was painting in 1497. Several inside the cathedral satisfy even after regilding; a fine Visitation stands in one of the ambulatory chapels, but the best, a very beautiful young bishop enthroned beside S. Martin, is blocked by a trumpery modern altar and can be neither seen nor photographed.

(11) Here are now a pair of tombs, corbelled out from the wall and covered on great days with velvet, gold-striped with the Catalan bars: those of Ramon Berenguer *el Viejo* and of his wife Doña Almodis.

(12) See note 22 on the Cathedral of Palma.

(13) S. Mary of the Sea was built by the merchants in 1329, burned in 1379, and rebuilt by them. The last keystone of the vault was placed in 1388, and Mass said August 15, 1384. The inscription, in Catalan and Latin, on either side the south door, says, on the right: " *En nom de la Santa Trinitat á honor de Madona Sancta Maria fo commençada la obra de questa esgleysa lo die de Sancta Maria de Mar en lany MCCCXXVIIII., regnant Nanfos [Alfonso] per la gracia de Deu Rey de Arago qui conquis lo ragne de Serdenya.*" The Latin of the left makes clear the day, the Feast of the Annunciation, VI. Kal. April. *See* p. 70, note 3.

(14) Read, 1630. It was dedicated the last day of that year. On the wall of the south ambulatory hang two panels from a great lost Catalan altar-piece of the third quarter of the fifteenth century, the Resurrection and Pentecost, in which the armour lightens and darkens and the tongues of flame rush down in a cataract of glory. It is an odd touch, that the Risen Lord should have come out, like the genie out of the bottle, from such a little coffer as Ramon Berenguer lies in upon the cathedral wall, locked with a great lock and fastened with a great chain.

(15) Santa Agueda belongs to the thirteenth and fourteenth century. On the wall of the apse are the shields of Jaime II. and Blanche of Anjou. 1302 the work was on; a little later it was directed by Riquer *carpintero;* in 1319 it must have been already finished. The roof may perhaps be explained by the master's being a carpenter, but it was a manner sympathetic to all the builders of the *language d'oc,* was propagated by the Dominicans, and was cheap. The church is now used for an Archæological Museum, to hold things not thought good enough for the Provincial Museum, and it contains, among others, the Retable of the Constable, 1464. This, authenticated by documents and provenance, offers the best point of departure for all study of the great Vergós family of painters. It has, unfortunately, so little charm as to throw suspicion on other and lovely work attributed to the atelier of the Vergós.

(16) Read " of both walls."

(17) The Carmen was demolished in 1873, San Miguel in 1874.

(18) The church and convent of S. Anthony Abbot were burned and with them a number of fine pictures collected and stacked away by the *Padres Escolapios,* in the rising of 1909. In this, which was so entirely a popular rising that the political leaders were all alike unprepared and unable to profit, the people held the city for three days, and while doing no damage to private persons or goods, they burned ecclesiastical property as a solemn expression of opinion. Later, when the police and the military regained the town, the criminal class had their innings. Since what happened in 1835-6 and in 1909 will happen again more often on a greater scale, here is one reason amongst others why more effort should be made to get the great early neglected pictures and other treasures out of the dark chapels of churches and the hands of chapters, into museums where they can be seen and cannot be sold, and where, being national property, they will not be endangered by any attitude that a Spaniard may take up towards priests.

(19) Made by Johan Jordi, 1400.

(20) At present the patios have all been pulled to pieces, and the whole place is under distressing restoration.

(21) It was begun 1357, finished July 5, 1392, according to D. Andres Avellino Pi.

(22) For other Catalan paintings, the Museum in the Park is worth some time. It contains, besides the Retable of the Councillors, strongly·Flemish in technique and types, finished in 1445 by Luis Dalmau, the altar-pieces from San Cugat, which is more French than Flemish and more Spanish than either. It contains also the eight panels of the Retable of S. Vincent of Sarría, painted by the Vergós

family through a long term of years, with the probable help of Jaime Huguet. A fragment of a Deposition shows the characteristic composition, with a stiff horizontal Christ and the heads horizontal above; and panels from a sixteenth - century Italianate retable, full of Umbrian suavity and pleasure, mark almost the last moment before the ruin began with the influence of what used to be talked about as the Roman School. There are, moreover, for such as fancy them, the retable of San Martin de Provensals, with its dry, merciless portrait head of the soldier-saint; some heads and other fragments of lovely Gothic sculpture in stone and alabaster, and some carved and painted Madonnas of Majesty in the ancient tradition. In the next room to these may be sought out a number of wooden altar frontals painted in the Byzantine tradition, that lingered on among the mountains as late as the fourteenth century—poor, rude, and touching. One among them shines like a star, where sainted abbots of his order are ranged about S. Benedict like the mosaics at Ravenna, their haloes faintly luminous like moonstones. It is impossible to photograph, but it is one of the very beautiful things in the world. Two of the ancient guilds preserve in their meeting places the panels of great and glorious altar-pieces of the Vergós School: in the Gremio de los Revendidores, near S. Mary of the Pine, the legend of S. Michael, told with more romantic chapters even than usual, and a Madonna with Virgin saints — SS. Lucy, Barbara, Agnes, and Petronilla. The Gremio de Curtidores is in the old town and hard to find, but I think it is not very far from the Capilla de Marcus, and no search were too long to find out the magnificent figures, painted probably between 1489 and 1493, that play through the pageant of the life of S. Augustine.

San Cugat and Pedralbes. The Benedictine monastery of San Cugat del Valle is served by a motor 'bus from Barcelona twice a day, or can be reached by taking the tram up to La Rabassada and walking through pine woods about three miles down into the next valley. Built on a Roman fort, and thence called *San Cucufate in Octaviano*, it looks, even after ruin and restoration, more than half a fortress. The nave and façade (with three fine roses) are Gothic, the head, with the cloister, Romanesque. In 986 the Moors killed the abbot and monks, destroyed the buildings, and burned papers and books. In the next year Abbot Otto began the present building. The cloister was built 1007 to 1050. Abbot Guitardo or Witardo, after taking counsel with the Bishops of Barcelona, Gerona, Vich, and Urgell, sold to the Counts of Barcelona, Don Ramon Borrell III. and Doña Ermesindis, in 1013, the ground that the monastery owned in Tarassa and Ullastrell, and pushed the work, building the chapter-room, etc., with the price. After this documents are wanting: we know simply that in the fourteenth century the church was still a-finishing, particularly the high altar, and in the next likewise; a Master Alfonso painted the pictures of the said altar in 1473 for 900 florins; in the eighteenth century the baroque south chapels were added. The church has no transepts but a nave and aisles, five bays of quadripartite vault, and three parallel apses; the lantern is placed over the fourth, and the sanctuary brought forward halfway down the fifth; the Coro fills the third.

The altar painting of the Martyrdom of San Medin, which is not in the least Catalan, is preserved now in the Museum at Barcelona. The Retable of All Saints was painted between 1411 and 1416 by a pupil of Luis Borrassá—a charming litany in which alternate choirs of young men and maidens, old men and angels, array themselves antiphonally. The theme is taken from the Golden Legend, the dream of the Keeper of S. Peter's. Madonna, enthroned with the Holy Child and ringed by angels, fills the great central panel, above which the Crucifixion, though irrelevant, holds its wonted place. In the tops of the side ranges she is adored as Queen of Angels, the heavenly host marshalled on one side by S. Michael with lance and shield, on the other by S. Raphael with the little Tobias. Below these, on the left, the Patriarchs are led by S. John Baptist in camel's hair, and on the right the Prophets, seven in all, count David among them, crowned and playing on a zither. Queen of Patriarchs, Queen of Prophets, Queen of Apostles, it goes, with S. Peter as pope at the head; Queen of Martyrs, and, as Jacques de Voragine says, " The soldiers are the martyrs and the multitude that follow are the holy confessors; " Queen of Virgins, led oddly by S. Anne with the little Mary on her arm, and numbering princesses and queenly nuns among them, and the opposite panel filled with more holy women. In the vertical divisions of the frame twelve more small saints are set, and in the predella great half-lengths of six saints and a Pietà, the Virgin straight from Siena. This is, or was, near the door on the south side. Outside, the apse has half-columns and corbels, the tower, pilaster strips and corbelling, the lantern, lancet windows under a pointed arch. The two-storied cloister lies along the whole north side, barrel-vaulted, the deep round arches set on pairs of columns wide apart, with superb historied capitals; a chapter-house on the east side is now the Chapel of the Blessed Sacrament; and the present chapter-room, on the north, was once the refectory. The workman on the last capital (*i.e.* the northernmost) of the east side carved himself at work, and on the inside face of the buttress adjoining engraved as follows: " *Haec est Arnalli sculptoris forma Catelli, qui claustrum tale construxit perpetuale.*" " This is the effigy of the carver, Arnaldo Cadell, who built this cloister, proof against time." The upper gallery was built at different times in the sixteenth century by Abbot Despuig and the Vicar General who governed the vacant abbey from 1573 to 1589; also in their time was built the little outer cloister that flanks the west side of the big one. Fallen from its high estate, San Cugat yet gives the idea of a great monastic establishment, and keeps still the gate tower, the belfry on the abbot's quarters, the tower of the prison, and the abbot's garden on the south sheltered by old walls.

The Convent of Pedralbes, near Sarría, possesses a fourteenth-century church of one nave, an apse and seven bays, with chapels between interior buttresses in the three bays east of the portal, a lovely tomb of the foundress, Doña Elisenda de Moncada, the wife of Jaime II., an equally lovely cloister, in three stories, of the delicate Catalan type, and a room inside the nunnery full of trecento frescoes by Ferrer Bassa that are amazingly Sienese. They were photographed for the book of Señor Sanpere y Miguel, but the *clausura* which was lifted for a moment on his account has shut down again even against women.

At *Palma* in Mallorca the work on the cathedral was begun in 1230. In 1232 the Chapel Royal was well advanced, and Don Jaime I. pleased with it. Then he died ; the kingdom was divided between Pedro III. the Great of Aragon and Jaime II. of Mallorca, and work stopped. When peace was made between the latter and Don Jaime II. the Just of Aragon, the work went on again ; the king fetched from Roussillon good workmen to turn into a palace the old Alcazar of the Almudaina, who made pictures and reliefs for the royal rooms and built the oratory of S. Anna. Francisco Camprodon, a sculptor of Perpignan, worked in the palace. But the king and bishops lacked money for the cathedral; the bishops squeezed the island and sold the right to have one's arms on any part of the building that one paid for, and on the keys of the nave vaults for a fixed price of a thousand libras. All through the thirteen hundreds work was going on. 1377 Camprodon went to Carcassonne for the chapter, but Beringuer Ostales continued his work on the stalls. The record of payments on account of the cloister begins June 3, 1346. On January 29, 1394, died Peter Morey, sculptor, head-master of the Gate of the Sea. The Virgin of the lintel must be his only work. 1422 Guillem Sagrera, who had finished Perpignan, was commissioned to do a S. Peter for the Portal of the Sea; it looks more Franco-Flemish than Toulousan, and before that date John of Valenciennes had worked in the place of the dead Peter, but not on the big statues, making probably the Last Supper, and the prophets and angels in the archivolts. The Puerta del Mirador, the only richly sculptured one, was begun in 1594. 1599, Juan Jordi put the glass in the western rose for nine thousand reals of Castile. The greater part of the church was built in the beginning of the sixteenth century. The nave and three aisles have eight bays and pentagonal chapels between the buttresses down both sides; the Coro occupies the central part of the nave in the fourth, fifth, sixth, and half the seventh. The sanctuary, which has two bays and a pentagonal apse, is flanked by a pair of like chapels, square on the outside, and is enough lower than the nave to allow, as at Gerona, space, where the vault drops, for a great rose. The Chapel Royal, of two bays and a pentagonal apse, opens to eastward behind the high altar. The vaulting is beset with intermediate ribs, not in star patterns, but cutting up good quadripartite structure, and six-ribbed chevets, with an intermediate rib everywhere: the pillars are far too slight for the church, but what is to be expected of the date?

The Lonja is of the Catalan type. In 1409 the merchants petitioned the King, Don Martin, and on March 3, in Barcelona, he gave them leave to form themselves into a royal college of twenty members, to meet to dictate rules and order business, to arm ships and impose a tax on outgoing and incoming merchandise, for the upkeep of the ships and the building of a Lonja which should ennoble their profession and the city. 1420, the master of the works of the cathedral, Guillermo Sagrera, undertook the work. *See* p. 333.

CHAPTER XV

GERONA—PERPIÑAN—S. ELNE

THERE are few Spanish towns which are altogether more interesting than the now insignificant and little-known city of Gerona. It not only contains several buildings of rare architectural interest, but it has, moreover, the advantage of being picturesquely placed on the banks of the rapid river Oña, and on the steep slope of the hills which bound it.

The Cathedral is the first object of attraction, and its history is so curious, that I need make no apology for proceeding without further preface to say the substance of what I have been able to learn about it.

There was a cathedral here at a very early period; and when Gerona was taken by the Moors, they converted it into a mosque, but, with their usual liberality, allowed the services of the Church still to be carried on in the neighbouring church of San Feliu, which for a time, accordingly, was the cathedral church. In A.D. 1015 this state of affairs had ceased, owing to the expulsion of the Moors, and the cathedral was again recovered to the use of the Church. Considerable works were at this time executed,[1] if, indeed, the cathedral was not entirely rebuilt, as the old documents declare, and the altered church was re-consecrated in A.D. 1038,[2] by the Archbishop of Narbonne, assisted by the Bishops of Vique, Urgel, Elne, Barcelona, Carcassonne, and others. In A.D. 1310 works seem to have been again in progress,[3] and in A.D. 1312 a Chapter was held, at which it was resolved to rebuild the head or chevet of the church with nine chapels,[4] for which, in A.D. 1292, Guillermo Gaufredo, the treasurer, made a

---

[1] See *España Sagrada*, xlv. 2-3. See also the deed executed by Bishop Roger in 1015. "Nostra necessitate coacti causa ædificationis prædictæ ecclesiæ, quæ satis cognitum cunctis est esse destructa," etc.—*Esp. Sag.* xliii. 423.

[2] See the act of consecration, *España Sagrada*, xliii. 432-437, which declares the church to have been rebuilt "*a fundamentis*."

[3] *Esp. Sag.* xliv. 43.

[4] "Capitulum Gerundense in cerca nova ecclesiæ Gerundensis more solito congregatum, statuit, voluit et ordinavit, quod caput ipsius ecclesiæ de novo construeretur et edificaretur, et circumcirca ipsum novem cappellæ fierent, et in dormitorio veteri fieret sacristia. Et cura ipsius operis fuit commissa per dictum capitulum, venerabilibus Raimundo de Vilarico, archidiacono, et Amaldo de Monterotundo, canonico."—*España Sagrada*, xlv. 3.

bequest in favour of the work.[1] In A.D. 1325 I find that an indulgence was granted by the Bishop Petrus de Urrea in favour of donors to the work of the cathedral;[2] and the work, so far westward as the end of the choir, was probably complete before A.D. 1346, inasmuch as in this year the silver altar, with its Retablo and baldachin, were placed where they now stand.[3] We know something of the architects employed during the fourteenth century upon the works just mentioned. In 1312 the Chapter appointed the Archdeacon Ramon de Vilarico and the Canon Arnaldo de Montredon to be the *obreros* or general clerical superintendents of the progress of the works. In A.D. 1316, or, according to some authorities, in February, 1320, an architect— Enrique of Narbonne—is first mentioned; and soon after this, on his death, another architect of the same city, Jacobo de Favariis by name, was appointed with a salary of two hundred and fifty libras[4] a quarter, and upon the condition that he should come from Narbonne six times a year[5] to examine the progress of the works. In A.D. 1325 Bart. Argenta was the master of the works, and he probably carried them on until the completion of the choir in 1346.[6]

[1] " Dimitto etiam ad caput prædictæ ecclesiæ, vel ad cimborium argenteum faciendum desuper altare Beatæ Mariæ illa decem millia solidorum Barchinon: quæ ad illud dare promisseram jam est diu."—Will of Guillermo Gaufredo, *Viage Lit. á las Iglesias de España*, xii. 184.

[2] *Esp. Sag.* xliv. 51, 320, 322.

[3] " Pateat universis," " quod die Lunæ 4 Idus Marti intitulata anno Domini 1346. Reverendus in Christo Pater " " S. Tarrachonensis ecclesiæ archiepiscopus, altare majus Beatissimæ Virginis Mariæ cathedralis Gerundensis ecclesiæ a loco antiquo ipsius ecclesiæ in quo construtum erat in capite novo operis ejusdem ut decuit translatum est," etc. " De quibus omnibus ad perpetuam rei memoriam venerabilis vir Dominus Petrus Stephani Presbiter de capitulo et operarius memoratæ ecclesiæ mandavit unum et plura fieri instrumenta per me Notarium infrascriptum præsentibus ad hoc vocatis testibus," etc., etc.—*España Sagrada*, xlv. 373, 374.

[4] Or " sueldos," Parcerisa. " Sous," V. le Duc.=1500 francs at the present day.

[5] Register entitled *Curia del Vicariato de Gerona, Liber notulorum ad anno 1320, ad 1322*, fol. 48, quoted in *Esp. Sag.* xlv. 373. See also Violiet le Duc, *Dictionnaire Raisonné*, i. 112. F. J. Parcerisa, *Recuerdos y Bellezas de España, Cataluña*, i. 146, says that the work was commenced in 1316, and that Enrique of Narbonne died in 1320.

[6] The list of architects given by D. J. Villanueva (*Viage Lit. á las Iglesias de España*, xii. 172 *et seq.*) does not agree with this. The first he mentions is Jayme de Taverant, a Frenchman from Narbonne (and no doubt identical with Jaques de Favariis), in 1320. Francisco de Plana, a Catalan, held the post after him, and was removed in 1368 in favour of Pedro Coma (de Cumba), who was employed also at San Feliu, Gerona; and in 1397 Pedro de San Juan, " de natione Picardiæ," was employed. Guillermo Boffiy succeeded him; in 1427 Rollinus Vautier, " diocesi Biterrensis," was master of the works, and in 1430 Pedro Cipres succeeded him.

In A.D. 1395 it was proposed to erect a Chapter-house, and the canons in charge of the fabric ("*canonigos fabriqueros*") presented in writing their reasons for not erecting it where proposed by the Chapter—at the south end of the refectory.   They said that the works of the church itself ought first of all to be gone on with, and that the proposed work would destroy a good and convenient refectory, and make it obscure and ridiculous: and it seems that their report had the effect of staying the work. In A.D. 1416 Guillermo Boffiy, master of the works of the cathedral, proposed a plan for its completion by the erection of a nave; and though the chevet had an aisle and chapels round it, he proposed to build his nave of the same width as the choir and its aisles, but as a single nave without aisles.   This proposition was deemed so hazardous, and created so great a discussion, that the Chapter, before deciding what plan should be adopted, called together a Junta of architects, and propounded to each of them separately certain questions, to each of which they all returned their answers upon oath.   In the September following, these answers were read before the Chapter by a notary, and it may be supposed carefully digested, for it was not until March 8, 1417, that Guillermo Boffiy, the master of the works, was called in and in his turn interrogated with the same questions.   Immediately after this, on the 15th of the same month, at a Chapter-meeting presided over by the Bishop, it was decided to carry on the work as proposed, with a single nave. The story is so well worth telling in full, that I have given in the Appendix a translation of the entire document, which equals in interest any with which I am acquainted, bearing on the profession of architect in the middle ages.[1]   It is valuable also, incidentally, as giving us the names of the architects of several other buildings, most of those who were examined having described themselves in a formal style as masters of the works of some particular church or churches.   It is difficult to say exactly when the nave was completed, but the great south door was not executed until A.D. 1458, and the key-stone of the last division of the vault seems to have been placed in the time of Bishop Benito, so late as *circa* 1579.[2]   In A.D. 1581 the same bishop laid the

[1] The original is in the *Liber Notularum*.   It is reprinted in *España Sagrada,* xlv., appendix, 227-244.   Cean Bermudez has again reprinted it in *Arq. de España,* i. 261-275; and D. J. Villanueva in the appendix to vol. xii. of the *Viage Lit. á las Iglesias de España*, prints it in the original Catalan dialect.

[2] This key-stone has a sculpture of San Benito.—*España Sagrada* xliv. 420.

first stone of the bell-tower, and in 1607 the west front and the great flight of steps leading up to it seem to have been commenced (1).

We have thus the story of the periods at which the church was founded, altered, and enlarged very fully told, and it now only remains to apply it to what is still to be seen in the existing building.

A reference to my ground-plan [1] will show that the church remains very much in the state which the documentary evidence describes. The choir has nine chapels round its chevet, as described, and has lofty arches, a series of very small openings in lieu of triforium, and a clerestory of two-light windows, of decidedly late but still good Middle-pointed character. The columns, in the usual Catalan fashion of this age, are clusters of rather reedy mouldings, with no proper division or subordination of parts, and consequently of poor effect, and there is no division by way of string-courses above or below the triforium. On the exterior the east end is not seen to much advantage, as it is built into and against a steep hill, so that at a distance of a few feet only the eye is on a level with the top of the walls of the chapels round the apse. The roofs, too, have all been modernised and lowered. The only peculiarities here are a series of trefoiled openings, just under the eaves of the roof, into the space over the vaulting, and perhaps devised for the purpose of ventilation: and the gurgoyles projecting from the buttresses, which are carved and moulded stones finished at the end with an octagonal capital, through the bottom of which the water falls, and which almost looks as if it were meant for the stone head of a metal down-pipe.

When the choir was built, some considerable portions of the church consecrated in A.D. 1038 were left standing. The nave was probably entirely of this age; and a portion of what was no doubt one of the original towers still remains on the north side, between the cloister and the nave. This tower has pilasters at the angles and in the centre, and is divided into equal stages in height by horizontal corbel-tables. An apse of the same age remains on the east side of what seems to have been the south transept of the early church: and from its position we may, I think, assume with safety that the church was then finished with three or five apses at the east, very much as in the church of San Pedro, close by, which I shall have presently to describe. In addition to these early remains there is also a magnificent and all but unaltered

[1] Plate XVIII., p. 104.

cloister. I cannot find any certain evidence of its exact date, though it seems to have existed in A.D. 1117, when an act of the Bishop Raymond Berenger was issued in the "cloister of the cathedral."[1] The character of the work confirms, I think, this date. The plan is very peculiar, forming a very irregular trapezium, no two of the sides being equal in length. It has on all four sides severely simple round arches carried on coupled shafts: these are of marble, and set as much as 20 inches apart, so as to enable them to carry a wall 3 feet 1½ inches thick. This thickness of wall was quite necessary, as the cloister is all roofed with stone, the section of the vaults on the east, west, and south sides being half of a barrel, and on the north a complete barrel vault. The detail of the capitals is of the extremely elaborate and delicate imitation of classical carving, so frequently seen throughout the south of France. The abaci are in one stone, but the bases of the shafts are separate and rest upon a low dwarf-wall, and square piers are carried up at intervals to strengthen the arcade. The columns have a very slight entasis.

This cloister deserves careful study, as it seems to show one of the main branches of the stream by which Romanesque art was introduced into Spain. It is impossible not to recognise the extreme similarity between such work as we see here, and that which we see in the cloister at Elne, near Perpiñan, and, to go still farther afield, at S. Trophime at Arles. And if any Spanish readers of these pages object to my assumption that the stream flowed from France westward, they must prove the exact converse, and assume that this Romanesque work was developed from Roman work in Spain, and thence spread to Elne and Arles, a position which none, I suppose, will be bold enough to take.

The nave remains to be described; and to do this well and adequately, it is necessary to use, not indeed many, but certainly strong, words. Guillermo Boffiy, master of the works, might well cling fondly to his grand scheme, for his proposal was not less, I believe, than the erection of the widest pointed vault in Christendom. Such a scheme might be expected to meet then in Spain, as it most certainly would now in this country,[2] a good deal of criticism, and many objections, on the score of its imprac-

---

[1] *España Sagrada*, xliii. 200, and Appendix, 453.
[2] In my first design for the Crimean Memorial church which I am building at Constantinople, I had a vault thirty-eight feet in clear span, and this was objected to by a really accomplished critic as too bold and hazardous an experiment! What would have been said then of a vault twice as wide?

GERONA CATHEDRAL
INTERIOR, LOOKING EAST

ticability; and it is to the honour of the Chapter that they had the good sense to consult experts and not amateurs as to the steps to be taken, and then, having satisfied themselves that their architect was competent to his work, that they left it entirely in his hands.

The clear width of this nave is 73 feet, and its height is admirably proportioned to this vast dimension.[1] It is only four bays in length; each bay has chapels opening into it on either side, and filling up the space between the enormous buttresses, whose depth from the front of the groining shaft to their face is no less than 20 feet. Above the arches which open into the side chapels is a row of small cusped openings, corresponding with those which form the triforium of the choir; and above these are lofty traceried clerestory windows. The groining-ribs are very large and well moulded. At the east end of the nave three arches open into the choir and its aisles; and above these are three circular windows, the largest of which has lost its tracery. And here it is that the magnificence of the scheme is most fully realised. A single nave and choir, all of the same enormous size, would have been immeasurable by the eye, and would have been, to a great extent, thrown away; here, however, the lofty choir and aisles, with their many subdivisions, give an extraordinary impression of size to the vast vault of the nave, and make it look even larger than it really is. In short, had this nave been longer by one bay, I believe that scarcely any interior in Europe could have surpassed it in effect. Unfortunately, as is so often the case among those who possess the most precious works of art, there is now but little feeling in Gerona for the treasure it possesses in this wondrous nave, for the stalls and Coro have been moved down from their proper place into the middle of its length, where they are shut in and surrounded by a high blank screen,

---

[1] I subjoin the dimensions of some of the largest French and other churches, in order that the dimensions of the nave of Gerona may be really appreciated.

Albi	.	.	58 feet between the walls.	
Toulouse Cathedral	.	63	,,	
S. Jean Perpiñan	.	60	,,	
Amiens	.	.	49	centre to centre of column of nave.
Paris	.	.	48	,,
Bourges	.	.	49	,,
Chartres	.	.	50	,,
Cologne	.	.	44	,,
Narbonne	.	.	54	,,
Canterbury	.	.	43	,, ,, of choir.
York	.	.	52	,, ,, of nave.
Westminster Abbey	.	38	,,	

painted in the vulgarest imitation of Gothic traceries, to the utter ruin, of course, of the whole internal perspective. It would be a grand and simple work of restoration to give up here, for once, the Spanish usage, and to restore the stalls to the proper choir. I say " restore," because it is pretty clear that they could not have been in the nave when they were first made, inasmuch as this was in A.D. 1351, sixty-six years before its commencement. A deed still remains in the archives of the cathedral, by which we ascertain this fact, for by it a sculptor from Barcelona agreed, on June 7, 1351, to make the stalls at the rate of 45 libras of Barcelona for each.[1] The detail of some parts of the woodwork is exceedingly good, and evidently of the middle of the fourteenth century, so that it is clear they are the very stalls referred to in the agreement. There is ample length in the proper choir for them, and they must have been moved into the nave in unwise obedience to the common modern Spanish arrangement, which was certainly never more entirely unfortunate and destructive of effect than it is here.

It will be seen, by reference to the Appendix, that though the architects consulted were fairly unanimous as to the possibility of building the single nave, they were by no means so in their recommendation of it as the best plan. The general feeling seems to have been decidedly adverse to it; and we may assume that the Chapter decided on it partly because it was already commenced, and partly because it promised to be a cheaper plan than the other. There seems also to have been great dread on the part of the Chapter of interfering in any way with the wall which now forms the east end of the nave, for fear lest, when it was cut into for the introduction of the respond of the nave arcade, the whole should give way.

Paschasius de Xulbe, one of the architects questioned, gives the valuable answer, that if the nave is of triple division in width, the groining of the choir must be raised in order that it may correspond in its measurements to its third; from which it is pretty clear that he spoke of a then recognised system of proportioning the height to the width of a building.

Guillermo Sagrera, master of the works at S. John, Perpiñan, tells us, in his answer, that the choir was originally built with the intention of having a single nave; and this will account for the otherwise unintelligible finish of its western wall, which it is clear, from the tenor of all the answers, was not prepared for any arches in the nave. I am not certain indeed whether

[1] *Liber Notularum*, fol. 31.

we are not to assume, in reading the questions asked by the Chapter, that the Romanesque nave was itself of the same plan and dimensions; and the vast width of the old nave of Toulouse Cathedral—sixty-three feet—affords an example, at no great distance from Gerona, of the fact that architects, even so early as the beginning of the thirteenth century, were not afraid to propose and execute works on so unusual a scale.

I will not quote farther from the answers of the architects, because they well deserve to be read in detail; but it is a satisfaction to be able to say that their conviction of the practicability of the work has been amply justified, inasmuch as, even to the present day, there is scarcely a sign of a settlement or crack throughout the entire building.

It is difficult to express a positive opinion as to the original intention of the architect in regard to the design and finish of the exterior of this part of the church. The gable walls have been altered, the roofs renewed, and the original termination of the buttresses destroyed. At no time, however, I think, can it have looked well. The position is charming, on the edge of a steep, rocky hill falling down to the river, and girt on its north side by the old many-towered city wall; yet with all these advantages it is now a decidedly ugly work, and the nave looks bald, and large out of all proportion to the subdivided, lower, and over-delicately-treated choir. On the west side the whole character of the church is Pagan;[1] and I well remember the astonishment with which, when I had climbed the long flight of broad steps which leads to the western door, I looked down the stupendous interior, for which I had been so little prepared!

The effect is not a little enhanced by the dark colour of the stone, which has never been polluted by whitewash; but there are some defects. The want of length has already been noticed; the entire absence of string-courses inside is not pleasant; and the lowering of the arches into the chapels in the second bay from the west wall, where there are three in place of the two in each of the other bays, breaks the main lines of the design very awkwardly. The mouldings too, as might be expected in work of so late a date, are nowhere very first rate, though they certainly retain generally the character of late fourteenth-century work.

The doorway on the south side of the nave is remarkable in one respect. It has in its jambs a series of statues of the Apostles, executed in terra-cotta; and the agreement for their execution,

---

[1] The church was originally intended to have octagonal towers at the angles of the west front. Of these the south-west tower has been built up in Pagan style, and the north-west has never been built.

made, in A.D. 1458, with the artist Berenguer Cervia, binds him
to execute them for six hundred florins, and " of the same earth
as the statue of Sta. Eulalia and the cross of the new doorway at
Barcelona." [1] This doorway is very large, but bald and poor in
detail; the statues to which the contract refers still remain, and
are in good preservation.

There is nothing more specially worth noticing in the fabric;
but fortunately the choir still retains precious relics in the Retablo behind, and the baldachin above, the high altar. There are
also said to be some frontals of the altar still preserved, which
are of silver, and which were originally adorned with precious
stones, and with an inscription which proves them to have been
made before the consecration of the church, in A.D. 1038. Unfortunately they were not in their place when I was at Gerona,
and so I missed seeing them. [2] The Retablo is of wood entirely
covered with silver plates, and divided vertically into three series
of niches and canopies; each division has a subject, and a good
deal of enamelling is introduced in various parts of the canopies
and grounds of the panels. Each panel has a cinquefoiled arch
with a crocketed gablet and pinnacles on either side. The
straight line of the top is broken by three niches, which rise in
the centre and at either end. In the centre is the Blessed
Virgin with our Lord; on the right, San Narcisso; and on the
left, San Feliu. The three tiers of subjects contain (a) figures of
saints, (b) subjects from the life of the Blessed Virgin, and (c)
subjects from the life of our Lord (2). A monument in one of the
chapels gives some account of this precious work; for though it
is called a ciborium, it is also spoken of as being of silver, which
I believe, the actual ciborium is not. [3] The date of this monu-

---

[1] *España Sagrada*, xlv. 8. Villanueva, *Viage Lit.* xii. 175, gives the
name of this artist as Antonio Claperos " obrer de ymagens."

[2] *See* the description of this silver frontal in *España Sagrada*, xlv. 8. The
Historia de S. Narciso y de Gerona, by P. M. Roig y Yalpi, is quoted as
authority for the statements given. *See* also the act of consecration of
the cathedral in A.D. 1038 (*España Sagrada*, xliii. 437), in which among
the list of signatures at the end occurs the following passage:—" S. Ermes-
sendis comitissæ quæ eadem die ad honorem Dei et Matris Ecclesiæ trescen-
tas auri contulit uncias ad auream construendam tabulam;" and in a
necrologium, from 1102 to 1313, occur the following entries: " 1254.
Pridie Kalendas Februarii obiit Guillelmus de Terradis, sacrista major,
qui tabulam argenteam altari Beatæ Mariæ Cathedralis fieri fecit." " 1229.
Kalendis Martii obiit Ermesendis Comitissa quæ hanc sedem ditavit et
tabulam auream ac crucem Deo et Beatæ Mariæ obtulit, et ecclesiam
multis ornamentis ornavit."

[3] " Hic jacet Amaldus de Solero, Archdiaconus Bisalduenensis qui etiam
suis expensis propriis fecit fieri cimborium seu coopertam argenteam super
altaro majori ecclesiæ Gerundensis. Obiit autem anno Dni. M.CCCXX.
sexto, viii. Kal. Augusti."

ment is 1362; but in the *Liber Notularum* for A.D. 1320, 21, and 22, it seems that the Chapter devoted 3000 libras for the reparation of the Retablo, though it was not till A.D. 1346 that

ALTAR, GERONA

the work was finished, and the altar finally fixed in its present position.[1]   The whole of the work is therefore before this date; and probably the Retablo and the baldachin date from the period between the two dates last given, viz. A.D. 1320 and A.D. 1348.

The baldachin is, like the Retablo, of wood covered with thin plates of metal. It stands upon four shafts, the lower portions of which are of dark marble resting on the moulded footpace round the altar.   These four shafts have capitals and   bands,   the   latter being set round with ena-melled coats-of-arms.   The canopy is a sort of very flat quadripartite vault covered with small figures; but on both my visits to Gerona it has been so dark in the choir as to render it impossible to make out the subjects.   The central subject seems to be the Coronation of the Blessed Virgin, and in the eastern division is a sitting figure of our Lord with saints on either side.   In order to show the figures on the roof of the baldachin as much as possible, the two eastern columns are much lower than the western, the whole roof having thus a slope up towards the west.   A singular arrangement was contrived behind the altar—a white marble seat for the bishop raised by several steps on either side to the level of the altar, and placed under the central arch of the apse.   Here, when the bishop celebrated pontifically, he sat till the oblation, and returned to it again to give the benediction to the people.[2]

The church is full of other objects of interest.   Against the

[1] *See* note 3, p. 93.
[2] See *Martene de Antiq. Eccl. Rit.* lib. i. cap. iv. art. 3.

north wall is a very pretty example of a wheel of bells: this is all of wood, corbelled out from the wall, and is rung with a noisy jingle of silver bells at the elevation of the Host. Near it is a doorway leading into the sacristy, I think, which is very ingeniously converted into a monument. It has a square lintel and a pointed arch above: bold corbels on either side carry a high tomb, the base of which is just over the lintel; this is arcaded at the side and ends, and on its sloping top is a figure of a knight. The favourite type of monument in this part of Spain is generally a coped tomb carried on corbels, which are usually lions or other beasts: there are good examples of this kind both in the church and cloister; and in

WHEEL OF BELLS, GERONA

the latter there is also preserved a great wooden cross, which looks as though it had originally decorated a rood-loft.

The windows have a good deal of very late stained glass, which consists generally of single figures under canopies. I have already mentioned the fine early woodwork in the Coro. In the fifteenth century this was altered and added to: and a seat was then made for the bishop in the centre of the western side of the Coro, which has enormous pieces of carved openwork on either side executed with uncommon vigour and skill. These, again, were added to afterwards by a Renaissance artist, so that it is now necessary to discriminate carefully between the work of various ages.

If, when the cathedral has been thoroughly studied, one goes out through the cloister, an external door at its north-western angle leads out to the top of a steep path from which an extremely picturesque view is obtained. The old town walls girt the cathedral on the north side; but in the eleventh century it was thought well to add to them, and a second wall descends, crosses the valley below, and rises against the opposite hill in a very picturesque fashion. This wall has the passage-way perfect all round, and occasional circular towers project from it. The eye is at once caught in looking at this view by a fine Romanesque church with a half-ruined cloister and lofty octagonal steeple, which seems to be absolutely built across and through the walls. This is the Benedictine church of San Pedro de los

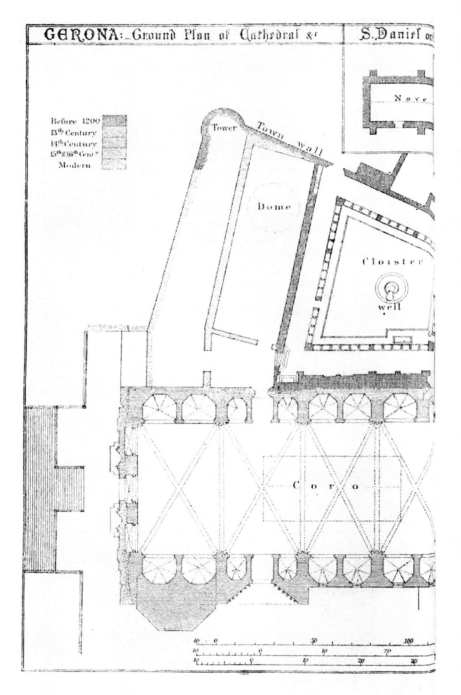

Before 1200
13th Century
14th Century
15th & 16th Cent y
Modern

Tower

Town wall

Dome

Cloister

well

Nave

Coro

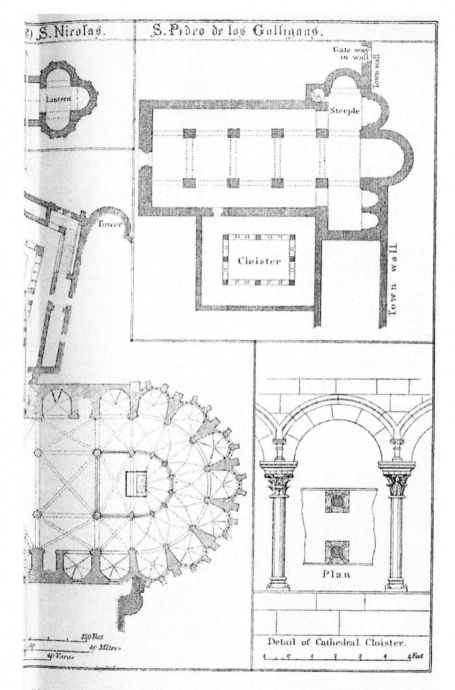

S. Nicolas.

S. Pedro de los Galligans.

Gate way in wall

Town wall

Lantern

Steeple

Tower

Cloister

Town wall

Plan

Detail of Cathedral Cloister.

150 Feet

40 Mètres

40 Varas

4 Feet

XVIII.

Galligans;[1] and a closer inspection shows that what at first
looks like the round-tower of the town walls, against which the
church has been built, is really the very apse of the church,
which when the new walls were built was raised and converted
above into a purely military work. The earliest reference to
this church that I have found is a statement that it existed in
the tenth century, and that, in A.D. 1117, the Count Ramon of
Barcelona gave it to the Benedictine convent of Sta. Maria de
la Crassa, in the bishopric of Carcassonne, of which his brother
was Abbat; and I think we may safely assume that the whole
of the existing church was built within a short time of its transfer
from the hands of the Secular to those of the Regular Clergy.

The church[2] consists of a nave and aisles of four bays, the
arches being very rude, and the piers plain and square. There
are north and south transepts, the former having one, and the
latter two eastern apsidal chapels; and the choir is also finished
with an apse. There is another apse at the north end of the
north transept. The nave is roofed with a round waggon-vault
with plain cross-ribs carried on engaged shafts; and there is a
clerestory of single-light windows which, on the inside, break up
partly into the vault of the roof. The aisles are roofed with
half-waggon or quadrant vaults, and the apses with semi-domes.
The octagonal steeple is built above the north transept, and has
in the eastern wall of its first stage two apsidal recesses, which
seem to have been intended for altars, and are roofed with semi-
domes. The detail of some of the work at the east end is of an
unusual kind: it is built in stone and black volcanic scoriæ, and
its rude character is evidence of its early date. Any one who is
acquainted with the noble church at Elne, near Perpiñan, will remember the similar use of volcanic scoriæ there, and will be led to
class the two monuments together as works of the same hand and
period. The view of the exterior of the church from the north-
west is very striking. There is a fine western door with a good
deal of carving very delicately and elaborately wrought, one of
the capitals having a very careful imitation of a fern-leaf on it;
above the doorway a horizontal cornice is carried all across the
front, and over this is a fine rose window. The side walls are
finished with dentil-courses; and the clerestory—which is carried
up very high above the springing of the vault inside—is finished

---

[1] " Galligans; in the old Latin, Galli Cantio. The name is taken from
a little stream which washes its walls and falls into the Oña."—Don J.
Villanueva, *Viage Lit.*, etc. xiv. 146.
[2] *See* ground-plan on Plate XVIII., p. 104.

SAN PEDRO, GERONA

EXTERIOR FROM THE NORTH-WEST

with an eaves-arcading also. There were no windows in the side walls of the aisle; and the clerestory windows, and a window at the west end of the north aisle, have bold splays on the outside as well as inside.

The steeple has been much altered; but the original design of the two upper (and octagonal) stages seems to have had a two-light window with a bold central shaft, angle-pilasters, and string-courses, with shallow arcading below them.

On the south side are the cloisters (3). They are locked up and in ruins; and though I tried two or three times, I was never able to gain admission to them; but I saw them from the hill above, and they looked at this distance as if they were designed very much after the pattern of those attached to the cathedral. The arches are round, and carried on coupled detached shafts. with piers in the centre of each side of the cloister. The roof seems to have been a barrel-vault, but great part of it has now fallen in. All this havoc and ruin is owing, like so much that one sees in Spain, to the action of the French troops during the Peninsular war.[1]

The whole character of this church is very interesting. The west front reminded me much of the best Italian Romanesque; and the rude simplicity of the interior—so similar in its mode of construction to the great church at Santiago in the opposite corner of the Peninsula—suggests the probability of its being one of the earliest examples of which Spain can boast.

Close to San Pedro, to the north-west, stands another church, which, though it is very small, is fully as curious (4). This is now desecrated and converted into workshops and dwelling-houses. It is transverse triapsal in plan (i.e. the transepts and the chancel are all finished with apses). The Crossing is surmounted by a low tower or lantern, square below, but octagonal above, and with some remains of an apparently old tiled roof. The transepts are ceiled with semi-domes, and the chancel was similarly covered, but its vault has now been removed in order to facilitate access to the steeple, in which a peasant and his family live. The nave is roofed with a waggon-vault, at the springing of which from the wall is a small moulding; and its walls are supported by buttresses, which do not seem to be earlier than the thirteenth century, though the rest of the church must date no doubt from the early part of the twelfth. The

---

[1] Don J. Villanueva, *Viage Literario*, xiv. 150, asserts that these cloisters are not earlier than the fourteenth century, though I notice that some of the inscriptions which he gives from them are of earlier date.

exterior is very plain; but the chancel apse is divided by pilasters which run up to and finish in a corbel-table at the eaves; and the tower has also an eaves' corbel-table. All the dimensions of this church are very small, but it is interesting, as being almost the only example I have seen in Spain of a transverse triapsal plan; and the central lantern is one of the earliest examples of what became in later days one of the most common features of Spanish buildings.[1]

We came down the hill north of the cathedral to see this church and San Pedro; and if we retrace our steps, and go out by the western door on to the platform at the top of the vast flight of steps which leads up to the cathedral, we shall be at once struck by the beautiful, though truncated, spire of San Feliu, which stands below, and to the west of the cathedral. Indeed, in nearly all views of the old city, this steeple claims the first place in our regard; and perhaps it is seen best of all in crossing the river at the other end of the town, where it stands at the end of the vista up the stream, which is edged on either side by the backs of the tall, picturesque, and crowded houses.

San Feliu[2] is one of the oldest collegiate foundations in the diocese of Gerona; and when, in the eighth century, the Moors converted the cathedral into a mosque, here it was that the Christian rites were celebrated. No doubt, therefore, a church stood here long before the first recorded notices of the fabric, for these do not occur before the early part of the fourteenth century, save such indications of work in progress as the bequest of ten solidos to the work by Bishop William in A.D. 1245, and such evidence of its damage or destruction as is the fact that the French, attacking the city in A.D. 1285, obtained possession of the church and did it much damage. In A.D. 1313, when the Chapter of the cathedral were obtaining royal

---

[1] Parcerisa describes this little church as that of S. Daniel, but I was unable on the spot to learn its dedication. I believe, however, that its dedication is to S. Nicolas, and that S. Daniel is a larger church of later date. In *España Sagrada*, xlv. 185 *et seq.*, some account is given of the foundation of S. Daniel. This took place in 1017, Bishop Roger having sold the church to Count Ramon, and Ermesendis his wife, for 100 ounces of gold, which were to be spent on the fabric of the cathedral. The Countess, after the death of the Count, endowed the church, and the deed still preserved recounts how that " Ego Ermesendis inchoavi prædictam ecclesiam edificare et Deo auxiliante volo perficere." An architectural description of the present church is given by Villanueva, *Viage Literario*, xiv. 158, from which it seems that it is a Greek cross in plan, and mainly of the fourteenth century, with an altar in a crypt below the high altar, constructed in 1343: and if this account is correct, this small twelfth-century church cannot be S. Daniel.

[2] S. Felix.

concessions towards the work of their own church, they granted an exemption to San Feliu, giving to its clergy the first-fruits of their benefices to spend on the work of their own church.[1] In A.D. 1318 there is evidence that the choir was completed, but other works were going on during the rest of the century. In A.D. 1340 the Chapter determined to erect cloisters, under the direction of an architect named Sancii, and bought a site for them to the north of the church; and the *operarius* or canon in charge of the work seems to have raised alms for them even so far off as at Valencia and in the Balearic Isles. The work was begun in A.D. 1357 and finished in 1368, in which year the Chapter entered into a contract[2] with an architect, one Pedro Zacoma, for the erection of the campanile. In A.D. 1363, however, it was deemed necessary, on account of the position of the church just outside the old walls, and on the north of the town, that it should be fortified; and to accomplish this work, and others of the same kind ordered in A.D. 1374 and 1385, the cloisters so recently built were destroyed. The steeple is said to have been finished in 1392,[3] Pedro Zacoma having acted as architect as late as A.D. 1376.

[1] *España Sagrada*, xlv. 41.

[2] Extract from the book entitled *Obra = Recepte et Expense, ab anno* 1365: "It.: Solvidisc°. R. Egidii Not. Gerunde v die Septembris, anno M.CCC.LX.VIII., pro instrumento facto inter Capitulum hujus Eccle. et P. Zacoma magistrum operis Cloquerii noviter incepti et est certum quod in isto instrumento continentur in efectu ista.—P°. Quod ille proficue procuret ipsum opus dictum evitando expensas inordinatas quantum in ipso fuerit, et hoc juravit. It.: Quod aliud opus accipere non valeat sine licencia operarii. It.: Quod quotiescumque fuerit in ipso opere factus apparatus operandi quod vocatus quocumque opere dimisso operetur in nostro opere: in premissis fuit exceptum opus Pontis majoris in quo jam prius extitit obligatus et convenit quando ipso fuerit in ipso opere Pontis vel in alio quod una hora diei sine lexiare—videat illos qui operabuntur vel parabunt lapides desbrocar in ipso opere. Et est sibi concessum dare pro qualibet die faoner quod fuerit in opere predicto IIII SS. et uni ejus famulo I vel II secundum ministeria ipsorum.—It.: Ulterius ammatim dare sibi de gratia CXL SS. (*sueldos*), segons lo temps empero que obraran. Car per lo temps que no obraran en lo Cloquer ne en padrera no deu res pendrer mes deu esser dedecet dels dets CXL SS. pro rata temporis, et quantitatis."—*España Sagrada*, App. xlv. 248. See Spanish translation do., p. 73. In an old Kalendar, of Gerona, printed in *España Sagrada*, xliv. 399, is the following paragraph, which refers to the works of Pedro Zacoma:—" An. 1368 fuit inceptus lo Pont nou de mense Madii; á 9 Aug. ejusdem anni fuit inceptus lo Cloquer de Sant Feliu."

[3] A memorandum in the book of the *Obra*, under date 1385, describes the various works in the fortification then in progress, and mentions " P. Comas, maestro mayor," *España Sagrada*, xlv. 45. Parcerisa, *Recuerdos y Bellezas de España, Cataluña*, says that the spire was finished in 1581. But I think he has been misled by some repairs of the steeple rendered necessary after the destruction of the upper part of the spire in this year by lightning, and mentioned in the *Actas Capitulares*.

The church bears evident marks of many alterations and additions. It consists of nave and aisles, transepts, central apse, and two apsidal chapels on the east side of the south, and one on the east of the north transept. The piers are plain square masses of masonry, and the main arches are semi-circular, unmoulded, and springing from a very plain abacus. There is a kind of triforium, an arcade of three divisions in each bay, and a fair pointed vault of ten bays — two to each bay of the nave arcade—carried on groin-ing-shafts corbelled out from the wall. The north transept retains a waggon-vault, the axis of which is north and south, whilst the south transept has two bays of cross vaulting. The eastern apse is circular in plan, but divided into seven groining bays, and lighted by three windows of three lights. The apses of the south transept are also circular, lighted by lancets, and groined with semi-domes, though the arches into the transept are pointed. The general character of the later part of this church is, I should say, that of late first-pointed work; yet it is pretty clear that it is almost all a work of the fourteenth century. There is a fine fourteenth-century south

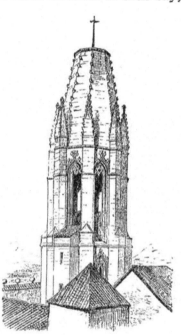

SPIRE OF SAN FELIU

porch, with some good arcading in its side walls, in which the tracery is all executed with soffit-cusping.

Of the western steeple I need not say very much, as my sketch shows the nature of its design, and the evidence as to its date is evidently very accurate. The character of the architectural detail is quite that of flamboyant-work, and the outline is bold, original, and good. It is seldom indeed that the junction of the tower and spire is more happily managed than it is here; and before the destruction of the upper part of the spire, the whole effect must have been singularly graceful. This is the more remarkable in a country where a genuine spire is so rare a feature; but the architect was fortunate in following the customs of the country when he made his steeple octagonal in plan, for it is extremely difficult—one may almost say impossible—to put a spire upon an octagonal tower the outline of which shall not be graceful. In an arch against the wall of this tower is a tomb resting on lions jutting out from the wall, and with the date 1387 in the inscription. It is a good example of the late date to which this early-looking type of monument continued to be used in Spain.

This church has a rather elaborate wooden Retablo, carved and gilt with subjects painted on its panels (5). The pulpit is also old, and has rich, late flamboyant tracery panels: it is placed against a pier on the south side of the nave, and a second modern pulpit faces it on the north. The old metal screen also remains: it is rather rude, and has prickets for candles along it, each of which has a sort of frame which looks as though it were meant to hold a glass.

There are also a few remains of old domestic buildings. A house near the cathedral has the usual Catalan features of trefoiled *ajimez* windows, and a doorway with a prodigiously deep archivolt. Another house near San Feliu has a broad window with a square-headed opening; the head is an ogee arch, with tracery in the tympanum, and over all is a square-headed label-moulding. It is not an elegant window, yet it has some value as an example of an opening as large as we usually adopt nowadays, and with a square head. The most interesting house, however, is the Fonda de la Estrella, the principal inn in the town. The windows here are capital examples of shafted windows of the end of the twelfth century. The shafts are very delicate (4¼ inches by 6 ft. 1 inch); the capitals are well carved with men and animals, and the carved abacus is carried from window to window. The windows are of three lights, and with only a narrow space of wall between them. The back of this house is less altered than the front: on the ground it has an arcade of four round arches, on the first floor five windows of the same sort as these just described, but simpler, and above this a series of pilasters, which now carry the roof. There must have been arches I think to this open upper stage.

There is another house in the same street, and just opposite the inn, of rather later date, but also with early *ajimez* windows, and this had also an open stage below the roof.

The whole city looks picturesque and old, and I dare say a more careful search than I had time for would be rewarded with

further discoveries of old remains. Most of the houses are
arcaded below, and their lower stories are groined, the cells of
the vaults being filled in with bricks laid in herring-bone patterns.

From Gerona to Barcelona there are two railways branching
from the station at Empalme. That which follows the coast
passes by several small towns facing the sea, in which there are
many remains of old walls and castles, and not a few *ajimez*
windows. It is, in short, a charming ride in every way. The
other line going inland also passes a very striking country, and
some old towns. Hostalrich is a very picturesque old walled town,
with its walls and towers all fairly perfect. Fornelles has a
good church, with a low crocketed spire on an octagonal steeple,
brought to a square just below the belfry-stage (6). Granollers
has a rather good fourteenth-century church, of the same general
character as the Barcelona churches of the same date. It has a
nave of five bays, and an apse of seven sides, with a tower at
the north-west angle. Some trace of an earlier church remains
in a round-arched western door. The western bay is occupied
by a late fifteenth-century groined gallery carried on an elliptic
arch, with a parapet pierced with richly-cusped circles. The
staircase to this gallery is in a sort of aisle or side chapel, and
has an extremely well managed iron hand-railing, supported by
occasional uprights, and quite worthy of imitation. The tower
has a delicate newel staircase in its angle: the newel has a
spiral moulding, and the under side of the steps is very carefully wrought. The upper part of the steeple is like those of
Barcelona cathedral—an irregular octagon, and has a traceried
parapet and low spire (7). There is a very rich late wooden
pulpit, corbelled out from the wall, through which a door is
pierced, and some rich woodwork is placed at the head of the steps
leading to it. The apse has two-light and single-light windows
in the alternate sides, and the nave the latter only. Small
chapels are formed between the buttresses, and these are also
lighted with small windows. On the whole this church has a
good many features of interest, and its very considerable height
gives it greater dignity than our own churches of the same class
have.

On the road from Gerona into France I have seen only one or
two churches. At Figueras the cathedral has a steeple extremely similar to that just described at Granollers, and evidently of the same date. The sides of the octagon are not equal,
and bells are hung in the windows, and one in an arched frame
at the top (8). This tower is on the north side of the nave,

II   H

which has four bays, transepts, and a Renaissance central dome covered with glazed tiles. The fabric of the nave seems to be of the thirteenth century, having lancet windows and buttresses of great projection rather well designed, chapels occupying the space between them. The west door label runs up to, and is terminated by, a long cross. At la Junquera, between Figueras and the frontier, the little Parroquia has the date of A.D. 1413 on the door. Its only feature of interest is the tower, which has a staircase carried on arches thrown from side to side of the tower, and having a square opening or well-hole in the centre. The same kind of staircase has been described in the church of San Roman at Toledo.

From hence a pleasant road among the mountains, beautifully clothed here with cork-trees, and disclosing charming views at every turn, leads by the frontier fortress of Bellegarde, over the Col de Pertús, and so on down the eastern side of the Pyrenees to Perpiñan. Here, if we look only at the map of modern France, my notes ought to stop. But Perpiñan was of old a Spanish city, and its buildings are so thoroughly Spanish in their character that I may venture to say a very few words about them.[1]

The church of San Juan is of very remarkable dimensions. The clear width of the nave is sixty feet, but in the easternmost bay this is gathered in to fifty-four feet, which is the diameter of the seven-sided apse. Guillermo Sagrera, master of the works of this cathedral, was one of the architects summoned to advise about the erection of the nave at Gerona, and I think there can be but little doubt that the plan of this church was his handiwork, and that it was erected, therefore, at the beginning of the fifteenth century. It will be seen that he was one of the architects who spoke most strongly in favour of the erection of a broad unbroken nave. The vault he erected here is of brick with stone ribs, and the brickwork is rather rough, with very wide mortar joints, and looks as if from the first it were intended to plaster and paint it. The roofs of the chapels which are built between the large buttresses have flat gables north and south, and the same arrangement is carried round the apse. The most striking feature in this cathedral is that very rare thing—a very fine mediæval organ. It is corbelled out from the north wall of the nave, and is of great size and height. The pipes are arranged in traceried compartments at five different levels (9). This compli-

---

[1] Roussillon belonged to the kings of Aragon from A.D. 1178. Perpiñan was taken, after a vigorous resistance, by Louis XI. in 1474, restored to Spain, and finally taken by the French in A.D. 1642.

cates the machinery for the supply of wind, but adds greatly to the picturesque character of the instrument. Originally this organ had great painted shutters, which are now nailed up against the wall close to the south porch. The width of its front is about twenty-five feet, its projection from the wall three feet six inches, and the organist sits in a gallery at its base.[1]

There are several good old houses here: but I must content myself with the mention of one only in the Rue de la Barre. Here we have the peculiarities of the Spanish houses, as they are seen along the coast from Gerona to Valencia, very decidedly developed: the windows are all *ajimez*, with the usual delicate trefoiled head to the lights, and slender shafts between them, and the arch-stones of the doorway are more than usually enormous, being little less than six feet in length.

A drive of a few miles from Perpiñan leads to the extremely interesting church at Elne, consecrated in A.D. 1058.[2] Here, as in San Pedro, Gerona, and to the east of it in the cathedral at Agde, there are occasional lines of black volcanic scoriæ used in the Romanesque steeple and west front, and with good effect. The nave of the church has a pointed barrel-vault, and the aisles half-barrel-vaults, but all the cross arches are semi-circular. At the west end is a sort of thirteenth-century narthex, and the three apses at the east have semi-domes. On the north side of the church is a noble cloister, planned just like that in the cathedral at Gerona with the most complete disregard to symmetry. It is extremely similar to it also in general design: but it is very remarkable as having its east and north sides erected about the end of the thirteenth century in evident and very close imitation of the earlier work on the other two sides. The vaulting throughout the cloister is of the later date, and raised considerably above the level of the old vault. The whole of this cloister is wrought in a veined white marble, and a door from it into the church is built in alternated courses of red and white marble (10).

On the whole S. Elne well deserves a visit, not only on account of the extreme interest of its church and cloister, but, to the student of Spanish architecture, on account of the very important link which it supplies in the chain which connects the early Spanish with the early French buildings of the middle ages.

[1] An illustration of this organ is given in M. Viollet le Duc's *Dictionary of French Architecture.*
[2] *Viage Literario á las Iglesias de España*, xiv. 106.

The history of Cataluña shows how intimate was the connection of the people and towns on both sides of the mountains, and it is here and elsewhere in the south of France that we see the germ of almost all the mediæval Spanish art (11).

NOTES

(1) " Ramon Berenguer II. *Cap de Estopa*, was buried in the cemetery called Galilee where now is the great stair." The present façade is of 1659 to 1793.

(2) This retable has since been remade, not for the first time: at present it is crowned by three magnificent gold crosses of various epochs, precious with gems, enamels, and workmanship. I. The bottom row has Madonna and Child between angels, in the manner of a triptych, four pairs of saints on each side; II. next, eight scenes of the Passion, from Palm Sunday to the Resurrection; a much later figure of the Risen Christ fills up the centre of this; and III. (where Street shows doors) eight scenes of the Early Life, the Annunciation, Nativity, Epiphany, and Presentation; the Baptism, Temptation, Transfiguration, and Raising of Lazarus. The top of the retable, between the three statues, is pieced out with a number of plaques, some of the Crucifixion, others of the Judge between the Tetramorph. The baldachin, silver and gilt on a core of wood (with silver plates on the upper part of the columns), has a Coronation on the centre, and on the east side, I believe, implausible though it sounds, S. Peter receiving homage from the donor of the retable: a double row of saints all round. On the walls of a northern nave chapel I found eight panels of saintly legend, pleasant and Italian-ate. Some of the tombs are as pure as they are splendid.

(3) The cloisters of San Pedro are now restored and used for the Archæological Museum. The Abbot's Palace adjoining is the Quartel de la Guardia Civil.

(4) This is San Nicholas; it is now a saw-mill and easy to examine. San Daniel is across the Gallegans, outside the walls. About San Nicholas, Mossén Baraguer gives some curious information; it stood in the cemetery, but had no right of burial, and on the four chief festivals must keep the door locked. It had the Sacrament of the Eucharist, but could not expose the Sacrament or raise monuments.

(5) It cannot be called interesting, being too late for gold and brocades and quite destitute of anything to take their place; a Spaniard, one could judge, had tried to imitate a German. By another and a better hand is a series of big predella pictures, below figures of the Risen Christ and the twelve apostles. In the retable proper six scenes relate the life and sufferings of S. Vincent; a statue of the Madonna and Child in the centre is accompanied by S. Vincent and S. Felix, both rather flat-faced, at the sides, under tall carved canopies.

(6) Fornells, a tiny village that had its prosperity in the eighteenth

century, offers more to a wandering artist than to the ecclesiologist. The church of S. James, without aisles, has four bays of quadripartite vaulting, resting on plain corbels, with a wide chevet of five and a western gallery. The keys of the vault are large and carved: Madonna, SS. James, Michael, Laurence, a bishop, S. George accompanied by another figure. Three chapels, north and south, contain one bay of ribbed, with one of barrel-vaulting: in addition there is a north-western chapel, two bays deeper, panelled and painted in 1796. A date, in the church, of 1730 is probably that of extensive rebuilding; 1565 is the façade. At present a flight of steps dated 1753 runs up the south wall to a neat window and door where apparently the priest has apartments above the vaults. The west front has a plain good Renaissance door under a triangular pediment, an *œil-de-bœuf* half framed in a round label, and an open arcade of six arches across the gable-end, opening into a sort of loft and showing the roof timbers. On the north side of this is a pepperbox turret; on the south, the belfry, the bell-chamber groined in a star. The only interesting objects inside are a carved retable of Santiago, and a dark red Romanesque holy-water stoop with the crudest carving of men at the corners.

(7) Like Barcelona, San Esteban crowns the tower with a fine frame for bells. In the priest's house next door are kept the precious panels of the Life of S. Stephen from the Retablo Mayor, replaced in the choir by modern paintings. It had been ordered from Pablo Vergós, the greatest of the house, who died before November 25, 1495, and his father, Jaime Vergós II., and his brother Raphael, finished it and receipted the bill, March 4, 1500. Four half-lengths of prophets from the *guarda polvo* are remarkably Burgundian in suggestion, magnificent, kingly figures of the Renaissance, who express all that Henry VIII. might have been and was not. Contemporary copies of these are in the Museum of the Hispanic Society, New York. The priest possesses also another version of the Peter Pan story, already noted at Tarragona. A Last Supper and Agony in the Garden from another source, and an interesting retable of S. Sebastian with SS. Roch, Eloy, Erasmus, and others —composed against the pestilence apparently—in which the protagonist is again a grave, bearded figure, not unlike S. James.

(8) At present two, in an arched iron frame of the Catalan type. Figueras is a rather charming town in the manner of the *langue d'oc;* I was sorry not to stay there long enough at least to drive over and see La Junquera, which lies far from the railway. That remains, in consequence, the one place where I have not set my foot in the track of my author.

(9) The Cathedral of Perpiñan has seven bays, transepts, and three parallel apses, but the chapels are set between buttresses, which project inward and cut off the view of the side apses, so that from the western part you get no sense of a cross. It is a real mercantile church, very broad and successful, but nothing like so fine in effect as Santa Maria del Mar. On the great organ doors are SS. Stephen and Laurence, Salome and the Baptist; in the north apse a good carved Gothic retable, and in the south apse a beautiful painted one, all but invisible.

(10) Elne is so close to the railway that travellers will remember the silhouette of the church and towers against the sky. The cloister is more magnificent than Street's tempered praise suggests: the carvings of the capitals breathe at moments the same sudden waft of eastern airs as at S. Gilles: precisely comparable to the marble reliefs of the bases there, are, for instance, a lion and a griffin here, set in *entrelacs*, to which the abacus is carved with a sort of palmette. Below the battlements the church carries the remains of a blind arcade across the front of the aisles and up the nave gable; inside there is the same feeling for largeness and breadth as at Cahors, and in addition the grandeur of the central apse; the bigness of the Languedoc type enhanced by the majesty of the Romanesque style. Between the buttresses on the southern side chapels are set, and in one of these a Catalan retable of S. Michael.

(11) It is unfortunate that, misled by the silence of Baedeker and the misinformation of a French priest now resident in Spain, I failed while in Narbonne to visit Fontefroid, the mother-house of the Spanish Cistercian abbeys. It seems that a large part of the abbey is still preserved in the purest and earliest Cistercian style: the church, of the end of the twelfth century, has a pointed barrel-vault in the nave and half-barrels in the aisles. In the chapter house, also of the twelfth, the great arches of the door and its two flanking windows open that whole side upon the cloister, and the opposite side has three round-headed windows as at Poblet. The ribbed vault is carried on four columns, the capitals formed of strong fleshy leaves overlapping. The cloister, five bays by four, belongs to the thirteenth century: the diagonal ribs are round, but the transverse and longitudinal arches are strongly pointed, and the last makes a pointed arch on the face of each bay, under which open three or four small round arches on coupled shafts of marble; the tympanum between being pierced by a moulded roundel, or sometimes more than one. The monastery, which is now in private hands, seems to lie on the flanks of hill-country, much like Val-de-Dios.

CHAPTER XVI

THE railway which connects Barcelona with Zaragoza enables the ecclesiologist to see some of the best buildings in this part of Spain with great ease. As far as Manresa its course is extremely picturesque, as it winds about among the Catalan hills, in sight, for a considerable part of the way, of that wonderful jagged mountain range of Montserrat, which, after much experience of mountains, strikes me more each time that I see it as among the very noblest of rocks. I know not its height above the sea, but its vast precipitous mass, rising suddenly from among the ordinary features of a landscape, and entirely unconnected with any other mountain range, produces an impression of size which may possibly be vastly in excess of the reality. Its sky-line is everywhere formed by grand pointed pinnacles, or aiguilles of rock, and the whole mass is of a pale grey colour which adds very much to its effect. The convent is a considerable distance below the summit; but as there appears, so far as I can learn, to be nothing left of any of its mediæval buildings, I was obliged to deny myself the pleasure of the climb to the summit of the rock, which a visit to the monastery would have excused, and in part, indeed, entailed. To the north of the line of the railway the hills rise gradually almost to the dignity of mountains, and suggest a beautiful situation for that old episcopal city—Vique—whose fine cathedral seems to have been destroyed and rebuilt, but where there is still to be seen a very rich late middle-pointed cloister (1). Everywhere the richly-coloured soil teems with produce; here vineyards and there corn-fields, all of them divided by long parallel lines of olives and standard peaches; whilst the deep river dells, clothed with cork-trees, stone pines, or underwood, add immensely to the interest of the road, which constantly crosses them.

Beyond Manresa the character of the country changes completely; and when he has once reached the frontier of Aragon, the traveller has his only pleasure in the fine distant views of the Pyrenees; and if his journey be made in the spring—in the sight of a vast extent of corn-fields, stretching on all sides as far as the eye can see.   In the summer nothing can be more saddening than the change which comes over this country; the corn is all cut before the end of May, and then the universal light-brown colour of the soil makes the landscape all but intolerably tame and uninteresting.

Two or three old buildings are seen from the railway. Between Sardanola and Sabadell is a house with a tower, in which is a very good round-arched *ajimez* window. At Tarrasa the churches evidently deserve examination. There is one with a lofty central lantern, and of transverse triapsal plan, which seems to be entirely Romanesque in character; and there is another of the usual later Catalan type, seven bays in length, with an apse of five sides, a tower on the south side of the choir, and a large rose-window at the west end (2). Near the same town, to the north, is a Romanesque village church (3) with a lofty belfry, which, like that of the early church in the town itself, has belfry-windows of two lights, with a dividing shaft, and a low square spire-roof. A church of the same type is seen near Monistrol—the station for Montserrat—and from this point there is nothing to be noticed until Manresa is reached, picturesquely situated on the steep hill above the river Cardener, with two or three churches and convents, and a great Collegiata—or collegiate church—towering up imposingly above everything else.   But if the situation of this church is noble, the building itself is even more so; and having passed it in my first journey, I was so much struck by its size and character that I made a point of going again to the same district, in order to examine it at my leisure.   The town is (4) poor and decayed; but I was there on a *festa*, and have seldom had a better opportunity of seeing the Catalan peasantry, who thronged the streets, the Plazas, and the churches, and made them lively with bright colours and noisy tongues.   There was a church consecrated on the same site in A.D. 1020, and it is of this probably that a fragment still remains on the north side. The rest has been destroyed, and Fr. J. Villanueva[1] says that the existing church was commenced in A.D. 1328—a date which accords very well with the detail of the earlier portion of the work—but he does not give his authority for the statement.   I have not been able to find any other evidence which would fix the date of the dedication or completion of the building; but as Arnaldo de Valleras, one of the architects consulted in 1416 as to the design for Gerona cathedral, speaks of himself as then engaged on the construction of the

[1] *Viage Lit. á las Iglesias de España,* vii. 179.

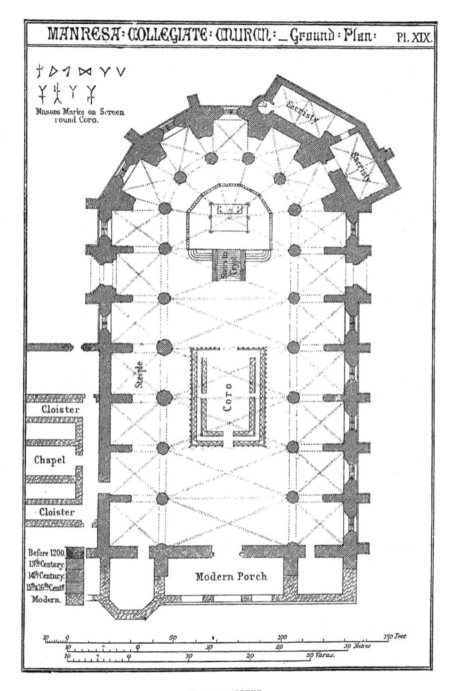

MANRESA·COLLEGIATE·CHURCH·—Ground·Plan· Pl. XIX.

Masons Marks on Screen
round Coro.

Sacristy

Sacristy

Steeple

Coro

Cloister

Chapel

Cloister

Before 1200.
13ᵗʰ Century.
14ᵗʰ Century.
15ᵗʰ & 16ᵗʰ Centᵗˢ
Modern.

Modern Porch

PLATE XIX.

church of Manresa, there can be but little doubt that at this time the Collegiata was still unfinished, having, as the detail of the design suggests, been a long time in progress (5). It is of the common Catalan type of the fourteenth century, and though it is one of the most important examples of its class, it presents so few new or unusual features that it hardly seems to require a very lengthy description. Its design is in nearly all respects of the same kind as those of the Barcelonese churches of the same age; but its plan[1] is very remarkable, as giving, perhaps, the widest span of nave anywhere to be seen in a church with aisles and a clerestory. Or perhaps I ought to limit myself to examples on the mainland, for at Palma in Mallorca the width of the nave of the cathedral seems to be even greater, and the plan is almost exactly the same. The scheme is very similar to that of Sta. Maria del Mar, Barcelona, but the width of the nave here is considerably greater, and the general effect of the interior is even finer. The buttresses are necessarily of vast size, and are formed partly inside and partly outside the church. A lofty tower is erected over one of the bays of the north aisle, and the two nave columns which carry it are in consequence built of larger dimensions than any of the others. A fine Romanesque doorway still remains in the wall, just outside this tower, and leads now into (6) the modern cloister court; but the principal entrances to the church are by grand doorways of the same age as the church, whose jambs and arches have rich continuous mouldings. These doorways are opposite each other, and just to the west of the apse, a position of much importance in regard to the ritual arrangements of the church. There is also a western doorway, but this, together with the rest of the west front, has all been modernised, whilst the cloister and its chapels appear to be entirely modern.

The magnificent scale of the plan is perhaps hardly supported as it should be by the beauty of the design in detail. In its present state it is hardly fair to judge of the original effect of the exterior, but inside one is struck by the enormous width and height, and not at all by the beauty of the details. The columns are of vast height and size: but plain piers, with poor bases and capitals, and poverty-stricken arches, seem out of place in such a church, and, owing to the enormous size of the vault, the clerestory windows are but little seen in the general view of the interior (7).

The columns are simple octagons in plan, and of great size:

[1] *See* Plate XIX., p. 121.

they have poor, shallow, carved capitals, which support the very thin-looking main arches, and the large moulded piers which carry the groining. This is quadripartite throughout, and has very bold ribs, with carved bosses at the meeting of the diagonal ribs. The window traceries throughout are of rich geometrical character, and savour rather of German influence than of French. Those in the aisles are generally of two lights, and in the clerestory of three and four lights—the window in the eastern bay of the apse being of four lights, whilst those in the other bays are only of three.

The whole roof of the aisles is paved with stone laid on the back of the vault, as at Toledo cathedral, with gutters following the lines of the vaulting ribs, and the water is carried down into the pockets of the vaults, and thence through the buttresses into gurgoyles. Over this roof—which seemed to me to be undoubtedly the old one—a modern wooden roof covered with pantiles has been erected, which blocks up all the lower part of the clerestory windows, and is carried in a very clumsy fashion on arches thrown across between the flying buttresses (8). The nave roof is now all covered with pantiles laid on the vault itself, so that from below the church has the effect, already noticed at Barcelona, of being roofless. This is certainly not the old arrangement, but whether of old there was any visible roof to any of these late Catalan churches I am wholly unable to say.

The flying buttresses are double in height, the lower arches abutting against the wall a few feet above the sills of the clerestory windows, and the upper somewhat above their springing. It is possible that this upper flying buttress is an addition to the original design, provided to meet some settlement in the fabric, for many of the buttresses have only the lower arch, which would hardly be the case if they had all been executed at the same time. The buttresses generally are finished with crocketed pediments, but there are now no traces to be seen of their pinnacles, or of the parapets between them. A lofty octagonal staircase turret is carried up to the height of the clerestory against one of the outer angles of the aisle wall, and a passageway from it to the clerestory roof is boldly carried upon an arch, which takes the place of a flying buttress.

The steeple is lofty: it is entered by old doorways opening on to the paved roof of the aisles, and is groined both under and above the bells. An old newel staircase in one angle has been destroyed, and steps projecting from the side walls have been ingeniously introduced instead. On the top of the tower a large bell is suspended from the intersection of four arched stone ribs; these ribs rise about twenty-five feet from the roof, are about one foot six inches thick, and abut against piers or dwarf pinnacles at the base, about four feet deep by one foot eleven inches thick. Two architects, said to be French—though their names seem to me to be those of Catalans—Juan Font and Giralt Cantarell, are said to have worked at this steeple from 1572 to 1590,[1] and no doubt it was this upper portion on which they wrought.

The sacristies on the south-east side of the apse are old, but not interesting. The only antiquities I saw in them were four fine processional staves, with tops of silver richly wrought with tracery in the sides, and crocketed gables over the traceries. Behind the openings of tracery the plate is gilt, the rest being all silver.

The arrangement of the interior of the church for service follows that usually seen in these enormously wide buildings. Within the apse the choir is formed by means of iron *grilles*, leaving a passage some ten feet wide all round it, and under the choir is a crypt as at Barcelona cathedral, approached in the same way, by a flight of steps from the nave. The Coro is placed, according to the common fashion, in the nave, occupying about two of its bays in length, and there is an equal space to the west (9) of it, between its eastern screen and the steps to the Capilla mayor. The width of the Coro is much less than that of the nave, and its enclosing walls are mainly old. At first sight, therefore, it seems to be a good example of an early introduction of this common Spanish arrangement: but on closer view it appears to have been taken down and rebuilt, and may not, possibly, retain its old position. But, on the other hand, the two great doors in the side walls would never have been placed where they are if the Coro had occupied its usual English position to the west of the altar enclosure. The plan of Barcelona cathedral has just the same arrangement of great doorways north and south between the Coro and the altar, and there, beyond any doubt, the Coro is in its old place; and seeing how close the points of similarity are in both churches, it must, I think, be assumed that even if this screen at Manresa has been rebuilt it still occupies its old place. It is a work of the fifteenth century, of stone, arcaded on either side of a central western doorway. The divisions of the arcade have figures painted within them of the apostles and other saints. The stalls and fittings of the Coro are all of Renaissance character.

[1] *Viage Lit. á las Iglesias de España*, vii. 180.

MANRESA
INTERIOR OF THE COLLEGIATE CHURCH

On either side of the altar there still remain three octagonal shafts with carved capitals, to which, no doubt, were originally hung the curtains or veils which protected the altar. They are of the same date as the church, and about ten feet six inches in height. The footpace is also old, and placed exactly in the centre of the apse. The richest treasure here is, however, still to be described. Among a number of altar-frontals, neither better nor worse than are usually seen, there is still preserved one which, after much study of embroidery in all parts of Europe, I may, I believe, safely pronounce to be the most beautiful work of its age. It is 10 feet long, by 2 feet 10¾ inches in height, divided into three compartments in width, the centre division having the Crucifixion, and the sides being each subdivided into nine divisions, each containing a subject from the life of our Lord.[1] An inscription at the lower edge of the frontal preserves the name of the artist to whom this great work is owing. It is in Lombardic capitals, and as follows:—

GERI: LAPI: RACHAMATORE: MEFECIT: INFLORENTIA.

The work is all done on fine linen doubled. The faces, hands, and many other parts—as, *e.g.*, the masonry of a wall—are drawn with brown ink on the linen, and very delicately shaded with a brush. The use of ink for the faces is very common in early embroidery, but I have never before seen work so elaborately finished with all the art of the painter. The faces are full of beauty and expression, and have much of the tender religious sentiment one sees in the work of Fra Angelico. The drawing is extremely good, the horses like those Benozzo Gozzoli painted, and the men dressed in Florentine dresses of the early part of the fifteenth century. The subjects are full of intricacy, the Crucifixion having the whole subject, with the crucifixion of the thieves, and all the crowd of figures so often represented.

[1] The subjects are as follows:—

1. The Marriage of the Blessed Virgin.
2. The Annunciation.
3. The Salutation.
4. The Nativity.
5. The Adoration of the Magi.
6. The Flight into Egypt.
7. The Presentation in the Temple.
8. The Dispute with the Doctors.
9. The Money-changers driven out of the Temple.
10. The Crucifixion.
11. The Entry into Jerusalem.
12. The Last Supper.
13. The Agony in the Garden.
14. The Betrayal.
15. Our Lord before Pilate.
16. The Scourging.
17. Our Lord bearing His Cross.
18. The Resurrection.
19. The Descent into Hell.

The subjects begin at the upper left-hand corner, and are continued from left to right, the subjects 1 to 9 being on the left, and 11 to 19 on the right of the Crucifixion.

The work is marvellously delicate—so much so that, passing the hand over it, it is difficult to tell exactly when it ends and the painting begins. The colours are generally very fresh and beautiful; but the gold backgrounds being very lightly stitched down are a good deal frayed. There are borders between and around all the subjects. Such a piece of embroidery makes one almost despair. English ladies who devotedly apply themselves to this kind of work have as yet no conception of the delicacy of the earlier works, and reproduce only too often the coarse patterns of the latest English school.[1]

In the choir-aisle is a wheel of bells in its old case, and under the organ is the favourite Catalan device of a Saracen's head.

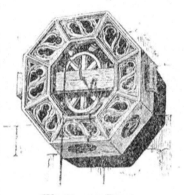

A picturesque effect was produced in the church here by the large white flannel hoods which all the women wore at mass. The church was crowded with people, and these white hoods contrasted well with the many-coloured bags or sacks—red and violet predominating—which the men always wear on their heads.

I saw two other old churches here. That "del Carmen" is of the same age as the Collegiata,

WHEEL OF BELLS

with a nave of six bays and an apse of seven sides (10). It is forty-seven feet wide in the clear, without aisles, has chapels between the buttresses, and is lighted by large clerestory-windows. Here, as at the cathedral, almost all the windows are blocked, and sufficient light seems to be obtained for the whole church by some ten or twelve holes about two feet square pierced here and there. The other church is of the same description, but less important (11).

Between Manresa and Lérida, the only town of any importance is Cervera. Here there is a vast and hideous university building going to ruin; and two churches, one of which, with a

---

[1] To those who know them I need hardly say that the remains of the Anglo-Saxon vestments found in S. Cuthbert's tomb, and preserved at Durham, are perhaps the most exquisitely delicate works in existence—so delicate that a magnifying glass is necessary in order to understand at all the way in which the work has been done. This Florentine work, of a later age, quite makes up in art for what it lacks in minute delicacy of execution when compared with S. Cuthbert's vestments.

square steeple, seems to be early in date, and the other—that
of Sta. Maria, I believe—of the usual Catalan fourteenth-century
type. This steeple was completed, in A.D. 1431, by an architect
of Cervera, Pedro de Vall-llebrera; but it must have been long
in progress, inasmuch as the principal bell—which was never to
be tolled save for the funeral of a peer, a royal officer, or a bishop
—was put in its place in A.D. 1377.[1] This bell has disappeared.
On another, however, is this inscription:—" I.H.S. . Mateus . de .
Ulmo . magister . cimbalorum . ville . Cervariæ . me . fecit .
anno . a . nativitate . Domini . millesimo . quadringentesimo .
vigesimo . quarto . Si . ergo . me . queritis . sinite . os . habire."
And on another—" + Barbara . nos . serva . Christi . sanctis-
sima . serva."

Between Cervera and Lérida the country is very uninteresting
until near the end of the journey, when a good view of Lérida,
and the cliff above the river, is obtained. I have twice visited
this interesting old city. In the autumn of 1861 I passed a
day there, when the greater part of my time was spent in
endeavouring to get admission into the cathedral, so that I
only saw enough to make me wish to repeat my visit; and this
I was fortunately able to accomplish in the spring of 1862.
My readers will agree with me, when they have realised to themselves what is to be seen, that such a cathedral as that of Lérida
is in itself worth the journey from England. Unfortunately its
examination will always be beset with difficulties—if indeed
it is allowed at all when visitors become more numerous than
they have been hitherto.

The town consists mainly of one very long, tortuous street
parallel with the river Segre, a broad, rapid stream, carrying the
waters of a large part of the southern slopes of the Pyrenees
into the Ebro at Mequinenza. There is an Alameda all along
the river-bank, and at about midway in its length a large stone
bridge across the river. Behind the town a hill rises rapidly
—in some parts abruptly—to an elevation of, I suppose, about
three hundred feet above the river; and on the summit of this
stand the old cathedral, and some remains of other coeval
buildings, now the centre of a formidable-looking, though really
neglected, system of fortifications. Two other old churches—
San Lorenzo and San Juan—remain, one in the upper part of the
city, and the other on the Plaza, near the bridge. A modern
cathedral, of the baldest and coldest Pagan type, but of great
size, was built in the main street, near the river, when the old

[1] *Viage Lit. á las Iglesias de España*, ix. 17.

cathedral was converted into a fortress; and I cannot do better than quote Mr. Ford's rather ironical statement of its history:— "The ruin," he says, "of the old cathedral dates from 1707, when the French made it a fortress: nor has it ever been restored to pious uses; for in the piping times of peace the steep walk proved too much for the pursy canons, who, abandoning their lofty church, employed General Sabatani! to build them a new cathedral below, in the convenient and Corinthian style." From the date of its desecration nothing whatever has been cared for; and it goes to one's heart to see so noble a work, and one so sacred. put to such vile uses. and to so little purpose: for even now when Spain bristles with soldiers, and the whole nation is bitten with the love of military sights and sounds. the desecration of a sacred building is all that has been accomplished ; for I believe that the Spaniards have seldom managed to hold possession of it against the French, and in its present dilapidated state are less than ever likely to do so.[1] The position is, however, a very strong one: and another hill to the west of the city is crowned with a second fort connected with it. Admission is only to be obtained by an order from the commandant of the district, who resides in the city below: and he very kindly sent a sub-officer to remain with me whilst I was in the fort, and with true Spanish courtesy came up himself to see that I gained admission to every part, and took great trouble to open doors some of which seemed hardly to have been opened since the Peninsular war!

The buildings now remaining consist of a church with an enormous cloister on its western side, and a lofty steeple at the south-west angle of the cloister. On the north side of the cloister is a large stone-roofed hall, and north of this again, and detached from the cathedral, are considerable fragments of what is called a castle, and these include another noble groined hall.

My ground-plan of the cathedral and its dependences will show at a glance how unusual and remarkable the whole scheme is. The south side of the church is built on the very edge of the precipitous cliff above the town and river, and the lofty tower is daringly balanced as it were on the most dangerous point of the whole ground. The mass of the whole group seen from below, and the vast height of the tower, are therefore singularly imposing, whilst the view obtained from the summit is one of

---

[1] I do not forget the successful defence of Lérida, in the sixteenth century, against the Prince de Condé; it is one of which the people may well be proud: but this was before the desecration of the cathedral.

rare magnificence. It is true that here the immediate neighbourhood is not lovely, but still the river does much towards con-
verting to fruitfulness the usually arid-looking Aragonese soil
of the district by clothing it with trees and verdure, and when
last I saw it not only was the Segre a torrent of rushing waters,
but on all sides the hills were covered with a wide expanse of
vineyards and corn-fields; and beyond these were to be seen
towering up in the far distance the grand range of the Pyrenees,
touched here and there—on the Maladetta and some of the other
high peaks—with lines of snow; whilst on the other side the
lower mountain ranges of Aragon completed one of the most
beautiful panoramas I have ever seen from church tower.

The site of the cathedral has long been occupied. It was an
important stronghold in the time of the Romans, and the first
cathedral was erected as early as in the sixth century. The
Moors in course of time gained possession of the city, and it was
not until A.D. 1149 that the Christians, under Ramon Berenguer,
finally drove them out and regained possession.

The documentary evidence as to the age of the existing buildings is fairly clear, and may as well be given at once. I derive
all my facts from the papers printed in *España Sagrada ;* [1] and
besides those which more particularly interest me as an architect, there are in the volume which relates to Lérida some most
interesting extracts from the proceedings of councils held there
from A.D. 1175 to 1418, and of diocesan synods from the year
1240. These are full of information as to the customs of the
church, and the rules affecting the clergy. [2]

The first stone of the new cathedral was laid in the time of
the third bishop after the restoration, and in the presence of the
king Don Pedro II. An inscription on a stone on the Gospel
side of the choir, which I did not see, gives the date [3] as the

---

[1] Vol. xlvii. De la Santa Iglesia de Lérida en su estado moderno. Su
autor el Doctor Don Pedro Sainz de Baranda.

[2] I give a few notes from the rules of this church as agreed on at the
Synods. In 1240: No priest to say mass more than once in a day, save in
case of great necessity. Priests to administer the sacrament of penance
in the sight of all in the church. Godchildren are prohibited from marrying
the children of the god-parents of baptism or confirmation. Mendicants
are forbidden to celebrate on portable altars (*super archas*). Clergy are
ordered to have a piscina near the altar, where, after receiving, they may
wash their hands and the chalice. In a Synod held in 1318, it is ordered
that, as many corpses are interred in churches which ought not to be, for
the future none shall be so save that of the patron, or of some one who
has built a chapel or endowed a chaplain.

[3] "Anno Domini мcciii. et xi. Cal. Aug. sub Innocentio Papa III.
venerabili, Gombaldo huic ecclesiæ presidente inclitus Rex Petrus II. et

22nd July, 1203; and in A.D. 1215 the cloister was, in part at any rate, built, one Raymundo de Segarra having desired that he might be buried within its walls.[1] From this time to the consecration we have no notice of the building, if I except the following inscription still remaining on the eastern jamb of the south transept doorway, which proves the existence of that part of the church at the time mentioned:—" Anno Domini M: cc° : xv xi : Kal : Madii : obiit Gulielmus de Rocas : cuj : aĵe : sit : " and there is a mention in *España Sagrada* of the burial of Bishop Berenguer, in A.D. 1256, by one of the doors, called thenceforward after him. On the last day of October, A.D. 1278, the church was consecrated by Bishop Guillen de Moncada, and the record of this on the west wall is now concealed, but I give a copy of it.[2]

In 1286 Pedro de Peñafreyta, who had been master of the works, died;[3] he had probably been employed on the central lantern and the cloister, for which latter work, on the 21st of August, 1310, the king Don Jayme II. gave the stone;[4] *circa* A.D. 1320 Bishop Guillen founded a chapel; in 1323 the work of the " cloister and tower " was still going on;[5] and in 1327 alms were asked for the completion of the same work;[6] and again in 1335 the vicar-general, in the absence of the bishop, appealed for alms, " pro maximo et sumptuoso opere claustri ecclesiæ catedralis."

In A.D. 1391 Guillermo Çolivella contracted to execute the statues for the doorway at the price of 240 sueldos each; and in A.D. 1490 Francisco Gomar contracted for the erection of a grand porch for 1600 sueldos. The steeple at the angle of the cloister seems to have been commenced about the end of the fourteenth century. The fabric-rolls for 1397 contain an item of 350 feet of stone from the river Daspe " for the work of the tower."

Ermengandus Comes Urgillen. primarium istius fabricæ lapidem posuerunt. Berengario Obicionis operario existente. Petrus Percumba Magister et fabricator."—*Esp. Sag.* xlvii. 17.

[1] *Viage Lit.* xvi. 81.

[2] " Anno Dñi MCCLXXVIII. ii Cal. Novembris Dominus G. de Montecatheno ix Ilerd. Eps. consecravit hanc Eccm. et concessit xl dies indulgencie per omnes octavas et constituit ut festum dedicationis celebraretur semper in Dominica prima post festum S. Luce."—*España Sagrada*, xlvii. 33.

[3] *Viage Lit.* xvi. 83.

[4] " Cum nos concesserimus dari operi claustri Ecclesie Sedis civitatis Illerde sex mille pedras somadals de petraria domus predicte de Gardenio : ideo vobis dicimus et mandamus quatenus dictas sex mille pedras de dicta petraria operario dicte Ecclesie recipere libere permitatis convertendas seu imponendas in opere supradicto. Datum Illerde duodecimo calendas Septembris anno Domini M.CCC.X.—*Ex. Arch. reg. Barc. grat.* 9 *Jacob. II.* fol. 145b.

[5] *Esp. Sag.* xlvii. 46.

[6] *Ibid.* p. 47.

Other similar notices occur, and among them the names of two masters of the works, Guillelmo Çolivella and Cárlos Galtes de Ruan. It was probably completed before 1416; for in this year Juan Adam, " de burgo Sanctæ Mariæ, Turlensis diocesis, regni Franciæ," contracted for the making of the great bell, which was finished in 1418, and commended by the chapter in these words—" Cujus sonitu et mentis vulnera sanari, et divinitatis singularis gratia possit conquiri."[1] There are no other notices of the main portion of the fabric; but we know that, in A.D. 1414, Pedro Balaguer was sent from Valencia to examine the tower at Lérida before he built the tower called the Micalete in his own city; and we may conclude therefore that before this date the work at Lérida had been completely finished.

It is easy to distinguish the works referred to in these notices. The church, of which the first stone was laid in A.D. 1203, and which was consecrated in A.D. 1278, still remains almost as it was built; and there can be but little doubt that the greater part of the cloister is of the same date. The works for which stone was given in A.D. 1310, were probably those in its western half, and possibly the lower part of the steeple; and the chapel, founded in A.D. 1320, must be one of those added on either side of the great south door, or on the east side of the south transept.

It is impossible not to feel greatly more interest in a church whose scheme is unusual, than in one of a common type, even when its detail is not of so high a value, or its scale less imposing. Here, however, we have both extreme novelty in the general scheme,[2] and extreme merit in all the detail. As one climbs the steep street which leads to the cathedral, where the open space around the fortifications is reached, the first general view of the buildings is most puzzling. The low outer wall of the cloister, with an enormous western doorway, the point of whose archway reaches to the top of the wall, the steeple on the extreme right, and the central lantern appearing to rise only just above the cloister wall, make a most unintelligible group. Making my way to the great doorway, I was astonished to find it to be the entrance, not of the church, as I at first assumed it to be, but only of the cloister; and not less disgusted to find that three

---

[1] The inscription on this bell was as follows:—" Christus. Rex. venit. in. pace. et. Deus. homo. factus. est. Chtus. vincit. Chtus. regnat. Chtus. ab. omn. mal. nos. defendat. Fuit. factum. per magistrum. Joannem. Adam. anno. Dñi. 1418 in mense. Aprili.—*Viage Lit. á las Iglesias de España*, xvi. 89.
[2] *See* plan, Plate XX., p. 136.

sides of this cloister had been turned into barracks, a floor having been inserted all round at the level of the springing of the vault, so as to afford ample accommodation for some hundreds of soldiers, who sleep, cook, and live within its walls; whilst the eastern side is now a store-house for arms and accoutrements, similarly divided by a floor, and without any visible trace of the doors of communication between church and cloister, which are said to be on this side (12). Yet this cloister is certainly, even in its present desecrated state, the grandest I have ever seen. Its scale is enormous, and much of its detail very fine. I have no doubt that it was a long time in progress, and this would account to some extent for the extreme irregularity of some of its parts. The bays, for instance, vary in width: the buttresses are variously treated; and the sculpture, which on the eastern side seems to be coeval with the earliest portion of the church, is evidently on the other sides of much later date—probably not earlier than A.D. 1300. The buttresses on the eastern side are carried on bold engaged columns with sculptured capitals, whilst most of the others are square in outline, with small engaged shafts in recesses at their angles. The arches are now all built up and plastered; but in two of those on the eastern side it is just possible to detect the commencement of traceries, from which it would seem that each arch had tracery above an arcade of three or four divisions. In its present state it is impossible to say more than this, or whether these traceries were original, though they seem to have been geometrical in style, and therefore probably later in date than the enclosing· arches. The eastern half of the cloister has the outer arches richly adorned with complicated chevron and cable ornament, and the remainder of the arches are finely moulded. The interior is more uniform in character, the vault being quadripartite throughout, with very boldly moulded ribs; and the main piers, and the piers at the angles, being very exquisitely planned, with a number of detached shafts with well moulded bases, bands, and capitals, the latter carved with foliage and heads. The capitals and bases are square throughout the cloister. On the south side this cloister has openings in the outer wall corresponding with those opening into the inner court; and these, I think, also had traceries. Owing to the fall of the ground towards the edge of the cliff, these windows are high above the terrace outside, and very bold buttresses are placed between each of them. The effect of the cloister on the south side is that of an enormous hall: and this, in truth, is what it is. Its clear internal width varies from 26 ft. 6 in. to 27 ft. 6 in., and the height is quite in proportion. Occupied as it now is by hundreds of soldiers, one is tempted to ask, whether a building so far larger than could be required for a mere cloister may not have been built in the first instance to serve some double purpose; being, for instance, not only an ambulatory, but a refectory, and dormitory also. The way in which some of our own old buildings were fitted, with

VIEW FROM STEEPLE, LÉRIDA OLD CATHEDRAL

a chapel at the end of a series of cubicles on either side under the open roof of a great hall (as, *e.g.*, S. Mary's Hospital at Chichester, Chichele's College, Higham Ferrers, and a hospital at Leicester), seems to point to the possibility of some such utilising of the vast space which these cloisters afford; and the more as it seemed to me that there were not the evidences that might have been expected of the existence at any time of the other dependent buildings required by a cathedral body in all cases, and more than usually here where the church was so far above and away from the city. I mentioned the western entrance of the cloister as being very large: it is a double doorway with niches for six statues in either jamb, and the orders of the archivolt are alternately of mouldings and niches for figures. The outer arch is crocketed between two great pinnacles. The carving has mostly been destroyed; but there is a poor sculpture of the Last Judgment in the tympanum. The doorway has evidently been added between two of the earlier buttresses of the cloister at about the end of the fourteenth century; its detail is extremely delicate and rich, and somewhat similar to that of the west doorway of Tarragona cathedral; and both are quite like very good French fourteenth-century work.

Unfortunately the doorways from the cloister to the church are now quite invisible, the wall being completely hidden by military packing-cases and arms.[1] This is the more to be regretted as the grandeur of the other doors leads me to suppose that the western doorway would be very fine.

It will be seen by reference to the plan that there is a steeple abutting against the south-west angle of the cloister; it is set against it in the most irregular fashion; and it is worth mention that the architect of the Micalete, at Valencia, who was directed to study this tower, imitated it even in this peculiarity. Here there seems, so far as I can see, to be no reason for the irregularity; and I can only conjecture that it may have been the consequence of some variation in the rock on which it stands. The entrance is by a staircase through a house, and thence by a newel staircase in the thickness of the wall. The steeple is octagonal in plan, and of five stages in height; the two lowest lighted by windows of one light; the third with windows of two; and the fourth with others of three lights, one in each face of the octagon. There is a rich parapet of open tracery, supported on corbels, to this stage, and a great pinnacle at each angle. The pinnacles are carried up from the ground, and are at present partly destroyed, and made to carry iron beacons instead of their old finish. The fifth stage stands entirely within the other; and its plan, as being the most interesting, is shown on my ground-plan of the whole building. Here each face of the octagon had a bold opening with a crocketed and traceried gable over it, and pinnacles at the angles, and probably a traceried parapet which no longer exists. The various stages are groined with stone vaults, and the whole construction is of the most dignified and solid description. The height from the terrace on the west side of the cloister to the top of the parapet is about

[1] There are said to be three doorways from the cloister to the church.— *Viage Lit.* xvi. 86.

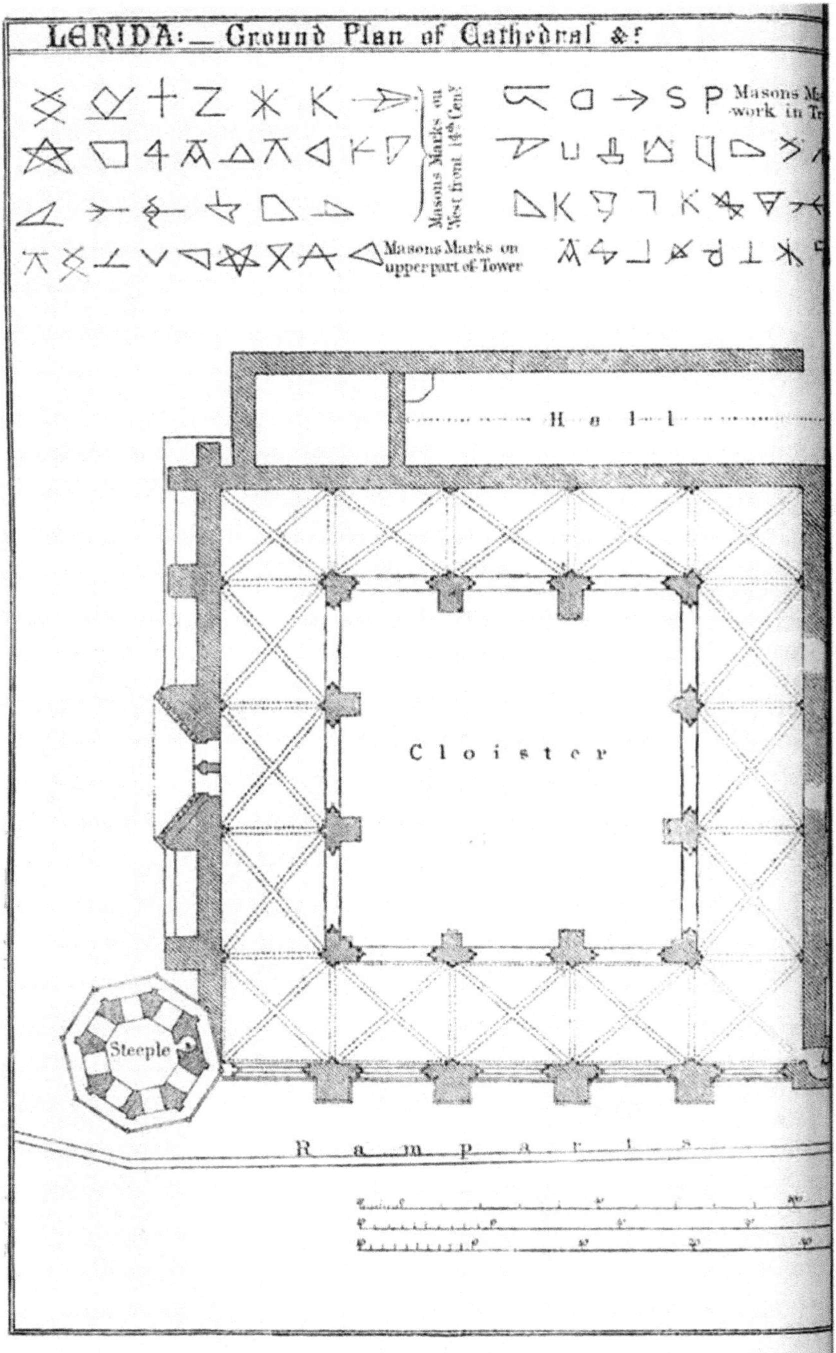

LERIDA:— Ground Plan of Cathedral &c

Masons Marks on West front 14th Cent.y

Masons Marks, work in Tr...

Masons Marks on upper part of Tower

Hall

Cloister

Steeple

R a m p a r t s

PLATE

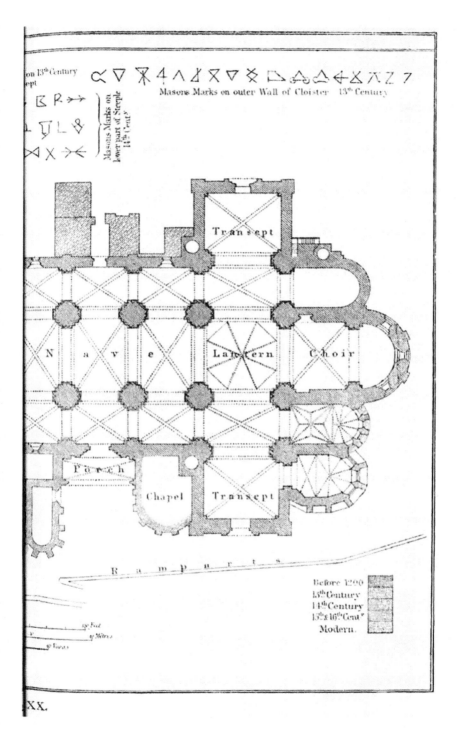

Masons Marks on 13th Century ...ept

Masons Marks on lower part of Steeple 14th Cent.y

Masons Marks on outer Wall of Cloister. 13th Century

Transept

Nave

Lantern

Choir

Porch

Chapel

Transept

Ramparts

Before 1200
13th Century
14th Century
15th & 16th Cent.y
Modern.

XX.

170 feet. The steeple looks much higher than this: but this is no doubt in great part owing to the enormous height above the city of the cliff on the edge of which it stands. The view of the church from the summit is so striking, and gives so clear an idea of its whole scheme, that I have engraved it. My drawing shows the cloister in the foreground, and the south-west view of the church beyond it. Here almost every part that is seen is of the earliest portion of the fabric, which seems to have been carried out on a regular plan from first to last. The church is cruciform, with a nave and aisles only three bays in length, and an octagonal lantern over the crossing. The choir and its aisles had three parallel apses east of the transept, and a fourth chapel was added in the fourteenth century, as were also two chapels on the south side of the nave. Two staircase-turrets on the west sides of the transepts (a favourite position for them in early Spanish churches) added much to the picturesqueness of the outline; but the upper part of one of these has unfortunately been destroyed, and the other was either carried up or altered at a later date—probably in the fourteenth century.

It will be seen that most of the windows are round-headed. Everywhere, however, the main arches are pointed; and this is, as I need hardly say, always characteristic of transitional buildings. The strange thing is, that in a church which was in building between A.D. 1203 and 1278 we should find such strong evidences of knowledge of nothing but twelfth-century art; and assuming the dates to be correct—as I think we must—it affords good evidence of the slow progress in this part of Spain of the developments which had at this time produced so great a change in the north of Europe. Either the whole building was built on the plan at first laid down, or else, having been commenced vigorously, and in great part finished, some delay must have been caused in its completion for consecration. The latter is no doubt the more probable supposition, because, whilst the whole of the walls up to the top of the clerestory seem to be of perfectly uniform character inside and out, the central lantern is evidently a work of *circa* A.D. 1260–78, and one which could not have been designed so early as 1203. The sculpture of all the capitals throughout the interior, as well as that of the doorways, must also be set down to the commencement of the century; and the date of A.D. 1215, which occurs on the south transept front, seems to make it probable that at that time the work in this part of the church was well advanced.

Here I may notice one of the remarkable features of this

building—that the external roofs are all of stone. Most of them indeed are modern; but those of the choir and lantern are undoubtedly original, and there can be little doubt that the whole church was covered in the same way. They are formed entirely of stones chamfered and weathered to a flat pitch, and lapping slightly over each other. Their effect is good, and they were evidently built by men who hoped their work would last for ever: yet this has not quite been the result of what they did; for, as I have said, most of the roofs have been relaid with slabs of stone carefully fitted together like pavement, and less likely therefore to withstand the weather than the old roofs were.

CORNICE OF SOUTH TRANSEPT DOORWAY

The entrances to the cathedral are at present three in number —a door in each transept and one in the south wall—in addition to the western doorway, which, if it exists, is now blocked up. These doors are all fine. That in the north transept is simple but effective: it has a simply-moulded semi-circular arch, above which is a pointed arch with a stone in the enclosed space carved with A and Ω; and above it a very finely-sculptured horizontal cornice. The doorway is set forward a few inches from the wall, in the Lombard fashion. In the gable of the transept over it is a large moulded but untraceried circular window, and enough of an original stepped corbel-table under the eaves to show that the old pitch of the roofs was very flat, though somewhat steeper than at present. The south transept doorway is much finer: it has a richly-sculptured round arch; and on each side of the arch are niches—one containing a statue of S. Gabriel, and the other one of the Blessed Virgin. Under the exquisitely sculptured cornice which surmounts the door is inscribed, in large incised letters, the angelic salutation; whilst on the right jamb of the door is the inscription of the year 1215, given at p. 131. Above the doorway is, as in the other gables, a circular window; and here the fine early tracery with which it was filled in still remains (13). The whole detail of this front is of the finest kind, and must have been executed by men who knew something of the best Italian Romanesque work. Nothing can exceed the delicacy and care with which the whole was executed. The wheel is divided by eight octagonal shafts radiating from the centre, and these carry an order of sixteen semi-circular cusps, two to each division. These cusps are covered with the billet ornament, and their spandrels have sunk carved circles. The mouldings which enclose the window are rich and delicate in character; and though it is unfortunately now walled up, it is well preserved, and still extremely effective.

The last and grandest of the doors—the " Puerta dels Fillols " or of the Infantes—is in the centre bay of the south aisle. This is an example of singularly rich transitional work, with an archi-volt enriched with mouldings, chevrons, dog-tooth, intersecting arches, and elaborate foliage. There is the usual horizontal cornice over the arch, and above this a fourteenth-century statue of the Blessed Virgin Mary and our Lord. The horizontal cornice is carried on moulded corbels, between which and the wall are carvings of wyverns and other animals; whilst the soffit of the cornice in each compartment is carved with delicate tracery panels, in some of which I thought I detected some trace of Moorish influence. The cornice has a delicate, trailing branch of foliage; and the label and two or three orders of the arch, in which sculpture of foliage is introduced, are remarkable for the singular delicacy and refinement of the lines of the foliage, and for the exceeding skill with which they have been wrought. There is none of that reckless dash which marks our carvers nowadays, but in its place a patient elabora-tion of lovely forms, which cannot too much be praised. The mouldings here are all decidedly characteristic of the thirteenth century. The whole is now protected by a later—probably fifteenth century—vaulted porch, which occupies the space

LÉRIDA OLD CATHEDRAL
SOUTH PORCH

between two added chapels.[1] The effect is very good and picturesque, as will be seen by the illustration which I give; but as this porch is the storehouse for rockets and shells, I fear its beauties are likely to be a sealed book to most travellers, though, owing to the extreme courtesy of the commandant, I was so fortunate as to be allowed to see and sketch it at my leisure.

The original windows are all simple round-arched, with moulded arches, and shafts, with caps and bases in the jambs; those in the lantern and at the west ends of the aisles are of later date, and pointed. The west window is circular and very large, but without tracery; and there is a small lancet below it which is now blocked up by the roof of the cloister. No doubt this roof was originally a gabled stone roof with a gutter against the wall, so as to leave this window open.

The lantern is octagonal above the roof, with a window in each side, pilasters at the angles, and an arcaded corbel-table at the eaves. The staircase-turret on its north-west side is also octagonal, and rises above the eaves. The roof is original, and of stone.

The chapels which have been added seem all to have been built in the fourteenth century, and are much mutilated: they are good works of their age, but rather mar the general effect of the church, and do not call for much notice; two of them were closed, and I was unable to obtain admission to them.

The interior of the church has been as completely encumbered with arrangements for soldiers' convenience as has that of the cloister. A floor has been erected all over the nave at mid-height of the columns, and in the south transept at the level of their capitals. The choir is boarded off, and not actively desecrated. The real floor of the church is now an artillery storehouse; on the raised floor of the nave a regiment of soldiers sleep and live; and in the south transept the bandsmen spend all their time making the most hideous and deafening discord. It is indeed a shameful use for a church, and there is only one small crumb of consolation in the fact that, soldiers notwithstanding, there has hitherto been no great amount of wilful damage done to any of the old work. The capitals throughout are extremely rich in sculpture, and are still perfect though obscured by whitewash, and the groining has nowhere been damaged. I know no style more full of vigour and true majesty than the earliest pointed, of which this interior is so fine an example. The lavish enrichment of the capitals, the fine section

[1] *See* reference to this porch at p. 131.

of the great clustered columns, the severe simplicity of the unmoulded arches, and the extreme boldness of the groining-ribs, all combine to produce this result. Almost all the principal shafts are coupled, and the groining-bays are kept very distinct from one another by very bold transverse arches; these, and indeed all the main arches, are pointed. There is no triforium, and but a small space between the arches into the aisles and the clerestory windows. The canted sides of the central lantern are supported on pendentives similar to those which occur under the angles of some of the early French domes.[1] Above these is an arcaded string-course, and then the windows: these are all double, and of varied tracery. There are monials and traceries nearly flush with both the internal and external face of the wall: this was a necessary arrangement for a work which was to be seen so entirely from below, where the external traceries would all have been lost to the view. There are groining-shafts in the angles of the octagon, and an octagonal dome or vault, with ribs at the angles. The choir is not used at all: it has a quadri-partite vault over its western half, and a pointed arch in front of the apse, which is covered with a semi-dome. The western bay is lighted by clerestory windows like those in the nave, and the apse by three windows, which on the outside have flat buttresses between them.

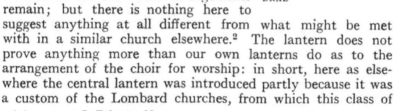

PENDENTIVE, ETC., UNDER LANTERN, LÉRIDA CATHE-DRAL

None of the old ritual arrangements remain; but there is nothing here to suggest anything at all different from what might be met with in a similar church elsewhere.[2] The lantern does not prove anything more than our own lanterns do as to the arrangement of the choir for worship: in short, here as else-where the central lantern was introduced partly because it was a custom of the Lombard churches, from which this class of

[1] As, e.g., at S. Etienne, Nevers.

[2] " During the episcopate of Romeo de Cescomes, 1361-80, the work of the principal altar was ordered to be concluded, and it was forbidden to say mass there from All Saints' day till the following month of May 1376."

Spanish church borrowed so much, and in the next place because it was especially suitable for a climate like that of Spain, where it afforded the chance not only of lighting the church in the most agreeable way, but also of ventilating it most efficaciously.

No doubt the external effect of this church was improved much by the addition of the great western steeple, though at the same time it is plain that its somewhat eccentric position has removed it so far from the main fabric of the church as to render the whole group of buildings less compact in its outline than it would have been had it been attached, like most of our own steeples, to the body of the church itself. On the other hand, nothing is more difficult, usually, than to build a steeple to a church which already has a central lantern, without entirely destroying the importance of this, which ought always, where it exists, to be a main feature; and here, as is generally the case in examples derived in any way from Italian examples, the central lantern is not very important in its dimensions, and required therefore more than usual caution on the part of the artist who ventured to add to it. Here, as happens often with detached campaniles, the grouping of the steeple with the church from various points of view is very diversified, and often very striking. From its great height above the valley it is seen on all sides, and generally at some distance. From the south, the grand size of the cloister, which connects the steeple with the church, gives it somewhat the effect of being in fact at the west end of an enormous building, of which the cloister may be the nave; whilst from the west, as the ground falls considerably, nothing of the church is seen but the central lantern rising slightly over the cloisters, whilst the steeple rears its whole height boldly to the right, and makes the whole scheme of the work utterly unintelligible until after a thorough investigation. Again, in the views of the cathedral from the east side the steeple has the effect of being, like that of Ely, at the west end of the nave, and here it groups finely with the central lantern. The same results will be found in some of our English examples, and the parish church of West Walton, near Wisbeach, illustrates, as well as any that I know, the extraordinary variety of effect which a detached tower, at some distance from the main building, produces.

The only portion of the building not yet described is a long hall on the north side of the cloister: this is vaulted with a pointed stone barrel-vault, and is gloomy-looking in the extreme, being lighted entirely from one end. A newel staircase has been taken away from the other end.

Near the north side of the cathedral, on slightly higher ground, is another fine fragment of a building of the same age, which looks as if it had always been built as a defensive work. It contains a magnificent hall, groined in four bays of quadripartite vaulting, and measuring about 24 feet by 96 feet. A smaller room next to this has a waggon-vault. The north and east walls of this hall, and of a building at right angles to it, are very boldly arcaded on the outside, and have a simple trefoiled corbel-table under the eaves: the hall windows are set within the wall-arcade. The bosses at the intersection of the ribs on the vault of the hall have interlacing patterns of Moorish character carved upon them, and afford the only distinct evidence of anything like Moorish influence that I noticed in any of the buildings here.

There are two other old churches in Lérida, San Lorenzo and San Juan. San Lorenzo is on the hill, not very far from the cathedral. It is a parallel triapsidal church, the nave vaulted with a pointed waggon-vault, divided into three bays by arches springing from coupled shafts in the side walls. The apse has a semi-dome, and is lighted by three round-headed windows, five inches wide in the clear, and has a corbel-table under the eaves outside. The side walls of the nave are eight feet thick (the nave being thirty-three feet wide), and through them very simple pointed arches are pierced, opening into the aisles. I have no doubt that these were additions to the original fabric. They have polygonal apses at their east end, with very good window-tracery of *circa* A.D. 1270-1300. On the south side an octagonal steeple was added in the fifteenth century, projecting from the aisle walls. This has a two-light window on each side of the belfry, a pierced parapet, and a simple octagonal spire. There is a fine fourteenth-century Retablo to the high altar. It has a niche in the centre with a figure of S. Laurence under a canopy, and a number of subjects and statues on either side. There is also one of the usual fifteenth-century galleries at the west end (14).

The interiors both of this church and of San Juan were so dark that I found it almost impossible to make even the roughest notes of their contents or dimensions.

San Juan (15) is another fine early church, perhaps a little later than San Lorenzo, and of about the same age as the cathedral; neither of them, however, show any signs of having been, as is the tradition, built as mosques, and converted into churches after the taking of Lérida from the Moors in A.D. 1149. The plan here is but little altered, and exhibits three bays of cross-vaulting and an apse.[1]   On the north side an aisle has been added; but on the south the façade is nearly unaltered, and the interior is similarly very perfect.   The mode of lighting with windows very high up is similar to that of the cathedral clerestory, and is worth the attention of those who wish to adapt the Pointed style for tropical climates.   The rose window and great south door are both very fine examples, and extremely peculiar in their arrangement.   The door, which is very large and imposing, occupies the whole of the central bay, and there are fine windows in the bays on either side of it: the impression produced at first sight is consequently that one is looking at the west end of a large church, upon one side of which an apsidal chancel has been added.   The door is in fact out of all proportion to the size of the church, though this very fact gives perhaps somewhat of that monumental character to the whole work which is so rare in small buildings.   It is worthy of notice that the very same design is to be seen in the church of la Magdalena at Zamora —already described; and there is indeed so much identity of character between the two churches as to make it more than probable that the same architect erected both.

In the street near San Juan is a very fine old Romanesque house of unusually good style.   It is of three stories in height, the lower story much modernised.   The intermediate stage has a very fine row of three-light *ajimez* windows with slender shafts and capitals very delicately sculptured.   The string under these windows is also elaborately carved: above is an eaves-cornice, resting on corbels, and above this a modern upper stage.   A stone with a Renaissance border to it, in the lower part of the wall, describes this building as the Exchange of Lérida, " built in 1589."   A more impudent forgery I do not know; but probably the architect of that day thought his ugly upper stage the only part worthy of notice, and meant only to record its erection.   The *patio* or court-yard behind is small. but has the same kind of windows as the front—though without any carving—and some good corbel-tables and archways.

I saw nothing else of architectural interest in Lérida; but I confidently recommend other ecclesiologists to examine its buildings for themselves.   They form an important link between the noble cathedral at Tarragona and the smaller but beautiful church of Tudela; and belonging as they do to the most interesting period of our art, the end of the twelfth and beginning of

[1] *See* plan, Vol. I., Plate VIII., p. 179.

the thirteenth century, they afford examples for our emulation
and study of even more value than the later works at Barcelona
and Manresa, which I have before had to describe.[1]

NOTES

(1) At Vich the magnificent Lombard tower of the cathedral
survives, with corbel tables and pilaster strips, six stages of graduated
window openings, and an open loggia above. The cloister, built 1324-
1400, has been completely restored, but Mossén Gudiol, the learned
curator, warrants the sculptured capitals and corbels as the identical
originals: the knight killing a dragon, angels making music, and all
the rest. The tracery is not really bad, and along the south walk
five corresponding windows, broken through the outer wall, look
across low houses and walls even to the mountains. The top story
is enclosed, the lowest story is a mere rectangle of great arches
plunged into a hillside, but this sudden outlook to the great sky, and
inlet for the green world, is more than half accountable for the charm
that hangs about the thought of Vich. Even from the train it is
seen to lie stately and episcopal in a hill-bordered world of its own.
The look of the town is old and yet fresh and fair, like some of the
women one meets in the clean, steep streets. I know there are late
Gothic bits everywhere, and I believe there are churches worth
entering, but my visit was made and my time devoted to the Museum.
It holds the spoil of the country-side, and the forged iron and enamels,
the vestments and textiles, the faïence and tiles, the goldsmith's
work and ivories, the miniatures even, I could not stop to study,
so many paintings drew me off. From the tenth to the eighteenth
century one may track down whatever one cares most about: series
of wooden painted altar frontals from the eleventh to the fourteenth;
and of wooden Madonnas called " of Majesty " (a *Magestad*, they
call it in the north-west), hieratic, eastern, enthroned, the Child
enthroned too on his Mother's knees, and presented solemnly for
adoration. From the tenth century well into the fourteenth these
keep the type pure: so does the Catalan Christ of Majesty, who, as
we say in England, *Reigns from the Tree*, robed and crowned—a
rare figure, of which five instances, here, range from the tenth to the
fourteenth century. Life-sized figures from groups of the Deposition like that at San Juan de las Abadesas, are late as the thirteenth
century in date, but Romanesque in technique. A retable of the
fourteenth century, its vermilion and gold yet clinging to the
alabaster, and deep blue glass to the background, under cusped
arcades encloses twenty scenes of the Passion, vividly and freshly
felt. This blue glass is mentioned in a Catalan document of 1367,
and was used in France the century before. Here also are fragments
from the alabaster Retablo Mayor of the cathedral, which was

[1] There is a very fair inn at Lérida, the Parador de San Luis, pleasantly
situated on the bank of the Segre; and the railway from Barcelona to
Zaragoza, passing by Lérida, makes it easy of access.

finished by Pere Oller in 1420, and altered when the church was rebuilt, in the last century. The twelve scenes, partly from the Life of Christ and the Blessed Virgin, partly from that of S. Peter, are in confusion now, but below a beautiful seated Madonna the prince of the Apostles, in chasuble and tiara, blesses with his right hand, while the other holds up a key as big and elaborate as a monstrance. Little saints under canopies are lined up everywhere, and Apostles and Evangelists occupy the predella. This is the only inducement, except some good music, to draw one into the cathedral, mercilessly rebuilt from foundation to roof-tree in 1803-21. The stack of episcopal buildings around the cloister houses both library and museum without incommoding the bishop. In the galleries of paintings one may visit authentic works of many of the great early Catalan painters, and many more as yet unidentified. The great retable from the convent of the Poor Clares, though broken up, is all in one room. The predella contains nine half-lengths of SS. George, Ives, Petronilla, Mary of Egypt, Restituto (a bishop), Thomas the Apostle, Delphina, Marcial, Matthias, and Paulinus of Nola. The body of the structure had three main divisions, presenting, at the left, SS. Peter Martyr, Martha, and Simon; at the right, SS. Jude, Perpetua, and Santo Domingo de la Calzada; in the centre between S. Michael slaying the dragon and S. Clare with abbatial staff and baronial coronet, Nuestra Señora de la Esperanza adored by SS. Cyprian and Cristina. Above these three sections were placed, respectively, the Massacre of the Innocents, S. Francis and the Three Orders, and the martyrdom of SS. Simon and Jude; above them again in the peaks a central Calvary, on the left King Abgar receiving the Veronica, and on the right S. Dominic saving a drowning man from the Rhone. For this Luis Borassá was paid, on July 7, 1415, two hundred florins. The paintings are invaluable for comparison, therefore, in all questions of the authenticity of other works, and for a high standard of spiritual loveliness, very close to the Sienese; they further serve to impress what photographs quite fail to convey, that the artist was no touching provincial follower of far-off beauty, but a man of power, of real and personal genius, living and intellectual imagination, of mastership in the work which he determined and accomplished. An Epiphany by Jaime Huguet shows the same delicately magnificent charm as Gentile da Fabriano imparted to his followers. A *Santa Faz*, Christ crowned with thorns and robed in purple (1491-5), is the one other painting attributed to Bermejo of which I am certain; a number of saints and scenes given to Joan Gasco of Navarre (1502-28) may want sorting out later into master's work and pupil's work, but meanwhile fix a strong Navarrese type of brown flesh tones and dark, clear colours, a little like some of the earlier Milanese. S. Augustine, in scholar's dress, writing at a desk, by Gabriel Guardia (1501), is, like the work of Ghirlandajo, not so interesting as he ought to be. Francesch Solivez (*circa* 1480), of Bañolas, whose greatest work, the retable of the Pietà at S. Lorenz dels Morunys, I have not seen, is represented here by two fragments of a retable—the Death of the Virgin and the discovery of a miraculous image—the latter one of those charming occasions for ritual and vestments that no Spaniard would miss.

He shows on the whole a more northern composition and emotion than his neighbours. The Museum is open regularly only in the summer months, because it is too cold at other times to keep any attendant there; notwithstanding, I found myself courteously admitted and escorted, not only in the month of January, but from breakfast time to dark, and the traveller will do well to provide woollen socks and a footstove, and lay his plans to stay five days at the least. A railway now runs up into the Pyrenees past Vich and Ripoll as far as San Juan de las Abadesas.

The Benedictine abbey of Ripoll was founded in the second half of the ninth century, by Wilfred the Shaggy. Unfortunately, in the first half of the nineteenth (1835) it was burned to the ground by the Spanish people, excepting the great portal. Parcerisa's print shows a good part of the cloister yet standing, but I believe that was pulled down for the restoration in 1887, and except for the façade not one of the ancient stones remains. The capitals, the vaults, the seven apses (which M. Enlart described as three), are new work of the architects, invented from other Catalan monuments. The outrage to antiquity and to antiquarians, even if more explicable, is not less shameful than the rebuilding at Périgueux and Angoulême, half a century earlier. The church has seven parallel apses, a lantern at the crossing, an elevated transept, and five aisles: the round-arched cloister on the south side of the nave had coupled shafts with storied capitals in the lower story and in the upper capitals of the familiar Catalan sort, as at Santa Aña in Barcelona. The Abbot, Ponce Mulnells, finished and dedicated it 1150. The west front is Lombard, with eaves-corbelling, a low tower on the north side, and a great south tower four-square, with corbel, string course, and pilaster strips, five stages of windows, and ajimez in the upper two. The penthouse porch of a later date, carried on clustered shafts, hardly obscures behind its wide, serene arches the famous screen of carved stone that it protects. The whole west face of the nave is covered with sculptures and treated, like those of Poitiers and Angoulême, like a plaque of jeweller's work or a page of miniatures. If the French examples ever were as coherent as this, earlier restorers than we know have confused the scheme. Here all, with study, becomes comprehensible. The door itself is easy to make out, S. Peter and S. Paul set against pillars and two other columns covered entirely with diaper. They are related to the sculptures of Moissac; and the little beasts crawling uncannily up a chamfered corner were also present at Moissac, and also uncanny. It is impossible to describe the richness of this door, which differs from the face of the wall chiefly in greater fineness and beauty of workmanship. The label of acanthus leaves was familiar at Zamora: directly inside that a scroll pattern that comes from Constantinople, if not further, enlaces, in alternate rounds, animals and leaves. The archivolt next, which springs directly over the heads of the apostles, is filled with little scenes from their lives, beginning on the left: (1) S. Peter with S. John cures a club-footed man ; (2) raises Tabitha ; (3) appears before Nero ; (4) Simon Magus falls ; (5) the saint is imprisoned ; (6) and crucified. The other half of the arch continues the story of S. Paul straight: (1) The journey to

Damascus; (2) he is baptised; (3) preaches to Greeks and Jews; (4) is bound (Acts xviii. 20); (5) prepared for execution; (6) beheaded. The work, being done for a literate class, is explained by inscriptions in this and the next row of scenes. These, however, read downward both ways from the centre on the subject of Jonah and Daniel. On the left of the top: (1) The word of the Lord comes to Jonah; (2) the whale swallows him; (3) renders him up again; (4) he preaches at Nineveh; (5) sits under his gourd. On the right: (1) Nebuchadnezzar's dream; (2) the idolatrous musicians about the golden statue; (3) the three Hebrew children in the fire; (4) Bel and the dragon; (5) Daniel in the lions' den. Separated from this only by a curious folded ribbon is the story of Genesis, that must be read across and across in corresponding scenes, starting from the middle with (1) The figure of the Creator, with (2) and (3) angels to whom (4) Cain offers a sheaf, and (6) being neglected kills Abel, and to whom (5) Abel offers a lamb in a cloth, but (7) is killed again. Up the door jambs, in a curious order which is capable of learned explanation, are set the labours of the months. The face of the church, though wrought all over, is composed in four great masses : (I) A great cornice; (II) three horizontal lines of narrative action ; (III) a row of important figures set in an arcade; (IV) a basement of rather Lombard beasts. The whole expounds the Triumph of Christ—a preciser formula would be hard to find, but one might also say, the *City of God*. In the centre is enthroned the Ancient of Days, and the cornice is lifted to leave him room; on either side angels adore, and one carries a scroll, and beside one the eagle perches on a book—these are Evangelists, whose companion-creatures fill the spandrels over the door. Twenty-two of the elders, crowned and making music, fill out the array, the two for whom there was not room standing around the corner. The band below these contains not only the twelve Apostles, the Precursor, and Isaiah, but holy women as well—perhaps the seven named in the canon of the Mass, SS. Felicitas, Perpetua, Agatha, Lucy, Agnes, Cecilia, and Anastasia. Old Testament scenes make up the other two horizontal bands: on the right, the smitten rock, the murmuring Israelites, the flight of quails, the fall of manna, and, below, Moses' hands held up, and the Amalekites consequently overthrown in a series of episodes. Around the corner, horses and riders are struggling together, and under S. John Baptist appears the Passage of the Red Sea. The corresponding scenes on the north side of the wall are taken from the Book of Kings, beginning in the lower range at the left. David escorts the ark to Jerusalem, dancing before it, while Michal mocks him from a tower ; and brings a plague upon Israel by numbering the people; the Prophet Gad brings the word of the Lord. On the range above, David, solaced by Abishag, promises to Bethsabe and Nathan the succession for Solomon, who is joyfully enthroned, and pronounces his famous judgment between the mothers. The series ends with a tree of Jesse, encircling the Son of Man. Around the corner are musicians, left over from the translation of the Ark, and the translation of Elijah, which makes a pendant in symbolism as well as position to the passage of the Red Sea. On this side in the five niches (III) we find David in the centre as king and poet directing the praise of God in the sound of the trumpet, on the lute and harp, and with a bell, which must stand for the well-tuned cymbals. On the south side corresponding to this the Eternal Word gives the tables to Moses, in the presence of Joshua, Aaron, and Caleb. Only in this last detail of this long account have I in following my own judgment departed from that of Mossén Gudiol, the learned curator of the Episcopal Museum at Vich, whose monograph on this amazing façade is unfortunately out of print, but whom I have to thank for a copy of it and for other kindness. The assemblage and the system of the Scripture, even were it not so beautiful, must make it, after Santiago, the finest Romanesque work in Spain.

The great abbey church of San Juan de las Abadesas, founded by Wilfred the Shaggy in the ninth century, and secularised by Pius II., was rebuilt for the third time by Abbot Ponce Mulnells in 1150; and though further alterations in the sixteenth century, with pilasters and cofferings and extra chapels, have done sad damage, one regrets to hear that a restoration is contemplated again. The main cloister is Catalan of the fifteenth century, with a bit of earlier arcade built into the wall, but there is a tiny precious earlier cloister, of low round arches and storied capitals, like those at Gerona, Elne, and San Cugat. The church is cruciform and barrel-vaulted, the choir and nave one immense height, the transepts lower with a pair of apsidal chapels to the east; in the ambulatory a deep Lady Chapel and two barrel-vaulted apsidal chapels, set at the curve of the aisle, at an oblique angle to it. This was, perhaps, to bring the altars nearer to an eastern position, or perhaps to keep them all on radii struck from the high altar; it goes back, of course, to the French plan referred to in Street's note on page 195, vol. i. A good arcade runs around the inside of them, and a tomb in that of the south, though late, shows a pure and lovely face; in the north ambulatory a wooden relief of Christ and the two SS. John has a curious reminiscence of the panel compositions of Mino da Fiesole. The Retablo Mayor carries statues of the two SS. John, and twelve scenes from their lives, Italian painting by a Spanish hand with reminiscence of Luini: the rood beam above the Sanctuary exhibits two dates, 1588, 1614, of which the former may belong to the altar-piece and the latter to further rebuildings. There is, for instance, a chamber contrived above the Lady Chapel to enshrine a thirteenth-century Deposition of enormous carved wooden figures, very archaic, for the sake of a Miraculous Host, which has remained for several hundreds of years uncorrupted, embedded in the forehead of the Christ. The short nave is entirely occupied by the coro, and the great transepts serve the needs of the congregation, the main door opening out of the northern arm, and that to the cloister from the southern. The town has other churches and a fine bridge. I regretted that I could not make a longer visit or drive thence to the Seo de Urgell.

(2) At Tarrasa the parish church is of the familiar Catalan type, immensely broad with a plain eighteenth-century western porch, small windows high in the walls, a crypt as at Barcelona, and a gigantic retable of the worst, filling the whole east end. The suburb

of San Pedro de Tarrasa, separated by deep ravines from the town proper, but only ten minutes to the left of the railway station as you emerge, is the site of the ancient citadel of Egara. There, cut off from the world by their own wall and cross-crowned gate, stands a group of three aged churches. San Pere is a triapsidal (*i.e.* trefoil) barrel-vaulted basilica, with transepts on original foundations, a semi-dome on pendentives, and a nave of five bays, which was probably once built with two aisles only. A long fourteenth-century chapel runs down the north side; the crossing and apse are of the tenth or eleventh century, the nave of the twelfth or thirteenth, according to Señor Lampérez. Señor Puig y Cataíalch claims a possible ninth-century date for the former. Santa Maria was consecrated by Raymond, Bishop of Barcelona, in 1112, but Señor Puig y Catafalch thinks the apse is Visigothic. It is square without, horse-shoe within; on the masonry of the transepts remain traces of eastern apses: the pointed barrel-vault is higher than the arch of the sanctuary. An oblong dome with lantern over the crossing, inside, appears on the outside as a high square drum with its corners chamfered off, carrying a tower of two stages, pierced by one and two windows, respectively. This gives the high-shouldered effect of so many Auvergnat churches: the façade is very Lombard, with arches and pilaster strips, small later windows, and an opening above them in the form of a Greek cross; the pilasters are continued around the sides of nave and apse. Doubt is hardly tenable that Lombard workmen did push across the southern flanks of the Pyrenees, from sea to sea, or else straggle down from France through every mountain pass; we found their mark in Galicia as in Catalonia, and the contract for building the Seo de Urgell [1] was drawn in 1175 between the Bishop and *R. Lambardo*, with four other Lombards. A better case for Visigothic origins exists in San Miguel, though M. Enlart would bring it down to the first half of the twelfth century. The ancient baptistery is built in the form of a Greek cross, the corners filled in with quarter-domes, and the horse-shoe apse projecting. The central square is raised into a dome, with a lantern on tiny *trompes* in the angles, carried by very stilted arches, on eight antique pillars. It is the very plan on which Germigny-des-Prés was built by a Spanish bishop in 806. In 1906, some Catalan architects dug here and found a piscina in the middle, and a crypt under the apse, of trefoil form, which had spherical vaulting in the apses, marks of windows, and a beginning of a nave. There may be a whole church below, but for want of money the gentlemen had to fill up and go away. On the outside, the sloping, tiled roofs at three different levels are picturesque in the little priests' garden, planted with cypresses and gay flowers. In the priests' house, which opens on the garden and is opened at request, are now stored the early retables from the churches, one of S. Peter, in fragments, one of S. Michael, insisting quaintly on the value of Masses for the souls of the dead, and one by Jaime Huguet of Sant Nin y Sant Non,—*i.e.*, SS. Abdon and Senen. For this he was paid on November 22, 1460, and again, March 27, 1461. The usual Calvary crowns the whole. The great predella shows SS. Cosmo and Damian, their martyrdom

---

[1] In *Villanueva y Geltru*, quoted in this volume, p. 263, note 2.

and the miracle of the Moor's leg, and the main concern of the altar dominates in five remaining panels. Two fair young lords who testify before the emperor are cast into a den of lions and bears, beheaded, and their relics translated. For their charm in face and bearing I was not prepared. The saints are young knights, poetic, standing easily for you to admire them, with no ungraceful sense of their own distinction, " delicate youths, with the hair not prickly on their chins." Any one who wanted to compare the composition, of a tiled terrace overlooking a landscape of hills and river, with that of Pollajuolo's SS. James, Eustace, and Vincent (1466), may particularly come to feel how exquisitely the sentiment in Spain is refined, romantic, and unreal. Another retable of Huguet's, containing six scenes and the figures of S. Julita and her little son, S. Quirico (Ciriacus), is at San Quirse de Tarrasa, within driving distance, indeed, but reached more easily, and on foot, from Sabadell.

(3) This is still to be seen on a lonely hill to the left. The house between Sardanola and Sabadell, and the church near Monistroll, though I have looked often, I have never succeeded in finding—but they may stand yet, for all that.

(4) The whole region is now prosperous with factories, but fairly unspoiled.

(5) On April 1, 1301, at a special meeting, the Municipal Council voted a new church for N. S. de la Aurora (or Alba), which was the name of an earlier church called *Canonica Aquisgranense*. In 1315 the Bishop of Mallorca conceded indulgences for gifts to it; in 1322 various confraternities joined, and the council voted extra funds; in the same year is mention of Berenguer de Montagud, *lapidista*. October 9, 1328, the first stone was laid, according to tradition—no documents mention it. In 1548 they were almost at the façade, when a great fall of vaulting occurred. In 1596 it was finished.

(6) Read: " into a passage which communicates with the cloister."

(7) Moreover, the glass is bad, but over one of the side altars stands Pere Serra's Retable of the Holy Ghost. Above the great central Pentecost is the Coronation and a Calvary, and four angels top the great ranges of panels, thirty-six small saints occupying the vertical lines that divide them. The twelve storied panels present, with a characteristic mingling of hieratic tradition and fresh imaginative conception: (1) The Creation, when " all the Sons of God shouted for joy"; (2) the Almighty admonishing Adam in a green wood, already clad in a skin, and looking like the Son of Man ; (3) the Annunciation ; (4) the Nativity ; (5) the Epiphany ; (6) the Presentation : then, on the other side, the supernatural moments of Christ's manhood : (1) Baptism ; (2) Transfiguration ; (3) Christ appears new-risen to His Mother ; (4) and to the Apostles in the inner chamber; (5) He is taken up to Heaven; (6) S. Peter preaches, having received the Gift of Tongues. The predella holds four large and six smaller saints. In spite of restoration and fresh gilding, the effect of this unspoiled trecento work is enchanting. Happier because forgotten, other retables and fragments are still in the archives. These are kept in a range of rooms over the west porch, and are most easily seen directly after

Mass, if one waylays one of the kind canons, or asks at the door of the Casa Rectoral. The retable of S. Mark is given to Benito Martorell on the strength of a contract he signed in 1437 with the shoemakers of Barcelona for one precisely like it. In connoisseurship, both in and out of Spain, this passes, I know, for evidence that the same man was hired to repeat himself, but I am not so sure. At any rate, I believe that two different men painted the retable of the Transfiguration at Barcelona and this at Manresa—the former's astonishing turn for sheer decorative composition, and the latter's immense sense for romance and temperament, are almost mutually exclusive. In 1432 the curriers acquired a chapel dedicated to S. Mark: that dates this retable, of which the three main divisions survive :

I. (1) S. Peter preaches, while S. Mark writes, and then sends him on an errand; (2) S. Mark is entering Alexandria when a cobbler wounds himself with an awl; S. Mark buys a pair of shoes, preaches to the whole household, and baptises the couple in a church. II. (1) Calvary; (2) S. Mark consecrates S. Anian. III. (1) S. Mark, celebrating, is surprised by two soldiers ; (2) dragged through the streets by ropes, and put to death; his soul in cope and mitre taken up by an angel dazzles a soldier; his funeral takes place in a church. The lost side pinnacles will have held an Annunciation. This is all the painting which has survived, and the type of S. Mark so fine that it is a pity we could not have retained the thoughtful scholar's face and silky beard. The retable of SS. Michael and Nicholas of Bari is not by the same hand. There is also a Catalan Deposition, rather wonderfully planned with the heads all on a row, showing a remote Lorezetti influence, but keeping the compacter silhouette; a retable of the Trinity by Gabriel Guardia, containing an admirable portrait of the donor, interesting for the choice of such scenes as the Creation of Eve, Abraham and the Angels, and the Burning Bush. The contract was signed September 24, 1501. Much more exists here, of lesser value, but considerable pleasantness, and here is kept the great Florentine frontal by Geri de Lapo.

(8) This is now gone; the mark of it still visible along the south wall.

(9) Read, " east of it," or supply " and " before " between." The paintings on the choir screen, between dilapidation and restoration, are of little moment.

(10) The Carmen was founded in 1300 by four ecclesiastics, Pedro Vidal, Jaime Joli, Garcia Gaucer, and Vicente Dalmau, to whom the city ceded a castle founded by Recaredo and rebuilt by various counts, one tower of which stood till 1822. In 1308 they began building. The retables are of the seventeenth century, carved and gilded, not remarkable for bad taste and rather systematic; the cloister of the middle of the eighteenth.

(11) This may be Santo Domingo, begun 1318, or it may be San Miguel, a smaller building, much more interesting, rebuilt 1384. It had originally a single nave of four bays and chevet of five; the quadripartite vault resting on corbels at the level of the string course below the clerestory. The windows are of two lights below a quatrefoil; it has a rose, a wheel of bells, and huge bosses carved

with S. Michael—the Annunciation, the Fall of the Angels, the Weighing of Souls, and the Defeat of the Dragon.

(12) The cloister is in better condition now: though the east walk is still a store-room, the southern is now a mess-hall in all its splendid breadth and height, and the stone of shafts and capitals is gradually being freed from the encumbering plaster.

(13) It is gone now like the statues. The carved capitals of the church, though respected, so far as I could see, by the soldiers, are fast being eaten away by whitewash.

(14) San Lorenzo may possibly have been in existence before the reconquest by Ramon Berenguer el Santo, though that would involve its building in the eleventh century. A whole baroque church continues to the north-east. As the retable of the cathedral was carved in 1344 by Ferrer Bassa of Barcelona, he and his pupils probably made this one as well, and the three delicate retables of SS. Lucy, Ursula, and the Madonna of Mercy (*de las Desemparados*) in as many little chapels on the north side.

(15) This has been rebuilt completely. The fragments I found in the Provincial Museum along with many other scraps—capitals, tombs, retables, and an altar-piece, called the " Retablo de los Pahers," painted, in imitation of that Dalmau made for the Councillors, in 1445-50 most probably, with the Madonna and the four Pahers of Lérida, between S. George and S. Michael. Most of the sculpture shows French qualities—a fine S. Peter series, for instance, of alabaster reliefs from the church of Combius—excepting one little Italianate series of the Ascension, Deposition, a group of sorrowing women, and a fine layman. Forgetting that there is always an Episcopal Museum, I failed to search that out at Lérida, and thereby missed, I am told, some other lovely remains, among them the twelve apostles that Guillem Çolvella made in 1391 for the west door of the cathedral.

To the north of the railway between Lérida and Zaragoza, and within easy distance of the stations of Monzon and Tardienta, are the two old Aragonese cities of Barbastro and Huesca. Monzon—a possession of the Knights Templars since A.D. 1143 —is still dignified by a castle on the hill, which rises steeply above the town, and in which there are said to be some remains of the residence of their superior in Aragon. The accounts I obtained of Barbastro made me think it hardly worthy of a visit (1). The cathedral was built between 1500 and 1533; and it is a small church (about 140 feet in length), without either triforium or clerestory, the groining springing from the capitals of the columns, and being covered with ogee lierne ribs.[1] Huesca seemed to promise more, so leaving the railway at Almudévar[2] I made an excursion thither. It is a drive of three or four hours from the railway; and the distant views of the old city are striking, backed as it is by a fine mountain range, on one of whose lower spurs it is built. The cathedral stands on the highest ground in the city; and the rocky bluffs of the mountain behind it look like enormous castles guarding its *enceinte*. These picturesque views are the more refreshing by the contrast they offer to the broad corn-covered plain at their feet. Two or three miles from Huesca, on another hill, are the remains of the great monastery of Monte Aragon, which was, however, rebuilt in 1777, and is not very likely therefore now to reward examination. The Plaza in front of the cathedral is surrounded by an important group of buildings—the palace of the kings of Aragon, the college of Santiago, and others belonging to the old university. They are mostly Renaissance in their design; but in the old palace is a crypt called " la Campana del Rey Monje," which seems to date from the end of the twelfth century. It has an apse covered with a semi-dome; and a quadripartite

---

[1] Parcerisa, *Recuerdos y Bellezas de España, Aragon*, p. 120.
[2] Almudévar has a picturesque castle, with a chapel on its eastern side, but I was unable to examine it.

vault of good character covers the buildings west of the apse. The arches are all semi-circular (2).

The cathedral was almost entirely rebuilt in the fifteenth century, from the designs of a Biscayan architect, Juan de Olotzaga.[1] The cloister on the north side is the principal remaining portion of the older church, and this is so damaged and decayed as to present hardly a single feature of interest save two or three of the picturesque tombs corbelled out from the walls (3), which are so frequently seen in the north of Spain.

The plan[2] of the cathedral consists of a nave and aisles of four bays in length, with chapels between the buttresses. The Coro is formed by screens which cut off the two eastern bays of the nave; it opens at the east into the rather grand transept, which, as is so invariably the case in the later Spanish churches, completely usurps the functions of the nave as the place of gathering for worshippers. To the east of the transept are five apsidal chapels opening out of it; that in the centre larger than the others, and containing the High Altar. Three broad steps are carried all across the church from north to south, in front of these chapels. It struck me that the plan of this east end was so very similar to that of some of the earlier Spanish churches[3] as to render it probable at any rate that Olotzaga raised his church upon the foundations of that which was removed to make way for his work (4). The steeple which takes the place of the westernmost chapel on the north side of the nave is octagonal in plan, but is much modernised, and finished with a brick belfry-stage: it is evidently of older foundation than the church. The columns between the nave and aisles are all clustered, and the main arches are boldly moulded. There is no triforium, the wall above the arcade being perfectly plain up to a carved string-course which is carried round the church below the clerestory; the windows in which are filled with flamboyant tracery. The groining is generally rather intricate, and has bosses at all the intersections of the ribs. There is no lantern at the intersection of the nave and transepts. It has been already said that the Coro occupies the usual place in the nave; and it is clear that it has never been moved, as there are small groined chapels formed between the columns on either side of it. The Reja at

[1] Cean Bermudez (*Arq.* i. 83) says that the work was commenced in A.D. 1400, and not finished until A.D. 1515.
[2] See plan, Plate XXI., p. 161.
[3] It will be seen that the plan is exactly the same as that of the church of Las Huelgas, Burgos (see Vol. I., Plate II., p. 52), and the cathedral at Tudela (Plate XXIV., p. 205).

the west end of choir is not old; the usual brass rails are placed
to form a passage from the Coro to the Capilla mayor, across the
transept.

The reredos behind the high altar is carved in alabaster: it
is of the latest Gothic, but certainly very fine.   Damian Forment, a Valencian sculptor, executed it between A.D. 1520 and
1533.[1]   It is divided into three great compartments, the centre
rising higher than the others.   Each compartment has a subject,
crowded lavishly with figures in high relief; whilst a broad band
of carving is carried round the whole, and many figures in
niches are introduced.   The subjects are: 1, The Procession to
Calvary; 2, the Crucifixion, with the First Person of the Holy
Trinity surrounded by angels in the sky; and, 3, the Descent
from the Cross.   Between these subjects and the altar are
statues of the twelve Apostles and our Lord, and a door on either
side of the altar opens into the space behind the reredos (5).

The west doorway is said by Cean Bermudez to be the work
of Olotzaga.   My own impression is that it is a work of *circa*
A.D. 1350.   It is a fine middle-pointed doorway of rich character.
The arch is of seven orders; three enriched with foliage, and
the remainder with figures under canopies, of—1, figures with
scrolls; 2, angels; 3, holy women; 4, apostles and saints.   The
tympanum has the B.V. Mary and our Lord under a canopy; she
is standing on a corbel, on which is a carved woman with asps
at her bosom; on either side of the canopy is an angel censing;
below, on the left, are three kings, and on the right the *Noli me
tangere*.   The lintel has some coats-of-arms; and there are seven
statues of saints in each jamb; and below them were subjects
enclosed within quatrefoils, all of which have been destroyed.[2]
The gable over the doorway arch is crocketed, and pierced with
tracery, and has pinnacles on either side.   The horn-shaped
leaf so often seen in English work is profusely used here, and in
the arches is generally arranged in the French fashion, *à crochet*.
The wooden doors are covered with iron plates beaten up into a
pattern, and nailed on with great brass nails.

The west end is finished at the top with a straight cornice,
with circular turrets at the angles, and pinnacles between, divid-

---

[1] This reredos cost 5500 crowns (escudos) or libras jaquesas.—Cean Bermudez, *Arq. de España*, i. 218.   Damian Forment is said to have studied
under Donatello, which seems, however, on a comparison of dates, to have
been all but impossible.   The epitaph on his monument in the cloister
here described him as " arte statuaria Phidiæ, Praxitelisque Æmulus," a
statement which must be accepted with the reserve usual in such cases.—
Bellas Artes en España, ii. 132.
[2] *See* Ainsa, *Historia de Huesca*, lib. 4.

ing it into three compartments. The detail of all this upper part
is very poor and late in style, and altogether inferior to that
of the west doorway. The clerestory is supported by simple
flying buttresses, finished with rich pinnacles.

There are two other old doorways. That from the cloister (6)
on the north side is round-arched, with dog-tooth, chevron, and
roses carved on it; yet the detail seems to prove that it cannot
be earlier than A.D. 1300, whilst some of the carving looks as if
it were even later than this. The other door is in the south
transept, and certainly deserves examination. It has a small
groined porch formed between two buttresses in front of it; over
the arch is the Crucifix, S. Mary, and S. John; whilst on the
west wall are the three Maries coming with spices, etc., to the
grave of our Lord, which is represented on the east wall of the
porch, with the angel seated on it.

The church of San Pedro el Viejo, which I now have to mention, is by far the most interesting in the city, being of much
earlier date than any part of the cathedral.[1] It has a nave
and aisles of four bays, a transept with a raised lantern over the
crossing, and three parallel apses at the east end. A hexagonal
tower is placed against the north wall of the north transept, and
a cloister occupies the whole south side of the church; whilst on
the east of the cloister is a series of chapels or rooms of early
date. There is, so far as I know, no evidence of the date of this
work; but judging by its style, it can hardly be later than the
middle of the twelfth century, with the exception of the raised
vault of the lantern, which was finished, however, before the
consecration of the church, which is said to have taken place (7)
in A.D. 1241.[2]

The nave and aisles are vaulted with continuous waggon-
vaults, the chapels at the east end with semi-domes, and the lantern with a quadripartite vault, the ribs of which are enriched
with the dog-tooth ornament. The waggon-vault of the nave
is divided into bays by cross arches corresponding with the
piers of the arcades. The vaulting of the lantern springs from
a higher level than the other vaults, and has ridge ribs as well as
diagonal and wall ribs. The lantern is lighted by four circular
windows, which have rich early thirteenth-century mouldings,
and are filled in with tracery which is evidently of Moorish origin.
A fine round-arched doorway, with three engaged shafts in each
jamb, leads from the transepts into the tower, which has groining shafts in each angle. The Coro here now occupies the

[1] *See* ground-plan on Plate XXI., p. 161.   [2] Parcerisa, *Aragon*, p. 157.

western bay of the nave, and is fitted up with fair fifteenth-century stalls, which, being carried across the end, block up the old western doorway.

The whole church is built of red sandstone, but is whitewashed throughout, and the exterior is much modernised, though the old work is still in part visible. The west front has a bold arch under the roof, which corresponds with the waggon-vault inside.

INTERIOR OF SAN PEDRO, HUESCA

The abacus from which this springs is carried across as a string-course, and in the space enclosed between it and the arch is a round-headed window, with a broad external splay and plain label moulding. A very plain western doorway is now (as also is this window) blocked up. The aisles have also small windows high up in the walls, and the whole church is covered with a roof of very flat pitch laid immediately on the stone vaults. The lowest stage of the tower had windows in each of its dis-engaged sides: it rises in four stages of equal height, divided by string-courses, but is capped with a modern belfry stage.

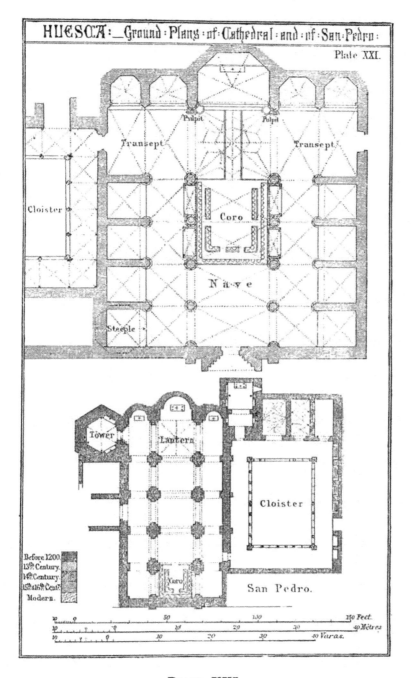

HUESCA:— Ground Plans of Cathedral and of San Pedro.

Plate XXI.

Pulpit · Pulpit

Transept · Transept

Coro

Cloister

Nave

Steeple

Tower · Lantern

Cloister

Before 1200.
13th Century.
14th Century.
15th & 16th Cent?
Modern.

Coro

San Pedro.

PLATE XXI.

II · L

The lantern is carried up to the level of the top of its vault, and then covered like the rest of the church with a flat tiled roof. A string-course, richly worked with a billet moulding, is carried round the outer walls of the aisles, and round their pilaster buttresses.

The cloister, though in a very sad state of dilapidation, is still very interesting. It is covered with a lean-to roof, and has round arches throughout springing from capitals, some of which are carved with figures, and some with foliage only, but all of rude character. Several arched recesses for monuments are formed in the outer walls, but none of the inscriptions that I observed were earlier than A.D. 1200. In the south wall six of these arches have enormous stone coffins, each supported on three corbels on the backs of three lions. These coffins are about two feet deep, by seven feet in length, and covered with a gabled stone cover. The columns in the arcades of this cloister are curiously varied, some being coupled shafts, some quatrefoil in section, some square, and some octagonal. Against the east wall are four chambers opening into the cloister. That nearest the church is the Chapel of San Bartolomé, and of the same style as the nave, covered with a low waggon-vault, and with the original stone altar still remaining against the square east end. The chapel next to this has a very late vault; the next, a quadri-partite vault; and the southernmost has a pointed waggon-vault, with three plain, pointed-arched recesses in each of the side walls.

Over the modern doorway from the cloister into the church is the tympanum of the original doorway, rudely sculptured with the Adoration of the Magi, above which two angels hold a circle, on which are inscribed the monogram of our Lord, and the letters A and Ω.

I could find nothing else of much architectural interest in Huesca (8). The Church of San Martin has a plain thirteenth-century west doorway, and that of San Juan—said to have been consecrated in A.D. 1204—seemed to have an apse of about that date, with a central lantern-tower carried on pointed arches. There are remains also of two of the town gateways, but they are of no interest.

In the distance, as I approached Huesca, I had noticed what looked like an old church at Salas, and, having time to spare, I walked there. The way lay along fields and by the muddiest of roads, where ruts were being levelled, and the whole made uni-formly muddy, in order to accommodate the Bishop of Huesca,

SALAS, NEAR HUESCA
WEST FRONT OF THE CHURCH

who was coming out in procession to have a service in the church there. I found the east and west ends of the church to be old, but the rest, inside and out, had been hopelessly modernised. The east end retains nothing beyond three very long slits for windows, about six inches wide, and not intended for glazing. The west end is very fine, and almost untouched. It has a noble doorway of six orders, very richly sculptured with chevrons, dog-tooth, mouldings of first-pointed character, and rich transitional foliage. The capitals have similar foliage, but the shafts and their bases have been destroyed, and a modern head to the door has been inserted within the arch. This door is set forward from the face of the wall nearly four feet, and has engaged shafts in the angles, and a richly-carved cornice. The gable (which is of flat pitch) is filled with a large circular window, the tracery of which has been destroyed. It has three orders of moulding round it, one moulded only, the others carved with a very bold dog-tooth enrichment. The label has rather ingeniously contrived crockets of very conventional design. The whole of this front is of very much the same character as the early work in the cathedral at Lérida. It is only about a mile and a half out of Huesca, and ought to be visited, as, with the exception of San Pedro el Viejo, it is certainly the most interesting work to be seen (9).

Travellers will find accommodation which is just tolerable in the Posada at Huesca. They should not return, as I was obliged to do, to Zaragoza, but should extend the journey to Jaca, where there seems to be a fair Romanesque cathedral. Near Jaca, too, Sta. Cruz de las Serós has a fine Romanesque church, with an octagonal raised central lantern, and a steeple of several stages in height on its north side. San Juan de la Peña, a monastery in the same district, has a fine Romanesque cloister, of the same character as that of San Pedro at Huesca: but the church is, I think, modern.[1]

I returned from Huesca to the railway (10), and thence to Zaragoza, hoping that, notwithstanding all it had suffered from wars and sieges, something might still be found to reward examination. I have seen no city in Spain which is more imposing in the distance, and yet less interesting on near acquaintance. A great group of towers and steeples stands up so grandly, that it is natural to suppose there will be much to see. But whether the French in their sieges destroyed everything, or whether it is

---

[1] Views of Jaca and San Juan de la Peña are given by F. J. Parcerisa, *Recuerdos y Bellezas de España, Aragon.*

that the city is too prosperous to allow old things to stand in the way, it is certainly the fact that but few old buildings do stand, and that none of them are of first-rate interest. The river here is rapid and broad, and the view of the distant mountains fine, whilst, partly owing to its being a centre for several railways, it is a fairly gay and lively city, and is year by year in process of improvement, in the modern sense of the word.

There are here two cathedrals, in which I believe the services are celebrated alternately for six months at a time, the same staff serving both churches. On the two occasions on which I have stopped in Zaragoza, it has fortunately happened that the old cathedral was open, and the exterior of the other promises so little gratification in the interior, that I never even made the attempt to penetrate into it.

The old cathedral is called the " Seu," *par excellence,* the other being the Cathedral " del Pilar." The Seu [1] is the usual term for the principal church, and the name of the second is derived from a miracle-working figure of the Blessed Virgin on a pillar, which it seems that the people care only to worship half the year (11).

The Seu is in some respects a remarkable church, but it is so much modernised outside as to be, with the exception of one portion, quite uninteresting, and the interior, though it is gorgeous and grand in its general effect, is of very late style and date, and does not bear very much examination in detail. It is very broad in proportion to its length, having two aisles on each side of the nave, and chapels beyond them between the buttresses; and there are but five bays west of the Crossing, and of these the Coro occupies two. There is a lantern at the Crossing, and a very short apsidal choir. The nave and aisles are all roofed at the same level, the vaulting springing from the capitals of the main columns, and the whole of the light is admitted by windows in the end walls, and high up in the outer walls of the aisles. In this respect Spanish churches of late date almost always exhibit an attention to the requirements of the climate, which is scarcely ever seen in the thirteenth and fourteenth centuries, and this church owes almost all its good effect to this circumstance, for it is in light and shade only, and neither in general design nor in detail, that it is a success. The detail, indeed, is almost as much Pagan as Gothic. The capitals of the columns, for instance, have carvings of fat nude cherubs, supporting coats-of-arms, and the groining, which is covered with ogee

[1] Seu, Sedes, See.

lierne ribs, has enormous bosses and pendants cut out of wood and gaudily gilded.

There is some interesting matter in the history of the Cimborio over the Crossing. It seems that in the year 1500 there was supposed to be some danger of the old Cimborio falling, and the Archbishop, D. Alonso de Aragon, and his Chapter, thereupon invited several artificers and skilled engineers to examine the works, and advise as to its repair. At this Junta there were present two *maestros* from Toledo—one of them Henrique de Egas; Maestro Font, from Barcelona; Carlos, from Montearagon (Huesca); and Compte, from Valencia; and they, having deliberated with the artificers attached to the cathedral, reported that it would be necessary to take down the Cimborio and rebuild it, and do other repairs to the rest of the church.

This report having been presented, the archbishop some time afterwards, in January, 1505, makes an appeal to the king on the subject, in order that he may obtain the services of Henrique de Egas as architect for the work. He says that he has had the advice of the most experienced and able architects of the day, and among them of Egas, and that they were all agreed that the Cimborio must be taken down, which had been done. And then he says that, inasmuch as the rest of the church seems to be much in want of repair, and as Egas seemed to be a man of great ability and experience, he was very anxious to procure his aid, but that Egas had excused himself on the plea that he had a certain hospital to build at Santiago in Galicia for the king, who required him to go there. Whereupon the archbishop begs the king, for the love of God our Lord, that he will have pity on him; and since there is no great necessity at Santiago, and a very great one at Zaragoza, that he will command Egas to undertake the work.

It is said that Egas did execute the work after all. But it is impossible not to be amused at the enormous contrast between those times and our own, if then it was necessary for an archbishop to appeal to the king to make an architect undertake such a work.[1]

[1] I am reminded by this of a curious passage of somewhat similar character in the life of Sir Christopher Wren, which is to be gathered out of the entries in the old parish books of S. Dionis Backchurch, Fenchurch Street. Here Sir Christopher built a steeple, and when it was nigh completion the grave question arose whether they should have an anchor for a weathercock. Sir Christopher preferred it, and some of the parishioners, of course, opposed it. They appealed to the bishop, and after many interviews it was at last decided that the bishop should meet them at Sir Christopher's at 8 o'clock a.m. to settle the matter, Sir Christopher's

The detail of the Cimborio is, as might be expected from its date, most impure. It is octagonal in plan, the canted sides being carried on semi-circular arches thrown across the angles. It is of two stages in height, the lower having square recesses for statues, and the upper traceried windows. The general scheme is Gothic, but the detail is all very Renaissance in character.[1]

The choir is apsidal, but the apse is concealed by an enormous sculptured Retablo, which, in spite of its very late date, is certainly dignified in its effect.

Externally there are evidences of the existence of an earlier church, the lower part of the apse being evidently Romanesque, a portion of the buttresses and one of the windows retaining their old character. The new work is of brick, the windows generally of four lights, with flamboyant tracery, and the walls crowned with rich cornices. The exterior of the Cimborio, as well as of the church, owes much of the picturesqueness which marks it to the fact that the brickwork is everywhere very roughly and irregularly executed.

One portion of the exterior of the church is, however, most interesting; for on the face of the wall, at the north-east angle, is a very remarkable example of brickwork, inlaid with coloured tiles, the character of which proves that it is, no doubt, part of the cathedral which was approaching completion in the middle of the fourteenth century, and earlier in date therefore than the greater part of the existing fabric. This wall is a lofty unbroken surface, about sixty-four feet in length from north to south, and is erected in front of a building of two stages in height, and pierced with pointed windows in each stage. It is built with bricks of, I think, a reddish colour (though I am a little uncertain, owing to their being now very dirty), which are all arranged in patterns in the wall, by setting those which are to form the outlines forward from one-and-a-half to two inches in advance of the general face of the wall. The spaces so left are then filled in with small tiles

---

"gentleman" (who was always treated to something to drink by the churchwarden when he came to the church) having made the engagement. The bishop was punctual to his appointment, but Sir Christopher seems to have gone out for an early walk and forgotten all about it; and finally, the Bishop of London, having waited an hour for the great man, retired in despair, but ordered Sir Christopher's weathercock to be adopted.

[1] The following inscription on the Cimborio fixes the date of its completion: "Cimborium quo hoc in loco Benedictus Papa XIII. Hispanus, patria Arago, gente nobili Luna exstruxerat, vetustate collapsum, majori impensa erexit amplissimus, illustrisque Alphonsus Catholici Ferdinandi, Castellæ, Arago, utriusque Siciliæ regis filius, q. gloria finatur, anno 1520."

set in patterns or diapers, the faces of which are generally about
three-quarters of an inch behind those of the brick outlines.   The
tiles of are various shapes, sizes, and colours, red, blue, green,
white, and buff on white.   The blue is very deep and dark in
tone, the green light and bright.   The patterns are generally
of very Moorish character; and there can be no doubt, I think,
that the whole work was done by Moorish workmen.   The
general character of this very remarkable work is certainly most
effective; and though I should not like to see the Moresque
character of the design reproduced, it undoubtedly affords
some most valuable suggestions for those who at the present
day are attempting to develop a ceramic decoration for the
exteriors of buildings.   Here I was certainly struck by the grave
quiet of the whole decoration, and was converted to some extent
from a belief which I had previously entertained rather too
strongly, that the use of tiles for inlaying would be likely to
lead to a very gay and garish style of decoration, foreign to all
dignity and repose in its effect.   There is an intersecting arcade
under the lowest windows, in which, as also in some other parts,
the ground of the panels is plastered; and in this plaster panels
of tiles and single sunk disks of tile are inserted on the white
ground.   The windows are pointed, and all of them have rich
borders to their jambs, which are continued round the arches.
Within their borders there appears to have been an order of
moulded brickwork, and then the window opening, which is
now blocked, but which may possibly have had stone monials and
tracery.   The bricks used here are of the usual old shape, about
1 ft. 1½ in. long by 6¾ in. wide.   They are generally built alternately long and short, but not by any means with any great
attempt to break the bond.   The mortar-joints are also not less
than half an inch in thickness, and this, it must be remembered,
in a work the whole characteristic of which is the extreme delicacy and refinement of the decoration.   The tiles are five-eighths
of an inch thick; some of them are encaustic, of two colours;
and all are, as is usual with Moorish tiles, glazed all over.   This
tile and brick decoration begins at a height of about eight feet
from the ground, and is carried up from that point to the top of
the wall.   Such work seems to be obviously unfitted to be close
to the ground; and the lower part of the wall is therefore
judiciously built with perfectly plain brickwork.

The most important church in Zaragoza after the cathedral
is that of San Pablo.   This is an early thirteenth-century
church of the same class as that of San Lorenzo at Lérida,

having a nave of four bays, and an apse of five sides with a groined aisle round it. The side walls of the nave, which are of enormous thickness, are pierced with pointed arches opening into the aisles, which seem to be of the same date, though from the enormous size of the piers they are very much cut off from the nave. The groining ribs are of great size, and moulded with a triple roll in both nave and aisles. Some trace of the original lancet windows is still to be seen in the apse; but most of them are blocked up or destroyed. The aisle is returned across the west end of the nave; and there is a western door and porch, with a descent of some eleven or twelve steps into the church. The Coro is at the west end of the nave, and is fitted with stalls executed *circa* A.D. 1500-20, with a Renaissance Reja to the east of them. There is a good reredos, rich in coloured and sculptured subjects, which is said to be a work of the beginning of the sixteenth century, by Damian Forment, of Valencia, who, as will be recollected, carved the reredos in the cathedral at Huesca. The fine octagonal brick steeple is evidently a later addition to the church, and rises from the north-west angle of the nave. It is very much covered with work of the same kind as the wall veil at the cathedral, which I have just been describing, though on a bolder and coarser scale; and it belongs, as far as I can judge by its style, to somewhere about the same period.[1] The brick patterns here, as there, are in parts filled in with glazed tiles; and the general effect of the steeple is very graceful, rising as it does with richly ornamented upper stages, upon a plain base, out of the low and strange jumble of irregular roofs with which the church is now covered (12).

The great steeple, called the Torre Nueva, in the Plaza San Felipe, is finer and loftier than that of San Pablo, and is, I suppose, on the whole, the finest example of its kind anywhere to be seen. It is octagonal in plan, and the sections of the various stages differ considerably in outline, owing to the ingenious manner in which the face of the walls is set at various angles. The face of most of the work is diapered with patterns in brickwork as in the other Zaragozan examples; but the most remarkable feature is, perhaps, the extraordinary extent to which the whole fabric falls out from the perpendicular. This, which is so common a fault with the Italian campaniles, arises here evidently from the same causes, the badness of the foundations,

---

[1] Don P. de la Escosura (*España Art. y Mon.* iii. 93) attributes this tower and the church to the twelfth century, but, I feel confident, without good ground for doing so, as far as the former is concerned.

and the absence of buttresses. A great mass of brickwork has been built up on one side, in order to prevent the further settlement of this steeple; and it is to be hoped that the remedy may be effectual; for Zaragoza can ill afford to lose so remarkable a feature out of the scanty number still left; and it is valuable also as one of the grandest examples of a very remarkable class. It is said to have been built in A.D. 1504 (13).

Another parish church in the principal street has a very small brick steeple of the same class, but very simple, and with it I think I must close my list of really Gothic erections here. The Renaissance buildings have often a certain amount of Gothic detail, and some Gothic arrangements of plan, but of so late and debased a kind as to make them little worthy of much study. Their real merit is their great size, and the rude grandeur of their treatment. They are usually built of rough brickwork, boldly and massively treated. They have always an arcaded stage, just below the eaves, which are very boldly corbelled out from the walls, and generally supported on moulded wood corbels, carrying a plate which projects some three or four feet from the face of the wall, and throws, of course, a very fine shadow over it. The *patios*, or court-yards, are lofty, and surrounded by columns which carry the open stages of the first and second floors. There is here no attempt at covering the brickwork with plaster or cement; and accordingly, though the detail is poor and uninteresting, the general effect is infinitely more noble than that of any of our compo-covered, smooth-faced modern London houses. The picturesque roughness of the work which was always indulged in by the mediæval architects was no sin, it seems, in the eyes of the early Renaissance architects; and it is, indeed, reserved for our own times to realise the full iniquity of any honest exhibition of facts in our ordinary buildings!

Among the buildings here which illustrate the transition from Gothic to Renaissance the cloister of the church of Sta. Engracia seems to be one of the most remarkable. It is said to have been constructed in 1536 by one Tudelilla of Tarazona, and an illustration is given of it in Villa Amil.[1] The Gothic element seems here to have been as much Moresque as Gothic, and hence the combination of these with Renaissance makes a whole which is as strange and heterogeneous as anything ever erected (14).

It will be seen that Zaragoza has not very much to interest

[1] Vol. ii. plate 45.

an architect or ecclesiologist. Travellers in Spain who find it necessary to recruit after roughing it in country towns may no doubt feel grateful for the creature comforts they will be able to enjoy there, and it is now rather a centre of railway communication, being on the line of railway which runs from Bilbao to Barcelona, and at the point where the line from Madrid joins it.

NOTES

(1) The cathedral affords another interesting comparison of the late Gothic in Spain and England, being covered with real Tudor fan-vaulting. The town has a stirring history of four centuries' struggle for the independence of its see against the claims of Huesca: in the first thirty-three years of the sixteenth century the cathedral was completely rebuilt, not by the munificence of princes and prelates, but by the diocese; after forty more years of effort its rights were confirmed by Philip II. and Pius V.

(2) These buildings, among other things, house the Provincial Museum, which includes the legacy of D. Valentin Carderera (1880). He had worked hard before 1873 to call the Museum into being, and his collection considerably more than doubled its value. Four sixteenth-century pictures from Sijena, in their flesh tones and their use of crimson and green, recall the north Italian schools, but the tiles and the lily-pot of the Annunciation are unquestionably Spanish industrial art. Burgundian influences are stronger here in Aragon than across the border: in one Virgin of the Rosary the angels have rainbow wings; in another she has all about her the rainbow tones of the Master of Moulins, and the moon set under her feet; SS. Catharine and Barbara on the sides. A fifteenth-century altarpiece shows in the Calvary the soldiers drawing straws for the seamless robe, and in the Glorification of S. Vincent a great carved throne, in the niches of which stand angels with the instruments of *his* passion—the millstone, X-cross, hammer, and scourges. He has beautiful hands, and a thin lovely throat, a touching *maladif* face. This piece is attributed to Pedro Aponte (working 1479-1517), not apparently by the good rule of putting the best picture and the best name together, but because Martinez says Ferdinand the Catholic ordered from him two fine pictures for the church of S. Laurence in Huesca. A pair of saints enthroned, SS. Stephen and Dominic, are good portraits, one of a middle-aged, the other of an elderly man. A S. Lucy, said to be signed by Vincent Carducci, the court painter of Philip III. and IV., is no better than one would expect. The Spanish fancy for realism determines, in a Retable of the Baptist of the fifteenth century, some heads of Herodias, her husband, and her daughter, which constitute a tract in the best manner of Zola. In the Museum are also preserved casts, and a very few stones, taken from the cloister of San Pedro before it was restored.

(3) One now—but others in recesses hardly less picturesque.

(4) The fuller history of the church confirms the conjecture. In the prelacy of D. Jaime Sarocco (1273-89) a new cathedral was begun; 1273 Jaime I. el Conquistador gave rents for the purpose. The square form may be that of the foundations of an earlier mosque, or may be in imitation of Romanesque abbey churches. It had three aisles (the chapels between the buttresses are of the fifteenth century) and the pillars and vaults of the aisles are strong and bold. Bishop Martin Lopez de Aslor (1300-13) built the portal, and the lateral doors are of his period. The middle of the fourteenth century finished the aisles and covered the nave with wood, the fifteenth, besides the chapels, added the cloisters and the belfry. Bishop John of Aragon (1484-1526) thought the cathedral looked mean, and after long consultation with masters from Aragon and Navarre the chapter gave the work to Juan de Olotzaga (of Navarre or of Vasconaga). He began April 22, 1497, and finished in 1515; he raised walls, opened windows, built the façade, flying buttresses, and vaults. In the chapels east of the transepts are superb dadoes of azulejos, and carved retables in the first one at the south, in a tiny chapel east of the transept door, in the westernmost chapels of the south and the north aisle. In the southernmost transept chapel, on a painted retable of the sixteenth century, there is Italian imitation of the wrong sort, but there is also the look that Lotto gives to his subtle women, sick at soul, and in a marriage of S. Catharine, on the right side, in two figures of bishops, there is the old Spanish feeling for rich textiles. In the second chapel of the north aisle an old processional banner is set into the middle of the retable, painted in tempera on linen in the purest French manner. All white and pale grey, this Madonna is *muy preciosa* in her lovely majesty. The bent head and sensitive hands, the Child on her left arm, turning its face up to hers, the folding of the drapery, all relate this to the painted tombs at Salamanca. The retables being for the most part contemporary with the finishing of the church, have a kind of homogeneity that fits them for greatly furnishing a king's house.

(5) It has a double predella: (1) at the extremities SS. Laurence and Vincent seated with books, the twelve apostles and the risen Christ, in a mandorla, blessing; (2) the Last Supper, Agony in the Garden, Betrayal, Flagellation, Buffeting, Ecce Homo, Pilate washing his hands. The doors have SS. Peter and Paul. The lowest stage of all is treated with rich Renaissance ornament, and set on the northern and southern panels with medallion heads of Forment and his wife, his a young and very fine Spanish face, with sharp nose, hollow cheek, and puckered upper lip. One could not ask for better than the small figures and scenes, free from fustian and grandiosity in their fresh and clear loveliness. The jamb statues of the west front are of the same style as those at Olite, and are set on corbels with a figure underneath in the French manner. I could only recognise SS. Laurence and Vincent and S. Orentius the Bishop, and, in one of the quatrefoils below, the Creation of Eve. The little figures in the archivolts are so charged with beauty that it is hard not to affirm the workmen knew the work of Forment.

(6) The north door has a Madonna in the tympanum, between angels, and remains of painting behind, filling in between the statues

of SS. George, Orentius, Urbicus, and perhaps Just and Pastor, with a background of tapestry pattern. The cloister is walled up into a dreary passage-way, but on the north side exist remains of an older one, three round bays in the inner wall and the great diagonal arch that carried a sloping timber roof. In the centre, where should be the cloister garth, stands the Parroquia, which contains another alabaster retable by Forment, fetched from Montearagon. Between the Transfiguration and the Ascension is the Last Judgment, and as predella the Epiphany, Christ among the Doctors, Deposition, Pietà, Massacre of the Innocents, and Resurrection, with small saints under canopies all the way up. The second and fourth of the predella scenes, though by the same hand, are in lower relief, subdued to hold a place behind statues now missing. The sweetness still of the early Renaissance clings about the forms, and the richness of the late Gothic charges the traceries and leafage.

(7) That may have been the consecration of the Retablo Mayor (the present one was consecrated 1603). Señor Lampérez thinks the church was built from 1134 to 1137. At any rate its history is a great one and typical. After the Reconquest of Huesca (1096), Benedictine monks were fetched to it from San Pedro de Tomares in Narbonne; therefore Ramiro II. loved it, who had been a monk there in France. It flourished in the twelfth century, declined in the middle of the thirteenth, in the fifteenth was secularised by Ferdinand the Catholic, in the sixteenth came down to a priorate and commandery. To-day it is a parish church. Lastly, it has been through a restoration, fairly conservative inside, but ruinous in the cloister. The chapels on the east wall are not vaulted as in Street's plan, but are still in the making over.

(8) San Martin was destroyed in 1865. The outline of the apse persists against the wall of a house, hardly so much in the memory of old women. The walls and gates have been destroyed, and the church of San Juan; the name of the Magdalena (of 1104), I believe, and the retable I hope, have been transferred to another church. S. Miguel, with a tower, is of 1238 and earlier, a good solid Spanish building, yet untampered with.

(9) The way is marked by pilgrimage crosses. Sancho of Castile (died October 13, 1173) built a sanctuary to N. S. de Salas. Jaime I. was distinguished for his liberalities to her. Pere Desvall, the treasurer of Pedro IV., had a silver altar made for the sanctuary, to replace the lamps he had taken for expenses of war. The present church was built in 1200, and rebuilt in 1727.

Santa Cruz de la Serós, near Jaca, is a ninth-century foundation for Benedictine nuns, who removed to Jaca in the sixteenth century. In 984 Sancho of Navarre and his wife Doña Urraca endowed it, in 1061 Ramiro I. of Aragon recommended it in a will to his daughter Urraca, 1076-96 his other two daughters—Sancha, Teresa, then widowed—made donations, and it was built in this last time. The vaults of the transept belong to a reconstruction not later than the twelfth century. The nave is ruined. The octagonal tower, which is still standing, is a true lantern, though this is not visible from below. A retable of 1490 was at last accounts still *in situ.*

Founded in 1040 by Ramiro I., the cathedral of Jaca was in 1063 the seat of a council whose decrees nine bishops signed after consecrating the new church. Of this only the apses and the transepts remain. To the end of the century belong the enclosing walls and the west door, with the beginning of the west tower. The aisles are of the late twelfth century, their vaults of the fifteenth, the vault of the nave sixteenth. The alternation of cylindrical pillars with cruciform piers is easily explained, as in French churches, and in San Millan of Segovia: the great piers carried the arches of the barrel-vault in the nave and the columns only the cross-vaulting of the aisles. Master Juan de la Abadia, painter of Huesca, received for the Retablo Mayor, of Santa Orosia (now in her chapel), 250 " sueldos jaquesas " in 1473, 610 more in 1495, and " the rest " the following year. In the cloister, all rebuilt, are preserved tombs of 1228 and 1253. The tympanum of the side portal contains some curious bits of symbolism—Christ taking empire of death; the lion respecting a fallen man, which means God's judgments disarmed by penitence.

San Juan de la Peña is Romanesque of the end of the eleventh century. The crypt remains from the ninth-century hermitage, founded by Sancho Garcés (842), also a door from the church to the cloister. At the end of the tenth Sancho el Mayor called one Paterno from France, who introduced the Rule of Cluny. The chapter-house was the seat of a council 1054 or 1062. Sancho Ramirez (1076) and his wife Doña Urraca rebuilt the church and cloister. In 1094 Peter I. left the siege of Huesca to go to the consecration of the new building; about the middle of the next century the cloister and dependencies were finished: the cloister has no roof because the jutting rock (peña) covers it; the storied capitals are of the first half of the twelfth century. The bell-tower was burned in 1676: the new ugly monastery dates from 1675-1717. On August 25, 1809, French troops burned most of the church, but the cloister and the head remain. It has one nave, opening by three arches into the head; the crypt contains tombs of abbots, the former sacristy those of kings of Aragon.

These three I did not see because it rained when I got to Zaragoza, and though I once pushed on to Huesca, I could not go further— partly because the original plan involved taking the diligence from Jaca to Sangüesa and the trolley thence to Pamplona, visiting on the way San Salvador de Leyre. This has a magnificent portal with two rows of statues and other sculptures above them (that M. Bertaux calls Toulousan Romanesque and Señor Madazo thinks may go back, some of them, to Carolingian times), and with northern reminiscences and barbaric archaism. The building is archaic Poitevin plus Cistercian: the portal belongs to the Cluniac church, consecrated Oct. 21, 1098, and perfect till after 1213; the present nave was built by Cistercians in the fourteenth century.

Sangüesa, though ignored by Baedeker, has a good electric service from Pamplona; and contains three fine churches—Santiago, of the twelfth and thirteenth centuries, in transitional style; San Salvador, of the fourteenth, with a Romanesque portal left from an earlier church; and Santa Maria la Real, built before 1131, restored in the end of the twelfth or beginning of the thirteenth century. The portal has a pointed arch set in a Romanesque façade and the same bossy splendour as Angoulême and Poitiers, Ripoll and San Salvador de Leyre.

(10) At Tardienta, now the junction for Huesca and Jaca, the inn is plain. The church, however, is Mudejar; not earlier than the fourteenth century, I suppose, though the south aisle has a pointed barrel-vault. The apses and a beautiful western tower are built in the characteristic arcaded brickwork of the region thence westward: the latter in four stages dwindling slightly and crowned with a low octagon, slightly concave and strongly moulded. It owns, besides the great baroque retable of S. James at the Altar Mayor, and a fourteenth-century wooden group of the Crucifixion in a recess under the tower, three painted altar-pieces, the worst of which is as good as much in the Prado.

(11) The *Virgin del Pilar* is beset by worshippers the year round. The retable by Damian Forment, 1509-11, is much more Renaissance in the worse sense of the word than that at Huesca. He was born in Valencia, and made the carved work of the retable and portal at Gandia in 1501, and in spite of Moralez, who says that he died in 1533, and the sacristan at Huesca, who shows his tomb in the cloister, he probably made the retable for Santo Domingo de la Calzada in 1536. He may have begun the retable for the cathedral of Barbastro and left it to a pupil, and he is said to have made the retable at Poblet, but I do not believe it.

(12) San Pablo is probably, as it stands, of the fourteenth century, tower and all. Señor Lampérez suggests, from the immense thickness of the piers, that it may have been built with one nave only in the Catalan way, and enlarged by the addition of aisles and ambulatory. The retable was carved 1516-24; the main scenes from the life of S. Paul, the predella from the passion of Christ. Mannered, of course, but dramatic in the same degree, if Raphael's tapestries are good, then these are, with less sham antique and sham grandeur, and a greater pleasure in telling clearly what was done and felt. Here is no such attitudinising to show off anatomy and draperies as had ruined, for instance, the Retablo Mayor at Valencia more than ten years earlier. Action is the sole interest. In this altar-piece again the Spanish spirit contrives a reconciliation between the passing age and the new; the canopies are late Gothic, interlaced and twisted like an old thorn-bush, the gilding is dim and the colour never more than suggested, like leather or lacquer. The central altar of the ambulatory has a delicious painted retable of S. Catharine with the Baptist and the Magdalen, in which the general treatment of faces and drapery both, while completely Spanish, yet shows more influence from Flanders than from Italy. It was painted, *circa* 1470, by Bonanat de Ortigia. An altar-piece of SS. Peter and Paul, in the south ambulatory, is completely Italianate in the golden and serene air of persons and landscape—north Italian rather than Tuscan. Bits of another retable which belongs here by Juan de Morales are now in the Archæological Museum at Madrid. Of alabaster touched with gold, it is faintly coloured about the heads: the Virgin a fine big woman

and a great lady; the Adoration of the Shepherds beautiful too, good as Italian work, but very different.

(13) The Torre Nuevo was taken down in 1894. The church next mentioned is San Gil, built in the second half of the fourteenth century, during the wars of Don Pedro the Ceremonious with Don Pedro the Cruel of Castile.

(14) The façade of Santa Engracia, by Juan de Morlanes and Diego Morlanes, his son, recalls Lombard work and has much beauty in the several statues. It is all that now remains of the original foundation. The church of S. Mary Magdalen has a tower of the fourteenth century, and that of S. Catharine a triptych of the school of Jacomart, dated 1454—a bishop between S. Paul the Hermit and S. Michael. An alabaster retable from the Archbishop's Palace, probably by Pere Johan de Vallfonoga, who began the Retablo Mayor of the Seo, was last heard of in Paris.

CHAPTER XVIII

I FOUND it a pleasant drive of two and a half hours, through vineyards and olive-grounds, from Tudela to Tarazona. In front all the way was the noble Sierra de Moncayo, which, according to one of my Spanish fellow-travellers, is the highest mountain in Spain, from which view, however, I humbly, and somewhat to his annoyance, dissented. But whether he were right or not, it is still of very grand height, and the more impressive in that it rises by itself in the midst of a comparatively flat country. Behind us was an admirable view of Tudela, backed by the brown and arid hills which skirt the Ebro; beyond them, in the far distance, the Pyrenees; whilst in the immediate foreground we had a rich green mass of olives and vines spread in a glorious expanse over the country.

The villages on the road have nothing to boast of if I except a pilgrimage church at Cascante, approached by a long covered gallery from below, and a brick tower at Monteacadeo, of the Zaragozan type. We passed, too, a newly-established convent for monks, who are already beginning to build, in spite of the ruin with which they have so lately been visited. But long before the end of our journey was reached, the towers and steeples of Tarazona rose attractively in front over the low hill which conceals the complete view of the city until you are almost close upon it.

Attractive as this general view undoubtedly is, this old city does not lose when it is examined more closely and carefully. It is not only in itself picturesque, but its situation on either side of the stream which a few miles below falls into the Ebro is eminently fine, and has been made the most of by the happy and probably unconscious skill of the men who have reared on the cliff above the water a tall pile of buildings on buildings, carried on grand arches, corbelled here and buttressed there, and with a sky line charming in itself, and rendered doubly beautiful by the sudden break in its outline caused by the lofty brick steeple of la Magdalena—one of the finest of its class—which rears itself, with admirable hardihood, on the very edge of the cliff. The streets and Plazas, too, of the old city are all picturesquely irregular, full of colour and evidences of national peculiarities, and climb the steep sides of the hills from the river-side to the high ground at the northern end of the city, which is crowned by the church of San Miguel. I call such skill as this " unconscious " because it is so much a characteristic of old works of this kind that their authors never exhibit any of that pert conceit which so distinctly marks the efforts of so many of us nowadays. Old architects fortunately lived in days when society was moderate in its demands, and had not ceased to care for that which is true and natural : sad for us that we live when every man wishes only to excel his neighbour, and that without regard to what is true or useful; so that, instead of obtaining those happy results which always reward the artist who does exactly what is needed in the most natural and unartificial manner, we, by our attempts to show our own cleverness, constantly end in substituting a petty personal conceit, where otherwise we might have had an enduring and artistic success.

The cathedral stands very much alone, and away from the busier part of the city, at the upper end of a grass-grown and irregular Plaza, on the opposite side of the river from the Alcazar, and indeed from the bulk of the houses. This Plaza, when I first saw it, on a Sunday afternoon, was thoroughly beautiful and characteristic as a picture of Spanish life. There was a fountain in the centre, around which hundreds of peasants were congregated in lively groups, talking at the top of their voices, and all gay with whitest shirt-sleeves, bright-coloured sashes, and velvet breeches, slashed daintily at the knees, to show the whiteness of the linen drawers; and when I went on into the church, I found in the Lady Chapel another group of them kneeling before the altar, and following one of their own class in a litany to the Blessed Virgin, the effect of which was striking even to one unable to join in the burthen of the prayer.

The cathedral here is said to have been restored by Alonso the First of Aragon, in the year 1110; but an old Breviary, cited by Argaïz, fixes the foundation of the present cathedral in 1235,[1] and with this date the earliest part of the existing church agrees very closely. The plan [2] is very good, consisting of a nave of six bays, with aisles and chapels between their buttresses, transepts, a lofty Cimborio over the Crossing, and a choir of two bays ended with a five-sided apse. The chapels in the chevet have mostly been altered, though the first on the north side

[1] Madoz, xiv. 595-599.   [2] *See* Plate XXII., p. 179.

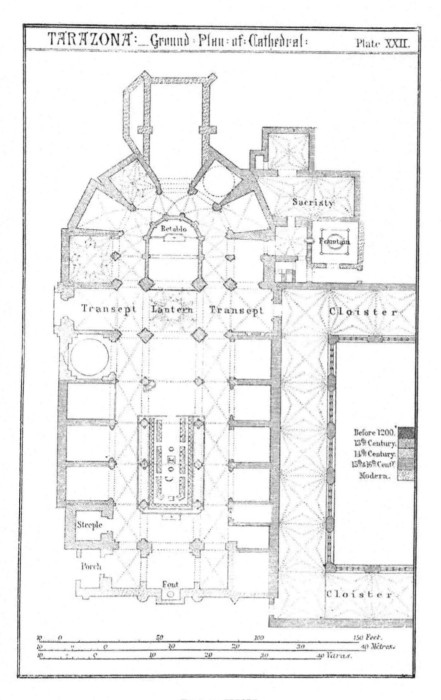

TARAZONA:_ Ground Plan of Cathedral: Plate XXII.

Sacristy

Retablo

Fountain

Transept Lantern Transept Cloister

Before 1200.
13ᵗʰ Century.
14ᵗʰ Century.
15ᵗʰ &16ᵗʰ Cent.ʸ
Modern.

Steeple

Porch

Font

Cloister

10   0   50   100   150 Feet.
10   "   0   10   20   30   40 Métres.
10   0   10   20   30   40 Varas.

PLATE XXII.

appears to be original, and proves that the outline of the plan of the chevet could never have been very good. This chapel is four-sided in plan, but much wider at one end than the other, and we must, I fear, give but scant credit to the architect who planned it. The Lady Chapel is a late and poor addition of a very inferior kind, and completely modernised—as indeed is the greater part of the church—on the exterior. On the south side of the cathedral there are old sacristies and a large cloister, of which more presently. The west end seemed to me to have been intended for two steeples, but one only has been completed, and this is on the north side of the north aisle.

The remaining portions of the thirteenth-century church have been so much altered that the general effect of the early work is almost entirely destroyed. The columns and arches generally are original; the former have carved capitals; many of the latter are slightly horse-shoe in shape, and have labels enriched with the dog-tooth ornament. The choir and transepts retain a good simple arcaded triforium, carried on detached shafts, and this returns across the gable-walls of the latter; it is of the simplest early pointed character; so too are the choir windows, which before their alteration appear to have been lancets, with engaged shafts in their jambs, whilst in the eastern wall of the transepts are windows of two lancet lights, with a circle above within an enclosing arch. Most of the arches of the nave are adorned with carved flowers on the chamfers, the effect of which is not good; indeed I half doubted whether they were not plaster additions, though they seemed to be just too good for this. The choir has two (and only two) flying buttresses; and as they are evidently of early date, with pinnacles of the very simplest pyramidal outline, they were probably erected to counteract a settlement which showed itself immediately after the erection of the church, for there is no evidence of any others having existed. The walls of the apse had originally a richly carved cornice, filled with heads and foliage. The groining of the aisles is generally simple and early in date, and quadripartite in plan: that of the whole of the rest of the choir and nave is of the richest description, and of the latest kind of Gothic.

Here, as is so frequently the case all over the world, the builders of one period used an entirely different material from that used by those of earlier times,[1] so that you may tell with

---

[1] The fact is worthy of record, because in these days, though it is often manifestly convenient to use a different material from that which was used by our ancestors, there are many well-disposed people who object

tolerable accuracy the date of the work by the material of which it is built. Here the early church was entirely built of stone, but in all the later additions brick is the prevailing material; and at first sight it is in these later additions that we seem to find almost all the most characteristic work in the church. Many of these additions, as for instance the Churrigueresque alterations of the clerestory, are thoroughly bad and contemptible; but some of them, though they damage the unity of effect of the building, and have taken the place of work which one would much rather have seen still intact, are nevertheless striking in themselves. Such is the singular and picturesque Cimborio erected by Canon Juan Muñoz[1] in the sixteenth century; it is certainly most picturesque, but such a curious and complex combination of pinnacles and turrets built of brick, and largely inlaid with green, blue, and white tiles, is perhaps nowhere else to be seen. It is octagonal in plan, and of three stages in height, the angles of the octagons in the several stages being all counterchanged. Enormous coats-of-arms decorate the fronts of the buttresses. The whole work is of the very latest possible Gothic, utterly against all rules both in design and decoration, and yet, notwithstanding all this, it is unquestionably striking in its effect. The mixture of glazed tiles with brickwork has here been carried to a very great extent, and the result does not, I think, encourage any one to hope for much from this kind of development. This work is not to be compared to that at the east end of Zaragoza Cathedral, where a plain piece of wall is carefully covered all over with a rich coloured diaper of brickwork and tiles, which are all harmonious and uniform in character, and—which is equally important—in texture, and it has, on the contrary, great similarity to some attempts to combine bricks and tiles which we see made in the present day, and seems to show that these attempts are not to be carelessly encouraged. For even when such work is first executed, and the brickwork is fresh and neat, I think we always feel that the smooth hard surface of the tile offers rather too great a contrast to the rougher texture of the bricks; and whilst the former is likely to remain almost unchanged for ever, the latter is certain gradually to grow rougher and ruder in its aspect, until, in the end, we shall have walls showing everywhere

to such a course as being an unwarrantable departure from old precedents; yet, if our forefathers' example is to be followed, we ought to do as they would have done in our circumstances.

[1] His name occurs in an inscription on it.

picturesque marks of age, and yet with their decorations as fresh as if they had but just been introduced. Nothing can well be worse than this; for if the appearance of age is to be venerated at all, it must be somewhat uniformly evident; and it no more answers to permit the decorations on an old and rugged wall to be always new and fresh-looking, than it does to allow a juvenile wig to be put on the venerable head of an old man!

The brick steeple of the cathedral is an inferior example of the same kind as that of la Magdalena, which I shall have presently to describe; its upper half is modern, and the lowest stage of stone. The west front is all modernised, and the north transept is conspicuous for a large porch of base design, erected probably in the sixteenth century, and exhibiting a curious though very unsuccessful attempt to copy—or perhaps I ought to say caricature—early work.

The whole of the clerestory walls have been raised with a stage of brickwork above the windows, which was added probably in the sixteenth or seventeenth century.

The cloister, built in the beginning of the sixteenth century, by D. Guillen Ramon de Moncada, is a remarkable example of very rich brickwork. It deserves illustration as being of an extremely uncommon style, and withal very effective. All the arches and jambs of the openings are of moulded brick, and there are brick enclosing arches, and a very simple brick cornice outside; but the delicate traceries which give so much character to the work are all cut in thin slabs of stone let into the brickwork. Of course such a work was not intended for glazing, and was an ingenious arrangement for rendering the cloister cool and unaffected by the sun, even when at its hottest. The forms of the openings here are certainly not good, and look much more like domestic than ecclesiastical work; but in spite of this one cannot but be thankful for novelty, whenever it is, as here, legitimately obtained. The bricks are of a very pale red tint, $12\frac{1}{2}$ inches long, $6\frac{1}{4}$ inches wide, and from $1\frac{1}{2}$ to $1\frac{3}{4}$ thick, and the mortar-joint, as usual, is very thick—generally about $\frac{3}{4}$ of an inch. The cloister is groined, and probably in brick, but is now plastered or whitewashed unsparingly, and its effect is in great degree ruined.

The sacristies are rather peculiar in their arrangement: they are all groined, and one of them has a small recess in one angle with a chair in it facing a crucifix, of which I could not learn the use. Another of this group of buildings contains a fountain under a small dome, the plashing of whose waters seemed to make it a very popular rendezvous of the people, and made itself heard everywhere throughout the sacristies and their passages.

The stalls in the Coro are of very late Gothic, the bishop's stall, with one on either side of it in the centre of the west end, having lofty canopies. The Coro is more than usually separated from the Capilla mayor, and there can be little doubt that it does not occupy its original position. The men who built so long a

CLOISTER, TARAZONA

nave would never have done so simply to render its length use-less by so perverse an arrangement of the choir. Here, in fact, the Coro occupies the same kind of position to which one so often sees it reduced in parish churches in Spain, where it is usually either in a western gallery, or at any rate at the extreme western end of the nave, behind everybody's backs, and apparently out of their minds!

A chapel on the north side of the nave, dedicated to Santiago, has a richly cusped arch opening from it to the aisle, and its vault springs from large corbels, carved with figures of the four evangelists, rudely but richly sculptured. It is mainly worthy of notice now on account of the beauty of a panel-painting still preserved over the altar: this is painted on a gold background, richly diapered, and the nimbi and borders to the vestments all elaborately raised in gold in high relief. The frame is richly carved with figures of saints, and gilt. The predella has on either side of the centre S. John and the Blessed Virgin, and four other holy women; in the centre a sculpture of our Lord and four saints which serves as a pedestal for a well-posed figure of Santiago; and on either side of the saint are two pictures with subjects illustrating his life. It is, on the whole, a very fine example of the combination of painting and sculpture, of which the Spaniards in the fifteenth and sixteenth centuries were so fond. The paintings are less realistic than German work of the same age, and, if not so delicately lovely as early Italian works, are yet of great interest and merit (1).

Returning from the cathedral to the town, and before one crosses to the opposite side of the river, a noble view of the buildings on the cliff above it is obtained from the bridge. The grandest of these is an enormous bishop's palace, once I believe the Alcazar; and close to it is the church of la Magdalena. The interior of this is entirely modernised, but the east end outside is a valuable example of untouched Romanesque. The eastern apse is divided into three by engaged shafts, stopping with capitals at the eaves-cornice, which is carried on a very simple corbel-table. To the west of this church is the steeple to which I have already alluded as giving so much of its character to Tarazona. It is a very lofty brick tower, without buttresses, with a solid simple base battering out boldly and effectively, and diapered in its upper stages with the patterns formed by projecting bricks, of which the builders of the brick buildings throughout this district were so fond. At a very slight expense a great effect of enrichment is obtained; the dark shadows of the bricks under the bright Spanish sunlight define all the lines clearly; and the uniformity of colour and the absence of buttresses make the general effect simple and quiet, notwithstanding the intricacy of the detail. The upper stage of this steeple is, as I need hardly say, a comparatively modern addition, but it no doubt adds to its effect by adding so much to the height, and in colour and design it harmonises fairly with the earlier work below.

The church of La Concepcion, not far from this, is a very late Gothic building, with a western gallery whose occupants are

TARAZONA
CAMPANILE OF LA MAGDALENA

quite concealed by stone traceries of the same kind as those in the cloisters of the cathedral. The sanctuary walls here are lined with glazed tiles, and the floor is laid with blue, green, and white tiles, the colour of each of which being half white and half blue or green allows of the whole floor being covered with a diaper of chequer-work, which is very effective and very easily arranged.

At the farther end of the city, and on the top of the long hill on which it is built, is a church dedicated to San Miguel. This has a simple nave with a seven-sided apse. The groining is all of very late date, the ribs curling down at their intersection as pendants, the under sides of which are cut off to receive bosses which were probably large and of wood. This groining is probably not earlier than the end of the sixteenth century, though the church itself is of the thirteenth or fourteenth century, having two doors of one of these dates: that on the north side has, in most respects, the air of being a work of the thirteenth, but its sculpture seems to prove that it cannot be earlier than the fourteenth century. ' It has the Judgment of Solomon carved on one of the capitals, angels in the label, and a figure of S. Michael above. The south doorway is executed in brick and stone, and is of the same date as the other. A brick belfry on the north side is enriched in the same fashion as that of la Magdalena, and, like it, batters out considerably at the base, but it is altogether inferior both in size and design (2).

From Tarazona I made a delightful excursion to the Abbey of Veruela. It is a two hours' ride, and the path takes one over a hill which conceals the Sierra de Moncayo from sight in most parts of Tarazona. The scenery on the road was beautiful. The town itself is always very striking; and as we ascended, the views of the distant hills and mountains beyond the Ebro were finer and finer. After riding for an hour and a half, a grand view of the whole height of Moncayo is obtained; below it to the right is a little village guarded by a picturesque castle keep, and on beyond and to the left a long line of roof, and towers, and walls girt around with trees, which seems to promise much to reward examination: and this is the old abbey of Veruela. At last the avenue is reached, which leads to the abbey gateway, in front of which stands a tall but mutilated cross, which forms the centre from which five paths—each planted with an avenue of trees—diverge.

The history of this abbey is interesting. It was the first Cistercian house in Spain, and was founded by a certain Don Pedro

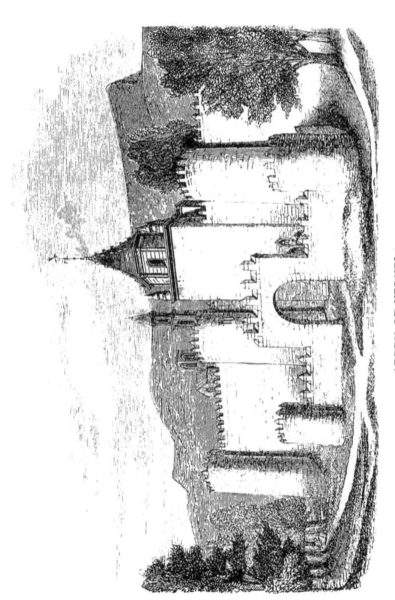

ABBEY OF VERUELA

ENTRANCE GATEWAY

de Atares, and his mother Teresa de Cajal, who commenced it in A.D. 1146, completed it in 1151, and obtained its formal incorporation in the Cistercian order on the 1st of September of the same year. There was a foundation for twelve monks, who were the first of their order to cross the Pyrenees, and who established themselves definitively here on the 10th August, 1171, under the direction of Bernard, Abbat of Scala Dei.[1]

I suppose the desolate situation of Veruela led to its being carefully fortified, though, indeed, at the date of its foundation, most religious houses were enclosed within fortified walls, and the severe rule of the early Cistercians will account fully for the remote and solitary situation chosen by the brethren who planted this house where we see it: at any rate, whatever the cause, it is now completely surrounded by walls, from which round towers project at intervals. The walls and towers are all perfectly plain, and surmounted with the pointed battlement so often seen in early Spanish buildings. A walled courtyard protects the entrance to the main gateway, and it is in front of this that the avenues mentioned just now all unite.

The view here is very peculiar. In front are the low walls of the outer court, with a raised archway in the centre; behind these the higher walls and towers, with a lofty and very plain central gateway, finished with an octagonal stage and low crocketed spire of late date, but pierced at the base with very simple thirteenth-century archways, leading into the inner court. Beyond this, again, is seen the upper part of the walls, and the steeple of the Abbey Church, backed by a bold line of hills. Passing through this gateway, a long narrow court leads to the west front of the church; and to the right of this court is a long range of buildings, all of which I think are of comparatively modern erection, though the brickwork in a *patio* entered by one of the openings is picturesque and good (3).

The west front of the church has a very noble round-arched doorway, boldly recessed, and with many shafts in the jambs. Above this is a small stone inscribed with the monograms X. P. and A. Ω.; and then, higher, a delicate line of arcading carried on slender shafts. All this work is set forward in advance of the general face of the wall. The nave and aisles were each lighted with a plain circular window, and the arcading up the eaves of the western gable still remaining shows that its pitch was always very flat. A steeple was built by an Abbat—Lope Marco—in the sixteenth century, against the western bay of

[1] Madoz, xv. 685.

VERUELA ABBEY CHURCH
INTERIOR

the north aisle, and before its erection there was, I suppose, no tower attached to the abbey.

In plan[1] the church consists of a nave and aisles six bays in length, transepts with eastern apses, and a choir with an aisle round it, and five small apsidal chapels.   To the south of the nave is a large cloister with a Chapter-house on its eastern side, and other ranges of buildings on the west and south.   To the east, too, are large erections now occupied as a private residence, and of which consequently I saw nothing properly, but without much regret, as they did not seem to show any traces of antiquity, and had probably been all rebuilt in those halcyon days in the seventeenth or eighteenth century, when Spaniards had more money than they well knew how to spend.

If we compare this church with one of the earliest French convents of the same order—as, for instance, Clairvaux—we shall find a very remarkable similarity in most of the arrangements.   In both the church is approached through a long narrow court, to which it is set in a slightly oblique line.   In both, the extreme simplicity, the absence of sculptures, the absence of a steeple, are observed in compliance with the fundamental rules of the Order.   Both have their cloisters similarly placed, with similar Chapter-houses, and lavatories projecting from their southern alleys.   The sacristies and the great libraries are in the same position—though here the latter has been converted into an enormous hall—and there are here groups of buildings all round the cloister, which were probably appropriated much in the same way as were those at Clairvaux.   Both, too, were enclosed in a very similar way with walls and towers, though at Clairvaux the enclosure was far larger than at Veruela.

It is clear, therefore, that the French monks who were brought here to found this first Spanish Cistercian house, came with the plan approved by their Order, and it is probable with something more than the mere ground-plan, for the whole of the work is such as might at the same date have been erected in France (4).

The whole exterior of the church is very fine, though severely simple.   The west front has already been described.   The exterior of the chevet is more striking.   The roofs of the chapels which surround it finish below the corbel-table of the aisle, which has a steepish roof finishing below the clerestory; and the latter is divided into five bays by plain pilasters.   All the eaves have corbel-tables, and the windows throughout are round-headed.   The chapels on the eastern side of the transepts are

[1] See Plate XXIII., p. 195.

of the same height as the aisle round the choir, and higher than the chapels of the chevet. The design of the interior, though very simple, is extremely massive and dignified. The main arches are all pointed, the groining generally quadripartite (save in the small apses, which are roofed with semi-domes), and the piers large and well planned. Many of the old altars remain; and among them the high altar in the choir, and those in the chapels of the chevet. The former is arcaded along its whole front, but has been altered somewhat in length at no very distant period. Near it is a double piscina, formed by a couple of shafts with capitals hollowed out with multifoil cusping.

CHAPEL ALTAR, VERUELA

The chapel altars are all like each other, and unlike the high altar, which is solid, whilst they are stone tables, each supported upon five detached shafts. They stand forward from the walls in the centre of the apses, and have rudely carved and planned piscinæ, and credence niches on the right-hand side as you face them.

The stones are marked in all directions by the masons, some of them with a mere line across from angle to angle, but mostly with marks of the usual quaint description. A number of examples of them are given on the engraving of the ground-plan.

Some part of the floor is laid with blue and white tiles, arranged in chevrons with good effect, and other parts with tombstones of Abbats, whose effigies are carved on them in low relief. They are flatter than the somewhat similar stones in some of the German churches (as *e.g.* at S. Elizabeth. Marburg), but are still a great deal too uneven on the surface to be suitable for a pavement.

The capitals are all very rudely sculptured, and the whole of the work has the air of extreme severity, almost of rudeness, which might be anticipated from the circumstances of its erection. A chapel was built in the sixteenth century to the north of the north transept by Ferdinand of Aragon, Bishop of Zaragoza, and nephew of Ferdinand the Catholic. It has nothing remarkable in its design (5). Later than this a large chapel was added to the east of the sacristy; and from what still remains of the fittings of the Coro in the nave, they seem to have been still later in date.

A fine late Romanesque door leads from the south aisle into the cloister, the whole of which is a good work of the early part of the fourteenth century, with well-traceried windows of four lights. The groining piers are clusters of shafts, and the buttresses on the outside are finished with crocketed gables and a bold cornice carved with foliage. The traceries are now all filled in with very thin panels of alabaster, which do not obscure the light much, whilst they effectually keep out the sun; but this precaution against sunshine does not seem to have been much needed, if the men were right who raised a second stage upon the old cloister, the Renaissance arcades of which are all left perfectly open. On the southern alley of the cloister there is a very pretty hexagonal projecting chamber, in which no doubt—if we may judge by the analogy of Clairvaux—was once the lavatory. The cloister has been built in front of, and without at all disturbing, the original Chapter-house, on its east side. The new groining shafts stand detached in front of the old arcade to the Chapter-house, and the combination of the two is managed very cleverly and picturesquely. This old arcade consists of the usual arrangement of a central doorway, with two openings on either side, all carried on clusters of detached shafts with capitals of foliage. The Chapter-house itself is divided into nine groining bays by four detached shafts; it is very low and small, and its three eastern windows are blocked up, but nevertheless its effect is admirable. One of its columns has been spoilt by the elaborate cutting in of the names of a party of Englishmen who ascended the Sierra de Moncayo to see the eclipse of the sun in 1860, and who recorded their not very hazardous or important achievement in this most barbarous fashion.

It is a fact quite worth notice here, that none of the old

windows are blocked up: the truth is that the churches from
which this was derived (6) were, in common with all Romanesque churches, taken straight from Italy, where the requirements of the climate were very similar to those of Spain. Yet
it was only very gradually that the northern architects discovered
their unfitness for a northern climate, and increased their dimensions. Here they give just enough and not too much light; but
at a later day, when the northern churches were all window
from end to end, the same fault was committed; and when their
architects were employed to build in other climates, they fol-

ENTRANCE TO CHAPTER-HOUSE, VERUELA

lowed their own traditions without reference to altered circumstances, as we see at Milan, at Leon, and elsewhere frequently.
  The church at Veruela seems now to be but little frequented,
the high altar alone being ever used. The stalls of the Coro are
gone, and a shattered fragment of the old organ-case standing
out from the wall serves only as a forlorn mark to show where
it once stood. The buildings generally are sadly decayed and
ruinous, and I have seldom seen a noble building less cared for
or respected. It is sad to see this result of the suppression of
religious orders, and one may be permitted to doubt whether it
can be for the interest of religion that this noble foundation
should now be nothing more than the private residence of a
Spanish gentleman, instead of—as it was intended it should be

by its pious founder—a perpetual refuge from the cares of the world of those in every age who aim to lead the holiest and most devoted lives.

I left Veruela with regret that I was unable to obtain more accurate notes of such portions of the monastic buildings as probably still remain overlaid with the poor additions of a too wealthy convent during the last three centuries. It is, however, easily accessible, and the plan which I give of the church will no doubt soon induce others to complete my examination where-ever it has been defective.

On the ride back to Tarazona, we made a short *détour* to look at what seemed to be an important church and village. Neither could well have been less so! The church was without anything worth remark save a band of tiles, set chevron fashion, in the cornice, and not harmonising at all well with the walls. The village was wretched in the extreme.

At Tarazona I was much struck by the extremely good char-acter of the common crockery in use in the inn and elsewhere. It is all painted by hand, never printed; and the result is that, even when simple diapers only are used, there is far greater life, variety, and vigour in the drawing than there ever is in our machine-made work. The colour seems generally to be used in such a way as that when burnt it varies charmingly in tint and texture. Every plate is different in pattern; and I fear that, uncivilised as we might think these good Spaniards in some things, they would be justly shocked were they to see the wretchedly inferior patterns with which, after many years of talking about art, we are still satisfied to decorate our earthen-ware. These people excel, too, just as much in form as in ornament. Their jugs are always quaint and good in outline, and made with the simplest regard to what is useful.

NOTES

(1) The chapel east of this has almost as good a retable, a Madonna of Mercy. Another, given by Sperandeo de Santa Fé, 1439, is now in the Lazáro collection in Madrid. The cloisters have not much of the pierced stone work, but in the church are still many good and great tombs. It is said that the first cathedral was where La Magdalena stands, and in 1473 a plan was abroad to move thither again and give up the other, where soldiers had to guard the doors against brigands daily: everything was prepared, the bull and the indulgences were ready, when the question rose how to move the tombs. They stayed with their dead.

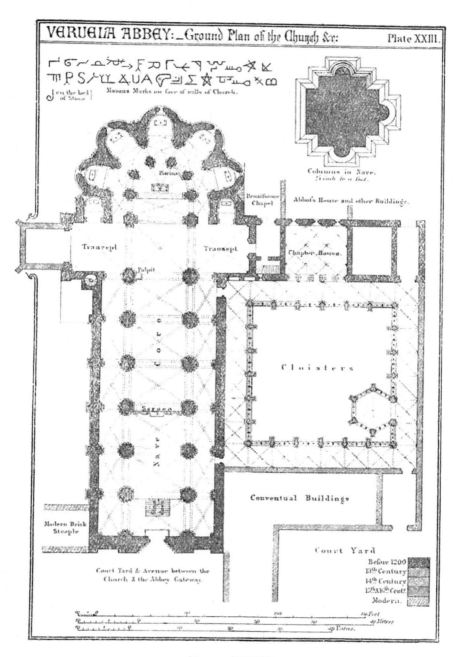

VERULAM ABBEY:_Ground Plan of the Church &c:

Plate XXIII.

Masons Marks on face of walls of Church.

on the bed of Stone

Columns in Nave.
½ inch to a foot.

Abbot's House and other Buildings.

Renaissance Chapel

Transept

Transept

Chapter House.

Pulpit

Cloisters

Nave

Screen

Conventual Buildings

Modern Brick Steeple

Court Yard

Before 1200
13th Century
14th Century
15 & 16th Cent.
Modern.

Court Yard & Avenue between the Church & the Abbey Gateway.

PLATE XXIII.

(2) San Miguel is of the fifteenth century.

(3) The approach and the palace are both changed now. Veruela is a house for Jesuit novices with a *clausura* against women which does not fortunately include the church, chapter-house, and cloisters, nor, I am told, the farm buildings. At these one can get homely but decent lodgings, established, or rather restored, for the visiting relatives of the young men. These, by the way, are not included in the *clausura*.

(4) Pedro Atares, the lord of Borja, brought monks from Scala Dei in Gascony as early as 1146, but they were not settled before 1171: the high altar was consecrated in 1211, and the church in 1224. It may well be the work of the same man who had already built Poblet, fetched from Scala Dei or Fontefroid. Though the church is now bare and sad, the cloister robbed of its alabaster panels, the nave stripped, cut off by a grille, and apparently unused, the miraculous Madonna still reigns beautiful at the high altar, and is at least four hundred years younger than the tradition admits.

(5) It has, however, a lovely alabaster tomb of the Abbot Lupi Marcos (died September 18, 1530), with his patrons, the sainted bishops Valerius of Zaragoza and Lupus of Sens.

(6) Derived—as Street himself would have admitted—at very long range, for he knew and said himself two pages back that the plan came from France, precisely as from France came the plans and the workmen for the great Italian abbeys of Fossanuova, Casamari, and San Galgano.

CHAPTER XIX

From Zaragoza the railway to Pamplona passes by Tudela. The line is carried all the way along the valley of the Ebro, the southern side of which is a fairly level open country, whilst on the north bold, barren hills, stream-worn and furrowed in all directions, rise immediately above the river. The broad valley through which the railway passes is well covered with corn-land, which, when I first passed, was rich with crops. To the south, as Tudela is approached, are seen the bold ranges of the Sierra de Moncayo, whilst in the opposite direction, far off to the north, soon after leaving Zaragoza the grand and snowy outlines of the Pyrenees come in sight.

Alagon is the only considerable town passed on the road, and there seems to be here an old brick belfry of the same character as the great steeple of Zaragoza, and, like it also, very much out of the perpendicular.

The cathedral dedicated to Sta. Maria at Tudela is one of the same noble class of church as those of Tarragona and Lérida, and quite worthy in itself of a long pilgrimage. It is said by Madoz to have been commenced in A.D. 1135, and consecrated in 1188, and was at first served by Regular clergy, but Secularised in 1238 (1). It is slightly earlier in date than the churches just mentioned, yet some of its sculpture, as will be seen, has, perhaps, more affinity to the best French work, and is indeed more advanced in style, than that with which the other two churches are decorated. This may be accounted for, most probably, by its more immediate neighbourhood to France. Its scale is fairly good without approaching to being grand, and thus it affords a good illustration of the great power which the mediæval architects undoubtedly possessed, of giving an impression of vastness even with very moderate dimensions, and of securing a thoroughly cathedral-like effect in a building much smaller in all its dimensions than the ordinary cathedral of the middle ages. No power is more to be desired by an architect; none marks more distinctly the abyss between the artist and the mere mechanical builder; and none has been more lost sight of during the three centuries which have elapsed since the eclipse of the Pointed style in the sixteenth century. We see here the usual subdivisions of parts, all well-proportioned and balanced. The nave[1] is of four bays only in length, and this is now, and perhaps was always in great part, occupied by the Coro: but, on the other hand, the proportions of the transept are very fine, and its internal perspective compensates in great degree for the loss of that of the nave. Out of this transept five arches in the east wall open to the choir and to four chapels, two on either side: and it is remarkable that two of these have square east ends, whilst all the rest have circular apses.

The plan of the columns is almost identical with that seen at Tarragona and Lérida: but it is one of which the eye is never satiated, inasmuch as it is well defined in its outlines, strong and massive-looking, and evidently equal to all that it has to perform. The vaulting is all quadripartite, except in the two eastern chapels on each side of the centre apse, or Capilla mayor, which are roofed with semi-domes, the Capilla mayor having its apse groined in five bays, with very bold groining ribs.

The arches are all pointed, very simply moulded with bold, broad, flat soffits, generally of only one order, and with labels adorned with dog-tooth. The bases and abaci of the capitals are all square. The former have the transition from the circular members to the square managed with admirable skill, tufts of foliage occupying the angles. The latter throughout the church are deep and boldly carved, as also are the capitals themselves. These seem to be of different dates: all those on the eastern side of the transept, and all the lower capitals of the nave, save the west end and first column, being very classical in their design, and probably dating from early in the thirteenth century, whilst the remainder appear to be generally of the latter part of the same century. In the earlier capitals the abaci are all set square with the walls, whereas in the later work they are set at right angles to the arch which they have to carry, and often, therefore, at an angle of 45° to the walls.

The groining ribs are very bold, and well moulded. There is no triforium, and the clerestory windows come down to a string-course just above the points of the main arches. They are of two lights, with a circle in the arched head, and their rear arches are moulded and carried on engaged jamb-shafts. The transepts have rose-windows in the bays next the choir, and lancet-windows in the north and south bays, and the carved

[1] *See* ground-plan, Plate XXIV., p. 205.

TUDELA CATHEDRAL
INTERIOR OF CHOIR

abacus is carried over these as a label. There seem to have been rose-windows round the principal apse at a lower level than the other clerestory windows; but only one of these is visible on either side, owing to the reredos: and I found it impossible to get any near exterior view of the east end, owing to the way in which it is built against by houses.

The west front had a large rose-window, which has been blocked up, and it still retains a noble doorway, of which I shall have to speak more in detail presently.

The north transept is now the least altered part of the church, and in the extreme simplicity of its bold buttresses, the refined beauty of its sculptured doorway, and the well-proportioned triplet which fills the upper part of the wall, it recalls to mind an English building of the thirteenth century. Unfortunately the gable has been destroyed, and the walls and buttresses are now finished with the straight line of the eaves. Almost the only peculiarity in the detail here is the wide, external splay of the windows between the glass and the jamb-shafts in the centre of the monials. The south transept has a triplet similar to that in the north transept, and has also lost its gable, and, being more shut in than the other, is perhaps the most picturesque in effect. A narrow lane leads up to it along the east wall of the cloister, and this, turning abruptly when it reaches the church, passes under a broad archway, which forms the south front of a porch, and then, out of an eastern archway, the street goes on again, twisting and turning in a fashion which is not a little eccentric. The exterior of the eastern apse retains its buttresses of slight projection, which run up to, and finish under, the eaves-cornice, which is carried, as all the cornices throughout the church are, upon boldly-moulded corbels.

It is only at some distance from the cathedral that anything is well seen of the turrets and tower, which give it most of the character it possesses. The west end had, I think, two small square towers, finished with octagonal turrets of smaller diameter than the towers. Of these the south-western still remains, but on the north side a lofty brick steeple was erected in the eighteenth century. Another turret is strangely placed over the centre of the principal apse. This is octangular in plan, with lancet-windows in the cardinal sides, and the sides of its spire pierced with two rows of small lights. The tile-roof of the apse slopes up on all sides from the eaves to the base of this turret; and, novel as its position is, it seemed to me to be well chosen and effective.[1] Other turrets rise out of the chapels which have sprung up round the church, and these, with the altered form of almost all the roofs, give a strange, informal, and disjointed look to the whole cathedral, which is eminently the reverse of attractive. Nevertheless the old work is there, and only requires a moderate amount of attention in order to understand the whole general character of the original scheme.

There are three grand doorways, one to each transept, and one at the west end. The former are not placed in the centre of the gable, but close to the western side of the transept, either, as is most probable, from a proper desire to leave space in front of the altars of the small transept chapels, or because then, as now, the ground was covered with houses, which made it impossible to place them centrally.

The finest of the three doorways is in the centre of the west front of the church, and its opening is more than nine feet in the clear, each of the jambs having eight shafts in square recesses. Two corbels support the tympanum, which has now no sculpture, nor any signs of ever having had any, and the arch has eight orders of sculptured moulding. The capitals of the columns in the jambs are all sculptured with subjects in a very exquisite fashion. There is here no grotesqueness or intentional awkwardness, but extreme beauty of design, simplicity of story, and fitness for the position chosen. The abaci are carved throughout with conventional foliage, well arranged and delicately cut. I know little even of French carving of the thirteenth century which surpasses this beautiful work, and none anywhere which more entirely deserves our admiration, or which may more worthily kindle our emulation. It is true, indeed, that here as elsewhere the cold formal critic may come and prove to his own satisfaction that some portions of the work are not academically correct: on the other hand, it is equally true that it is not academically cold and soulless, for the men who wrought here wrought of their love and enthusiasm, and not merely because they were drilled and paid, and they afford us, therefore, an example not to be despised of the truths, that in art enthusiasm is worth more than skill, and feeling more than knowledge; truths specially valuable in these days, when men fancy they can convert all who call themselves architects into

---

[1] The lead *flèche* in a similar position at Reims cathedral will no doubt be remembered by many of my readers. No doubt, however, this work at Tudela is earlier, and being of stone is even more remarkable.

artists, not by making them rejoice in their work, but simply by teaching them how to draw (2).

The subjects in the capitals are arranged in the following order:—Nos. 1 to 8 are those in the left or northern jamb, and Nos. 9 to 16 those in the right or southern jamb. Nos. 1 and 9 are next the opening, and Nos. 8 and 16 the extreme capitals right and left of the centre.

1. The Creation of Angels.
2. Do. of Earth, Stars, etc.
3. Do. of Trees.
4. Do. of Birds and Beasts.
5. Do. of Adam.
6. Do. of Eve.
7. The Fall.
8. Eve sleeping with a fig-leaf in her hand, and the Serpent mocking her.

9. Expulsion from Paradise.
10. Adam tilling, Eve spinning.
11. Cain and Abel sacrificing.
12. Cain killing Abel.
13. God cursing Cain.
14. Cain, a fugitive.
15. Entry into the Ark.
16. The Sacrifice of Abraham.

The two corbels which support the tympanum have on their face angels blowing trumpets, and under them two lions, eating, one of them two wyverns, the other a man. The archivolt has a series of eight figures carved on key-stones at its intersection. There are—beginning with the lowest—(1) the Agnus Dei, (2) the Blessed Virgin, (3) an angel, (4) a martyr, (5) a king, (6) a bishop, and (7) another king. On the sides the archivolt has on the left the Resurrection, and the happiness of the blessed, who are all represented in pairs; and on the right, the tortures of the damned, full of terror and horror of every kind. In the first rank of these unhappy ones are two bishops and an abbat learning the truth of our Lord's awful saying, " Where their worm dieth not, and their fire is not quenched "—a saying practically ignored by our sculptors and carvers at the present day, who seem to believe in no Last Judgment, no masculine saints, and nothing but female angels; so far, at least, as one can judge by the figures with which they cover so profusely the walls of some of our new churches. The outer order of the archivolt has angels all round it, with crowns and sceptres in their hands. There can be little doubt, I suppose, that the tympanum was intended to have a sculpture, or, perhaps, had a painting of a sitting figure of our Lord in Judgment; without this figure the whole scheme wants the key-note, to give tone and significance to all its varied story. With it there would be few doorways which would be altogether finer or more worshipful than this.

The transept-doors are rightly much more simple than the western door, and the character of their sculpture has so much Byzantine feeling that there can be no doubt they are of somewhat earlier date.

The north transept doorway has on its eastern capitals: 1. The Baptism of our Lord by S. John; 2, Herod's Feast; 3, The head of S. John brought in a charger;—and on its western capitals: 4, S. Martin giving his cloak to a beggar; 5, Our Lord holding a cloth (?), and two angels worshipping; 6, S. Nicholas restoring the two children to life. The door-arch is pointed, and all its orders and the label are very richly carved, but with foliage only. The south transept door is round-arched, and its tympanum is not filled in. On the capitals of the western jamb are: 1, S. Peter walking on the Sea; 2, The Last Supper; 3, The Charge to S. Peter;—and on the eastern jamb: 4, The Incredulity of S. Thomas; 5, The Walk to Emmaus; 6, The Supper at Emmaus.

The west front has two large square turrets, one of which only is carried up above the line of the roof. Its highest stage is octagonal, with a lancet opening on each face, and is finished with a low spire. A bold row of corbels is carried round the turret between the octagonal and square stages, as if for the support of a projecting parapet which no longer exists. The western rose-window was inserted under a broadly-soffited and bold pointed arch, which spans the whole space between the turrets and rises nearly to the top of the walls.

The internal furniture of this church is not interesting. The metal screens are of the sixteenth and seventeenth centuries. The Coro occupies the second and third bays of the nave, and iron rails are placed from its eastern door to the doorway in the Reja or screen of the Capilla mayor, so as to preserve a passage for the clergy. The reredos of the high altar contains sixteen paintings, enclosed within a complicated architectural frame-work of buttresses, pinnacles, and canopies. In the centre is an enormous canopy and niche, in which is a modern effigy of the Blessed Virgin. This combination of rich architectural detail with paintings is not satisfactory to the eye; and it is evident that sculptured subjects would have been much more in harmony with the framework (3).

In the south-east chapel of the south transept there is a magnificent monument to the " Muy Hoñorable Señor Môsen Francis de Villia Espepa, Doctor, Cabalero, et Chanceller de Navarre," and his " Muy Hoñorable Duenya Doña Ysabel," who died in 1423. The two effigies lie under a deeply-recessed arch filled in with tracery, the recess being adorned with sculptured subjects on its three sides. There are eight Weepers in the arcade on the side of the tomb. It was too dark to see what all the subjects were; but at the back our Lord is seated and censed by angels; and below this He is represented in His tomb, with His arms bound, with a weeping angel on either side.

I have left to the last all notice of the beautiful cloister on the south side of the nave (4). The arcades, which open into the cloister-court, are carried on columns, which are alternately coupled and tripled or quadrupled; larger piers are introduced in the centre of each side, in order to give additional strength. The arches are generally simple and pointed, but on the north and south sides they are chevroned on the inside. The engraving

which I give of the south-east angle of this cloister will show how elaborate the whole of the work is. The capitals throughout are carved with subjects and foliage, and most of the latter is of extremely delicate character. The acanthus-leaf is largely introduced. I had not time to catalogue the subjects carved in the capitals ; but so many of them are concealed and so many damaged, that I fear it would be almost impossible at present to do so at all completely.

I may with safety class this small church at Tudela among the very best it has been my good fortune to visit in any part of Europe; and there is much in

ANGLE OF CLOISTER, TUDELA

its Iconography and in its sculptured detail which would reward a much more lengthened examination than I was able to afford.

I saw but one other old church here—that of la Magdalena, in the Calle de Sta. Cruz (5). It consists of a nave and choir, vaulted with a pointed waggon roof, with bold transverse ribs carried on carved capitals built in the side-walls. The chancel makes a very decided bend to the north. There is a simple tower on the north side, with a round-arched window of two lights in the belfry stage, and a window of one light in the stage below it. The west doorway is very fine: it is round-arched, and has in the tympanum our Lord seated in a quatrefoil, surrounded by the emblems of the four Evangelists. The label is carved, and the orders of the arch are in part carved with acanthus, and in

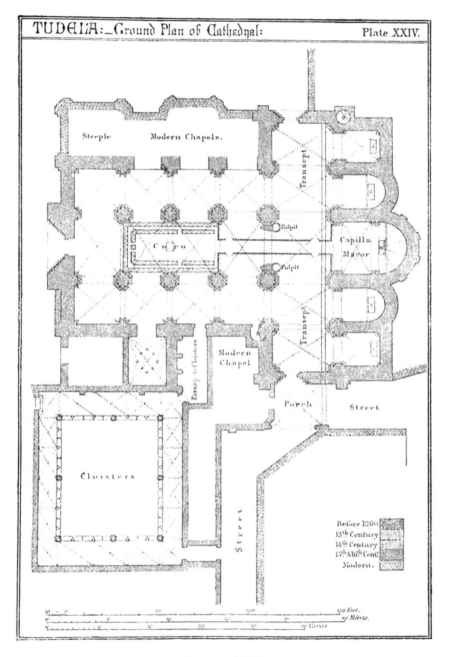

TUDELA:—Ground Plan of Cathedral: Plate XXIV.

Steeple

Modern Chapels.

Transept

Coro

Pulpit

Capilla Mayor

Pulpit

Passage to Cloisters

Modern Chapel

Transept

Porch

Street

Cloisters

Street

Before 1200
13th Century
14th Century
15th & 16th Cent.
Modern.

100 Feet.
40 Metres.

PLATE XXIV.

part with figures. Among the latter are the twelve Apostles and (apparently) the Descent of the Holy Ghost. The capitals are also storied.[1]

From Tudela I availed myself of a special train on the railway to Pamplona, which ran solely for the purpose of carrying the passengers of a diligence from Madrid, and in which the station-master obligingly gave me a seat. On the road we passed the towns of Olite and Tafalla, the view of the former of which gave so much promise that I returned there in order to examine its remains properly.

Tafalla and Olite were of old called the Flowers of Navarre. Olite now is dreary, desolate, and ruinous; and though Tafalla looks a little more thriving, it too has lost all its former claim to the title of a flower!

In Olite there are the extensive remains of a very fine castle, which was built as a palace by the kings of Navarre, and two interesting parish churches, Sta. Maria and San Pedro. Sta. Maria consists of a wide nave of four bays in length, and a small apse at the east end. On the west side is a small cloister in front of the principal entrance, which gives great picturesqueness to the whole work. The cloister is a work of the fifteenth century, an irregular square in plan, and arcaded with a good simple open arcade. The east side has been destroyed, in order to allow of the grand western doorway of the church being seen. This is protected by a penthouse roof, supported on two tall columns, which have taken the place of the old arcade. The church was built within the walls of the castle, but the cloister seems to have been thrown out beyond their line on the town side. There is a tower on the south of the nave, finished with a gabled roof, and pierced with some good early-pointed openings.

The west front is a very elaborate work of the fourteenth century. It has a central doorway, and a row of niches with figures on each side of it, above a string-course, which is on the same level as the springing of the doorway. The tympanum of the door has sculptures of the Blessed Virgin Mary and our Lord under a canopy in the centre; on the (proper) right, the Baptism, the Flight into Egypt, and the Massacre of the Innocents; and on the left, the Presentation, the Annunciation, and the Nativity. The carving of the archivolt is rich, mainly of foliage, but with two or three figures under niches introduced capriciously in its midst. The jambs, too, are covered with

---

[1] There is, I believe, a fine old bridge of seventeen arches over the Ebro, near Tudela: unfortunately I did not see it.

carvings of subjects arranged in the oddest way; *e.g.* there are in succession an Agnus Dei, an Annunciation, the Creation of Eve, Adam tilling the ground, wyverns, an elephant and castle, the Fall, a pelican vulming its breast with a goat standing on its hind-legs and looking on; and so on with subjects which seem to exhibit nothing but the odd conceits of the workman, and to be arranged in no kind of order. The carving is all of that crisp, sharp, clever kind, so seldom seen in England, but so common in the fourteenth-century buildings of Germany, and in which some of the Spanish sculptors were unsurpassed by all save perhaps their own successors in the latest period of Gothic art, whose works I have already described at Burgos, Miraflores, and Valladolid. There are extensive traces of old painting on the stonework of this doorway; and I noticed that the detached shafts (of which there are four in each jamb) were covered with a trailing branch of ivy, with green leaves and red stems (6).

The interior of Sta. Maria is not very interesting, though its scale is good, the groined nave being 36 feet wide by 108 feet in length. The groining-shafts are commendably bold and dignified. There is the usual late western gallery, and a modern chapel and large irregular porch on the south side.

Sta. Maria stands, as I have said, partly within the walls of the ancient castle or palace. This was dismantled in the course of the Peninsular war, but is still an imposing ruin, with a vast extent of enclosing wall, out of which rise several fine towers. These are generally very simple, but lofty, and capped with projecting machicoulis. I give an illustration of one in which the finish is unlike any that I remember to have seen.[1] The window here is a good example of a traceried domestic window, a straight stone transome being carried across under the tracery, so as to make the window-opening square-headed.

Two grand towers on the eastern face of the castle are oct-angular in plan, and one of them rises in three stages, each slightly within the other, and each finished with fine corbelled machicoulis.

The gateways have extremely small and low pointed arches, looking like little holes in the great walls. Some of the walls are finished with the common Arab type of battlement, the coping of which is weathered to a point. The keep is a large pile, with square towers at the angles; and near it is a large hall with battlemented side-walls, which has the air of being

---

[1] *See* illustration on next page.

the earliest part of the castle, but into which I was unable to gain admission.

At the other extremity of the town (or village as it ought rather to be called) is the church of San Pedro. This forms an important feature in the picturesque view of the place, owing to its fine and peculiar tower and spire. This is built against the south side of the church, is quite plain until it rises above the roof, and then has two stages each pierced with windows; above this a pierced overhanging parapet, carried upon very bold

CASTLE, AND CHURCH OF SAN PEDRO, OLITE

corbels, and then a low octagonal stage, each side surmounted by a crocketed gable, and the whole finished with a spire, the entasis of which is very distinctly marked. An original design, such as this is, deserves illustration. The height of the spire bears, it will be seen, but a small proportion to that of the tower, as is often to be observed in the case of good steeples; but the most unusual feature is the enormous parapet, and taking into account the position of the church just at the extreme angle of the town, it may be supposed to have been built with some view to military requirements. The greater part of the steeple is a work I suppose of the fourteenth century—much later than the church, which, saving modern additions, is a fine work of quite the beginning of the thirteenth century, if not earlier. The west doorway is round-arched, having three shafts in each jamb, with sculptured capitals, and an arch of six orders alternately carved and moulded. The tympanum is sculptured with our Lord and two censing angels, and below are subjects from the life of S. Peter: (1) His commission; (2) His walking on the sea; (3) His trial; and (4) His crucifixion. Above the doorway is a string-course carved in the fourteenth century, and in the gable a wheel window within a pointed enclosing-arch. The plan of the nave and aisles is of the same kind as that of the church at Tudela, though on a smaller scale. A curious difference in the design is the carrying up of the aisle groining almost to the same level as that of the nave, whilst the transverse arches across the aisle are at a much lower level, and have pointed and circular windows pierced in the walls between the arches and the groining. The eastern part of the church is all modern and very bad (7).

Olite is a very squalid and miserable place; but a few hours may be well spent here; and the castle in particular, which has been very badly treated within a few years, ought to be carefully examined and drawn before it is too late. I was there on a hot day in June—so hot as to make it difficult to work—and yet on the summit of the hills, lying to the south-south-west of the town, a good deal of snow was lying, and in the evening, as the sun went down, the cautious Spaniards put on their great cloth cloaks, and stole about muffled up to the eyes as though it were mid-winter.

From Olite to Tafalla there was once, or was once intended to be, a continuous subterranean communication. The distance must be some three or four miles, so that the story would appear to be rather improbable. The intention of Charles III. of Navarre to make such a communication between the great palace he was building at Tafalla and the already existing castle of Olite, is mentioned by Cean Bermudez under the date of 1419; but he gives no authority for his statement.

I was unable to stop at Tafalla: it is a more important place than Olite, and has two churches, both apparently of the latest Gothic, with square-ended transepts, and windowless apsidal choirs like those of the late Burgalese churches.

After leaving Tafalla the country becomes at every step wilder and more beautiful. The hills rise grandly on either side, and are bare and rocky. The railway passes under an aqueduct, which in height, length, and simple grandeur of design, is worthy to be ranked among the finest European aqueducts.   It was built at the end of the last century by D. Ventura Rodriguez.   The only old church I saw on this part of the road was close to Las Campanas station.   Its west front had a good doorway, and above this a great arch rising almost to the point of the gable, with a circular window pierced within it.   The same design is repeated in one of the churches of Pamplona.

The towers and walls of Pamplona are seen for some time before they are reached.   The railway follows the winding of a pretty stream, and the city stands well elevated above it.   The situation is indeed very charming, the whole character of the country being thoroughly mountainous, and the city standing on an elevated knoll rising out of an ample and prosperous-looking valley surrounded by fine hills.

The views from the cathedral and walls are very beautiful, and as the town is large and rather handsomely laid out with a grand arcaded Plaza in the centre, it gives a very favourable impression of Spain to those who make it their first resting-place on a Spanish tour.

The cathedral stands on the outside of the city and close to the walls.   It was commenced in A.D. 1397 by Charles III. of Navarre who pulled down almost[1] the whole of the old church (built *circa* A.D. 1100).   The planning of this church is both ingenious and novel.   Its chevet is entirely devised upon a system of equilateral triangles, and, as will be seen by reference to my plan,[2] the apse has only two canted sides, having a column in the centre behind the altar; and though it is perfectly true that this two-sided apse is in itself not a very graceful scheme, it is at the same time equally true that the combination of the chapels with the central apse is very ingenious and clever.   The distortion of the chapel next to the transept is very objectionable, and seems to be without reason or necessity.   There are transepts and a nave and aisles of six bays in length, with side chapels along the greater part of the aisles.   The extreme shortness of the constructional choir makes it certain that the church was planned for the modern Spanish arrangement of the Coro, which now occupies two bays of the nave, leaving one bay between its eastern Reja and the Crossing.   The Reja of the Capilla mayor is under the eastern arch of the Crossing, so that the low rails

[1] I believe a portion of the old cloister remains.   I was not aware of this, and seeing the fine late cloister, assumed, unfortunately, that there was nothing else to be seen.
[2] Plate XXV., p. 216.

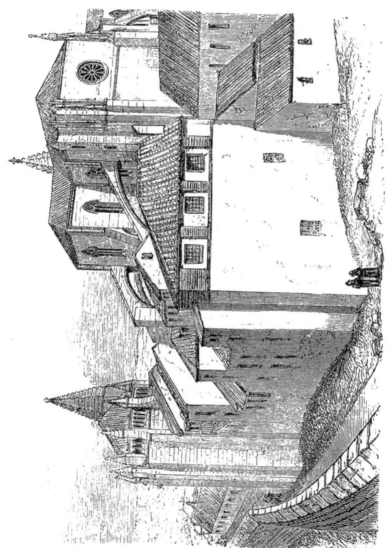

PAMPLONA CATHEDRAL

EXTERIOR FROM THE NORTH-EAST

marking the passage from the Coro to the Capilla mayor are very long. The detail of all the architecture is characteristic of the late date at which the church was built. The columns are large, but composed of a succession of insignificant mouldings, so as to produce but little effect of bold light and shade: those in the choir are cylindrical, with clusters of mouldings supporting, and continued on as, the groining ribs, and they all lack that definiteness of arrangement and plan which is one of the surest tests of the difference between good and bad Gothic architecture generally, as it is between the work of men of the thirteenth and fifteenth centuries almost everywhere.

The internal effect of the cathedral is certainly very fine. The peculiar scheme of the apse allows of the erection of a Retablo of unusual height with less interference with the architectural features than is common; and the whole design has the merit which I have so often had to accord to the latest school of Gothic artists in Spain, of having been schemed with an evident intention of meeting and providing for the necessities of the climate; and one consequence of this is that almost all the windows are left as they were originally designed, and have not been blocked up in order to diminish the glare. The clerestory windows throughout are small, those in the transepts are only small roses, and owing to the steep slope of the aisle roofs there is a great space between these openings and the main arcades. The three eastern bays of the nave have geometrical traceries, whilst in the western bays and the choir they are flamboyant in character; but I do not imagine that this slight difference in character betokens any real difference in their age. They all, in short, have somewhat of late middle-pointed character, though their actual date and their detail would make us class them rather with works of the third-pointed style.

The stalls in the Coro are of Renaissance character, but founded closely on the older models; and the Reja, to the east of them, is of wrought iron, old, but with a Renaissance cresting. The Reja in front of the Capilla mayor is much finer; it is of wrought iron, and is made, as is so usual, with vertical bars, set rather close together, and alternately plain and twisted. What the lower part lacks in ornament the cresting more than atones for; it is unusually ornate, consisting of interlacing ogee arches with crocketed pinnacles between them, all very elaborately hammered up. The horizontal bars and rails are also all covered with traceries in relief, and at regular intervals on these there are small figures under canopies. The whole stands upon a moulded and panelled base of stone. The total height of this screen is not less than thirty feet, of which the cresting is about a third.

Of the other furniture I may mention some of the glass in the clerestory, which is fine; and the old Retablos. Two of these in the south chapel of the chevet are especially worthy of notice. One of them has a crucifix (with the figure draped in modern drapery) which has the feet half plated with silver, and behind it are twelve prophets in rows of four over each other, and all of them with inscriptions referring to the Crucifixion—such as the texts beginning " Foderunt manus," " Vere languores nostros ipse tulit," " Post ebdomadas sexaginta dies occidetur," " Quid sicut plage iste," etc.

The western front is a poor Pagan work utterly out of keeping with the remainder of the fabric, and erected in the last century from the designs of D. Ventura Rodriguez. The rest of the exterior is Gothic, but not at all striking. It was once well garnished with crocketed pinnacles above its flying buttresses, but they have now for the most part disappeared. The roofs are flat and tiled, and hipped back in an ungainly fashion even at the transepts. The north transept door has an unusually fine example of a latch-handle or closing ring; the handle has writhing serpents round it, and the plate is perforated all over with rich flamboyant traceries.

This cathedral is fortunate in retaining many of its old dependent buildings in a very perfect state, but unfortunately I have spent only one day in Pamplona, and I did not see by any means all that is to be seen. For Cean Bermudez[1] says that some portions of the first cathedral, founded in A.D. 1100, still remain; particularly the small cloister and some of the buildings attached to it (8). This was the last cathedral in Spain that observed the rule of S. Augustine, and the canons always lived in common; the refectory, said to be of the thirteenth century, the kitchen and offices, all still remain. Of about the same age as the cathedral are the beautiful cloisters on its south side, and the Chapter-house to the east of the cloister. It is said, indeed, that a part of this cloister had been built some seventy years before the fall of the old cathedral rendered it necessary to rebuild it from the ground, and the style of much of the work encourages one to believe the statement. It is certainly a very charming work in every way: it is a square in plan, each side having six traceried windows towards the centre court, and a small chapel breaks out

[1] *Arq. de España*, i. 83.

into this at the south-west angle. The windows are all of four lights, filled with geometrical traceries, with crocketed labels to some and canopies to others, and delicate buttresses and pinnacles dividing the bays. The low wall below the open windows is covered with small figures in niches, and the walls above the windows with panelling, as is also the parapet of the modern upper cloister. The general conception is very ornate, and at the same time very delicate and light in its proportions; and it is rendered very interesting by the number of rich doorways, monuments, and sculptures with which the walls are everywhere enriched. The door called " Of our Lady of the Refuge " opens from the transept to the cloister; its front is in the cloister, of which it occupies the north-western bay. In its tympanum is a sculpture of the burial of the Blessed Virgin, whose statue, with the figure of our Lord in her arms, occupies the post of honour against the central pier. The reveals of the jambs are filled with little niches and canopies in which are figures and subjects; and below the bases, in a band of quatre-foils, are on the one side the Acts of Mercy; on the other, figures playing on instruments. Angels in the archivolt bear a scroll on which is inscribed—" Quæ est ista que ascendit de deserto deliciis affluens, innixa super dilectum suum? Assumpta est Maria in cœlum." Against the east wall of the cloister is a sculpture of the Adoration of the Magi, and next to this the grand triple opening to the Chapter-house—a richly moulded door with a two-light window on either side. In the southern alley are a fine tomb of a bishop, the door of the Sala Preciosa adorned with a series of bas-reliefs from the life of the Blessed Virgin, and another door with the Last Supper and the Entry into Jerusalem; and close to the latter, but in the western wall, is a doorway with the Crucifixion, and the Maries going to the Sepulchre. Between these sculptured doorways the walls are all arcaded with tracery panels corresponding to the windows; and as all the mouldings are rich and delicate in their design, and the proportions of the cloister very lofty, it will be seen that I cannot be very far wrong in considering this to be, on the whole, one of the most effective and striking cloisters of its age. The projecting chapel on the south-west angle is exceed-ingly delicate in its construction, and is screened from the cloister with iron *grilles* (9). A quaintly trimmed box-garden occupies the cloister-court to the no small improvement of its effect.

On the eastern side is the Chapter-house; a very remarkable

work of probably the same age as the cloister, though of a simpler, bolder, and much more grand kind of design. It is square in plan, but the vault is octagonal, the angles of the square being arched and covered with small subordinate vaults below the springing of the main vault. Buttresses are placed outside to resist the thrust of each of the eight principal ribs of the octagonal vault; and these buttresses, being all placed in the same direction as the ribs, abut against the square outline of the building in the most singular and, at first sight, unintelligible manner. They are carried up straight from the ground nearly to the eaves, where they are weathered back and finished with square crocketed pinnacles; whilst between them an open arcade is carried all round just below the eaves. On the exterior this Chapter-house seems to be so far removed from the east end of the church as to have hardly any connection with it; they are separated by houses built up close to their walls, and present consequently a not very imposing effect from the exterior; and standing, as the Chapter-house does, just on the edge of the city walls, it is strange that it has fared so well in the many attacks that have been made on Pamplona. The interior is remarkable only for the grand scale and proportions of the vault with which it is covered.

There are several other old churches here which deserve notice, though none are on a very fine or grand scale. That of San Saturnino—the first Bishop of Pamplona—is remarkable chiefly for the very unusual planning of its eastern end, which has three unequal sides, out of which three unequal polygonal chapels open.[1] My impression is that there was never any altar under the great apse, but that the high altar stood in the central chapel, at its east end. The Coro is, and probably was always intended to be, in the western gallery, the under side of which is groined, and any arrangement of stalls on the floor of such a church would be obviously inconvenient and out of place. Two towers are built against the eastern bay of the nave. The window tracery is of good geometrical middle-pointed character, and the mouldings and other details all seem to prove that the church was built about the middle of the fourteenth century (10). The south doorway has the rare feature at this period of capitals *historiés* ; on the left hand are the Annunciation, the Salutation, the Nativity, and the Flight into Egypt; and on the right our Lord bearing His Cross, the Descent from the Cross, the Resurrection, and the Descent into Hell. The

[1] *See* ground-plan on Plate XXV., p. 216.

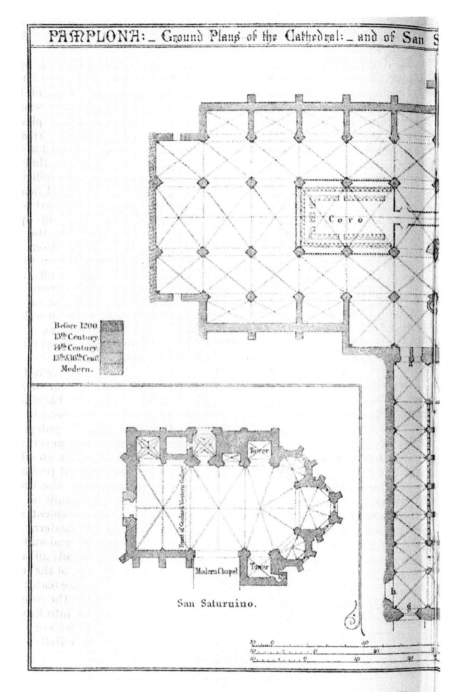

Before 1200.
13th Century.
14th Century.
15th & 16th Cent.
Modern.

Coro

Tower

Chapel of Gentiana

Modern Gallery

Modern Chapel

Tower

San Saturnino.

h

g

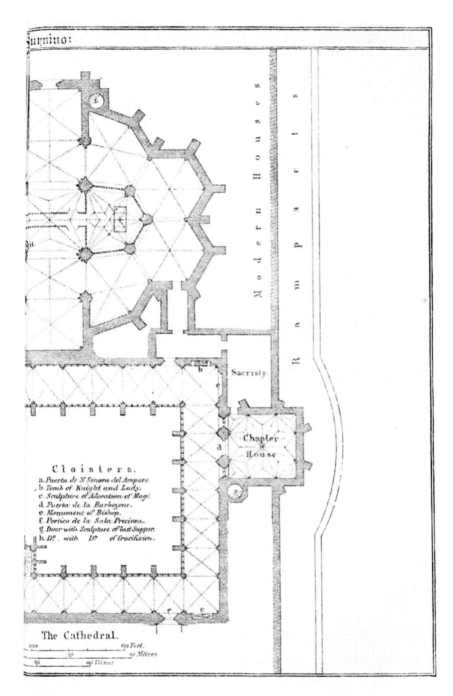

Modern Houses

Ramparts

Sacristy.

Chapter House

C l o i s t e r s.

a. Puerta de N. Senora del Amparo
b. Tomb of Knight and Lady.
c. Sculpture of Adoration of Magi.
d. Puerta de la Barbezone.
e. Monument of Bishop.
f. Portico de la Sala Preciosa.
g. Door with Sculpture of Last Supper.
h. D? . with D? of Crucifixion.

The Cathedral.

XXV.

Crucifixion forms the finial of the canopy over the doorway, and three or four other subjects are concealed by the modern framework round the door.   There seems to be no reason why the idea of such a plan as this should not be adopted again: the termination of the nave by a kind of apsis, from one side of which the chancel projects, is extremely good, and perhaps, on the whole, the best way of effecting the change from the grand span of so broad a nave to the moderate dimensions (just half those of the nave) of the chancel.   Such a church would probably hold about six hundred worshippers, all in sight of the altar, and might, with advantage to its proportions, be lengthened by the addition of another bay; and, simple as all its parts would be, it would be a relief to eyes wearied by the flimsy weakness of our modern Gothic work to look upon anything which could not possibly be constructed without solid walls, massive buttresses, and some degree of constructive skill.

The church of San Nicolas (11) is of Romanesque date, but much altered and added to at later periods.   It consists of a nave and aisles of three bays, a Crossing, and a short eastern polygonal apse.   The nave aisles retain their original waggon vaults, with transverse ribs at intervals; but the other vaults are all quadripartite.   The clerestory of the nave, too, consists of broad unpierced lancets, which are probably coeval with the arcades below them.

The exterior of this church is very much obscured by modern additions and excrescences, but still retains some features of much interest.   There is a fine early western door, and above this a rose-window filled with rich geometrical tracery, over which is a very boldly projecting pointed arch, which abuts against a tower on the north and against a massive buttress on the south.   The walls appear to have been finished at the eaves with very bold machicoulis.   At a much later date than that of the church a lofty open cloister, with plain pointed arches, was added on the western and northern sides.

On either side of the apse of this church, in front of the Retablo and altar, are what look like two tabernacles for the reservation of the Sacrament: but I had no opportunity of learning the object of this double arrangement.

The views from the walls of Pamplona are eminently lovely; I remember looking across to the east, over the flat which stretches away from them to where the mountains begin to rise boldly beyond; and, as my eyes wandered on, I began to turn my thoughts eagerly homewards, and much as I had enjoyed the

Spanish journey which ended at Pamplona, there was perhaps no part of it which I enjoyed more than this, where I was ungrateful enough to Spain to allow everything to be seasoned by the near prospect of home.

NOTES

(1) The collegiata was a cathedral only from 1783 to 1851.

(2) Details in the portal, of women's dress, for instance, are French beyond dispute, but all influenced by the Spanish regional types. There, as at Leon and Santiago, the carvers wrought what they saw.

(3) I cannot agree in disapproval of this retable of N. S. la Blanca, which was ordered by the chapter in 1489 from the architect and painter Pedro Diaz of Oviedo, and finished in 1494. All the retables in this church I vastly admired, even that of the fifteenth century in the south aisle, devoted to S. Catharine and rich in unedited scenes borrowed from miracle plays of her life and Our Lady's. That in the south-east transept chapel was ordered by Mosén Francés de Villa Espesa, chancellor of Navarre under Charles the Noble, who was buried there in 1427. The predella contains eight panels of the Passion, the pinnacles and divisions Christ in Glory, two prophets and twenty-eight small saints; the central part, under the inevitable Calvary, an Epiphany and great Madonna of Mercy, with donors, flanked on the Gospel side by the Annunciation, Noli Me Tangere, and Pentecost, and on the Epistle side by the Nativity, Ascension of Christ, and Dormition of the Blessed Virgin. Beyond these, again, remain, in panels as fine as the central one and nearly as large, three scenes each from the lives of S. Francis and S. Giles. The chancellor's tomb M. Bertaux thinks came from the workshop at Pamplona of Janin Lome of Tournai.

(4) The cloister is very easily missed, being separated from the nave, in the Benedictine manner, by a closed door and a passage. It is in the Cluniac tradition of Castile and Navarre, with special characteristics of its own.

(5) La Magdalena, of the thirteenth and fifteenth centuries, keeps its thirteenth century barrel-vault; the portal, set inside the present door, is in the French style of the twelfth century and earlier than that of the collegiata.

(6) The apostles are ranged, six on a side, along the west wall of the church. They are unquestionably of the French school, but they are not apparently all of one set. It is customary to compare them with Santo Sepulcro of Estrella and San Saturnino of Artajona, of which I have seen neither, and here record the names because if comparable they are worth seeing. The façade and door belong, I believe, well along in the fourteenth century. It is easier to conceive of the apostles belated than of the grotesques anticipated. Inside, an immense Italianate painted retable, dark and luminous, in twenty-eight or thirty-two compartments, besides saints, belongs in the same way I suppose to the sixteenth century. The painter bore the same relation to his Italian-trained master that Lo Spagna

and Mariotto Albertinelli did to theirs; he is sometimes very imitative, but you can never confront him with what he imitates, and he is sincere and conscientious.

(7) Señor Madrazo dates San Pedro in the end of the twelfth century along with the tower on the south ; that on the north in the fourteenth or fifteenth.

(8) Except a few capitals behind a wire netting in a niche of the cloister I could hear of nothing else, nor could another ecclesiologist who had lately been over the ground, Professor Desdevises of Clermont-Ferrand.

(9) This was once the fountain house, for washing. The *Sala Preciosa* was probably the canons' library. The refectory is of the fourteenth century—the Hue and Cry after the Unicorn is carved under the lector's pulpit, and the kitchen adjoining, that looks thirteenth century, is probably a hundred years later. Since 1902 it shelters the alabaster tomb of Charles the Noble and Eleanor his queen, which was begun in 1416 by Janin Lome, image-carver, of Tournai, who ranged mourners in niches round about, like those at Dijon. But in 1411, when the tomb of Philippe le Hardi was finished, Janin Lome was already established at Pamplona and had made for the king a S. John Baptist. By him also may be the tomb of the Infants of Luna in the north-east corner of the cloister, Messire Lionel of Navarre, who died 1413, and his wife Doña Elfa de Luna. Six little saints and the Crucified in the midst are as vigorous as the great portal figures of Champmol; and charming painted saints on the wall above are as completely French as a curious thirteenth-century painting kept with a few other pictures in a room opening from the inner sacristy. It is hard to get leave to see these, " because people were always asking." In the rococo sacristy itself, that looked like a favourite's dressing room, one can count in rapid passing fourteen mirrors, and there may have been more. In the cloister the door of the Barbazana, which must have been once the chapter-house, was carved by the same sculptor as an Epiphany on the wall close by, who signed " Jaques Perut fit cest estoire." He also may have made *la Preciosa*. In 1349, a merchant of Pamplona named Martin fetched from Paris a marble Virgin which he gave to his native village of Huart-Araquil. This has disappeared only lately, and a photograph in Michel looks, in effect, native Spanish work, done under the prevalent French influence. The cloister had been begun under a French prince, Philippe d'Evreux, in the first half of the century, and finished by a French bishop, Arnold of Barbazan, toward the end of it.

(10) San Saturnino is the oldest Gothic church in Navarre, and belongs to the second half of the thirteenth century. The traveller will be spared bewilderment if told that this church, like S. Pedro at Olite and San Lorenzo at Lérida, has a whole church, larger and later though less lovely, growing out of it like a fungus.

(11) Restored past remedy.

CHAPTER XX

It is time, now that I have described so many Spanish Gothic buildings in detail, to undertake a somewhat more general classification of them, both in regard to their history and their style. Hitherto I have spoken of each building by itself, only endeavouring to give so clear and concise an account of each as was necessary in order that their general character might be understood. But this kind of account would be incomplete and almost useless without a more generalising and more systematic summary of the whole. And to this I propose to devote this chapter.

There are, indeed, few parts of Europe in which it is more easy to detect the influence of History upon Art than it is in Spain. I dismiss from consideration the period of the Visigothic rule, which lasted from A.D. 417 to 717; for though it is possible that some works of this age still exist, as *e.g.* part of the walls of Toledo, and the metal votive crowns of Guarrazar, they do not really come within the scope of my subject, inasmuch as there is no kind of evidence that they exercised any influence over the architecture of the Christian parts of the country after the Moorish interregnum.

From the first invasion by the Moors in A.D. 711 down to their expulsion from Granada in A.D. 1492, their whole history is mixed up with that of the Christians; and, as might be expected, so great was the detestation in which the two races held each other, that neither of them borrowed to any great extent from the art of the other, and accordingly we see two streams of art flowing as it were side by side at the same time, and often in the same district—a circumstance, as I need hardly say, almost, if not quite, unknown at the same period in any other part of Europe. The Mosque at Cordoba in the ninth century, the Alcazar and Giralda at Seville in the thirteenth, the Court of Lions in the Alhambra in the fourteenth, some of the houses in Toledo in the fifteenth century, are examples of what the Moors were building during the very period of the Middle Ages in which all the buildings which I have described and illustrated were being erected; the only exception to be made to this general statement being that when the Christians vanquished the Moors they usually continued to allow them to build somewhat in their own fashion—as, for example, they did in Toledo—whilst on the other hand, the Moors seem never to have imitated this example, though they were of course utterly unable to suppress all evidence in their work of any knowledge of Gothic buildings (1).

The reason of this was, no doubt, that throughout this period any contrast drawn between the Moors and Christians in regard to civilisation would generally, if not always, have been in favour of the former.   They were accomplished both in art and science: their architectural works would have been impossible except to a very refined people, and their scientific attainments are evidenced even to the present day by the system of artificial irrigation which they everywhere introduced, and which even now remains almost unaltered and unimproved.   The Christians, on the contrary, were warlike and hardy, and in the midst of constant wars had but scant time for the pursuit of art; and finally, when they had re-established their supremacy, they wisely allowed the Moors to remain under their rule when they would, and employed them to some extent on the works in which they could not fail to see that they excelled.

Again, the subdivision of the country into several kingdoms, administered under varying laws, owing no common allegiance to any central authority, and inhabited by people of various origin, might well be expected to leave considerable marks on the style of the buildings; though, at the same time, the antipathy which the inhabitants of all of them felt for the Moors rendered this cause less operative than it would otherwise have been.   Some portions of the country had never been conquered by the Saracens: such were the regions of the Pyrenees lying betwixt Aragon and Navarre, the Asturias, Biscay, and the northern portion of Galicia.[1]   And though it was by degrees that the other states freed themselves from their conquerors, it happened fortunately that the Christian successes generally synchronised as nearly as possible with that great development of Christian art which at the time covered all parts of Europe with the noblest examples of Pointed Architecture.   Toledo was recovered by the Christians in A.D. 1085, Tarragona in 1089, Zaragoza in 1118, Lérida in 1149, Valencia in 1239, Seville in 1248, whilst Segovia, Leon, Burgos, Zamora, and Santiago suffered

[1] *Morales*, lib. 12, cap. 76.

more or less from occasional irruptions of the Moors down to the beginning of the eleventh century, but from that date were practically free from molestation. By the middle of the fifteenth century the number of states into which the country had been divided was reduced to four, Castile, Aragon, Navarre, and the Moorish kingdom of Granada. Of these Aragon and Castile are the two of which I have seen the most, and, I may venture to add, those in which the History of Gothic Architecture in Spain is properly to be studied. For though it is true that Seville was recovered in the thirteenth century, and Cordoba about the same time, it is equally so that most of their buildings are Moorish or modern, the Gothic cathedral in the former not having been commenced until A.D. 1401, and the Moorish mosque in the latter still doing service as the Christian cathedral; and generally throughout the South of Spain, so far as I can learn, there are but few early Gothic buildings to be seen; whilst the late examples of the style were designed by the same architects, and in precisely the same style, as those which were erected in the parts of Spain which I have visited.

Of these two great divisions of the country, Aragon included the province of that name, together with Cataluña and Valencia; and owing to the great political freedom which the Catalans in particular enjoyed at an early period, to the vast amount of trade with Italy, the Mediterranean, and the East carried on along its extensive seaboard, and to its large foreign possessions —which included the Balearic Isles, Naples, Sicily, and Sardinia—the kingdom of Aragon possessed great wealth and power, and has left magnificent architectural remains.

The kingdom of Castile in course of time came to include, in addition to the two Castiles, Leon, Biscay, the Asturias, Galicia, Estremadura, Murcia, and Andalusia: and here there was not only a larger Spanish territory, but one peopled by a much more varied population than that of Aragon, and which naturally, I think, left a less distinct architectural impress than we see in the other.

Each of these kingdoms of course inherited a certain number of buildings erected under the rulers who had formerly held the country. It is possible that some portion of the walls of Toledo were built by the Goths; and at any rate we know by the fortunate discovery of the crowns at Guarrazar,[1] that, whatever may have been the state of the people in respect of other arts, that of working in precious metals was in an advanced state.

[1] *See* Vol. I., p. 302.

The Moors who succeeded them undertook undoubtedly large works in many parts of the country. They first built the Bridge of Alcantara across the Tagus at Toledo, and enclosed several towns with strong walls, among others Valencia and Talavera. They erected mosques and other public buildings, and before the Christian conquests of the eleventh century had no doubt imported much of a very advanced civilisation into the country which they ruled. The mosque " *Cristo de la Luz*," at Toledo, is a remarkable example of delicate skill in design and construction, and certainly in advance of the coeval Christian works. The ingenuity of the planning of the vaults is extreme, and though, at the same time, there is to our eyes an error in trying to do so much in so very small a space—nine vaulting compartments covered with varied vaults being contrived in a chamber only 21 feet square—it is to be observed that this is just one of the mistakes which arises from over-great education and skill, and is in marked contrast to the kind of design which we see in the simple, grave, but rude buildings which the less cultivated Christians were erecting at the same period.

Of the early Christian buildings I think there can be but little doubt that some at least still exist. There is no one year in Spanish history which can be used as that of the Norman Conquest is in England. Here people are accustomed to argue as though before and after A.D. 1066 two entirely different styles existed, with few, if any, marks of imitation of one from the other, though of course both must have had the same common Roman origin. This cannot be said in Spain; and where we find distinct and good evidence of the erection of churches in the ninth and tenth centuries, and the buildings still standing, with every architectural evidence of not being more modern than the eleventh century, I see not why we should doubt their greater antiquity. For looking to the solid way in which all these early works were built, it seems to be extremely unlikely that they should have required rebuilding so soon, or that, if they were rebuilt, not only should older stones with inscriptions recording the dates be inserted in the new walls, but also that no kind of evidence—documentary or other—should be forthcoming as to their reconstruction.

Several inscriptions on foundation-stones are given by Cean Bermudez,[1] and I regret never having been able to examine the buildings in which they occur. One of the earliest of these, Sta. Cruz de Cangas, is described as having a crypt (2); and a

[1] *Noticias de los Arq. de España*, i. 1-14.

long inscription, with the date 739, on a stone in it is given by Florez.[1] But I gather from Mr. Ford that the church has now been modernised. Cean Bermudez describes it as "strong, arched, and without ornament." Another church at Santiañes de Pravia has a labyrinthine inscription of A.D. 776, recording its erection by the King Silo (3). This church was very small, but had a Capilla mayor, two side chapels, a Crossing, and three naves; in fact, was in plan completely and exactly what the Spanish churches of the twelfth century were; and in this case it may, perhaps, be doubted whether the inscription referred to the church described, and was not taken from some older building. But the most interesting probably of these early churches is that of Sta. Maria de Naranco, near Oviedo. This is described and illustrated by Parcerisa,[2] and is undoubtedly a most remarkable example, though unfortunately I can find no reliable evidence as to its probably very early date. It seems to be planned with a view to a congregation outside the church joining in the worship within, there being galleries and open arches at the ends through which the altar might be seen. I confess that the details which I have seen, as well as the plans and views of this church, and of some portions of Oviedo Cathedral, to which a similarly early date is ascribed, do not give me the impression of work which is sufficiently distinct in style to be pronounced, as the Spanish writers have it, "obra de Godos," or work of the Goths. Yet it is undoubtedly of early date, and probably, at any rate, not later than the tenth or eleventh century. The detail is Romanesque, and the modification of plan in such a building seems to point to some special use for it rather than to some special age for its erection. On the other hand, there is some reason to suppose that the church at Santiago, which existed before the erection of the present cathedral, was very similar in its plan;[3] and if so, it would seem to fortify the claim for a very early date for Sta. Maria de Naranco.

I have thought it right to refer to these buildings on account of the great age ascribed to some of them; but I have done so with some hesitation, because I have not seen them myself, and it is impossible to form any good opinion upon such questions as arise in connection with them without careful personal examination.

It is a relief, therefore, to turn now to more certain ground, and to speak of churches which I have myself seen. I think

[1] *Esp. Sag.* xxxvii. 86-87.
[2] *Recuerdos y Bellezas de Esp., Ast. y Leon*, pp. 76 and 244.
[3] *See* the account of it in the *Historia Compostellana*, lib. i. cap. 78.

II P

the earliest of these are the two old churches of San Pablo and San Pere, at Barcelona, said to have been built in A.D. 914 and 983. I see no reason whatever to doubt these dates; at least it is improbable that if San Pablo was built in 914 it should have required rebuilding before the end of the next century; and no one I suppose would suggest a later date for it than this. In any case it is a valuable example. The ground-plan is cruciform, with a central lantern and three eastern apses; and the roofs are all covered with waggon vaulting and semi-domes. The plan is quite worthy of very attentive considera-tion, since with more or less modification of details it is that which more than any other may be said to have been popular in Spain in the twelfth and thirteenth centuries.

The question as to the quarter from whence it was derived is one of the greatest possible interest, and admits, I think, of but little doubt. It must be remembered that in considering these questions there are no Pyrenees. The towns on what is now the French side of the mountains were not then French; and such places as S. Elne were not only really Spanish, but so intimate was the connection existing between them and places at a greater distance (as e.g. Carcassonne), that for our purpose they may fairly be considered as being in the same country. The plan which we see in San Pablo del Campo is one which, having its origin in the East, spread to the north of Italy, was adopted largely in Provence, Auvergne, and Aquitaine, and was probably imported from thence to Barcelona. The central lantern and the three eastern apses are rather Byzantine than Romanesque in their origin; and though they are not common in Italy, they are occasionally met with; whilst in the parts of France just mentioned they are of frequent occurrence. The church which I coupled with this—San Pedro de las Puellas, in the same city—was consecrated in A.D. 983; it is also cruci-form, but has no chapels east of the transepts. Here, too, we have waggon-vaults, and a central dome.

The little church of San Daniel,[1] at Gerona, not much later probably in date than those first mentioned, is mainly remarkable for the apsidal north and south ends of its transepts. This common German arrangement is most rarely seen in Spain, and deserves especial notice. Here it is coupled with a central octagonal lantern, which has a very good effect. It is repeated very nearly in the church at Tarrasa, and so far as the apses

[1] See p. 109. I am not certain as to the dedication. I refer to the small church near San Pedro de los Galligans.

at the end of the transept, in the church of San Pedro, Gerona; and there is considerable similarity between the latter and the cathedral at Le Puy en Velay.

The succeeding century shows us the same type of plan becoming much more popular, and developed again in such close imitation of some foreign examples as to make it almost impossible to doubt its foreign origin. In these buildings the nave has usually a waggon-vault, and this is supported by half barrel-vaults in the aisles. There is no clerestory; a central lantern rises to a moderate height; and three eastern apsidal chapels open into the transepts, and are roofed with semi-domes. San Pedro, Huesca—probably not later in date than A.D. 1096-1150—is a remarkably good and early example of the class; and will be found to be extremely similar to some of the churches built about the same time on the other side of the Pyrenees. The plan of the steeple [1]—which is hexagonal—deserves special record; and it may not be amiss to observe, that at Tarbes, in the Pyrenees, the principal church not only has three eastern apses, but also a central octagonal steeple; and the same type is again repeated at San Pedro, Gerona—said to have been commenced in A.D. 1117—though here there are two apses on each side of the principal altar, and all the detail of the design is very Italian, or perhaps I should rather say Provençal, in its character. If we compare some of these churches with the earlier portions of the cathedral at Carcassonne, we shall find them to be almost identical in character and detail, and cannot avoid coming to the conclusion that they were all designed by the same school of architects or masons. Carcassonne Cathedral has a nave and aisles divided by columns formed of a square block, with an engaged shaft on each face: the covering of the nave is a waggon-vault with square ribs on its under side, and that of the aisles is a quadrant. It is, in fact, almost identical with San Pedro at Gerona. Go farther east, and in the church at Monistrol, between Le Puy and S. Etienne, the same design precisely will be seen in a remote French village far from Spain.

About this period a type of church varying but little from this became extremely common in Aquitaine and Auvergne; and this again evidently influenced at least one of the Spanish architects very much indeed: I allude to such churches as those of Notre Dame du Port, Clermont Ferrand, and S. Sernin at Toulouse—to name two only out of a large number. In these

---

[1] For illustration, etc., see p. 160 and Plate XXI., p. 161.

the ground-plan has usually nave and aisles, transepts, central lantern, and a chevet consisting of an apsidal choir with a surrounding aisle, and chapels opening into it, with spaces between each chapel. This plan, as I have already shown, is absolutely repeated at Santiago with such close accuracy that one can hardly avoid calling it merely a reproduction of S. Sernin at Toulouse.[1] It is the more remarkable because for some reason the early Spanish architects almost always avoided the erection of a regular chevet, and adhered strictly to their first plan of separate apsidal chapels on the eastern side of the transept. But whilst the early French chevet was only copied at Santiago, the other features of the French churches to which it belonged were copied not unfrequently—these are the waggon-vaulted nave, supported by half waggon-vaults over the aisles, and the central lantern. Gradually the design of these various parts was developed into a sort of stereotyped regularity, the instances of which extend so far across to the Peninsula as to be very surprising to those who have noticed the remarkable way in which local peculiarities generally confine themselves to the particular districts in which they originated. In course of time the groining was varied, and in place of the round barrel-vault, one of pointed section was adopted, and in place of it again the usual quadripartite vault. The examples which I have described, and which belong to this class, are—San Isidoro, Leon; San Vicente and San Pedro, Avila; several churches in Segovia; the Old Cathedral at Salamanca; Lérida old Cathedral; Sta. Maria, Benavente; and Santiago, la Coruña. Other churches of precisely similar character exist at Valdedios, near Gijon; Villanueva and Villa Mayor, near Oñis; San Antolin de Bedon, between Ribadella and Llanes; Sandoval, on the river Esla (4); San Juan de Amandi, and Tarbes, on the French side of the Pyrenees. Those in Segovia may be accepted as the best examples of their class, and they are so closely alike in all their details as to lead naturally to the belief that they were all executed at about the same period, and by the same workmen. The sack of the city by the Moors in 1071, when it is said that thirty churches were destroyed, seems to point to the period at which most of these churches were probably erected

---

[1] Both these churches are planned upon precisely the same system of proportions founded upon the equilateral triangle. Taking the width of the nave and aisles as the base, the apex of the triangle gives the centre from which the vault of the nave is struck; and all the subordinate divisions are also so exactly marked that there is hardly room for doubt that the system was distinctly recognised, and intentionally acted on.

to take the place of those that had been destroyed; and it seems to be certain that their leading features remained generally unaltered until about the end of the twelfth, if not far into the succeeding century. Indeed it is remarkable in Spain, just as it is in Germany, that the late Romanesque style, having once been introduced, retained its position and *prestige* longer than it did in France, and was only supplanted finally by designs brought again from France in a later style, instead of developing into it through the features of first-pointed, as was the case in England and France.

In this general similarity there are several subordinate variations to be observed. At Santiago, for instance, we see an almost absolute copy of the great church of S. Sernin, Toulouse, erected soon after its original had been completed. At Lugo it is clear, I think, that the architect of the cathedral copied, not from any foreign work, but from that at Santiago: he was probably neither acquainted with the church at Toulouse, nor any of its class. At San Vicente, Avila, again, though we see the Segovian eastern apses repeated with absolute accuracy, the design of the church is modified in a most important manner by the introduction of quadripartite vaulting in place of the waggon-vault, and the piercing the wall above the nave arcades with a regular triforium and clerestory. The same design was repeated with little alteration at San Pedro, in the same city; and in both it seems to me that we may detect some foreign influence, so rare was the introduction of the clerestory in Spanish buildings of the same age (5). Sta. Maria, la Coruña, again, though it evidently belongs to the same class as the cathedral at Santiago, has certain peculiarities which identify it absolutely with that variation which we see at Carcassonne and Monistrol:[1] for here there are narrow aisles; and the three divisions of the church are all covered with waggon-vaults, those at the sides resisting the thrust from the centre, and, owing to their slight width, exerting but slight pressure on the outer walls (6). The distinction between this design and one in which the aisles are covered with quadrant-vaults is very marked; and the erection of the cathedral at Santiago would not have been very likely to lead to the design of such a church as this.

In all these churches the proportion of the length of the choir to that of the nave is very small. Usually the apses are either simply added against the eastern wall of the transept,

[1] The Monistrol I refer to is the village between S. Etienne and Le Puy, and not the place of the same name at the foot of Montserrat, in Cataluña.

or else, whilst the side apses are built on this plan, the central apse is lengthened by the addition of one bay between the Crossing and the apse. It is very important to mark this plan, because, however it was introduced—whether in such churches as that of the abbey of Veruela, where the conventual arrangement of Cîteaux was imported, or in those earlier churches of which San Pedro, Gerona, may be taken as an example, in which from the first no doubt the choir was transferred to the nave, and the central apse treated only as a sanctuary—the result was the same on Spanish architecture and Spanish ritual. The Church found herself in possession of churches with short eastern apses and no choirs; and instead of retaining the old arrangement of the choir, close to and in face of the altar, she admitted her laity to the transept, divorced the choir from the altar, and invented those church arrangements which puzzle ecclesiologists so much. In our own country the same system to some extent at first prevailed; but our architects took a different course; they retained their choirs, prolonged them into the nave, and so contrived without suffering the separation of the clergy from the altar they serve, which we see in Spain.[1] In one great English church only has the Spanish system been adopted, and this, strangely enough, in the most complete fashion. Westminster Abbey, in fact, will enable any one to understand exactly what the arrangement of a Spanish church is. Its short choir, just large enough for a sumptuous and glorious altar, its Crossing exactly fitted for the stalls of the clergy and choir, its nave and transepts large enough to hold a magnificent crowd of worshippers, are all misused just as they would be in Spain; whilst the modern arrangements for the people—much more mistaken than they are there—involve the possession of the greater part of the choir by the laity, and the entire cutting off by very solid metal fences of all the worshippers in the transepts from the altar before which they are supposed to kneel, and the placing of the entire congregation between the priest and the altar.[2]

This digression will be excused when it is remembered how universally this tradition settled itself upon Spain, and how completely the perseverance in Romanesque traditions has affected

[1] *E.g.* S. Albans, Winchester Cathedral, S. Cross Chapel.

[2] The parallel holds good in very small matters. At Westminster the clergy and choir assemble in the choir, and begin the service so soon as the clock strikes. In several Spanish churches the same custom obtains. I think it would be a great gain if the metal screens across the transepts were moved so as to form the narrow central passage from the choir to the altar, so common in Spain. They would then have some meaning and use, which they certainly have not now.

her ritual arrangements, and with them her church architecture from the twelfth century until the present day. The long choirs which were naturally developed in England and France were never thought of there; the choir was merely the "Capilla mayor"—the chapel for the high altar; and the use of the nave as the people's church was ignored or forgotten as much as it was—very rightly—in some of our own old conventual churches, where the choir was prolonged far down into the nave, and the space for the people reduced to a bay or two only at its western end.

I must now bring this discussion to a close, and proceed with my chronological summary; and here the Abbey Church at Veruela ought to be mentioned, if regard be had to the date of its erection—*circa* A.D. 1146-71—though I must say that I have not been able to discover that it exercised any distinct influence upon Spanish buildings. It is in truth a very close copy of a Burgundian church of the period, built by French monks for an order only just established in Spain, under the direction probably of a French architect, and in close compliance with the rather strict architectural rules and restrictions which the Cistercians imposed on all their branches and members.[1] The character of the interior of this church is grand and simple, but at the same time rather rude and austere; but the detail of much of the exterior is full of delicacy; and the design of the chevet, with its central clerestory, and the surrounding aisle roofed with a separate lean-to roof, and the chapels projecting from it so subordinated as to finish below its eaves, recalls to memory some of the best examples of French Romanesque work.[2] The beauty and refinement of the little Chapter-house here lead me to suppose that it cannot be earlier than the end of the century.

There are some of these churches which require more detailed notice as being derived to some extent from the same models, but erected on a grander scale, and if documentary evidence can be trusted, whose erection was spread over so long a time as to illustrate very well indeed the slow progress of the development in art which we so often see in these Spanish buildings. The old cathedral at Salamanca was building from A.D. 1120 to 1178; Tarragona Cathedral was begun in 1131; Tudela, com-

[1] *See* p. 190.
[2] The design of this chevet is almost a repetition of that of the church at Avenières, near Laval, which is said to have been commenced as early as A.D. 1040, though most of it is certainly later by a century than this.

menced at about the same time, was completed in 1188; Lérida, whose style is so similar to that of the others as to make me class them all together, was not commenced until 1203, nor consecrated until 1278; and Valencia Cathedral, of which the south transept of the original foundation still remains, was not commenced until A.D. 1262. Yet if I except the early and Italian-looking eastern apse at Tarragona, most of the features of these churches look as though they were the design of the same man, and very nearly the same period; and it is altogether unintelligible how such a work, for instance, as Lérida Cathedral could be in progress at the same time as Toledo and Burgos, save upon the assumption that the thirteenth-century churches in an advanced Pointed style, such as these last, were erected by French workmen and artists imported for the occasion, and in a style far in advance of that at which the native artists had arrived.

Yet I think few churches deserve more careful study than these. I know none whose interiors are more solid, truly noble, or impressive; and these qualities are all secured not by any vast scale of dimensions—for, as will be seen by the plans, they are all churches of very moderate size—but by the boldness of their design, the simplicity of their sections, the extreme solidity of their construction, and the remarkable contrast between these characteristics and the delicacy of their sculptured decorations; they seem to me to be among the most valuable examples for study on artistic grounds that I have ever seen anywhere, and to teach us as much as to the power of Pointed art as do any churches in Christendom.

In all there is a very remarkable likeness in the section of the main clustered piers. They are composed usually of four pairs of clustered columns, two of them carrying the main arches, and two others supporting bold cross arches between the vaulting bays, whilst four shafts placed in the re-entering angles carry the diagonal groining ribs both of the nave and aisle. The arches are usually quite plain and square in section, the groining ribs are very bold and simple, and the whole decorative sculpture is reserved for the doorways and the capitals and bases of the columns. The windows have usually jamb-shafts inside and out; and the eastern apses are always covered with semi-dome vaults. Permanence being the one great object their builders set before them, they determined to dispense as far as possible with wood in their construction, and they seem to have laid stone roofs of rather flat pitch above the vaulting, and in some cases very ingeniously contrived with a view to preventing any possible lodgment of wet, and so any danger of decay. It may be said, perhaps, that fragments only of these roofs remain, so that after all timber roofs covered with tiles would have been equally good; but this is not so. The very attempt to build for everlasting is in itself an indication of the highest virtue on the part of the artist. The man who builds for to-day builds only to suit the miserable caprice of his patron, whilst he who builds for all time does so with a wholesome dread of exciting hostile criticism from those grave unprejudiced men who will come after him, and who will judge, not consciously perhaps, but infallibly, as to the honesty of his work. In England we have hardly a single attempt at anything of the kind, though in Ireland, in S. Cormack's Chapel at Cashel, we not only have an example, but one also that proves to us that we may build in this solid fashion, so that our work may endure in extraordinary perfection come what may—as it has there—of neglect, of desolation, and of desecration! Yet of all the virtues of good architecture none are greater than solidity and permanence, and we in England cannot therefore afford to affect any of our insular airs of superiority over these old Spanish artists!

Look also at the thorough way in which their work was done. The Chapter-houses, the cloisters, the subordinate erections of these old buildings, are always equal in merit to the churches themselves, and I really know not where—save in some of the English abbeys which we have wickedly ruined and destroyed— we are to find their equals. Nothing can be more lovely than such cloisters as those of Gerona or Tarragona, few things grander than that desecrated one at Lérida, whilst the Chapter-house at Veruela, and the doorways at Valencia, Lérida, and Tudela, deserve to rank among the very best examples of mediæval art.

There are yet two other grand early churches to be mentioned which do not seem to range themselves under either of the divisions already noticed, and which yet do not at all belong to the list of churches of French design with which my notice of thirteenth-century Spanish work must of necessity conclude. These are the cathedrals of Sigüenza and Avila.[1] Both of these are, so far as I can see, but to a slight extent founded upon other examples. Sigüenza Cathedral seems to have had originally three eastern apses: the plan is simple and grand, and its scale, either really, or at any rate in effect, very magnificent

[1] I might perhaps add Tarazona Cathedral to this list (?).

The great size of the clustered columns, their well-devised sections, the massive solidity of the arches, the buttresses, and all the details, make this church rank, so far at least as the interior is concerned, among the finest Spanish examples of its age. At Avila, on the other hand, we see a remarkable attempt to introduce somewhat more of the delicacy and refinement of the first-pointed style; and just as if the architect had been exasperated by the obligation under which he lay to end his chevet within the plain, bald, windowless circular wall projecting from the city ramparts which was traced out for him, we find him indulging in delicate detached shafts, a double aisle round the chevet, and subsequently in such strange as well as daring expedients in the way of the support of the groining and the flying buttresses, as could hardly have been ventured on by any one really accustomed to deal with the various problems which the constructors of groined roofs ordinarily had before them. I venture therefore to place these two churches at Sigüenza and Avila among the most decidedly Spanish works of their day; I see no distinct evidence of foreign influence in any part of their design, and they seem to me to be fairly independent on the one hand of the early Spanish style of Tarragona, Lérida, Salamanca, and Segovia, and on the other of the imported French style of Toledo, Burgos, and Leon.

And now I must say a few words on the three last-named churches. I have already expressed my opinion as to their origin, which seems to me to be most distinctly and undoubtedly French. The history of the Spanish Church at the end of the twelfth and beginning of the thirteenth century, points with remarkable force to such a development as we see here. What more natural than that the country which looked, on the recovery from its troubles—on the expulsion of the Saracen—to its neighbour the French Church to supply it with bishops for its metropolitan and other sees—should look also to it for a supply of that instruction in art which had grown and flourished there, whilst men were fighting and striving with all their might and main here? And what is there more natural than that French architects, sent over for such works, should first of all plan their buildings on the most distinctly French plan, with French mouldings and French sculpture; and then—as we see both at Burgos and Toledo, in the singular treatment of the triforia—should have gradually succumbed to the national and in part Moresque influences by which they were surrounded? At Leon the evidences of imitation of French work are so remarkable, that no one capable of forming a judgment can doubt the fact; and if at Burgos and Toledo they are not quite so strong, the difference is slight, and one only of degree. I have already spoken upon these points in describing the churches in question; and here I will only repeat that, as the features of which I speak are exceptional and not gradually developed, it is as certain as anything can be that their style was not invented at all in Spain. We have only to remember the fact, that at the same time that Lérida Cathedral was being built, those of Toledo and Burgos were also in progress, whilst that of Valencia was not commenced until much later, to realise how fitful and irregular was the progress of art in Spain. It is, in fact, precisely what we see in the history of German art. There, just as in Spain, the Romanesque and semi-Romanesque styles remained long time in quiet possession of the field, and it was not until the marvellous power and success of the architects of Amiens and Beauvais excited the German architects to emulation in Cologne Cathedral, that they moved from their Romanesque style into the most decided and well-developed geometrical Gothic. And just as Cologne Cathedral is an exotic in Germany, so are those of Burgos, Leon, and Toledo in Spain; so that, whilst Spaniards may fairly be proud of the glory of possessing such magnificent works of art, their pride ought to be confined to that of ownership, and should not extend to any claim of authorship.

The demands of these three great churches upon our admiration are very different. The palm must be awarded to Toledo, which, as I have shown, equals, if it do not surpass, all other churches in Christendom in the beauty and scale of its plan. Undoubtedly, however, it lacks something of height, whilst later alterations have shorn it also of some of its attractiveness in design, the original triforium and clerestory remaining only in the choir. Nevertheless, as it stands, with all its alterations for the worse, it is still one of the most impressive churches I have ever seen, and one in which the heart must be cold indeed that is not at once moved to worship by the awfulness of the place.

I have already, in my account of this great church, entered somewhat fully into a description of the peculiarities of its plan, and the evidence which they afford of its foreign origin. The unusual arrangement of the chevet, in which the vaulting bays in both the surrounding aisles of the presbytery are made of nearly the same size,[1] by the introduction of triangular vaulting

[1] *See* ground-plan, Vol. I. Plate XIV. p. 346.

compartments, and in which the chapels of the outer aisle are alternately square and circular in plan, renders it, however, not merely an example of a French school, but one of the very highest interest and peculiarity. There is no church, so far as I know, similarly planned, though some are extremely suggestive as to the school in which its architect had studied. The cathedral at Le Mans has triangular vaulting compartments in the outer of its two aisles, arranged somewhat as they are at Toledo, but with inferior skill, the aisle next the central apse having the unequal vaulting compartments, which have been avoided here; but the surrounding chapels in these two examples are utterly unlike. Notre Dame, Paris, also has triangular vaulting compartments, but they are utterly different in their arrangement from those in Toledo Cathedral.[1] Neither of these examples, in short, proves much as to the authorship of the latter. A far more interesting comparison may, however, be instituted between the plan of this chevet and that rare example of a mediæval architect's own handiwork, which has been handed down to us in the design for a church made by Wilars de Honecort, under which he wrote the inscription, " Deseure est une glize a double charole. K vilars de honecort trova & pieres de corbie." In English: " Above is (the presbytery of) a church with a double circumscribing aisle, which Wilars de Honecort and Peter de Corbie contrived together."[2] In this plan we find these two old architects, not only introducing alternate square and circular chapels round their apse, but also an arrangement of the groining which looks almost as though they were acquainted with some such arrangement as that of the triangular vaulting compartments of Le Mans and Toledo. The diligent and able editors of Wilars de Honecort—M. Lassus and Professor Willis— say that no such plan as this is anywhere known to exist; and I believe they were nearly, though not, as I have shown, absolutely correct in this assertion. At Toledo they still exist in part, and once, no doubt, existed all round the chevet; and it may well, I think, be a question whether Peter, the architect of Toledo, had not studied in the French school, and with these very men— Wilars de Honecort and Peter de Corbie—who, " inter se disputando," as they wrote on this plan, struck out this original scheme. At the same time it will be seen, on comparison of

---

[1] The round portion of the Temple Church, London, has its aisle groined with alternate bays of square and triangular outline. The latter have no ribs, and are constructed differently from those at Toledo.

[2] Facsimile of the *Sketch-book of Wilars de Honecort*. Eng. edit. Edited by Professor Willis. Plate XXVIII.

the two plans, that if he derived his idea from his brethren, he developed it into a much more scientific and perfect form.

It will be recollected that though I claim a French origin for Toledo Cathedral, I allow that it is not only possible, but probable, that, as the work went on, either Spaniards only were employed on it, or (which is more likely) that the French architect forgot somewhat of his own early practice, and was affected by the work of other kind being done by native artists around him. The evidence of this change is mainly to be seen in the triforium and clerestory of the choir and transepts.

The religious gloom of the cathedral at Toledo is strangely different from the religious brightness of that of Leon; for in the latter, where the sole end of the architect seems to have been the multiplication of openings and the diminution of solid points of support, the artist in stained glass has fortunately come to the rescue, and filled the windows with some of the most gorgeous colouring ever seen, so as to redeem it from its otherwise utter unfitness for its work in such a climate as that even of Northern Spain. I have already said that this church has not stood well. It was, in truth, too daring, and has in consequence failed to some extent. Yet, in spite of this, I cannot but admire immensely the hardihood and the skill of the man who could venture—knowing as much as he did—upon such a daring work as this; and I know not to whom to liken him so well as to the first architect of Beauvais Cathedral, though certainly the work at Leon has not failed so conspicuously as it did there. In both these churches the arrangement of the ground-plan of the chevet is so nearly similar as to allow of their being classed together as at any rate works of the same style, if they are not indeed both works of the same school. Both have pentagonal chapels round the apse, and square chapels to the west of them, and they were built within a few years of each other.[1] The detail at Leon is almost all very French, and the windows of its clerestory are, in their general design as well as in their detail, almost reproductions of those at Saint Denis, in the peculiar mode adopted there of strengthening the principal monials by doubling the smaller monials in width, without any change in their thickness.

The cathedral at Burgos is certainly in most respects a somewhat inferior work to that at Leon. It, too, is French; but its architect was familiar not with the best examples of French art in the Ile de France and Champagne, but only, I think, with

---

[1] Beauvais Cathedral was commenced in A.D. 1225.

those of the somewhat inferior Angevine school. The plan of this chevet[1] was probably never so fine as that of Leon, though it was very similar to it. Here, too, I think, we see some local influence exerting itself in the design of the triforia throughout the church, whereas at Leon the original scheme seems from first to last to have been faithfully adhered to. But if Burgos Cathedral is far inferior in scale to that of Toledo, and somewhat so to that of Leon in skilfulness of design, it is in all other respects equally deserving of study, and is in its general effect at present far more Spanish than either of them. The many additions have to a great extent, it is true, obscured the original design; but the result is so picturesque, and so far more interesting than an unaltered church usually is, that one cannot well find fault. The main failure of the design is the smallness of the scale, and the loss of internal effect owing to the alteration of the primitive arrangements by the placing of the Coro in the nave, and the leaving of the ample choir unoccupied save by the altar at its eastern end.

The succeeding great division of Gothic art is much more distinctly marked and more uniform throughout Spain, whilst at the same time it is even less national and peculiar. There are in truth very considerable remains of fourteenth-century works, though, perhaps, no one grand and entire example of a fourteenth-century building. All these examples are extremely similar in style; and I think, on the whole, more akin in feeling and detail to German middle-pointed than to French. The west front of Tarragona Cathedral, the lantern and north transept of Valencia Cathedral, the chapel of San Ildefonso, the Puerta of Sta. Catalina, and the screen round the Coro at Toledo, Sta. Maria del Mar and the cathedral at Barcelona, the chevet of Gerona Cathedral, the north doorway and nave clerestory of Avila Cathedral, and the cloisters of Burgos and Veruela, afford, with many others, fair examples of the design and details of churches of this period. The traceries are generally elaborately geometrical and rather rigid and ironlike in their character, the carving fair but not especially interesting—dealing *usque ad nauseam* in diapers of lions and castles—and the whole system of design one of line and rule rather than of heart and mind. Yet, in this, Spain reflected much more truly than before what was passing elsewhere in the fourteenth century; and exhibited, just

---

[1] *See* the plan, Vol. I., Plate I., p. 40. The chapel marked B is, I think, the only original one; and this repeated five times will probably give the exact plan of the original chevet.

as did Germany, France, and England [1] at the same moment, the fatal results of the descent from poetry and feeling in architecture to that skill and dexterity which are still in the nineteenth century, as they were in the fourteenth, regarded—and most wrongly regarded—as the elements of art most to be striven after and most taught. Art, in truth, was ceasing to be vigorous and natural, and becoming rapidly tame and academical!

Yet if these works are not very national, they are at any rate most interesting and deserve most careful study. He was no mean artist who made the first design for Barcelona Cathedral, who completed the chevet of Gerona, or who designed the steeple at Lérida, or the cloisters of Burgos, Leon, or Veruela. At this time indeed art was cosmopolitan, and all Europe seems to have been possessed with the same love for geometrical traceries, for crockets, for thin delicate mouldings, and for sharp naturalesque foliage, so that no country presents anything which is absolutely new, or unlike what may be seen to some extent elsewhere. There are perhaps only two features of this period which I need record here, and these are, first, the reproduction of the octagonal steeple, which, as we have seen, was a most favourite type of the Romanesque builders; and, secondly, the introduction of that grand innovation upon old precedents, the great unbroken naves, groined in stone, lighted from windows high up in the walls, and inviting each of them its thousands to worship God or to hear His word in such fashion as we, who are used to our little English town churches, can scarcely realise to ourselves. [2] But on this point I will say no more because its consideration more naturally arises in the succeeding period, in which the problem was more distinctly met and more satisfactorily settled.

The survey of Spanish art in the fifteenth century is, I think, on the whole, more gratifying than it is in the fourteenth. In the earliest churches, as the models from which they were derived were first of all built in hot climates, the windows were small and few, the walls thick, the roofs flat-pitched, and the whole construction eminently suited to the physical circumstances of the country. But these models, having been taken to

---

[1] The commerce of the south of Spain with England was considerable; and it is just possible that some of the middle-pointed work in Valencia may have an English origin. The English sovereigns encouraged the Catalan traders by considerable immunities to frequent their ports during the fourteenth century.—Macpherson, *Annals of Commerce*, i. 502, etc.

[2] I speak only of town churches here: our little English village churches are the most perfect in the world, so thoroughly characteristic, and at the same time so suitable for their work, that we may always study them with greater gain than any others elsewhere in Europe.

the north of Europe, and there largely and perhaps thoughtlessly copied, in spite of the vast difference of climate, were soon found to be unfitted for their purpose, and were consequently, in due course of time, developed into that advanced style of Gothic of which the main characteristic is the size and beauty of its windows. Of course this development was just that of all others which ought not to have been tolerated at all under a southern sun; and we must allow the fifteenth-century architects the credit of having discovered this, and of having returned very much to the same kind of design as that in which their thirteenth-century predecessors had indulged.

The examples of this age which I have described will have given a fair idea of their main characteristics. The magnificent size, the solid construction, and the solemn internal effect of such churches as those of Segovia, Salamanca, Astorga, Huesca, Gerona, Pamplona, and Manresa, would be sufficient to mark the period which produced them as one of the most fertile and artistic the world has ever seen. We may approach such buildings full of prejudice in favour of an earlier style of architecture, of a purer form of art; but we cannot leave them without acknowledging that at least they are admirable in their general effect, and if not conceived in the very purest art, still conceived in what is at any rate a true form of art. By the time in which they were erected, Spain had become far more powerful than ever before; she was quite free from all fear of the Moors, and was so rich as to be able to expend vast sums of money in works of art and luxury. She had also more trade and communication with her neighbours; and no doubt their customs and their schools of art had become so familiar to Spanish architects as to lead naturally to some imitation of them in their works. In their later works we find, at any rate, a development beyond that point at which Spaniards had before arrived, and noticeably an affection for the French chevet or apsidal choir surrounded by a procession-path and group of chapels. This arrangement, which, when it was adopted at Veruela, Santiago, Burgos, Leon, and Toledo, was evidently only adopted because the architects of these churches were French, was a favourite one of the artists of the fifteenth century. Huesca and Astorga alone of the great churches mentioned just now are founded upon the old Spanish type of parallel apses at the east end: the others are all founded upon that of the French chevet with some modifications in the details of their design. Of these, few are more interesting than that which we see in the cathedral at Pamplona, the chevet of which is, to the best of my belief, unique in its curious use of the equilateral triangle in the plan. This is perhaps the most novel modification of the French plan; but among all of them it is impossible not to award the palm, most decidedly, to the really magnificent works of the Catalan School. In other parts of Spain the great churches of this period had no very special or marked character; nothing which clearly showed them to be real developments in advance of what had been done before or elsewhere. In Cataluña, on the other hand, there was a most marked impulse given by a Mallorcan artist at the latter part of the fourteenth century; and to the influence of his school we owe some of, I suppose, the most important mediæval churches to be seen in any part of Europe. Their value consists mainly in the success with which they meet the problem of placing an enormous congregation on the floor in front of one altar, and within sight and hearing of the preacher. The vastest attempt which we have made in this direction sinks into something quite below insignificance when compared with such churches as Gerona Cathedral, Sta. Maria del Mar, Barcelona, or the Collegiata at Manresa. The nave of the former would hold some two thousand three hundred worshippers, that of the next hard upon three thousand, and that of the third about two thousand. Their internal effect is magnificent in the extreme; and if, in their present state, their external effect is not so fine, it must be remembered, first of all, that they have all been much mutilated, and, in the next place, that their architects had evidently mastered the first great necessity in church-building—the successful treatment of the interior. In these days it is impossible to say this too strongly: men build churches everywhere in England, as though they were only to be looked at, not worshipped in; and forget, in fact, that the sole use of art in connection with religion is the exaltation of the solemnity of the ritual, and the oblation of our best before the altar, and not the mere pleasing of men's eyes with the sweet sights of spires rising among trees, or gables and traceried windows standing out amid the uninteresting fabrics of nineteenth-century streets!

In our large towns in England there is nothing we now want more than something which shall emulate the magnificent scale of these Catalan churches. They were built in the middle ages for a large manufacturing or seafaring population; and we have everywhere just such masses of souls to be dealt with as they were provided for. But then, of course, it is useless to recommend such models if they are only to be used as we use our churches, for four or five hours on Sundays, instead of, as these Spanish churches were and still are, for worship at all sorts of hours, not only on Sundays, but on every day of the week also. When English Churchmen are accustomed to see churches thoroughly well used; when no church is without its weekly, no great church without its daily Eucharist; and when they see none, great or small, without their doors open daily both for public and private prayer—then, and not till then, can we expect that they will allow architects any chance of emulating the glories achieved by these old men. Till then we shall hold fast to our insular traditions of little town churches and subdivided parishes, and shall doubt the advantages of enormous naves, of colleges of clergy working together, and of those other old Catholic appliances, which must be tried fully and fairly before we give up in despair the attempt to Christianise the working population of our large cities.

The general idea of these great fifteenth-century churches has no doubt already been grasped by my readers. Worship at the altar appears to me to be the key to the design and arrangement of many of them, for nowhere else in Europe, I suppose, can we find a church on so very moderate a scale as the Cathedral at Barcelona crowded in the way it is with altars, and so planned and fitted up as to make it absolutely useless as a place of gathering for a large number of persons at one service. But if this multiplication of side altars was here carried to excess, one of the most remarkable examples of an attempt to glorify the high altar, and at the same time to provide for one enormous and united congregation, is unquestionably that which is presented by Sta. Maria del Mar in the same city. This church has its prototype at Palma in Mallorca, and I much regret that I have never yet been able to visit that island, for, so far as I can learn, it seems that the mainland owed much to it in the way of architectural development, and that some of the finest examples of the Catalan style in this age are still to be seen there.

The special devotion to the altar service which is exemplified in Barcelona Cathedral led naturally to other architectural developments. Such are the remarkable church of Santo Tomás at Avila, with its western choir and eastern altar both raised in galleries, and its arrangement for the congregation of worshippers below. Such again is the church of El Parral, Segovia, with its deep western gallery for the choir, its dark, gloomy, and austere nave, and the concentration of light and window round the altar. Indeed, the institution of the western gallery, so common—I might almost say so universal—in small churches at this period in Spain, arose from the same feeling as did the removal of the choir into the nave in the larger churches. The object of all these changes was to give the people access to the altar, and usually they seem to have been made upon the assumption that no one would care to assist at the services in the choir itself. I am very much inclined to think that the rise of this feeling was to a great extent an accident, and the result of the fact that almost all the early Spanish churches were founded on models in which the eastern limb of the Cross was so very short that the choir or Chorus Cantorum must almost always have occupied the eastern part of the nave, or the Crossing under the central lantern. This must have been almost a necessity in such cathedrals as those of Lérida, Tudela, and Sigüenza: whilst in others, as those of Tarragona, Tarazona, and Avila, the space must always have been cramped, though a choir might have been accommodated. Of the larger churches Burgos alone has a really large constructional choir. In Toledo it is very short, and in Leon certainly below what we usually find in a French church of the same age and pretensions.

The cathedrals of Segovia and Salamanca are the two latest great Gothic churches in Spain, and in some respects among the grandest; and here, as might be expected, the Spanish custom as to the position of the Coro had become so thoroughly fixed and invariable, that the choir proper is very short, and built only for the altar. The plan of Segovia Cathedral is very fine and well proportioned; whilst that of Salamanca has been unhappily ruined by the erection of a square east end, in place of the apse which was first of all intended: and this, in place of emulating at all the noble design of any of our English eastern ends, is contrived with but little skill, the aisle returning across behind the altar, whilst beyond it to the east there is a line of chapels similar to those beyond the aisles.

Of the later styles I need say but little. They are not Gothic, and this is a summary of Gothic architecture only; yet it is interesting to look into their history if only to notice how curious the fact is that at the same time that men like Berruguete were designing in the most thoroughly Renaissance style, Juan Gil de Hontañon was still painfully superintending the erection of a great Gothic cathedral. The remarkably Gothic staircase to the Hall at Christ Church, Oxford (A.D. 1640); the Gothic window traceries of Stone Church, Kent, of the same date; the rebuilding of Higham Ferrers steeple by the great

Archbishop Laud, and of the spire of Lichfield Cathedral by good Bishop Hacket in 1669, are well-known instances of the remarkable love for Christian art which Englishmen retained long after the fashion for Pagan and Renaissance art had set in. And it is not a little interesting to find the same contest going on in Spain, and the same love for the old and hallowed form of art exhibited.

I cannot see much—I might almost say I can see nothing—to admire in the works of the Renaissance school in Spain. It was in their time that the discovery of America raised the country to the very summit of her prosperity, and right nobly did she acknowledge her duty by the offerings she made of her wealth. Few Spanish churches are without some token of the magnificent liberality of the people at this time, and one is obliged to acknowledge it in spite of the horror with which one regards the works they did, and the damage which their execution did to the older buildings to which they were added.

It would be dreary work to follow the stream of Spanish art down by Berruguete and Herrera to Churriguera and so on to our own time; and the only fact of interest that I know is that the old scheme of cruciform church with a central lantern is still the most popular, and that down to the present time almost every modern church has been so planned, with a lantern dome rising from above the intersection of the nave and transepts.

Fortunately, down to this time the tide of " Restoration " has hardly reached Spain, and one is able therefore to study the genuine old records in their old state. There are no Salisbury Chapter-houses or Worcester Cathedrals to puzzle us as to whether anything about them is old, or whether all may be dismissed or discussed as if it were perfectly new; and so it affords a field for study the value of which cannot be overrated, and which ought not to be neglected (8). It must not be supposed that this field of study is limited to the general scheme of the churches. On the contrary, their fittings and furniture, their appendages and dependent buildings, are unsurpassed in interest by those of any other land, and in addition to these there are several other heads under which my subject naturally presents itself.

First among them is that of church furniture. No country is perhaps now so rich in this respect as Spain. Few of course—if any—of her churches retain their old furniture in its original place earlier in date than the fifteenth century. It is true that the magnificent baldachin and Retablo at Gerona, the screens round the Coro at Toledo, and the beautiful painted Retablo in the old cathedral at Salamanca, are earlier than this; but these are exceptions to the rule. The great glory of the country in this respect are such Retablos—rich in sculpture, covered with gold and colour, and in paintings of no mean merit, and lofty and imposing beyond anything of the kind ever seen elsewhere— as those of Toledo Cathedral or the Carthusian Church of Miraflores. In these one hardly knows whether to admire most the noble munificence of the founders, or the marvellous skill and dexterity of the men who executed them. It is not only that they are rich and costly, but much more, that all the work in them is usually good of its kind, and far finer than the work of the same age and style which we see in the Netherlands and Germany. The choir stalls, again, are often magnificent. Nothing can be more interesting than the contemporary chronicle of the capture of Granada which we see in the lower range of stalls at Toledo; they are full of character and spirit, and represent what was no doubt felt to be a truly religious enterprise, with at least as much fidelity as any view of our own military operations at the present day ever attains to. Other churches have choir fittings, like those of Zamora, full of curious interest to the student of Christian iconography; like those at Palencia, remarkable for the exceedingly elaborate character of their traceries and panelling; and like those of Gerona, valuable for the fine character of the rare fourteenth-century woodwork which has been re-arranged in the modern Coro. Turn again from the choir stalls to the other fittings of the choir. Seldom elsewhere shall we see the old columns for the curtains at the side of the altar still standing as they do at Manresa. Nowhere shall we see such magnificent choir lecterns, in brass as that of Toledo, or in wood as that of Zamora; nowhere else such pretty and sweet-sounding wheels of bells for use at the elevation of the Host; nowhere, perhaps, so many old organs, many of which, if not Mediæval, are at any rate not far from being so; nowhere else so many or such magnificent Rejas or metal screens and parcloses, as in this country. In every one of these works Spanish workmen excelled, because they devoted themselves to them. We have lists of men who made screens, of others who carved the choir stalls, of others who made Retablos, and of others, again, who painted and gilded them. Each class of men is named after the furniture to the execution of which they devoted themselves, and occasionally individuals rose to rare eminence from this kind of work. The time was late, indeed, when it happened, but see

how Borgoña and Berruguete strove for mastery over their work
on the upper stalls at Toledo, or how the poor Matias Bonifé, at
Barcelona, was bound to carve no beasts or subjects on his stalls,
to which we may suppose he was addicted; and how his successor
died of distress because the Chapter did not like the pinnacles
he added to the canopies; and consider how people interested
themselves in the matter, how they were excited in the contest
between Borgoña and Berruguete, and no doubt in the others
also, and we see at once how different was the position which
these men occupied from that which, so far as we know, their
contemporaries in England held.

The monuments in the Spanish churches are not the least of
their glories. From one of the earliest and finest, that of Bishop
Maurice at Burgos, there is a sequence illustrating almost every
variety of Gothic down to that exquisite Renaissance monument
of the son of Ferdinand and Isabella at Avila, in which—in
spite of the date and style—the old spirit still breathes an air
of grace, refinement, and purity over the whole work. Such
chapels as those which enshrine these monuments—that of
the Constable at Burgos, of Santiago at Toledo, of Miraflores
near Burgos—are well fitted to hold the most magnificent of
memorials; for were it not that such a work as the tomb of
Juan II. and Elizabeth is almost unmatched anywhere for the
skill and delicacy of its workmanship, and that some of the
others are almost equally sumptuous, the chapels within which
they are erected would appear to be in themselves the noblest
remembrances of the dead.

Of the dependent buildings of these great churches I have
had to speak over and over again. The ground-plans which I
have given will show how complete they usually are. Their
arrangement varies very much. The cloister, for instance, is on
the north-east at Tarragona; the north at Sigüenza, Toledo, and
Leon; the west at Lérida and Olite; the south at Santiago,
Palencia, Tudela, and Veruela; and the south-east at Burgos.
The Chapter-houses by no means always stand on the east of the
cloister, though they usually retain the old triple entrance, and
the remaining buildings seem to vary very much in the positions
assigned to them.

The roofing of Spanish churches has been incidentally noticed
in various places throughout this volume. It was almost always
of stone. So far as the interior roofing is concerned, the changes
that are seen are of course very much the same as those which
marked the vaults of most other parts of Europe at the same

period. At first the cylindrical Roman vault, then the same vault supported by quadrant vaults over the aisles, then simple quadripartite vaults, and finally vaults supported on very elaborate systems of lierne ribs. But there are some minor peculiarities in these vaults which deserve record. The waggon vaults generally have transverse ribs on their under side, and occur usually in buildings in which all the apsidal terminations are roofed with semi-domes—and they are sometimes (as in Lugo Cathedral, and Sta. Maria, la Coruña) pointed. The early quadripartite vaulting is generally remarkable for the large size of the vaulting-ribs, and for the very bold transverse arches which divide the bays. Ridge-ribs are hardly ever introduced, and the ridge is generally very little out of the level. The vaults of Leon Cathedral are filled in with tufa in order to diminish the weight, but I have not noticed any similar contrivance elsewhere. Down to the end of the fourteenth century the vaulting seldom if ever had any but diagonal, transverse, and wall-ribs; and even in many of the works of the succeeding century the same judicious simplicity is seen. But usually at this time it became the fashion to introduce a most complicated system of lierne ribs, covering the whole surface of the vault, dividing it up into an endless number of small and irregularly shaped compartments, and very much damaging its effect. My ground-plans of Segovia and (new) Salamanca Cathedrals show how extremely elaborate these later vaults very frequently were. There is another form of vault which is not unfrequently met with: this occurs where a square vaulting bay is groined with an octagonal vault. In these examples a pendentive is formed at each angle of the square, and thus the octagonal base is formed for the vault. Examples of this are to be seen in the Chapels of San Ildefonso and Santiago at Toledo Cathedral, in three of the late Chapels at Burgos Cathedral, and in the Chapter-house of Pamplona Cathedral. The fashion for this vault arose probably from the custom which had obtained of building central lanterns, which were frequently finished with octagonal stages, and consequently vaulted with octagonal vaults. So far as to the internal roofing. The evidence I have found of the old external roofing in some cases is even more interesting. It is clear that many of the early churches were intended from the first to be built entirely of stone in the roof as well as in the walls. Avila, Toledo, and Lérida Cathedrals, and the Collegiata at Manresa, still retain some of their old stone covering; and though it is true that in none of these cases has the attempt to construct an absolutely imperishable building been perfectly successful, it appears to me that the workmen and architects who attempted to carry such plans into execution deserve all our admiration. I have described these roofs in the course of my notes upon the churches in which they occur, and here I need only refer to my descriptions and illustrations.

In sculpture Spain is not so rich as France, but on the whole probably more so than England. The best complete Gothic work that I have seen is at Leon; but it offers no variety whatever from the best of the same age in France. I have given the various iconographical schemes, so far as I could manage to do so, in describing the several works, and here I will only repeat that, to my mind, the triple western doors at Santiago[1] —completed in A.D. 1188—are among the finest works of their age, and deserving of the greatest care and tenderness on the part of their guardians. Most of us are conscious how much good sculpture adds to the interest of good architecture. Usually, however, we spread our modern sculpture too lavishly in all directions if we have the money to spend. But even in this there may be too much of a good thing; the mind and eye become satiated, and sicken; and not half the real pleasure is felt in seeing some modern works that would be if the work had been somewhat less lavishly applied, somewhat more thoughtfully, or as at Santiago, in one spot, leaving the whole of the rest of the church in its stern, rude simplicity.

The domestic architecture of Spain in the middle ages is, as might be expected, very much less important than the religious architecture. Probably the wealth of the fifteenth and sixteenth centuries was even more damaging to the former than it was to the latter. At any rate, no country—Italy excepted—contains a greater number of showy Renaissance palaces in all its principal towns than Spain does; and there can be little doubt that they took the place of Gothic houses to a very considerable extent. Either I was very unlucky, or, if I saw what is to be seen, I must pronounce Spain to be unusually barren of old examples of domestic buildings. Of the twelfth and thirteenth centuries I have hardly seen a single example, save the house which I have described at Lérida; whilst of the two following centuries, the best examples seem to be confined very much to

---

[1] *See* Vol. I., frontispiece. In so small an engraving—putting out of view the extreme difficulty of getting a faithful transcript of a careful sketch of sculpture—it is impossible to do justice to such a work; and I must ask my readers rather to accept my statement then to pass judgment by aid only of the illustration.

the Mediterranean seaboard. In this part of Spain are the simple houses lighted by *ajimez* windows, which I have described and illustrated; they extend all along the coast from Perpiñan to Valencia, and are usually so much alike as to produce the impression that they are all made from the same design. Later than this, the public buildings at Barcelona and Valencia, the palace of the Dukes del Infantado at Guadalajara, the museum and other convents at Valladolid, the house of the Constable Velasco at Burgos, and the great hospital at Santiago, are no doubt magnificent examples of their class. In these the buildings are generally arranged round courtyards, which are surrounded by passages opening to the court, and lighted either with open arches or with traceried windows. Rich and noble as some of these buildings are, there is little that is interesting or picturesque in them, and they seldom attain the degree of importance of which one would suppose such an architectural scheme skilfully treated would admit. Their date is rarely earlier than *circa* A.D. 1450, and the detail of their mouldings and sculpture is consequently of the latest kind of Gothic. There is, however, a rude barbaric splendour in some of the courts or *patios* at Valladolid, where this kind of building is seen to perhaps greater advantage than anywhere else.

The castles of Spain deserve, apparently, much more attention, and are in every way more important, than the other domestic buildings. Those at Olite, Segovia, and Medina del Campo have been already described; and there is, no doubt, a vast number of buildings of somewhat similar character to be seen, especially in those parts of the country which formed for a time the frontier land between the Moorish and Christian kingdoms. Generally, they are remarkable for the unbroken surface of their lofty walls, crowned with picturesque and complicated projecting turrets at the angles. The scale on which they are built is magnificent, and their walls still stand almost untouched by the ages of neglect from which they have suffered. In the same way the walls which encircle the Spanish cities are often still so perfect throughout their circuit that it is almost possible to persuade oneself that they have been untouched for three hundred years. Avila, Lugo, Segovia, Toledo, Pamplona, Astorga, Gerona, Tarragona, and many other towns are girt round with so close an array of tower and wall as to make them still look fit for defence. The age of these walls varies much; but most are probably of early foundation, owing their first erection to the days when the Moors still from time to time rode raiding across the land. They are always of extraordinary solidity, and consist usually of plain walls with circular projecting towers at short intervals.

The materials used by Spanish architects and builders seem to have been granite, stone, and brick. Granite was used in some of the very earliest constructions; but after the introduction of Christian art into the country, nothing but stone was used for two or three centuries, when granite was again made use of. We see the same thing in England; and no doubt the admirable masons who played so important a part in the development of Christian architecture must have detested the hard, coarse, and unyielding material, when they compared it with the more easily-wrought free-stones which lent themselves so kindly to their work. The Spanish masons were always, I think, skilful; and in the fifteenth century, when Gothic art was glowing forth in all the glory of decay, pre-eminently so. I know no mere execution of details more admirable in every way than that which we see, for instance, in the work of Diego de Siloe. It reaches the very utmost limit of skilful handiwork. It is not very artistic, but it is so clever that we cannot but admire it; and I doubt much whether the best of our own works of the same age can at all be put in comparison with it. It is generally marked by the extraordinary love of heraldic achievements which is so characteristic of the Spaniards. There are some of the façades of the later churches which are adorned with absolutely nothing but coats-of-arms and their supporters; and I know no work which is less interesting in spite of its extraordinary elaborateness. The decorations of parts of our Houses of Parliament give some idea of this sort of work, though they are by no means so painfully elaborate.

The masons seem to have worked together in large bodies, and the walls are marked in all directions with the signs which, then as now, distinguished the work of each mason from that of his neighbour, but I have been unable (save in one or two cases) to detect the mark of the same mason in more than one work; and from this it would seem to be probable that the masons were stationary rather than nomadic in their habits, a deduction which is fortified by the difference of general character which may, I think, be detected between the groups of marks in different buildings. Occasionally the number of men employed on one building seems to have been unusually large, and it is clear therefore that there were great numbers of masons in the country. In the small church of Sta. Maria, Benavente,

there are the marks of at least thirty-one masons on the eastern
wall; as many as thirty-five were at work on the lower part of
the steeple at Lérida; whilst in one portion of Santiago Cathedral
there appears to have been as many as sixty. These numbers
would be large at the present day; and are very considerable
even if compared with such a building as Westminster Abbey,
where, in A.D. 1253, when the works were in full progress, the
number of stone-cutters varied from thirty-five to seventy-
eight.

The use of bricks was not, so far as I have seen, very great.
They were used either in combination with stone, plaster, or
tiles, or by themselves. Examples of their use in combination
with stone may be seen at Toledo. Here, in all the Moorish or
Moresque examples, the walls are built of rubble stone, with
occasional bonding-courses of brick, and brick quoins. This
kind of construction, which has been sometimes adopted of late
years in England, is obviously good and convenient, but wanted,
to some minds, the authority of ancient precedent ; and here
at Toledo we are able to show it from a very early period. In
the very early Puerta de Visagra (*circa* A.D. 1108–36) single
bonding-courses of brick are used at a very short distance apart,
whilst in the later works, such as the steeples of San Roman and
La Magdalena, the bands are farther apart, and consist frequently of two or three courses of brick, whilst the string-courses
and corbel-tables are formed of projecting bricks, which are
seldom, if ever, moulded. This, indeed, may almost be said to
be the special peculiarity of Spanish brickwork; for in every
other part of Europe, so far as I have seen, where bricks are much
used, they were always more or less moulded. These examples
are useful, however, as showing how very much richness of effect
can be obtained by the use of the simple rough material in the
simplest way. At Zaragoza, at Tarazona, at Calatayud, and
elsewhere, the buildings and their steeples are covered with
panels and arcades, formed by setting forward some of the bricks
a few inches in advance of the face of the wall. In some cases,
as in the Cimborio of Tarazona Cathedral, and the east wall of
Zaragoza, the spaces so left are filled in with extremely rich work
in coloured tiles, the effect of which is far less garish and strange
than might have been expected.

The most curious feature that I have noticed about Spanish
brickwork is that it always, or almost always, appears to have
been the work of Moorish workmen, and not of the Christian
workmen by whom the great churches throughout the country

were erected. The Moors continued to live and work in many towns long after the Christians had recovered them; and wherever they did so, they seem to have retained, to a great extent, all their old architectural and constructive traditions. We see this most distinctly in the markedly different character of the old Spanish brickwork both from the other Spanish architectural developments of the day, and also from any brickwork of the same period that is seen in other parts of Europe. If after leaving Zaragoza the traveller were to cross the Pyrenees, and then make his way to Toulouse, he would find himself again in the midst of brick buildings, erected at various times from the twelfth to the sixteenth century; but he would find them utterly different in style from the brick buildings of the Zaragozan district, and thoroughly in harmony with the stone buildings which were being erected at the same time in the same neighbourhood. And this brings us in face of one of the most curious evidences of the extremely exotic character of most Spanish art. Spain was the only country in Europe, probably, in which at the same time, during the whole period from A.D. 1200 to A.D. 1500, various schools of architecture existed much as they do in England at the present day. There were the genuine Spanish Gothic churches (derived, of course, from Roman and Romanesque), the northern Gothic buildings executed by architects imported from France, and in later days from Germany, and the Moresque buildings executed by Moorish architects for their Christian masters. Of these schools I have already discussed two in this chapter, and I must now say a few words about the third.

I do not propose to speak here of Moorish art, properly and strictly so called, but only of that variety of it which we see made use of by the Christians, and which throughout this work I have called " Moresque." Of these, the most remarkable that I have seen are in that most interesting city of Toledo, which, so far as I can learn, seems to surpass Seville in work of this kind, almost as much as it does in its treasures of Christian art. Here it is plain that, though Christians ruled the city, Moors inhabited it. The very planning of the town, with its long, narrow, winding lanes; the arrangement of the houses, with their closed outer walls, their *patios* or courts, and their large and magnificent halls, speak strongly and decidedly in favour of the Moorish origin of the whole. And when we come to look into the matter in detail, this presumption is most fully supported; for everywhere the design of the internal finishing and decorations of the houses and rooms is thoroughly Moorish, executed with the remarkable skill in plaster for which the Moors were noted, and with curious exhibitions here and there of a knowledge, on the part of the men who did them, of the Gothic details which were most in vogue at the time.

It may well be supposed that if the Moors were thus influenced by the sight of Christian art, the Christians would be not less so by the sight of theirs. I fully expected when I went first to Spain that I should find evidences of this more or less everywhere; I soon found that I was entirely mistaken, and that, though they do exist, they are comparatively rare and very unimportant. This will be seen if I notice some of the most remarkable of the examples.

(1.) In Toledo Cathedral the triforium of the choir is decidedly Moresque in its design, though it is Gothic in all its details, and has carvings of heads, and of the ordinary dog-tooth enrichment. It consists of a trefoiled arcade; in the spandrels between the arches of this there are circles with heads in them; and above these, triangular openings pierced through the wall; the mouldings of all these openings interpenetrate, and the whole arcade has the air of intricate ingenuity so usual in Moorish work. It might not be called Moresque in England, but in Toledo there can, I think, be no question that it is the result of Moorish influence on the Christian artist. So also in the triforium of the inner aisle of the same Cathedral the cusping of the arcades begins with the point of the cusp on the capital, so as to produce the effect of a horse-shoe arch: and though it is true that this form of cusping is found extensively in French buildings in the country between Le Puy and Bourges, here, in the neighbourhood of the universal horse-shoe cusping of the Moorish arches, it is difficult to suppose that the origin of this work is not Moorish also. The same may be said with equal truth of the triforium at the east end of Avila Cathedral.

(2.) The towers of the Christian churches in Toledo, at Illescas, at Calatayud, at Zaragoza, and at Tarazona, all appear to me to be completely Moresque. Those in Toledo make no disguise about it, the pointed arches of their window openings not even affecting to be Gothic in their mode of construction. So also in some of the churches of Toledo much of the work is completely Moresque. The church of Sta. Leocadia is a remarkable example of the mixture of Romanesque and Moresque ideas in the same building.

(3.) In many buildings some small portion of Moorish orna-

ment is introduced by the Christian workman evidently as a
curiosity, and as it were to show that he knew how to do it, but
did not choose to do much of it. Among these are (a) the traceries
in the thirteenth-century cloister at Tarragona,[1] where the
Moresque character is combined with the Christian symbol; (b)
the interlacing traceries of the circular windows in the lantern
of San Pedro, Huesca;[2] (c) the carving of a Moorish interlacing
pattern on the keystone of a vault at Lérida; (d) the filling in
of the windows of the Cloister at Tarazona with the most elaborate pierced traceries;[3] (e) the traceries of the clerestory of the
aisle of the chevet of Toledo Cathedral; (f) and similar semi-
Moresque traceries inserted in Gothic windows at Lugo, and
many other places, where everything else is purely Gothic.

(4.) The introduction of coupled groining ribs, as in the vault
of the Templars' Church at Segovia, and in that of the Chapter-
house at Salamanca. The Moorish architects seem always to
have been extremely fond of coupled ribs. We see them in
several of the vaults in the church or mosque called *Cristo de
la Luz*;[4] and the principal timbers of the wooden roofs of the
synagogue "*del Transito*" are similarly coupled. It is an
arrangement utterly unknown, so far as I remember, in Gothic
work, and there can be no doubt that in these examples it is
Moresque. The vault of the Chapter-house at Salamanca, which
also has parallel vaulting ribs, produces, as will be seen[5] in the
centre, the sort of star-shaped compartment of which the Moorish
architects were always so fond.

(5.) The Moorish battlement is used extensively on walls
throughout Spain. It is weathered on all sides to a point, and
covers only the battlements, and not the spaces between them.[6]

(6.) The Moorish system of plastering was considerably used,
not only at Toledo, but also to a late period on the Alcazar and
on houses and towers at Segovia. Here, however, though the
system of design and the mode of execution are altogether
Moorish, the details of the patterns cut in the plaster are generally Christian.

(7.) The Moorish carpentry is very peculiar, and is constantly
introduced in late Gothic work. Most of my readers have
probably seen the ingenious puzzles which the Moors contrived
with interlacing ribs in their ceilings at the Alhambra, illustrated

[1] *See* p. 33 and illustrations on ground-plan, Plate XV., p. 40.
[2] *See* p. 161.   [3] *See* p. 183.   [4] *See* Vol. I., p. 305.
[5] *See* ground-plan, Vol. I., Plate IV., p. 104.
[6] *See* illustration of this battlement at Las Huelgas, Vol. I., page 45, and
on the walls at Veruela, page 187.

with so much completeness by Mr. Owen Jones; these patterns are constantly used in Gothic buildihgs for door-framing; and examples of this kind of work may be seen frequently, and especially in towns—like Valencia and Barcelona—on the eastern coast.

These evidences of Moorish influence upon Christian art in Spain are, it will at once be seen, rather insignificant, and serve on the whole to prove the fact, that Christian art was nearly as pure here as it was anywhere. This is precisely, I think, what might have been expected. For where a semi-religious war was for ages going on between two nations, and where art was, as it almost always is—God be praised—more or less religious in its origin and object, nothing can be imagined less probable than that their national styles of art should be much mixed one with the other. It is probable, on the contrary, that each would have a certain amount of pride in this practical way of protesting against his enemy's heresies, so that art was likely to assume a religious air even greater and deeper than it did elsewhere.

The mention of the religious element in art leads naturally to the consideration of that art which most objectively ministered to the teaching of religious truths and history—the art of Painting. The admirable and interesting work of Mr. Stirling [1] begins just where I leave off, and almost treats the painters before Velasquez, Murillo, and Joánes as though they had never existed. But in truth I suppose it is necessary that the whole subject should be studied from the beginning; and though we can never hope for such a mine of information about mediæval Spanish painters as Messrs. Crowe and Cavalcaselle have given us about their Italian contemporaries, it is not, I think, unreasonable to suppose that a good deal of information might still be obtained. I regret very much that in all my Spanish journeys my time has been so fully occupied with purely architectural work that I have never been able to pay so much attention as they seemed to deserve to the early paintings that I saw. Yet the works of Borgoña at Avila, the paintings round the cloister and choir-screen at Leon, the painted Retablos at Barcelona, Toledo, and elsewhere, seemed to me to be often very full of beauty both of drawing and colour. Their number is very great, and most of them are still in the very places for which they were originally painted. Their character appears to me to be utterly different from that to which we are accustomed as marking Spanish painting. Almost all our ideas are formed, as it seems to me,

[1] *Annals of the Artists of Spain,* 1848.

on the work of a school of painters who, adopting religious art as their special vocation, and shutting themselves out almost entirely from any representation of any other kind of subject, contrived unfortunately to take the gloomy side of religion, and to paint as though an officer of the Holy Office was ever at their elbow. How contrary this spirit to that of the earlier men, who, so far as I have seen, painted just as naturally religious men, cheerful, hearty, and unaffected by the souring influence of the Inquisition, might be expected to paint! Their work appears to me to give them an intermediate place between the tenderly delicate treatment of the early Italian masters, and the intensely realistic and consequently very mundane style of the early German painters; but it is always bright, cheerful, and agreeable both in manner and choice of subject. The names of but a few of these early men are preserved, and unfortunately next to nothing beyond their names. Among them are Ramon Torrente of Zaragoza, who died in 1323; Guillem Fort, his pupil; Juan Cesilles of Barcelona, who at the end of the fourteenth century contracted for the painting of the Reredos at Reus, and some of whose handiwork may not impossibly remain among the Retablos still preserved in the cloister chapels of Barcelona Cathedral; Gherardo d'Jacobo Starna (or Starnina), born at Florence in 1354, who before the end of the fourteenth century spent several years painting in Spain; Dello, also of Florence, and a friend of Paolo Uccello, who died somewhere about 1466–70;[1] Rogel, a Fleming, who painted a chapel at Miraflores in A.D. 1445; Jorge Ingles (probably an Englishman), who was painting in Spain circa A.D. 1450; Antonio Rincon,[2] who was born at Guadalajara in 1446, studied under Ghirlandaio for a time, and, subsequently residing at Toledo, painted in A.D. 1483 the walls of the old sacristy, and died circa 1500, with the reputation of being the painter who had most contributed to the overthrow of the mediæval style; finally, Juan de Borgoña, who may be mentioned as one of the latest and greatest of the earlier school, and almost the only one of them whose known works are still to be seen. His great work appears to have been a series of paintings round the cloister of Toledo Cathedral, which have all been

---

[1] The paintings at Leon seem to me to be such as one might expect at the hands of Dello Delli. He is said to have made Seville his place of residence during the many years that he spent in Spain. But the period of his abode there is just that during which the paintings at Leon were executed.

[2] See the short account of these painters in Mr. Stirling's *Annals of the Artists of Spain*, vol. i. chap. ii.

destroyed; besides which he executed other works in the sacristy, chapter-house, and Mozarabic chapel there, and in the Cathedral at Avila. The feature which strikes one the most in these early works is the strange way in which sculpture and painting are combined in the same work. The great Retablos which give so grand an effect to Spanish altars are frequently adorned with paintings in some parts and sculptured subjects in others. The frames to the pictures are generally elaborate architectural compositions of pinnacles and canopies, and consequently the art is altogether rather decorative than pictorial in its effect. Sometimes, when the altar is small, and the Retablo close to the eye, this is not so much the case, and I have seen many of the pictures in these positions look so thoroughly well as to give a very high impression of the men who produced them. They are almost all painted on panel, and, as might be expected, on gold grounds. Old wall-paintings are comparatively rare: I have seen no important series save that which I have described at Leon, and of the later of these some at least appeared to me to be extremely Florentine in their character.

This general review of the whole course and history of Spanish art seemed to be necessary in order to give point and intelligible order to the various descriptive notices which have been given in the previous chapters of this book. It is probable that some of my readers may after all think that I have had but little that was new to tell them. Possibly this may be so. The history of art repeats itself everywhere in obedience to some general law of progress; and it might have been assumed beforehand that we should find the same story in Spain as in France, Germany, or England. But the real novelty of my account is, I take it, this—that whereas generally men credited Spain with forming an exception to a general rule, my business has been to show that, on the whole, she did nothing of the sort. Just as we obtained a French architect for our Canterbury, as the people of Milan obtained one from Germany for their cathedral, as the architect of S. Mark at Venice borrowed from the East, as he of Périgueux from S. Mark, as he of Cologne from Amiens or Beauvais, so Spain profited, no doubt, from time to time, by the example of her French neighbours. But at the same time she formed a true branch of art for herself, and one so vigorous, so noble, and so worthy of study, that I shall be disappointed indeed if her buildings are not ere long far more familiar than they now are to English ecclesiologists.

I think, too, that the occasional study of any ancient school

II R

of architecture is always attended with the best possible results to those who are themselves attempting to practise the same art. It recalls us, when necessary, to the consideration of the points of difference between their work and ours; and thus, by obliging us to reconsider our position, may enable us to see where it is defective, and where the course we are pursuing is evidently erroneous. I have already noticed incidentally, in more than one place in this work, the noble air of solidity which so often marks the early Spanish buildings; I need hardly say that in these days none of us err on this side, and that in truth our buildings only too often lack even that amount of solidity which is necessary to their stability. And this leads me naturally to another questionable feature in modern work, which is to a great extent the cause of our failing in the matter of solidity. These noble Spanish buildings were usually solid and simple; their mouldings were not very many, and their sculptures were few, precious, and delicate. There was little in them of mere ornament, and never any lavish display of it. Sculpture of the human figure was but rarely introduced, and whatever sculpture there was, was thoroughly architectural in its character. How different is the case now! Hardly a church or public building of any kind is built, which—whatever its poverty elsewhere—has not sculpture of foliage and flowers, birds and beasts, scattered broadcast and with profusion all over it. However bad the work, it is sure to be admired, and as it is evidently almost always done without any, or with but little interference of the architect, he is often tempted to secure popularity for his work in this easiest of ways. I know buildings of great cost which have been absolutely ruined in effect by this miserable practice; and I know none in the middle ages in which so much carved work has been introduced, as has been in some of those which have recently been erected. I believe it to be a fact that more carving—if the vulgar hacking and hewing of stone we see is to be called carving—has been done in England within the last twenty years than our forefathers accomplished in any fifty years between A.D. 1100 and 1500! And I believe equally that, if we limited ourselves to one-tenth of the amount, there would be more chance of our having time to think about it and to design it ourselves.

The same misfortune that has befallen us with foliage will soon befall us with figures. It has suddenly been discovered that every architect ought to be able to draw the human figure, and soon, I fear, we shall see it become the fashion to introduce figures without thought or value everywhere. If men would but look at some of our own old buildings, they would see how great is still the work which has to be done before we understand how to emulate the merits of those even among them which have no sculpture of any kind in their composition, and how great the architect may be who despises and rejects this cheap kind of popularity.[1] And they ought to take warning, by the comparison of old work and old ways of working with new, of those too attractive but most dangerous schemes for seducing them from the real study of their art into other paths, certain, it is true, of popularity, but full of snares and pitfalls, which, as we see on all sides, entrap some of those even who ought to have been aware of their danger.

Sculpture in moderation is above everything beautiful. Sculpture in excess is very offensive. These Spanish churches teach us this most unmistakably if they teach us anything at all; and as the main object of the study of ancient art—the main object of those who wish to " stand in the old ways where is the truth "—is to derive lessons for the present and future from the practice of the past, I am sure that, in applying the results of my study of Spanish art in the warning which I here very gravely give, I am only doing that which as an artist I am bound to do, if I care at all for my art.

NOTES

(1) There is, however, a parallelism in the changes that, for instance, Moorish capitals went through, century by century, curiously like the contemporaneous development of Gothic. I had better admit, moreover, explicitly, what Street implies not very clearly, a Mudejar type of church architecture in brick, most easily to be studied about Zaragoza and Sagahún.

(2) Santa Cruz de Cangas (in Asturias, to be reached from Oviedo) was rebuilt in 1632, and is abandoned at present.

(3) The ancient Romanesque church of S. John Evangelist at Santiañes de Pravia was completely restored a few years ago. Don Silos was king in Pravia 774-783; he brought back from Mérida, and enshrined, bones of Santa Eulalia.

(4) In Asturias, San Pedro de Villanueva, of the twelfth century. The church retains only the head and the portal, the rest being

---

[1] I venture to regard the stern simplicity of Mr. Butterfield's noble church of S. Alban as his silent protest against the vulgarity in art to which I here refer. Without any sculpture, this church is from first to last the work of a great master of his art, and one for which his brother artists owe him a great debt of gratitude.

remade in 1687 and the three aisles thrown into one. It has three semi-circular apses opening together and historied capitals; three arches on coupled columns, with Attic bases and very simple leafage, are the remains of the entrance to the chapter-house.

Santa Maria de Villamayor keeps a magnificent semi-circular apse with a blind arcade inside below, and a great sanctuary arch. It is certainly of the thirteenth century: the capitals have grand leaves.

San Antolin de Bedón, built by Abbot John or James, 1175 or 1176, is Romanesque in type, with pointed arches and a groined vault in the crossing. It has three aisles, a transept and a lantern, and three semi-circular apses of rough masonry, with lines of ashlar. It sounds rather fine and is perfectly accessible from the railroad between Santander and Gijon.

Sandoval, in Leon, a Cistercian foundation of 1167, has three rich parallel apses with fine clustered shafts, and two columns in the jambs of the moulded windows. The aisles are very high, the main arcade and aisle vaults pointed, the transepts short and high with gables; the nave has a barrel-vault carried on engaged Romanesque shafts, and was finished westward in the fifteenth century. A pointed door in the transept has Romanesque mouldings.

(5) History and style both show this influence to have been Burgundian.

(6) Señor Lampérez says that San Martin of Segovia is unique in this—but the aisles are about of a height.

(7) It might be better to say that Zaragoza created a regional style, and from it are derived the Collegiata of Santa Maria at Cala-tayud, the cathedral of Tarazona, and that of Teruel as far as the transepts.

(8) This is no longer quite true; the rebuilding of Ripoll and repairing of Santa Maria la Blanca in Toledo, for instance, have falsified the evidence beyond remedy. Still, on the whole, Spain has suffered less wanton wrong than either France or Italy.

CHAPTER XXI

THE history of the architects of the middle ages has never been written, and so few are the facts which we really know about them, that it may well be doubted whether it ever can be. Yet were it possible to do so, few subjects would be more interesting. To me it always seems that the most precious property of all good art is its human and personal character. I have always had an especial pleasure in tracing out what appear to be such similarities between different buildings as seem to prove, or at least to suggest, that they were designed by the same artist; for, just as in painting a work becomes far more precious if we know it to be really the handiwork of a Giotto or a Simone Memmi, so in the sister art a building is far more precious when we know it to be the work of an Elias of Dereham, an Alan of Walsingham, or an Eudes de Montreuil; and if we are able, as in their case, to start with the knowledge that certain men did certain works, the interest of such investigations is at once manyfold enhanced.

This is precisely the point at which we have now arrived in regard to Spanish buildings; for the notices of their architects which I have given in various parts of this book are so numerous that I think I shall do well to collect them together in their order; and to sum up, as much as one can learn from the documents relating to them, as to the terms on which they carried on their work, and generally, indeed, as to the position which they held.

In the earliest period, and just when any information would have been more than usually interesting to us, I have been able to learn next to nothing of any real value as to the superintendents of Spanish buildings.

One of the first notices of an architect is that contained in an inscription in San Isidoro, Leon, to the memory of Petrus de Deo, of whom it was said, " Erat vir miræ abstinentiæ, et multis florebat miraculis; " and, what is even more to our purpose, he is said to have built a bridge. He " superædificavit " the church of San Isidoro, and, from the reference to his saintly life, one is inclined to suspect that he must have been a priest and probably a monk; if so, it is important to note the fact, inasmuch as almost all the other architects or masters of the works referred to in all books I have examined, seem to have been laymen, and just as much a distinct class as architects at the present day are. The expression " superædificavit " does not tell us much as to the exact office of Petrus de Deo; but the next notice of an architect is not only one of the earliest, but also one of the most curious; this is in the contract entered into by the Chapter of Lugo with their architect Raymundo of Monforte de Lemos, in A.D. 1129; and from the terms of his payment, which was to be either in money or in kind, it is clear that, whatever his position was, he could not leave Lugo, but was retained solely for the work there. The terms of the contract are very worthy of notice, and may be compared with some of the similar agreements with the superintendents of English works, who frequently stipulated for a cloak of office and other payments in kind, though I doubt whether we know of any English contract of so early a date. It is clear from the payment of an annual salary, and an engagement for the term of his life, that Maestro Raymundo was distinctly an architect, not a mere builder or contractor; it seems that he was a layman, and that his son followed the same profession. The title given him in the contract, " Master of the works," is, as we shall find, that which in course of time was usually given to the architect; though I am not inclined to think that it makes it impossible that he should also have wrought with his own hands. Indeed, the very next notice of an architect is of one who certainly did act as sculptor on his own works. This was Mattheus, master of the works at Santiago Cathedral. The warrant issued by the king Ferdinand II., in A.D. 1168, granted him a pension of a hundred maravedis annually for the rest of his life,[1] and, though the amount seems to be insignificant, the fact of any royal grant being made proves, I think, not only the king's sense of the value of a fine church, but also somewhat as to the degree of importance which its designer may have attained to, when he was recognised at all by the king. On the other hand, when twenty years later the same man (no doubt) wrote his name exultingly on the lintels of the church doorway, which was only then at last finished,[2] there can be no doubt that he had been acting there both as sculptor

[1] See Appendix. The maravedi was, I believe, a more valuable coin then than it is now, so that it is difficult to say what amount of money at the present day this grant really represents.

This inscription is referred to in Vol. I., p. 192.

and architect: and if, from a modern point of view, he lost caste as an architect, he no doubt gained it as an artist; and even now, if one had to make the choice, one would far rather have been able honestly to put up one's name as the author of those doorways, than as the builder of the church to which they are attached. It will be noticed that here, just as at Lugo, the master of the works was appointed at a salary for his lifetime, and held his office precisely in the same way as do the surveyors of our own cathedrals at the present day.

Much about the same time, in A.D. 1175, a most interesting document was drawn out, binding one Raymundo, a "Lambardo,"[1] to execute certain works in the cathedral at Urgel, in Cataluña. It is very difficult to say whether this Raymundo was the architect and builder, or only the builder, of the church, though I incline to believe he was both. He was to complete his work in seven years, employing four "Lambardos," and, if necessary, "Cementarios," or wallers, in addition; and in return he was to be paid with a Canon's portion for the rest of his life. The mode of payment, the engagement for life, and the fact that there is no mention whatever of any materials to be provided by Raymundo, as well as the absence from the contract of any reference to a master of the works, lead, I think, to the conclusion that he was in truth the architect, but that he also superintended the execution of the works, and contracted for the labour.[2]

---

[1] I do not know the meaning of this term: it is evidently the name of a trade or calling, and probably corresponds with " masons," as distinguished from " wallers; " the two terms, " Lambardos " and " Cementarios," being used somewhat in opposition to each other.

Cementarius is one of the earliest terms used in documents referring to English buildings, and no doubt would be properly translated by the word " mason; " but in the case of the Urgel contract, it seems there were to be several " Lambardos," and, as " Cementarios " were only to be employed if absolutely necessary, there must have been some distinction between them, which was more probably of grade or degree than of profession. Possibly the " Lambardos " may have been members of a guild, " Cementarios " common masons.

[2] This contract is given by Don J. Villanueva, *Viage Literario a las Iglesias de España*, ix. 298-300. I extract from it the parts which are especially interesting:—

" EGO A. DEI Gratia Urgellensis episcopus, cum consilio et comuni voluntate omnium canonicorum Urgellensis ecclesiae, commendo tibi Raymundo Lambardo opus beatae Mariae, cum omnibus rebus tam mobilibus quam immobilibus, scilicet, mansos, alodia, vineas, census, et cum oblationibus oppressionum et penitentialium, et cum elemosinis fidelium, et cum numis clericorum, et cum omnibus illis, quae hucusque vel in antea aliquo titulo videntur spectasse sive spectare ad prephatum opus beatae Mariae. Et preterea damus tibi cibum canonicalem in omni vita tua, tali videlicet pacto, ut tu fideliter et sine omni enganno claudas

The next notice I find of an architect is in A.D. 1203, when the architect of Lérida Cathedral, one Pedro de Cumba, is described as " Magister et fabricator," and there can be no doubt, therefore, that he not only designed but executed the work, which, as we go on, we shall find to have been a not very uncommon custom; but it is rare, nevertheless, to see this title of " Fabricator " given to the architect, who is usually " Magister operis," and no more; [1] as, indeed, we see in the case of the successor

nobis ecclesiam totam, et leves coclearia sive campanilia, unum filum super omnes voltas, et facias ipsum cugul bene et decenter cum omnibus sibi pertinentibus. Et Ego R. Lambardus convenio Domino Deo, et beatae Mariae, et domino episcopo, et omnibus clericis Urgellensis ecclesiae, qui modo ibi sunt, vel in antea erunt, quod hoc totum, sicut superius scriptum est, vitâ comite, perficiam ab hoc presenti Pascha, quod celebratur anno dominicae incarnationis M.° C.° LXXV.°, usque ad VII. annos fideliter, et sine omni enganno. Ita quod singulis annis habeam et teneam ad servitium beatae Mariae, me quinto, de Lambardis idest IIII. lambardos et me, et hoc in yeme et in estate indesinenter. Et si cum istis potero perficere, faciam, et si non potero addam tot cementarios, quod supra dictum opus consumetur in prephato termino. Post VII. vero annos, cum iam dictum opus, divina misercordiâ opitulante, compievero, habeam libere et quiete cibum meum dum vixero, et de honore operis et avere stem in voluntate et mandamento capituli postea. Preterea nos, tam episcopus, quam canonici, omnino prohibemus tibi Raymundo Lambardo, quod per te, vel per submisam personam, non alienes vel obliges aliqua occasione quicquam de honore operis, quae modo habet, vel in antea habebit. De tuo itaque honore, quem nomine tuo adquisisti, et de avere, fac in vita et in morte quod tibi placuerit post illud septennium. Si forte, quod absit, tanta esterilitas terrae incubuerit, quod te nimium videamus gravari, liceat nobis prephato termino addere secundum arbitrium nostrum, ne notam periurii incurras. Sed aliquis vel aliqui nostrum praedictam relaxationem sacramenti facere tibi non possit, nisi in pleno capitulo, comuni deliberatione et consensu omnium. Et quicquid melioraveris in honore operis, remaneat ad ipsum opus. Si vero pro melioracione honoris operis oporteret te aliquid impignorare vel comutare, non possis hoc facere sine consilio et conveniencia capituli. Juro ego R. Lambardus, quod hoc totum, sicut superius est scriptum, perficiam, et fidelitatem et indempnitatem canonicae beatae Mariae Urgellensis ecclesiae pro posse meo, per Deum, et haec sancta evangelia=Sig + num R. Lambardi, qui hoc iuro, claudo et confirmo=Sig + num domni Arnalli Urgellensis episcopi," etc., etc.

[1] E.g. at San Cristobal de Ibeas—

Era M. C. LXX.
Fuit hoc opus fundatum
Martino Abbate regente
Petrus Christophorus
Magister hujus operis fuit.

Or another at Ciudad Rodrigo—

Aqui yace Benito Sanchez,
Maestro que fue de esta obra, é
Dios le perdone. Amen.

So too the inscription given in Vol. I., p. 325, of the architect of Toledo. The same term was used extensively at the same time over the greater part of Europe.

In France we have these among others:—" Ci git Robert de Coucy, of Pedro de Cumba, one Pedro de Peñafreyta, who is described on his monument by this title only.

In the thirteenth century we have the names of several architects, but nothing more than their names; and the only point which seems worthy of special note is that, so far as I can learn, none of them were ecclesiastics; whilst, from first to last, I have found no reference to anything like freemasonry. Indeed, on both these points, the history of Spanish architects seems to be singularly conclusive; and there can be little doubt that they carried on their work entirely as a business, and always under very distinct and formal engagements as to the way in which it was to be done.

In the fourteenth century the earliest notice is that contained in an order of the king, in 1303, dated at Perpiñan, and directed to his lieutenant in Mallorca, requiring him to go at once " cum Magistro Poncio " to Minorca, to arrange about the building a town hall, which the king wishes to have built with round towers, " sicut in muro Perpiniani; " and two years later the king writes again, " Item audivimus turrim nostram Majoricarum, ubi stat angelus ictu fulgens fuisse percussam et aliquantulum deformatam. Volumus quod celeriter sicut magister Poncius et alii viderint faciendum celeriter restauretur." [1] Here it is, to say the least, doubtful whether Master Ponce was architect and adviser only, or also the mason who was to do the work. But this could not have been the case with the two architects of Narbonne, employed in the rebuilding of the cathedral at Gerona, one of whom was appointed in A.D. 1320-22 at a salary of two hundred and fifty sueldos a quarter, and under agreement to come from Narbonne six times a year. Here, whilst the old plan of making the architect enter into a kind of contract is adhered to, we seem to have a distinct recognition of a class of men who were not workmen, but really and only superintendents of buildings—in fact, architects in the modern sense of the word.

Maître de Notre Dame et de Saint Nicaise, qui trépassa l'an 1311." In A.D. 1251, at Rouen, " Walter de St. Hilaire, Cementarius, magister operis," is mentioned; and in A.D. 1440, in the same city, we have this inscription: " Ci gît M. Alexandre de Berneval, Maistre des Œuvres de Massonerie au Baillage de Rouen et de cette église." In Italy the same term was commonly used, as, *e.g.*, in the Baptistery at Pisa, which has the inscription, " Deotisalvi magister hujus operis; " and again in the church at Mensano near Siena, which has " Opus quod videtis Bonusamicus magister fecit." But in England, according to Mr. Wyatt Papworth, who has devoted much pains to the elucidation of the subject, the term " Master of the works " appears to be very seldom employed, and sometimes of the officer called the " operarius " in Spain, rather than of the architect.

[1] Villanueva, *Viage Lit.* xxi. 106.

About the same time, Jayme Fabre (or Fabra), a Mallorcan, seems to have been one of the greatest architects of his day, and to have given a very important impulse to the principal provincial development of architecture of which we see any evidence in Spain—that of Cataluña. From a contract entered into in A.D. 1318, between him and the Superior and brethren of the convent of Santo Domingo at Palma, in Mallorca, it seems that he was bound by an older agreement to execute the works of their church; and that he then promised to come back whenever required to Palma, from Barcelona, whither he was going to undertake another work at the desire of the king and the bishop. This " other work " was the cathedral, and here we know that Fabre was employed till A.D. 1339, when he and the workmen [1] of the church put the covering on the shrine which contained the relics of Sta. Eulalia, in the crypt. It is impossible to read the account of the completion of the shrine of Sta. Eulalia at Barcelona without feeling that Fabre superintended a number of masons, and acted in fact as their foreman, though this is no reason whatever why he should not also have designed the work they executed. He seems to have carried on the two works at Barcelona and Palma at the same time; for, on the 23rd June, A.D. 1317, a year only after his agreement with the convent of Santo Domingo at Palma, he was appointed master of the works of Barcelona Cathedral, with a salary of eighteen sueldos each week, and payment of his expenses on his voyages to and from Mallorca. Soon after this time, in A.D. 1368, the fabric rolls of the cathedral at Palma, in Mallorca, record the name of Jayme Mates, who was " Maestro Mayor " of the work at Palma, and had a salary of twenty pounds a year, besides six sueldos a day for the working days, and two for festivals.[2]

In the same year we have the very interesting contract between the Chapter of San Feliu, Gerona, and Pedro Zacoma, the master of the works of the steeple; by this, it seems, he did not contract for the work, but had permission to employ an apprentice on it, and he was not to undertake any other work without the consent of the " Operarius," or Canon in charge of the works, save a bridge on which he was already engaged. He was to be paid by the day, with a yearly salary in addition. I have given the contract at p. 110 of this volume. Zacoma is

[1] Fabre is spoken of in the inscription on the shrine as Jacobus " Majoricarum, cum suis consortibus."
[2] These fabric rolls contain the names of Martin Mayol, G. Scardon, Bernardo Desdons, and Jayme Pelicer, as painters of pictures between A.D. 1327 and 1339.

called in it the " Master of the work of the belfry." He must have been employed constantly at the church, or it would not have been necessary to prevent his undertaking other works; and in such a building a man could hardly have been constantly employed without absolutely working as a mason.

It may be thought that the " Operarius " was the real architect; but I find, at this time, that most collegiate and cathedral churches had a Canon whose special duty it was to make arrangements with the master of the works. Sometimes they are called " Canonigos fabriqueros," at others " Obreros," or else, as in this case, " Operarii." Some examples of the application of these terms may be given to prove what I say:—In A.D. 1312, for instance, the Chapter of Gerona appointed two of their own body—one an archdeacon, the other a Canon—to be the *obreros* of their works.[1] In A.D. 1340 the " Operarius " was gathering alms in Valencia and the Balearic Isles for the works at Gerona Cathedral.[2] In an inscription of A.D. 1183, at S. Trophime at Arles, Poncius Rebolli is called " Sacerdos et operarius; " at Palencia, in A.D. 1321, there was an " Obrero," or Canon in charge of the works, as he is described by Dávila.[3] In the inscription on a stone in the choir of Lérida Cathedral,[4] the two offices of the " operarius " and the " magister et fabricator " are contrasted, and the double office of the latter seems to make it impossible that the former can have been the architect. The fabric rolls of Exeter Cathedral contain, in A.D. 1318, a payment to the " Custos operis " for the adornment of the high altar: and, no doubt, he held the same post as the Operarius in Spain.

At the end of this century Juan Garcia de Laguardia was named " Master-mason " of the kingdom of Navarre, by a royal writ, at the wage of three sueldos a day. His title adds another to those already mentioned.

In A.D. 1391 Guillermo Çolivella undertook to make twelve statues of the apostles, at Lérida, at the price of 240 sueldos for each statue; and subsequently, in A.D. 1392, he is styled " Magister operis " of the see of Lérida, and " Lapicida," and he had the superintendence of the stained glass windows which Juan de San Amat was making for the apses of the church, with the stories of the apostles.[5] He was evidently, I think, a builder,

---

[1] *See* p. 93. [2] *See* p. 110. [3] *See* Vol. I., p. 69. [4] *See* p. 130, note 3.
[5] Villanueva, *Viage Lit. a las Iglesias de España*, xvi. 99, says that " Lapicida " does not really mean a cutter of stones, which would be described as " pica petras." In vol. xxi. p. 107, however, he speaks of " Lapicida " as the Latin term corresponding to " picapedres " in the vulgar tongue; and he says sculptors of figures called themselves " Imaginayres."

and yet held very much the office of a modern architect as super-intendent of the whole work. Jayme Fabre describes himself as " Lapicida," but was also the " Master of the fabric " at Barce-lona; whilst Roque, who succeeded Fabre at Barcelona, was also called master of the works only, and received three sueldos and four dineros a day, besides a hundred sueldos a year for clothing.

Just about this period we have what appears to be a rather important reference to the separate offices of the architect and builder in the same work; for it seems that during the construction of the tower of the cathedral at Valencia, one Juan Franck acted as architect, with a succession of men as builders and contractors under him.[1] I confess I do not adduce this example with much confidence, inasmuch as one of them was Balaguer, whose mission to Lérida has already been mentioned, and who is moreover termed, in a contemporary document, an " accomplished architect."

In the fifteenth century, the notices of architects are more numerous, and their position becomes much more clearly defined.

In A.D. 1410 a contract was entered into by one Lucas Ber-naldo de Quintana—master mason, as he is called in it—for the rebuilding of the church at Gijon in the Asturias. In this contract[2] there is no reference of any kind to plans, or to a directing architect or superintendent of any kind; but the dimensions and form of the building are all carefully described in such a way as to lead to the conclusion that the notary who drew up the contract had some sort of plan before him. It is said, for instance, " that the church is to be twenty-five yards long by twelve and a half wide, with three columns on each side, three vaults each with three ribs crossing them, and all the arches, pilasters, etc., as well as the door (which is to be twelve and a half feet high by eight wide), to be of wrought stone. There is to be a turret for two bells over the door, etc." " Item, the ' master ' is to be allowed to use the materials of the old church." The contract was entered into on March 10, 1410, and the key of the building was to be delivered up on the 1st of May, 1411, and finally two sureties were bound with the contractor. The whole deed is so very formal and careful in its terms, that there can be no doubt that Quintana acted as architect as well

---

[1] See p. 8.
[2] The contract is given at length by Cean Bermudez, *Arq. de España*, i. 257-261.

as builder, for otherwise the name of the architect would necessarily have been mentioned.

It was in A.D. 1415 that the Valencian authorities sent their architect on a tour of inspection among church steeples in Cataluña, and as far as Narbonne, on the other side of the Pyrenees, in order that they might be sure of a good design for their own; but this is a very rare, if not a unique, instance of such a proceeding. In the year following the Junta of Architects was assembled at Gerona, and we have in it the first example of that habit so common in this day, of consulting bodies of men, instead of trusting in one skilled man, which from this time forth seems to have been extraordinarily popular in Spain. Incidentally, the records of the proceedings of this Junta are valuable, as giving the names of many architects and the works on which they were then engaged; but they are still more valuable as showing how decided and independent of each other in their opinions these men were. All of them probably were architects; but it is observable that all but two call themselves "Lapicidæ;" that two of them held somewhat inferior offices —one being the "Socius" of the magister operis, and the other, "Regens," in the place of the master. Another is "Magister sive sculptor imaginum;" and two only—Antonino Antigoni and Guillermo Sagrera—call themselves masters of the works. Their answers seem to prove that they were all men of considerable intelligence, but at the same time generally disposed, just as a similar body would be now, to declare rather for the usual than the novel course. It is to their credit that they all maintained the perfect practicability of the work proposed, and the judgment of the Chapter seems to have been as much influenced by economical considerations as by artistic, seeing that a majority of the architects decided against the proposed plan on artistic grounds, whilst some of them said that it would certainly be the least costly. It was intended at first that two of the architects consulted should be asked to prepare a plan for the work; but this does not seem to have been done after all, the plan of the master of the works at the cathedral having been agreed to and carried into execution.

There cannot be a shadow of doubt that at the beginning of the fifteenth century most of the superintendents of buildings, in Cataluña at any rate, were sculptors or masons also. Their own description of themselves is conclusive on this point; at the same time their answers are all given in the tone and style of architects, and it is quite certain that, had there been a superior

class of men—architects only in the modern sense of the word—
the Dean and Chapter would have applied first of all to them.
The answers which these men gave ought to be carefully read, as
they are valuable from several points of view. Several of them
seem to speak of some recognised system of proportioning the
height of a building to its width; one of them suggests using
light stone for the vaulting; and another, Arnaldo de Valleras,
was evidently anxious to supplant the existing master of the
works, and announced what he would do if the works were
intrusted to him. I cannot help thinking that they had before
them the plans of Guillermo de Boffiy, and that the similarity
of the suggestions made by some of them as to the position
of the windows and the proportions of the work are to be taken
as an evidence of their desire to affirm what he had proposed.

In the same year in which this Junta of architects assembled
at Gerona, one of their number—Guillermo Sagrera—was acting
as the architect of the church of S. John, Perpiñan, a building
which is still remarkable for the enormous width of its nave.
Ten years later he contracted for the execution of the Exchange
at Palma, in Mallorca, according to plans which he presented,
and upon certain specified conditions, from which it appears
very clearly that Sagrera was both builder and architect, being
bound to find scaffolding and all materials. The only difference
one can see between Sagrera and an ordinary builder or contractor of the present day is, that he presented the plans himself,
and that there is no trace whatever of any architect or superintendent over him. It is doubted by some whether this mixture
of the two offices of builder and architect was ever allowed in the
middle ages; but this agreement (of which I give a translation
in the Appendix) is conclusive as regards this particular case,
and we may be tolerably sure that such a practice must have
been a usual one, or it would hardly have been adopted in the
case of so important a building.

Sagrera seems to have remained a long time at Palma, but
having quarrelled with his employers there, and his dispute
having been carried before the King of Aragon, at Naples, for
settlement, the completion of the work was intrusted to one
Guillermo Vilasolar, " lapicida et magister fabricæ," who bound
himself on March 19th, A.D. 1451, to complete the works which
had been commenced. Two of the clauses in this agreement
are worth quoting; they are as follows:—

1st. " That I, the said Guillermo Vilasolar, am bound to
execute within the next coming year all the traceries and termina-

tions of cornices which I have to make in the six windows of the said Exchange of Felanix stone, in the following form:—The traceries of two of the said windows according to the design which I have delivered to you, and the traceries and the cornices of the remaining four windows just as they were commenced by Master Guillermo Sagrera, formerly master of the fabric of the said Exchange; which traceries and cornices of all the said six windows I am bound to make entirely at my own cost, with all necessary scaffolding, stone, lime, gravel, and wages for the complete finishing of the said traceries and cornices.

" *Item.*—That for making all the said traceries and cornices as described, in the said six windows, you, the said honourable guardians, shall be bound to give and pay of the goods of the college to me, the said Guillermo Vilasolar, two hundred and eighty pounds of Mallorcan money in the following way, viz.: fifty pounds down, and the remainder of the said two hundred and eighty pounds when the said traceries and cornices to the said six windows shall have been executed."

So that here again, just as in the case of Guillermo Sagrera, we have a mason contracting for his work, and himself making the drawing according to which it is to be done.

After his quarrel with the authorities at Palma, Sagrera seems to have undertaken work for the King in the Castel Nuevo at Naples, for which he used stone from Mallorca, and where he was styled " Proto-Magister Castri Novi." His work at Palma seems, from the accounts I have been able to obtain, to have much resembled that of the Lonja at Valencia, which I have described and illustrated in this work.

In A.D. 1485, when Calahorra cathedral was rebuilt, an architect seems to have been so formally appointed, that the words used appear to me to be quite worth transcribing here: " Miércoles á ocho dias del mes de junio, año à nativitate Domini, millessimo quatorcentessimo octuagessimo quinto cœpit ædificari Capella mayor S. Mariæ de Calahorra. Composuerunt primum lapidem Johannes Ximenes de Enciso decanus, et Petrus Ximenes archidiaconus de Verberiego, et ego Rodericus Martini Vaco de Enciso, canonicus ejusdem ecclesiæ, et artium et theologiæ magister, dedi duplam unam auri in auro, dicens hæc verba magistro Johanni ædificatori principali prædictæ capellæ; accipite in signum vestri laboris, et en protestationem, quod Dominus Deus ad cujus gloriam et honorem ecclesia et capella ista fundari incipit, implebit residuum ad preces gloriosæ Virginis Mariæ matris suæ, et Sanctorum martirum Hemeterij et Caledonij, in quorum honore fundata est ecclesia. In quorum testimonium supradicta manu propria subscripsi. Rodericus artium et theologiæ magister."

It is remarkable that in the case of so important a city as Seville there is no mention of an architect to the cathedral before A.D. 1462, in which year Juan Norman was appointed, with Pedro de Toledo as assistant (" *aparejador* ") till A.D. 1472, when the Chapter appointed three " Maestros Mayores " or principal masters, to the end that the work might go on faster: but it seems, as might be expected, that these men were none of them architects, for in A.D. 1496 the archbishop, being at Guadalajara, was persuaded that it was not well to trust such ill-informed persons, as their employment would end in loss to the fabric, and so he called in one Maestro Jimon, who went to Seville and was made Maestro Mayor until A.D. 1502.

The works at the Parral, Segovia, A.D. 1472–94, afford another example of an architect acting also as contractor for the work; and about the same time a monk of this convent, Juan de Escobedo, superintended the repair of the aqueduct, and was afterwards sent to the Queen (Isabella) to report to her on the state of various buildings in Segovia.

In 1482 Pedro Compte, of Valencia, said to be " *Molt sabut en l'art de la pedra,*" was the architect of the Exchange at Valencia—a building evidently copied to some extent from Sagrera's Exchange at Palma; and at a later date he was employed upon some water-works for the keeping up the waters in the Guadalaviar at Valencia. He held the post of Maestro Mayor of the city, with an annual salary. In him we seem to have not only an architect and engineer, but one of so much character and influence as to hold important posts, being " *alcaide perpetuo* " as well as Maestro Mayor of the city.

In the beginning of the sixteenth century the new cathedral at Salamanca was commenced, but only after a vast amount of consultation among architects. The King had to order Anton Egas of Toledo, and Alfonso Rodriguez of Seville, to go to Salamanca and decide upon the plan for the church, and these two men drew up a joint plan which they presented to the Chapter; two or three years later, nothing having been done in the meantime, a Junta of nine architects was assembled, who jointly agreed on a very elaborate report, detailing all the parts and proportions of the church; and their report having been presented, the Chapter forthwith proceeded to elect a master of the works.[1]

[1] *See* the translation of these documents in the Appendix.

Rodrigo Gil de Hontañon was appointed; and by his will, dated in May, A.D. 1577, it appears that he had a house rent free, as well as his salary of 30,000 maravedis a year.[1]   He had also liberty to undertake other works; for, a few years later, he designed the cathedral at Segovia, and by his will it seems that he had several other churches in hand, in some of which it is evident that he acted as contractor, as he complains bitterly of the difficulties he had been put to by the large sums he had paid for the work at the church of San Julian at Toro, without being repaid by the authorities.   It is remarkable that the works at Salamanca were examined from time to time by two architects, who reported whether Hontañon was following the instructions laid down for his guidance by the Junta, and this supervision rather leads to the inference that the design was not made by Hontañon, but prepared for him; and that it was necessary, as it is nowadays, to employ some one to see that he executed his work properly. The curiously exact terms of the report of the Junta, which specifies the height, thickness, and proportions of all the walls in the church, could not have been adopted as they are unless the Junta had some plans before them when they drew up their report, and on the whole I think it probable that the plan which Egas and Rodriguez prepared formed the basis on which they proceeded.   This plan is still said to be preserved in the archives, and it would be very interesting to see how far it agrees with the church which has been erected.[2]

But, on the other hand, there is a report upon the state of the works in A.D. 1523, given by Cean Bermudez, which tends to confirm Hontañon's position as a real architect.[3]   It is signed by three architects, Juan de Rasinas, Henrique de Egas, and Vasco de la Zarza.   They go into the question of the height to which the vaults ought to be carried, they say the walls are built properly, and, finally, that they were shown a plan of Juan Gil de Hontañon's for some alteration of the work, and that in their opinion it is good, and they have, therefore, signed it with their names.

There are other instances at this time of the assemblage of Juntas of architects, of which one or two may properly be mentioned here; one of these was in reference to the Cimborio of the cathedral at Zaragoza which fell in A.D. 1520, when a number

---

[1] This sum would probably be equal to about £90 or £100 per annum at the present day.
[2] Other plans still preserved in Spain are, the original design for the church of San Juan de los Reyes, Toledo, and that for the west front of Barcelona Cathedral.   I have tried in vain to obtain copies of these plans.
[3] *Arq. de]España*, i. 282-284.

of architects were at once called together to advise as to its reconstruction; and again, in the same way, when the Cimborio at Seville fell, in A.D. 1511, several architects were consulted, and after they had reported, one of them—Hontañon, the fashionable architect of the day—was selected to manage the execution of the work.[1]

At this late date we have, I believe for the first time, the singular description of a man as " master maker of churches." This occurs in the contract entered into by Benedicto Oger, of Alió, for the erection of a church at Reus. From the terms of the contract Oger seems to have been a mason: he was to have three others with him, and was bound not to undertake any other work. And if the authorities desired it they were to have his work examined by another " master," though whether by one of his own grade, or a superior man, does not appear.

Another contract of a somewhat similar kind was entered into in A.D. 1518 by Domingo Urteaga for the erection of the church of Sta. Maria de Cocentaina, in Valencia. He bound himself to go with his wife and family to Cocentaina, where the town was to give him a house rent free. He was to do all that a " master " ought in the management of such a work, without attending to other works, and was to receive each day for himself five sueldos, and was to provide two assistants and two apprentices, the former to have three sueldos each, and the latter one and a half. He was to be every day at the work, having half an hour for breakfast, and an hour for dinner in winter, and an hour and a half in summer. Here again, though Urteaga was evidently only a foreman of the works, there is no reference to any superintendent or architect, and nothing is said about any plans which are to be followed. I conclude, therefore, that in this case too the foreman of the masons was really the architect.

In addition to the men I have here rapidly mentioned, there

[1] We have accidental evidence of the fact that Hontañon was an architect, for the " Master of the Works " of La Magdalena, Valladolid, contracted in A.D. 1570 to build the tower and body of the church according to his plan for a specified sum. But it will be observed that the date of this agreement is very late, and that, whilst the maker of a plan had become an architect in the modern sense of the word, the Maestro Mayor had descended to be, in fact, nothing more than the contractor for the work, also in the modern sense. Somewhat in the same way we know that when the lantern of Burgos Cathedral fell, in A.D. 1539, Felipe de Borgoña was summoned from Toledo to superintend the two cathedral masters of the works: from which it seems probable that they executed the work which Borgoña designed. So again at an earlier date, in A.D. 1375, Jayme Castayls executed some statues for the west front of Tarragona cathedral, under the direction of Bernardo de Vallfogona, the Maestro Mayor.

were many others whose work was confined to the design and execution of certain portions of buildings; such a one was Berengario Portell, "*lapicida*" of Gerona, who in A.D. 1325 entered into a contract for the execution of the columns of the cloister of Vique Cathedral, and who is commonly said to have executed the columns and capitals for the cloister at Ripoll also. Such, in later days, was Gil de Siloe, who both designed and executed the monuments at Miraflores; and such, though in a less eminent position, were the various wood-carvers, decorators, painters on glass, makers of metal screens, and the like, the names of a great number of whom are still preserved in the volumes of Cean Bermudez.[1]

There is also another officer who ought not to be forgotten here—the "*aparejador*" or assistant of the architect—clerk of the works as we should call him. About his office there is no doubt, but it will have been observed that some men who held it—as *e.g.* Juan Campero—have at other times acted as architects or contractors, which is precisely what might be expected.

There are a few but not very important cases of competition among artists recorded in the work of Cean Bermudez; but generally they seem to me to have been rather competitions for the execution of work than for its design. Such, for instance, was the competition for the execution of the monument of D. Alvaro de Luna and his wife in Toledo Cathedral, when the design of Pablo Ortiz was selected.[2] Cristóbal Andino is said to have competed unsuccessfully with other men, in A.D. 1540, for the execution of the iron screens of Toledo Cathedral. Cean Bermudez speaks also of a competition among architects as to the rebuilding of Segovia Cathedral;[3] but I doubt whether his statement can be depended on.

The result at which we arrive after this *résumé* of the practice of Spanish architects is certainly that it was utterly unlike the practice of our own day. Whether it was either better or worse I can hardly venture to say; it seems to me, indeed, to be of comparatively little importance whether an architect is paid as of old by the year, or as now by a commission on the cost of the works; probably the difference in amount is seldom serious; but on the other hand it is possible that where special contracts are made the sums paid are not always the same, and so the

---

[1] *Bellas Artes en España.* This catalogue of artists includes those who lived before the year 1500, the names of fifty sculptors, thirty painters, several silversmiths, workers in stained glass, and others.

[2] *See* Vol. I., p. 346.   [3] *See* Vol. I., p. 258.

absurd rule by which at present the best and the worst architect both get the same amount of pay for their work is avoided; one result of this rule is, that the architect of the highest reputation, in order to reap the pecuniary reward to which he is entitled, is tempted to undertake so much work that it is impossible for him to attend to half of it, and so in time, unless he have an extraordinary capacity for rapid work, his work deteriorates, and his reputation is likely to suffer.

The other old custom common in Spain—of architects contracting for the execution of their own works—does not seem to deserve much respect; yet one cannot but see that it was a natural result of the universal feeling and taste for art which seems to have obtained in the middle ages; and though it would now certainly be mere madness to ask any chance builder to execute an architectural work, there are undoubtedly many builders who are at least as well fitted to do so as are a large number of those who, without study or proper education, are nevertheless able, unchallenged by any one, to call themselves architects.

On the whole, then, it is vain to regret the passing away of a system which is foreign to the nature and ideas of an artistic profession such as that of the architects of England now; though if these old men, whose art and whose interests pulled opposite ways—seeing they were architects and contractors—did their work so honestly that it still stands unharmed by time, we may well take great shame to ourselves if the rules for our personal respectability, about which we are all so jealous, are yet in practice so often compatible, apparently, with a system of shams and makeshifts, of false construction and bad execution, of which these old architect-builders were almost wholly guiltless.

The questions between ourselves and them, when simply stated, are these—Whose work is best in itself, and whose work will last the longest? If these questions cannot be answered in our favour, then it is absurd to protest vigorously against the practice which we see pursued by such men as Juan Campero, Martin Llobet, Juan de Ruesga, Guillermo Sagrera, or Pedro de Cumba, and we shall do well to admit, whenever necessary, that he is the best architect who designs the best building, whatever his education; though it is undoubtedly true that he is most likely to be the best architect who is the best taught, the most refined, and the most regularly educated in his art.

It is often, and generally thoughtlessly, assumed, that most of the churches of the middle ages were designed by monks or clerical architects. So far as Spain is concerned, the result at which we arrive is quite hostile to this assumption, for in all the names of architects that I have noticed there are but one or two who were clerics. The abbat who in the eighth or ninth century rebuilt Leon Cathedral is one; Frater Bernardus of Tarragona, in A.D. 1256, another; and the monk of El Parral, who restored the Roman aqueduct at Segovia, is the third; and the occurrence of these three exceptions to the otherwise general rule proves clearly, I think, that in Spain the distinct position of the architect was understood and accepted a good deal earlier than it was, perhaps, in England. In our own country it is indeed commonly asserted that the bishops and abbats were themselves the architects of the great churches built under their rule. Gundulph, Flambard, Walsingham, and Wykeham, have all been so described, but I suspect upon insufficient evidence; and those who have devoted the most study and time to the subject seem to be the least disposed to allow the truth of the claim made for them. The contrary evidence which I am able to adduce from Spain certainly serves to confirm these doubts. I was myself strongly disposed once to regard the attempt to deprive us of our great clerical architects as a little sacrilegious; but I am bound to say that I have now changed my mind, and believe that the attempt was only too well warranted by the facts. In short, the common belief in a race of clerical architects and in ubiquitous bodies of freemasons, seems to me to be altogether erroneous. The more careful the inquiry is that we make into the customs of the architects of the middle ages, the more clear does it appear that neither of these classes had any general existence; and in Spain, so far as I have examined, I have met with not a single trace of either. I am glad that it is so; for in these days of doubt and perplexity as to what is true in art, it is at least a comfort to find that one may go on heartily with one's work, with the honest conviction that the position one occupies may be, if one chooses to make it so, as nearly as possible the same as that occupied by the artists of the middle ages. So that, as it was open to them—often with small means and in spite of many difficulties—to achieve very great works of lasting architectural merit, the time may come when, if we do our work with equal zeal, equal artistic feeling, and equal honesty, our own names will be added to the list, which already includes theirs, of artists who have earned the respect and affection of all those whose everyday life is blessed with the sight of the true and beautiful works which in age after age they have left behind them as enduring monuments of their artistic skill.

APPENDIX

A

CATALOGUE OF DATED EXAMPLES OF SPANISH BUILDINGS, FROM THE TENTH TO THE SIXTEENTH CENTURY INCLUSIVE

NOTE.—*The dates of those Examples which are printed in Italics appear to me to be very uncertain, or are those of buildings which I have not visited.*

DATE.	PLACE.	REMARKS.
914	BARCELONA	Church of San Pablo del Campo said to have been built.
983	BARCELONA	San Pedro de las Puellas consecrated.
1017	GERONA..........	*Church of Saint Daniel commenced.*
1038	GERONA..........	Consecration of first Cathedral, of which remains exist.
1058	ELNE	Consecration of Church.
1063	LEON	The Panteon, San Isidoro, appears to have been finished in this year.
1078	SANTIAGO	Cathedral commenced.
1078	SANTIAGO	South transept doorways erected.
1085	TOLEDO	The Church " Cristo de la Luz " existed before this date.
1090	AVILA	Town walls commenced.
1091	AVILA	Cathedral commenced.
1109	TOLEDO	Outer circuit of walls.
1117	GERONA..........	*Church of San Pedro de los Galligans commenced.*
1117	GERONA..........	Cloisters of Cathedral erected.
1108 to 1126	TOLEDO	Puerta de Visagra erected.
1120	SALAMANCA.......	Old Cathedral commenced.
1128	SANTIAGO	Fabric of Cathedral so far finished as to be used.
1129	LUGO	Cathedral commenced.
1131	TARRAGONA	Cathedral commenced.

DATE.	PLACE.	REMARKS.
1136	SALAMANCA......	*Santo Tomé de los Caballeros consecrated.*
1146	BARCELONA	Collegiata of Sta. Aña founded.
1146	VERUELA........	Abbey commenced.
1149	LEON	Church of San Isidoro consecrated in this year.
1156	SALAMANCA	*Church of San Adrian consecrated.*
1171	VERUELA........	Abbey first occupied, and probably completed in this year.
1173	BARCELONA, ...	*Royal Chapel of Sta. Agueda, attached to the palace of the Counts of Barcelona, completed.*
1173	SALAMANCA......	*Church of San Martin consecrated.*
1174	ZAMORA	Cathedral completed.
1175	SANTIAGO	Chapel beneath west front of Cathedral finished about this year.
1177	LUGO	Cathedral finished.
1178	SALAMANCA......	Cloister of old Cathedral in course of erection; Chapter-house probably erected at same time.
1179	SALAMANCA......	*Church of S. Thomas of Canterbury consecrated.*
1180	BURGOS	Convent of Las Huelgas commenced; inhabited in 1187; formally established as a Cistercian Convent in 1199.
1180	POBLET	*Benedictine Monastery founded.*
1188	SANTIAGO	Western doors of Cathedral finished.
1188	TUDELA	Cathedral consecrated.
1203	LÉRIDA	First stone of Cathedral laid.
1208	SEGOVIA	Templars' Church consecrated.
1212	TOLEDO	Bridge of San Martin erected.
1219	MONDOÑEDO	*Cathedral commenced.*
1221	BURGOS	First stone of Cathedral laid.
1221	TOLEDO	Church of San Roman consecrated.
1227	TOLEDO	First stone of Cathedral laid.
1230	BURGOS	Cathedral first used in this year.
1235	TARAZONA	Cathedral founded.
1239	BARCELONA	Chapel of Sta. Lucia, and doorway from cloister into south transept of Cathedral.

Date.	Place.	Remarks.
1252–84	Avila	Central Lantern of San Vicente built.
1258	Toledo	Bridge of Alcantara rebuilt.
1262	Valencia	First stone of Cathedral laid. South transept and apse of this date.
1273	Leon	Cathedral in progress.
1278	Lérida	Cathedral consecrated.
1278	Tarragona	Nine of the statues of the Apostles in west front of Cathedral executed.
1287	Barcelona	Nuestra Señora del Carmen founded.
1292	Avila	Considerable works in the Cathedral under Sancho II., Bishop of Avila, 1292-1353.
1298	Barcelona	New Cathedral commenced.
1303	Leon	Cathedral finished (save the towers) before this date.
1310–27	Lérida	Western side and entrance to cloister of Cathedral, and tower at S.W. angle of cloister, erected between these years.
1316–46	Gerona	Chevet of Cathedral in course of building.
1318	Gerona	Choir of San Feliu completed before this date.
1321	Palencia	First stone of Cathedral laid.
1328	Barcelona	Sta. Maria del Mar commenced, and completed in 1383.
1329	Barcelona	North transept of Cathedral.
1329	Barcelona	Sta. Maria del Pi commenced, and *consecrated in* 1353.
1332	Guadalajara	Chapel of Holy Trinity in the Church of Santiago.
1339	Barcelona	Crypt and Chapel of Sta. Eulalia in the Cathedral completed.
1345	Barcelona	SS. Just y Pastor commenced.
1346	Gerona	Retablo of Altar and Baldachin erected.
1349	Valencia	Puerta de Serranos erected.
1350	Lugo	Church of Santo Domingo consecrated.

Date.	Place.	Remarks.
1350	Zaragoza	*East wall decoration executed.*
1351	Gerona..........	Stalls in Choir of Cathedral executed.
1366	Toledo	Synagogue (now Church "del Transito") completed.
1368–92	Gerona..........	Steeple of San Feliu in course of building.
1369	Barcelona	Casa Consistorial commenced; finished in 1378.
1374	La Coruña.......	Chapel of the Visitation in Church of Sta. Maria.
1375	Tarragona	Completion of Statues in west front of Cathedral.
1380	Toledo	Bridge of Alcantara repaired.
1381	Valencia	First stone of the Micalete (tower of the Cathedral) laid.
1383	Barcelona	Sta. Maria del Mar completed.
1383	Barcelona	The Casa Lonja, or Exchange, founded.
1388	Barcelona	West doorway of San Jayme.
1389	Alcalá de Henares	Tower of Archbishop's Palace.
1389	Toledo	Cloister and Chapel of San Blas completed.
1389	Toledo	Bridge of San Martin built.
1391	Lérida	West doorway of Cloister completed.
1397	Lérida	Steeple of Cathedral in course of erection.
1397	Pamplona	Cathedral commenced.
1399	Burgos	*Chancel and Aisles of San Gil founded.*
1400	Huesca	Cathedral commenced.
1404	Valencia	Lantern or Cimborio of Cathedral completed.
1405	Toledo	Synagogue (now Church of Sta. Maria la Blanca) converted into a Church, and much altered.
1410	Palencia	Stalls in Choir of Cathedral executed.
1415	Burgos	Church of Convent of San Pablo erected.
1416	Barcelona	San Jayme in progress.
1416	Lérida	Steeple of Cathedral completed.

Date.	Place.	Remarks.
1416	Manresa	The Collegiata in progress at this date.
1416	Perpiñan	Cathedral in progress.
1416	Tarragona	Reredos of High Altar.
1417	Gerona.........	Nave of Cathedral commenced.
1418	Toledo	West front of Cathedral commenced.
1424	Valencia	Tower of Cathedral completed.
1425	Toledo	The N.W. Steeple of Cathedral commenced.
1431	Cervera	*Steeple of Sta. Maria.*
1435	Burgos	Convent of San Pablo commenced.
1436	Barcelona	Casa de la Disputacion erected.
1438	Olite	Considerable works in progress.
1440	Avila	Tower of San Vicente completed.
1440	Medina del Campo	Castle " de la Mota."
1442	Burgos	Spires of Cathedral commenced.
1442	Toledo	Chapel of Santiago (built by D. Alvaro de Luna) erected.
1442	Valladolid	San Pablo commenced.
1444	Barcelona	The Hala de Paños completed.
1444	Valencia	Puerta de Cuarte.
1448	Barcelona	Cloister of Cathedral completed.
1453	Barcelona	Sta. Maria del Pi consecrated.
1454	Burgos	Convent of la Cartucca, Miraflores, commenced.
1458	Gerona.........	South door of nave of Cathedral.
1459	Toledo	Façade " de los Leones " (South transept).
1459 to 1482	Valencia	West end of nave of the Cathedral erected, and (probably) the Chapter-house.
1461	Guadalajara	Palace del Infantado.
1463	Valladolid	San Pablo completed.
1465	Avila	Canopy over the Shrine of San Vicente.
1471	Astorga	First stone of Cathedral laid.
1472	Segovia	Capilla Mayor of El Parral commenced.
1476	Toledo	San Juan de los Reyes, Toledo, commenced.
1480	Burgos	Stalls in the Coro of Chapel at Miraflores.

DATE.	PLACE.	REMARKS.
1480-92	VALLADOLID	College of Sta. Cruz.
1482	VALENCIA	The Casa Lonja commenced.
1482-93	AVILA	Convent of Santo Tomás.
1483	TOLEDO	Doorway of old Sacristy.
1484	TOLEDO	Bridge of Alcantara fortified.
1485	SEGOVIA	Vaulting of El Parral finished.
1487	BURGOS	Chapel of the Constable.
1488-96	VALLADOLID	College of San Gregorio.
1489	TOLEDO	Monument of Alvaro de Luna in Chapel of Santiago in Cathedral.
1489-93	BURGOS	Monument of Juan and Isabel in the Church at Miraflores.
1490	LÉRIDA	South Porch.
1494	SEGOVIA	Tribune in Church of El Parral rebuilt.
1495	TOLEDO	Lower range of Stalls in Coro of Cathedral.
1497	ALCALÁ DE HENARES	Church of SS. Just y Pastor commenced.
1497-1512	BURGOS	Stalls in Coro of Cathedral.
1498	ALCALÁ DE HENARES	College of San Ildefonso commenced.
1499	VALLADOLID	Church of San Benito.
1500	TOLEDO	Retablo of High Altar.
1503	MEDINA DEL CAMPO	Capilla Mayor of Church of S. Antholin.
1504	SANTIAGO	Hospital of Santiago.
1504	TOLEDO	Entrance to Winter Chapter-room.
1504	ZARAGOZA	The Torre Nueva in course of construction.
1504-10	PALENCIA	Cathedral completed.
1505	ZARAGOZA	Cimborio, or Lantern, of the Seu commenced.
1507	SAN SEBASTIAN ...	Church of San Vicente commenced.
1507	SIGÜENZA	Cloister of Cathedral completed.
1508	IRUN	Church commenced.
1509	ALCALÁ DE HENARES	Church of SS. Just y Pastor completed.
1513	LEON	San Isidoro, new Choir erected.
1513	SALAMANCA.......	First stone of new Cathedral laid.
1514	PALENCIA	Cathedral Chapter-house and Cloister.

DATE.	PLACE.	REMARKS.
1515	HUESCA	Cathedral completed.
1518	AVILA	Monument of Don Juan in the Church of Santo Tomás.
1520	HUESCA	The Retablo of the Principal Altar commenced.
1520	TARAZONA	*Cathedral Cloister.*
1520	ZARAGOZA	Cimborio of the Seu completed.
1525	SEGOVIA	Cathedral commenced.
1531	TOLEDO	Chapel de los Reyes Nuevos.
1533	SANTIAGO	Cloisters.
1536	ZARAGOZA	Sta. Engracia, Cloister erected.
1543	TOLEDO	Upper range of Stalls in Coro of Cathedral.
1548	TOLEDO	Rejas of Capilla Mayor and Coro of Cathedral.
1550	TARAZONA	Cimborio of Cathedral.
1553	ALCALÁ DE HENARES	Patio of University.
1567	BURGOS	Lantern or Cimborio completed.
1572–90	MANRESA	Steeple of the Seu or Collegiata completed.
1576	VALLADOLID	Church of La Magdalena.
1579	GERONA..........	Vault of Cathedral finished.
1586	BURGOS	Capilla Mayor in the Church of San Gil.

B

CATALOGUE OF ARCHITECTS, SCULPTORS, AND BUILDERS OF THE CHURCHES, ETC., MENTIONED IN THIS WORK

ABIELL [GUILLERMO]. One of the Junta of Architects consulted at *Gerona* in A.D. 1416. At this time he was Master of the Works at *Sta. Maria del Pi, San Jayme,* and the Hospital of *Santa Cruz* in *Barcelona.*

ALAVA [JUAN DE]. One of the Architects summoned to the Junta at *Salamanca* in A.D. 1513. He was a native of Vitoria, and master of the works of the Cathedral at *Placencia.*

ALEMAN   [JUAN].   Sculptor. Wrought at the western and southern doorways of *Toledo* Cathedral, A.D. 1462–66.

ALFONSO   [JUAN].   Sculptor. Wrought on the façade of *Toledo* Cathedral in A.D. 1418.

ALFONSO [RODRIGO].   Maestro Mayor of *Toledo* Cathedral, probably the Architect of the Cloister and Chapel of *San Blas*, the first stone of which was laid August 14, 1389. He designed the *Carthusian Convent* of *Paular*, near *Segovia*, in A.D. 1390.

ANDINO [CRISTÓBAL DE].   Made the iron Screen of the Capilla Mayor in *Palencia* Cathedral in A.D. 1520; the Screen of the Chapel of the Constable at *Burgos* in 1523; and in 1540 he competed unsuccessfully with other men for the erection of the Screens and Pulpits of *Toledo* Cathedral.

ANTIGONI [ANTONIO].   Master of the Works in the town of *Castellon de Empurias*, and one of the Junta of Architects consulted at *Gerona* in A.D. 1416.

ARANDIA [JUAN DE].   Probably a native of Biscay. Architect (?) and Builder of the Church of *San Benito* at *Valladolid*, which was commenced in A.D. 1499. He contracted for the first part of the work for 1,460,000 maravedis, and for the remainder for 500,000.

ARFE   [ANTONIO DE].   Silversmith; a native of Leon. His work is thoroughly Renaissance, and, though much praised, really very uninteresting. *Circa* 1520–77.

ARFE   [ENRIQUE DE].   A German; father of Antonio, born in 1470-80; dec. *circa* 1550. A famous Silversmith. Worked at *Leon, Toledo*, etc.

ARGENTA [BARTOLOMÉ].   Master of the works, *Gerona* Cathedral, 1325 to 1346. He seems to have superintended the erection of most of the Choir now standing.

BADAJOZ [JUAN DE].   Sculptor and Master of the Works of *Leon* Cathedral. Architect of Choir of *San Isidoro, Leon*. In A.D. 1512 he was one of the Junta of Architects consulted as to rebuilding *Salamanca* Cathedral. In 1513 he went to *Seville* to examine the fabric of the Cathedral, for which he received a fee of 100 ducats. In 1522 he went to *Salamanca* to see that the works at the Cathedral were being properly executed. In 1545 he was Architect of the Monastery at *Exlonza* near *Leon*, and calls himself " Architector " in an inscription on its wall.

BALAGUER [PEDRO]. Architect of the Tower of *Valencia* Cathedral in A.D. 1414. He is called an " Arquitecto perito " in a contemporary document, and was paid for going to *Lerida, Narbonne*, and elsewhere to examine their steeples with a view to his own work.

BARTOLOMÉ. Sculptor, *Tarragona*. Executed in A.D. 1278 nine of the Statues of the Western Doorway.

BARTOLOMÉ. Silversmith, who executed part of the Retablo of *Gerona* Cathedral in A.D. 1325.

BENES [PEDRO]. Made the Canopy over the ·Altar at *Gerona* Cathedral before A.D. 1340.

BERNARDUS [FRATER]. Magister Operis of *Tarragona* Cathedral in A.D. 1256.

BERRUGUETE [ALONSO]. Architect, Sculptor, and Painter. Went to Italy in A.D. 1504, and studied at Rome and Florence: afterwards, in A.D. 1520, returned to Spain, and held the appointment of Maestro Mayor to Charles V. Executed the Stalls and Retablos of *San Benito, Valladolid*, in 1526-32, and the upper range of Stalls on the Epistle side of *Toledo* Cathedral in 1543. His works are numerous, and he was· the great reviver of Pagan architecture in Spain.

BLAY [PEDRO]. Architect of the Casa de la Disputacion, *Barcelona*. in 1436 according to Cean Bermudez. But this seems impossible, unless there were two of the same name, as one was Maestro Mayor of the Cathedral in 1584.

BOFFIY [GUILLERMO]. Architect of Nave of *Gerona* Cathedral in A.D. 1416. It was to discuss and advise upon his plan that a Junta of twelve Architects was summoned; their opinions are given in the Appendix H, and in the end his plan was carried into execution.

BONCKS [ARNAU]. A native of Ax (in the county of Foix).

Directed the works at the Mole of *Tarragona*, for which he was also the contractor, in A.D. 1507.

BONIFACIO [MARTIN SANCHEZ]. Maestro Mayor of *Toledo* Cathedral from 1481 to 1494. He executed the doorway of the old Sacristy, *circa* 1484.

BONIFACIO [PEDRO]. Painter on Glass. Executed some of the windows in the nave of *Toledo* Cathedral in A.D. 1439.

BONIFE [MATIAS]. Made the lower range of Stalls in the Coro of *Barcelona* Cathedral in A.D. 1457.

BORGOÑA [FELIPE DE]. Sculptor of the upper range of Stalls on the Gospel side of *Toledo* Cathedral. He was consulted as to the design for the Cimborio or lantern of *Burgos* Cathedral, and executed the Sculptures under the arches of the apse in the same church. He is said to have been Maestro Mayor of *Seville* Cathedral (?), and was one of the Architects consulted as to *Salamanca* new Cathedral in A.D. 1512. He died in 1543.

BORGOÑA [JUAN DE]. Painted in A.D. 1495 the Cloister of *Toledo* Cathedral. In 1508 painted five subjects for *Avila* Cathedral. He dec. *circa* 1533.

BRUXELAS [JUAN DE]. Executed the Retablo of the Chapel of *San Ildefonso, Toledo*, in A.D. 1500.

CAMPERO [JUAN]. One of the Junta of Architects consulted at *Salamanca* in A.D. 1512, and afterwards appointed assistant to the Architect there. In 1529 he was engaged as builder at *El Parral, Segovia*. In 1530 he contracted with the Chapter of *Segovia* for the removal and re-erection of the old *Cloisters*. He had been employed by Cardinal Ximenes as Architect and Builder at *Torrelunga*.

CANET [ANTONIUS]. Sculptor of *Barcelona*. One of the Junta at *Gerona* in 1416, and Master of the Fabric of the Cathedral at *Urgel*.

CANTARELL [GIRALT]. Architect engaged on Steeple at *Manresa* from A.D. 1572 to 1590.

CARPINTERO [MACIAS]. A native of Medina del Campo, and Architect and Sculptor of the College of *San Gregorio, Valladolid*, in A.D. 1488. He is said to have committed suicide in A.D. 1490.

CARREÑO [FERNANDO DE]. Master of the Works at the *Castle, Medina del Campo*, 1440.

CASTAÑEDA [JUAN DE]. Architect at *Burgos* A.D. 1539. He was one of the Cathedral architects, and wrought under Felipe de Borgoña in the rebuilding of the Cimborio, which he completed in A.D. 1567. He is said to have designed the *Gateway of Sta. Maria at Burgos*.

CASTAYLS [MAESTRO JAYME]. Sculptor, *Tarragona*, in 1375. Executed by contract some of the Statues in the Western Doorway of the Cathedral, under the direction of Bernardo de Vallfogona, the Master of the Works. He executed three of the Apostles and all the Prophets, and bound himself to make them all life-size.

CEBRIAN [PEDRO]. Master of the Works, *Leon* Cathedral, A.D. 1175.

CENTELLAS [EL MAESTRO]. Made the Stalls for the Choir of *Palencia* Cathedral in A.D. 1410. A native of Valencia.

CERVIA [BERENGUER]. Made the terra-cotta Statues in the South Door of *Gerona* Cathedral in A.D. 1458. He also made a Statue of Sta. Eulalia and a Cross of terra-cotta for a doorway in *Barcelona* Cathedral.

CESPIDES [DOMINGO]. Maker of the iron Reja, east of the Coro, *Toledo* Cathedral, in A.D. 1548.

CIPRES [PEDRO]. Maestro Mayor of *Gerona* Cathedral in A.D. 1430.

COLIVELLA [GUILLERMO]. Master of the Works at *Lerida* Cathedral, A.D. 1397. He had contracted in A.D. 1391 for the execution of some Statues for a doorway, and was evidently therefore a working Sculptor.

COLONIA [FRANCISCO DE]. Said to have been related to Juan and Simon de Colonia. He was an Architect of Burgos, and was employed in A.D. 1515, and again in 1522, by the Chapter of *Salamanca* Cathedral, to go there and examine the works to see that J. G. de Hontañon was executing them according to the plan.

COLONIA [JUAN DE]. Designed the upper part of the Western Steeples of *Burgos* Cathedral. They were commenced in A.D. 1442, and in 1456 one

Spire was completed, and the other nearly so. *San Pablo, Valladolid*, is also said by some to be his work in 1463. He was Architect of the Chapel of the Constable at *Burgos* in 1487, and made the design for the Church at *Miraflores*, for which he was paid 3350 maravedis. He is said to have been a German by birth, and to have been brought to Spain by Bishop Alonso de Cartagena when he returned from the Council of Basel.

COLONIA [SIMON DE]. Completed the Church at *Miraflores* from A.D. 1488 to 1500. He was son of Juan de Colonia, and died before A.D. 1512.

COMAS· [PEDRO]. Maestro Mayor, *San Feliu, Gerona*, in A.D. 1385. He seems to have been Maestro Mayor of *Gerona* Cathedral from A.D. 1368 to 1397.

COMPTE [PEDRO]. Architect at *Valencia*, employed on the Cathedral, and one of the Architects consulted as to the rebuilding of the Cimborio of *Zaragoza*, and the Architect of the Lonja at *Valencia*. In 1486 he superintended the laying of a marble pavement in the Cathedral there. He is described in a contemporary MS. as being " Molt sabut en l'art de la pedra." He was made perpetual " Alcaide " of the Lonja, or Exchange, in 1498, with a salary of 30 sueldos a year. He was " Maestro Mayor " of the city, and was employed on some engineering works for it: one of them was the bringing the waters of the river Cabriel to augment those of the Guadalaviar, and in A.D. 1500 he was engaged on another similar work.

COVARRUBIAS [ALONSO DE]. A native of Burgos. He was one of the Architects consulted as to the erection of *Salamanca* Cathedral in 1513. He competed with Diego de Siloe for the erection of the *Chapel " de los Reyes Nuevos," Toledo* Cathedral, and succeeded, 1531-34. Was Maestro Mayor of *Toledo* from 1534 to 1566. Employed on the Archbishop's Palace at *Alcalá*. Employed by the King on the Alcazars at *Madrid* and *Toledo* in 1537. He was paid 25,000 maravedis a year, and compelled to attend his work six months in the year, during which time he received four reals a day for maintenance. He married Maria de Egas, a daughter, it is thought, of Anequin de Egas; and his son was afterwards Bishop of Segovia. Various Royal writs in reference to his work and payment are given by Cean Bermudez, *Arq. de Esp.*, i. 304-7.

CRUZ [DIEGO DE LA]. Assisted Gil de Siloe in his works in the church at *Miraflores, Burgos*, A.D. 1496 to 1499.

CUMBA [PEDRO DE]. " Magister et fabricator " of the Cathedral at *Lérida* in A.D. 1203.

DEO [PETRUS DE]. Master of the Works at *San Isidoro, Leon*, in A.D. 1065. He also built a bridge called " de Deo tamben," and seems to have had a great repute for sanctity.

DOLFIN [EL MAESTRO]. Painter on Glass. Commenced painting the windows of *Toledo* Cathedral in A.D. 1418.

EGAS [ANEQUIN DE]. Of Brussels. Maestro Mayor of *Toledo* Cathedral in 1459, and erected the façade " de los Leones " about that year. He had an " aparejador " (or clerk of the works), Juan (or Alfonso?) Fernandez de Llena.

EGAS [ANTON]. In 1509 was engaged at *Toledo* Cathedral, and received two writs from the King ordering him to go to *Salamanca* to assist other Architects in deciding on the plan of the new Cathedral. In A.D. 1510, conjointly with Alonso Rodriguez, he drew a plan for the Cathedral.

EGAS [ENRIQUE DE]. Succeeded his father as Maestro Mayor of *Toledo* in A.D. 1494, and held the office until his death in A.D. 1534. He was summoned with other Architects to decide what should be done after the fall of the Cimborio at *Seville*. He built the Hospital " de los Espiritos," at *Toledo*, in 1504-14, and the Royal Hospital at *Santiago* in 1519. Altered the Mozarabic Chapel at *Toledo*, and built the Hospital of *Sta. Cruz, Valladolid*, went in 1515 with two other Architects to examine

J. G. de Hontañon's work at *Seville*, for which he was paid 120 ducats of gold. He and Juan de Alava then made plans together for the *Capilla Mayor* at *Seville*. He was ordered by the King to go to *Zaragoza* to examine the Cathedral, but endeavoured to excuse himself on the ground that he had the Royal Hospital at *Santiago* in hand. In 1529 he appears to have gone again to *Salamanca* to see whether the work at the Cathedral was being done perfectly by J. G. de Hontañon. He went to *Malaga* on another occasion with the same object. In a Royal writ issued in his favour, in A.D. 1552, he is called " Maestro de Canteria "—Master of Masonry.

ESCOBEDO [FR. JUAN DE]. A monk of the Convent of El Parral, Segovia. He repaired the Roman Aqueduct at *Segovia* in A.D. 1481.

ESTACIO. Native of Alexandria, Engineer, constructed the Mole at *Barcelona*, 1477.

FABRE, OR FABRA [JAYME]. Was Architect of the Dominican Convent at *Palma, Mallorca*, in A.D. 1317. This seems to have had a single nave of enormous width. He was ordered in 1307 to go to *Barcelona* to act as Architect at the Cathedral. In 1339 he assisted at the translation of the remains of Sta. Eulalia to the crypt under the high altar. He is said to have died *circa* 1388. He seems to have been the architect from whose work most of the later Catalan buildings were derived.

FAVARIIS [JACOBO DE]. A · native of Narbonne, and Architect of the Chevet of *Gerona* Cathedral in A.D. 1320.

FONT [CARLOS]. Of Montearagon. Was consulted with others as to the rebuilding of the Cimborio of *Zàragoza* Cathedral in A.D. 1500.

FONT [JUAN]. Architect engaged on Steeple at *Manresa* in A.D. 1572-90.

FORMENT [DAMIAN]. Executed the alabaster Reredos of *Huesca* Cathedral in 1520-33.

FRANCES [PEDRO]. Painter on Glass. Executed some of the windows of *Toledo* Cathedral, *circa* 1459, in company with two Germans, Pablo and Cristóbal.

FRANCK [JUAN]. One of the Architects employed on the Tower of *Valencia* Cathedral, between A.D. 1381 and 1418. He was employed in 1389 at the Monastery of *Guadalupe*.

GALLEGO [JUAN]. Master of the Works at *El Parral, Segovia*, in A.D. 1459-72.

GALLEGO [PEDRO]. " Gobernador de los Torres " at *Leon* Cathedral in A.D. 1175.

GARCIA [ALVAR]. Architect of *Avila* Cathedral in A.D. 1091, a native of Navarre.

GOMAR [FRANCISCO]. Executed the Porch in front of the South doorway of *Lérida* Cathedral, in A.D. 1490.

GOMEZ [ALVAR]. Maestro Mayor of *Toledo* Cathedral; in A.D. 1418 he designed the West Front and Tower of the Cathedral. The papers in the archives of the Cathedral speak of him as " aparejador de las canteras," which seems to imply that he was a superintendent of masons. He was appointed to this office in A.D. 1425, and is the first recorded to have held it; from his time the names of the architects of Toledo Cathedral are all known.

GUADALUPE [PEDRO DE]. Made additional Stalls for *Palencia* Cathedral, and moved the old stalls from the choir into the nave, in A.D. 1518.

GUAL [BARTOLOMÉ]. One of the Architects summoned to the Junta at *Gerona* in A.D. 1416. At this date he was Maestro Mayor of *Barcelona* Cathedral, and calls himself " lapicida et magister operis."

GUAS [JUAN]. Architect of the Convent of San Juan de los Reyes, *Toledo*, commenced in A.D. 1476. His portrait (together with those of his wife and children) is preserved in a mural painting in the Convent.

GUINGUAMPS [JOANNES DE]. " Lapicida " of the town of *Narbonne*, and one of the Junta of Architects at *Gerona* in A.D. 1416.

GUMIEL [PEDRO]. Architect of SS. Just y Pastor, at *Alcalá de Henares*, in A.D. 1497-1509. He was " Regidor " of the city in 1492, and Architect to Cardinal Ximenes, and both their names were inscribed on the first stone of the

College of *San Ildefonso* at *Alcalá*, which was laid in 1497. He died *circa* 1516.

GUTIERREZ [ANTONIO]. Executed the Entrance to the Summer Chapter-house, *Toledo* Cathedral, in A.D. 1504.

HENRICUS " Magister operis " of *Leon* Cathedral; he deceased in A.D. 1277.

HOLANDA [ALBERTO DE]. Painter on Glass, of Burgos. Executed several windows in A.D. 1520 for *Avila* Cathedral at a charge of 82 maravedis the foot.

HONTAÑON [JUAN GIL DE]. Was Maestro Mayor of *Salamanca* Cathedral when it was resolved to rebuild it. He made plans, which are still (it is said) preserved, with the signatures of four Architects who were called in to advise upon them. He seems, however, to have followed some plans prepared in A.D. 1510 by Alonso Rodriguez and Anton Egas, and to have been appointed Architect in 1513, after having given a joint report with nine other Architects on the mode of construction of the Cathedral. Subsequently other Architects, Martin de Palencia, Francisco de Colonia, Juan de Badajoz, and others, were summoned to *Salamanca* by the Chapter to certify that he was adhering to the plan originally agreed to. In one of their reports they speak of a plan made by Juan Gil, of which they approve. In 1513, after the fall of the Cimborio at *Seville*, he was summoned (after a Junta of four Architects had reported) to superintend the work, and before 1522 he made plans for the new Cathedral at *Segovia*, which was commenced in that year. He deceased in 1531.

HONTAÑON [JUAN GIL DE]. Son of Juan Gil. Assisted his father in his work at *Salamanca*.

HONTAÑON [RODRIGO GIL DE]. Second son of Juan Gil. Continued his father's works at *Salamanca* (with a salary of 30,000 maravedis and a house) and *Segovia* : he erected the Pagan façade of the College at *Alcalá de Henares*, and churches in various towns. In the paper appointing him " Maestro Mayor " of *Salamanca* Cathedral, he is called " Master of Masonry." His will proves that he contracted for as well as designed some buildings, as he complains bitterly of the losses he has sustained in this way, especially in the Church of *San Julian* at *Toro*, for which he could not get paid. This will is dated May 27, 1577.

JUAN [PEDRO]. Sculptor. Executed the Reredos of *Tarragona* Cathedral in 1426-36.

LAPI [GERI]. Embroiderer, of Florence. He made an Altar-cloth for the Collegiate Church at *Manresa*, which still exists, and is inscribed with his name.

LLENA [JUAN FERNANDEZ DE]. " Aparejador " or assistant to Anequin de Egas, Architect of *Toledo* Cathedral in A.D. 1459.

LLOBET [MARTIN]. Completed the Micalete at *Valencia* in A.D. 1424. He seems to have been a mason, and contracted for the execution of the work.

LOQUER [MIGUEL]. Made the Canopies of the Upper Stalls in the Coro of *Barcelona* Cathedral in A.D. 1483.

LUNA [HURTADO DE]. Maestro Mayor of the Church at *Irun* in A.D. 1508.

MAEDA [JUAN DE]. Assistant to Diego de Siloe, who by his will, in A.D. 1563, left him all his plans and designs.

MANS [PEDRO]. Enlarged the Reredos in *Palencia* in A.D. 1518.

MATHEUS. Master of the Works of *Santiago* Cathedral, from A.D. 1168 to 1188.

MATIENZO [G. FERNANDEZ DE]. Architect of Church at *Miraflores*, from A.D. 1466 to 1488, after the death of Juan de Colonia.

MOTA [GUILLERMUS DE LA]. " Socius magistri" of *Tarragona* Cathedral, and one of the Junta of Architects at *Gerona* in A.D. 1416. He completed the Retablo of *Tarragona* Cathedral (commenced by Pedro Juan in 1426).

NARBONNE [ENRIQUE OF]. Architect of Chevet of *Gerona* Cathedral in A.D. 1316.

NAVARRO [MIGUEL]. Contracted for the erection of the Cloisters of *San Francesco el Grande*, *Valencia*, in A.D. 1421.

NIETO [ALONSO]. Appointed " Obrero Mayor " of the Works at the Castle " de la Mota," *Medina del Campo*, in A.D. 1479.

OLOTZAGA [JUAN DE].   Designed and commenced the Cathedral at *Huesca* in A.D. 1400. He is said to have carved the statues for the façade.

OROZCO   [JUAN DE].   One of the Junta of Architects assembled at *Salamanca* in A.D. 1512.

ORTIZ   [PABLO].   Executed the Monuments of the Constable Alvaro de Luna and his wife, in the *Chapel of Santiago* in *Toledo* Cathedral. He obtained this work in a competition, and contracted for its execution in A.D. 1489.

PARADISO   [MATEO].   Architect of the Tower on the Bridge of Alcantara, *Toledo*, in A.D. 1217.

PEÑAFREYTA [PEDRO DE].   Master of the Works of *Lérida* Cathedral, deceased in A.D. 1286.

PEREZ   [PEDRO]   or   " PETRUS PETRI." Master of the Works of *Toledo* Cathedral. He deceased in A.D. 1290.

PITUENGA [FLORIN DE].   Superintendent of Works in building the Walls of *Avila* in A.D. 1090. He is said to have been a Frenchman.

PLANA [FRANCISCO DE].   A Catalan, Maestro Mayor of *Gerona* Cathedral *circa* A.D. 1346-68.

RAYMUNDO.   Master of the Works of *Lugo* Cathedral, which was commenced in A.D. 1129. The agreement for his payment is given in Vol. I., p. 171. He was evidently the Architect, and not the builder, of the Cathedral.

RIO [FRANCISCO DEL].   Built the Steeple of La Magdalena, *Valladolid*, under contract, and according to the plans of Rodrigo Gil de Hontañon, in 1570.

ROAN [GUILLEN DE].   Maestro Mayor of *Leon* Cathedral; he deceased in A.D. 1431, and on his monument he is called " Maestro " of Leon and " aparejador " of a chapel at *Tordesillas*, in which he was buried.

RODRIGO.   Sculptor of the lower range of Stalls in the Coro of *Toledo* Cathedral in A.D. 1495.

RODRIGUEZ [ALONSO].   Maestro Mayor of *Seville* Cathedral in A.D. 1503. In 1510, at the command of the King, he went to *Salamanca* with Anton Egas, and prepared a plan for rebuilding the Cathedral, and afterwards went to the island of *San Domingo* to build a Church at *Sanlucar*.

RODRIGUEZ [GASPAR].   Made the Iron Screen across the Coro of *Palencia* Cathedral in A.D. 1555.

RODRIGUEZ [JUAN]. Built the Church of *San Pablo, Burgos,* between A.D. 1415 and 1435.

ROMANO [CASANDRO]. Superintendent of Works in building the Walls of *Avila* in A.D. 1090.

ROQUE [EL MAESTRO]. Built the Cloister of *Barcelona* Cathedral, which was completed in A.D. 1448. He was appointed Master of the Works in A.D. 1388.

RUAN [CARLOS GALTES DE]. Master of the Works at *Lérida* Cathedral A.D. 1397 to 1416. He was employed on the Campanile.

RUESGA [JUAN DE]. An inhabitant of *Segovia.* Was employed by the monks of *El Parral* to reconstruct the Gallery for the Coro in their Church in A.D. 1494; he also completed *Palencia* Cathedral A.D. 1506-10, and seems to have been a builder rather than an architect.

SAGRERA [GUILLERMO]. Master of the Works of *S. John, Perpiñan,* in A.D. 1416. In the same year he served on the Junta of Architects at *Gerona.* In 1426 commenced the Lonja or Exchange at *Palma* in *Mallorca,* for which he was both Architect and Contractor, and carried it on until A.D. 1448 or 1450, when he quarrelled and went to law with his employers. He then went to *Naples,* and commenced the *Castel Nuovo* there in 1450, of which he is described as "Protomagister" in a Royal writ of that year.

SALÓRZANO [MARTIN DE]. Contracted to complete *Palencia* Cathedral in A.D. 1504, and deceased in 1506.

SANCHEZ [BONIFACIO]. Was Maestro Mayor of *Toledo* Cathedral in A.D. 1481-94, and designed the Entrance to the old Sacristy.

SANCHEZ [MARTIN]. Executed the Stalls in the Coro of the Church at *Miraflores,* near *Burgos,* in A.D. 1480.

SANCHEZ [PEDRO]. "Mayordomo" of the Castle at *Burgos* during its construction in A.D. 1295.

SAN JUAN [PEDRO DE]. A native of Picardy, and Maestro Mayor of *Gerona* Cathedral in A.D. 1397.

SANTA CELAY [MIGUEL DE]. Architect of the Church of *San Vicente, San Sebastian,* in A.D. 1507.

SANTILLANA [JUAN DE]. Executed the painted glass at *Miraflores, Burgos, circa* 1480.

SARAVIA [RODRIGO DE]. One of the Junta of Architects assembled at *Salamanca* in A.D. 1512.

SILOE [DIEGO DE]. Son of Gil de Siloe the Sculptor. One of the revivers of Pagan art in Spain. He executed various works in *Granada, Seville,* and *Malaga,* and deceased in A.D. 1563.

SILOE [GIL DE]. Sculptor of the Monuments of Juan and Isabel, and of Alfonso their son, in the Church at *Miraflores, Burgos,* and of the Retablo in the same Church, between A.D. 1486 and 1499.

TORNERO [JUAN]. One of the Junta of Architects at *Salamanca* in A.D. 1512.

TUDELILLA. Of *Tarazona.* Architect of the Cloister of *Sta. Engracia, Zaragoza,* in A.D. 1536.

URRUTIA [JUAN DE]. Architect of the Church of *San Vicente, San Sebastian,* A.D. 1507.

VALDEVIESO [JUAN DE]. Executed Stained-glass in the Church at *Miraflores* in A.D. 1480.

VALDOMAR. Architect of West end of Nave of *Valencia* Cathedral in A.D. 1459.

VALLEJO [JUAN DE]. One of the Architects of *Burgos* Cathedral. He was consulted as to the rebuilding of *Salamanca* Cathedral in 1512, and wrought under Felipe de Borgoña in rebuilding the Cimborio of *Burgos* Cathedral, between A.D. 1539 and 1567. He built the Renaissance Gateway on the East side of the South Transept between 1514 and 1524.

VALL-LLEBRERA [PEDRO DE]. Architect of the Steeple of *Sta. Maria Cervera,* A.D. 1431.

VALLERAS [ARNALDUS DE]. " Lapicida " and " Magister operis " of the Collegiata at *Manresa.* One of the Junta of Architects consulted at *Gerona* in A.D. 1416.

VALLFOGONA [BERNARDO DE]. Maestro Mayor of *Tarragona* Cathedral in A.D. 1375.

VALLFOGONA [PEDRO DE]. Executed Reredos of High Altar, *Tarragona,* and was one of the Junta of Architects at *Gerona* in A.D. 1416.

VALMESEDA [JUAN DE]. Executed the Statues in the Reredos, *Palencia* Cathedral, in A.D. 1518.

VANTIER [ROLLINUS]. Maestro Mayor of *Gerona* Cathedral in A.D. 1427.

XULBE [JOHANNES DE]. One of the Junta of Architects assembled at *Gerona* in A.D. 1416. He describes himself as son of Paschasius de Xulbe and "Lapicida."

XULBE [PASCHASIUS DE]. Master of the Works of Church at *Tortosa*, and one of the Junta of Architects at *Gerona* in A.D. 1416.

ZACOMA [PEDRO]. Architect of the Tower of *San Feliu, Gerona*, in A.D. 1368.

C

DOCUMENTS RELATING TO THE CONSTRUCTION OF THE NEW CATHEDRAL AT SALAMANCA

Royal Order of Ferdinand the Catholic, requiring Alfonso Rodriguez to go to Salamanca to choose the site and to make a design for the Construction of the Cathedral.

The KING to the MASTER MAJOR of the Works of the Church of Seville.

SINCE it has now to be decided how the Church of Salamanca may be made, in order that the building and its design may be made as it ought, I agree that you may be present there. I charge and command you that, instantly leaving all other things, you may come to the said city of Salamanca, and, jointly with the other persons who are there, you may see the site where the said church has to be built, and may make a drawing for it, and in all things may give your judgment how it may be the most suited to the Divine worship and to the ornature of the said church; which, having come to pass, then your salary shall be paid; which I shall receive return for in this service.

Done in Valladolid, the 23rd day of the month of November, 1509, etc.[1]

Order of the Queen Doña Juana to the same.

Recites that the King, her Lord and Father, had given an order, which she repeats, quoting the document above given, and then proceeds:—" And now, on the part of the Church of the said city of Salamanca, relation has been made me, that, although the said order was notified to you, until now you have not come to do anything in

[1] Cean Bermudez, *Arq. de Esp.* i. 285.

the business of which mention is made therein, making various excuses and delays; and it has been demanded of me, as for this cause of your not having come there is much delay in the work of the said church, to order you at once to come to the said city of Salamanca to make yourself acquainted with the affairs contained in the said order, as was by it commanded, or as my will might be; which, being seen by those of my council, it was agreed that I should order this my letter to be given for the said reason; and I find it good, as I command you, that immediately that this my letter shall be made known to you, without making any excuse or delay, you shall go to the said city of Salamanca, according and as by the said order was commanded, in order that, conjointly with the other persons who have to make themselves acquainted with the before-said matter, thou mayest give a plan how the said church may be made, which done, the salary will be paid you for the said church, which you are entitled to have for the coming, and staying, and returning to your house; and thou mayest not fail in this, under pain of my displeasure, and of 50,000 maravedis for my treasury.

" Given in the most noble city of Valladolid, 26th day of the month of January, from the birth of our Saviour Jesus Christ 1510 years." [1]

Writ of Ferdinand the Catholic to Anton Egas, ordering him to go to Salamanca to choose the site and make the plan for the Cathedral, November 23rd, 1509.

Anton Egas is ordered to go at once, and, jointly with the other architects there assembled, make a plan, etc.; which done, his salary, which he receives on service, shall be paid him there. This writ is endorsed as having been served on his two maids, Maria and Catalina, he and his wife being both away.

Declaration or Information which Alonso Rodriguez and Anton Egas made before the Chapter of Salamanca on the mode of constructing the Cathedral.

In Salamanca, the second day of the month of May, 1510, Señor Gonzalo de San Vicente, representative of S. A., being with the Chapter, present the Reverend Señors D. Alfonso Pereira, Dean of Salamanca, and other persons, dignitaries and beneficiaries, who were in Chapter, in order to acquaint themselves touching the order and plan of their church, oath being taken in the due form by the Señors Alonso Rodriguez, Maestro of Seville, and Anton Egas, Maestro of Toledo, persons deputed by his Highness for the ordering and

[1] Cean Bermudez, *Arq. de Esp.* i. 286.

planning of the said church, that all affection and passion, partiality and interest, or any other cause, being well and faithfully postponed, they determine and declare, according to God and their conscience, the most commodious plan and site that may be fitting for the adornment of the said church, and for the utility of it and of this city, without prejudice and wrong to the Schools of this University of Salamanca; both of whom made the said oath, and replied to its confession, and said, " So I swear, and Amen."

And under the said oath they presented a plan and outline of the said church, drawn on parchment to the heights and widths of the naves, and thicknesses of the walls, and projections of the buttresses, the whole taken in writing by me the said notary; the which they affirmed by their names in my presence, and said that the site marked out by them for where the said church—our Lord permitting—ought to be, would not do any wrong or prejudice to the said Schools, rather they would be benefited and adorned, because the site of the said church commences ten feet further from the gate " del Apeadero " of the Schools, being set back from the street by the said Schools fifty feet, in front of the said church, from the line of the church as it now is. And because there was a diversity in the opinion of these Masters as to the proportion of length to breadth in the Capilla mayor, they agreed to meet in Toledo in ten days, and to select an umpire between them if it were necessary, so that the decision should be arrived at with more circumspection, and sent within fifteen days to the said Señor San Vicente, or to this Chapter.[1]

Declaration or Judgment which was pronounced in Salamanca in a Junta which was held Sept. 3rd, 1512, by the Masters of Architecture Anton Egas, Juan Gil de Hontañon, Juan de Badajos, Juan de Alava, Juan de Orozco, Alonzo de Covarrubias, Juan Tornero, Rodrigo de Saravia, and Juan Campero, as to the mode of constructing the Cathedral.

That which appears to the Masters who were called and assembled by the most reverend and most magnificent in Christ, Father and Lord Don Francisco de Bobadilla, by the grace of God, and of the Holy Church of Rome, Bishop of Salamanca, and of the Council of the Queen our Lady, and by the Reverend the Dean and Chapter of the Church of Salamanca, to give the plan of the site and building of this holy church and temple, which it has been unanimously decided by the said Lord Bishop and Chapter—our Lord helping—to make and begin, is as follows:—

Firstly, the said Masters decided that the site of the church

[1] Cean Bermudez, *Arq. de Esp.* i. 287.

should be in length as far as the church of San Cebrian, and in width as far as the Schools.

Item.—That the three clear naves should begin from the line of the tower unto the place of the Schools, so that all the three doors of the front may show themselves and be clear of the tower.

Item.—They determine that the church should be directed and turned as much as possible to the east; and it appears to them that it can turn directly to the said east.

Item.—They determine that the principal nave may have fifty feet in width in the clear, and a hundred and ten in height.

Item.—That the side naves shall have thirty-seven feet in clear width, and seventy feet in height, or seventy-five, not being of the height of the other.

Item.—They determine that the chapels opened in the side walls may have twenty-seven feet in clear width, and forty-three or forty-five in height.

Item.—That the three gable walls of the west front may have all three seven feet of thickness, and the side walls throughout the church six feet; but to some of the said Masters it appeared that the end walls should be eight feet in thickness.

Item.—That the buttresses of the end walls may project beyond the wall twelve feet, and in thickness may have seven feet in front.

Item.—That the buttresses of all the side walls of the church may be five feet thick in front, and project six feet beyond the wall outside.

Item.—That the divisions of the chapels in the walls may be seven feet thick.

Item.—That the four principal columns of the Cimborio may be eleven-and-a-half feet thick.

Item.—They determine that the head of the Trascoro may be octagonal.[1]

Item.—They determine that the Capilla mayor may have in length and breadth two chapels of the sides.

Item.—That the chapels in the walls of the Trascoro may be twenty-seven feet in depth from wall to wall, and that in the spaces of the walls and buttresses in the angles of the octagons, which are formed between the chapels on the outside, sacristies for each chapel may be made.

Item.—They declare that the feet of which in this their declaration and determination mention is made, are to be taken as the third of a yard; and (marking out the form of the said church) the said Masters declare that from the mark towards the door of the

---

[1] In the margin of this paragraph is written, in the hand of Maestro Juan del Ribero Rada—" It has been built square." The word "Trascoro" seems to be used here of the east end of the church.

Schools to the first step there may be seven yards and a third, which is twenty-two feet.

Item.—They declare that the wall of the west front within the tower has to be begun forty-nine feet from the corner of the said tower on the inside, and should be in thickness from there forward so much as to leave forty-nine feet of the tower visible.

Item.—They declare that the wall of the side nave, from towards the old church, has to come with the side of the tower, and has to contract itself the thickness of the said wall in the said tower.

And inasmuch as some persons, as well members of the Chapter as out of it, have held certain opinions in regard to the site of the said building, and where it ought to stand, the said Lord Bishop and Chapter, desiring to avoid and escape such opinions as at present and in future may impede the order and form of the said building, command the said Masters to give the reasons and motives that may have moved them to direct and propose the site and position determined on by them, and not the other places, lines, or sites suggested; and that they should say specifically for their satisfaction why, with all quietness and willingness, the order, form, and site laid down by them may be followed. The which said Masters, in order to satisfy the persons who either held or might hold opinions contrary to their own, gave the following reasons:—

Firstly. That making or putting the church in another part or site than that determined on by them, it and its cloister would be separated from the view of the city, and would be concealed; that it could not be seen round about, only the end wall by itself, and the Chevet by itself, and there would be no entire view.

The second reason is, that the said church would be put behind the schools from the Crossing almost to the end, where the best view and the most frequented part of the church ought to be, because there the doors have to be placed.

The third reason is, that of the cloister—which already exists— the two parts are so placed that it would leave a narrow passage between the church and the Archbishop's chapel, and the library and Chapter-house, and the said chapels would remain separated, and one would enter them from the narrow passage, and in a roundabout way; for though it might be desired to make a door from the Chevet, it could not be done, because the sacristy would prevent it.

The fourth reason which they give is, that if the said church has to be moved to another site opposed to that declared and determined on by them, the tower would have to be destroyed, which is a good and singular work, and could not be rebuilt without a great sum of maravedis, and the church could not be without a tower.

The fifth reason is, that if the said church has to be moved to another site, it will be necessary to take down the house of the said Lord Bishop, and to restore it opposite the front of the church; and in order to restore it, besides the great sum of maravedis it would cost, it would be necessary to destroy fourteen houses, the rent of which is of much value, and this would be costly to the church, and involve loss to the treasury of the Chapter.

The sixth reason is, that in order to make the cloister on another site contrary to their determination, many houses must be taken; and in order to make it on the south, it would be necessary to go into it by what is called the River-door, and afterwards to be more away from the city, and out of view, and it would be very costly to make the foundations of such great depth, and to raise the walls to the level of the church.

The seventh reason which they give is, that the Chevet of the church would cover the door of the chapel of the Archbishop and the library in order to join them.

The eighth reason which they give is, that the Crossing would not come in the line of any street, and there would be no way out by way of the cloister, because the new and old cloister would stop it; and supposing a remedy to be sought, by separating the new cloister, it would be so high when they had to go out, that it would have at least more than fifteen steps, and the entrance would be by a narrow passage; because on one part would be the new cloister, and on the other part of the old cloister the chapel of the Archbishop.

The ninth reason which they give is, that the church would encroach upon the principal street of the schools, which comes before the house of his Lordship, and the other street, " *del Desafiadero;* " so that if there was none at the apse of the church there would be no way out; and the height of the church, putting it so much between the sun and the schools on the south, would take away much of their light, and darken them much.

The which reasons they give against the opinions of them who say or desire to say that the site of the said church should be towards the house of the Lord Bishop, and towards the street " *del Desafiadero ;* " and in order to answer the other opinion of some who argue that the site of the said church could go through the cloister, which is already built to the River bridge, because this would not be a convenient site for the church; and in order to oppose the opinion for it, they give the following reasons:—

Firstly. That it would be more separated from the city, and would not go well with the schools, and would lack the appearance which it would have going, as is agreed, towards the schools.

The second reason which they give is, that it would stand at an angle with the schools, and would be an ugly thing, and the façades of the church and the schools would not be harmonised together by the said arrangement of the plan.

The third reason which they give is, that the Plaza of the Lord Bishop's house would be narrowed in great part, so that the Plaza would be a street; and the height of the church would shut out the sun from the said house of his Lordship, and would stifle it very much; and the doors of the church would be behind the tower in the view as one comes from the city through the Street of the Schools.

The fourth reason which they give is, that the west front of the church would have to join the wall of the Archbishop's chapel, and through its inequality and depth it would be necessary to have many steps through that part, and towards the town not any, and this would be a defective and ugly thing.

The fifth reason which they give is, that, making the cloister towards the Schools, all the view of the church would be shut out, and the cloister would be gloomy, and it would be without the harmony and order of good churches, and without grace.

The sixth reason which they give is, that the church standing close to the chapel of the Archbishop and the library, its height would shut out the light from the small chapels in the walls, and there would be no exit for the water from the roof of the middle of the church at that part.

The seventh reason which they give is, that in order to make the new church it would be necessary to clear out immediately all the church and the cloister, and the chapel of the Doctor of Talavera, and of Sta. Barbara, and the Chapter-house; and in their opinion it would be a grand inconvenience to be so many years without having where to celebrate the Divine offices.

The eighth reason which they give is, that if the church is separated from above, and put as in a corner, part in the shade through the one part of the tower and cloister, and through the other of the library and the chapel of the Archbishop, it could not have as much of its walls in light as is convenient.

The ninth reason which they give is, that the door of the transept would come out so high from the street, in their opinion, as more than ten or twelve steps, and would cut across the street " *del Chantre*," and would be bad in its arrangement, and a place where nuisance would be caused.

This opinion having been given, it is then pronounced by the deputies appointed by the Chapter to confer with the architects, that as they were all agreed both as to the site and as to the general form of the church, and as they are such learned and skilful men, and experienced in their art, their opinion ought certainly to be acted on. But for the more certainty it was thought well to make every one of the architects take an oath, " by God and S. Mary, under whose invocation the church is, and upon the sign of the cross, upon which they and each of them put their right hands bodily," that they had spoken the entire truth, which each of them did, saying " So I swear, and amen."[1]

The report of the architects having been received, the Chapter then say that the many singular and great Masters of the Art of Masonry (canteria) who had been consulted had agreed on a plan, but that it will be necessary to choose and elect a Master (Maestro) and an overseer (aparejador).[2] On the same day, Sept. 3rd, 1512, Juan Gil de Hontañon, " Master of Masonry," was appointed principal master of the works (Maestro principal), and Juan Campero, mason, overseer, with a salary to the former of 40,000 maravedis a year, and 100 maravedis more for each day that he assisted at the works; and to the latter of 20,000 maravedis a year, and 2½ reals per day.[3] And on the 10th May, 1538, Rodrigo Gil de Hontañon was appointed principal master of the works, with the salary of 30,000 maravedis a year. Alonso de Covarrubias seems to have been joined with Rodrigo Gil de Hontañon as master.[4] By R. G. de Hontañon's will it seems that he also had a house rent free from the Chapter.[5]

D

SANTIAGO CATHEDRAL

Warrant of King Ferdinand II., issued in 1168, in favour of Mattheus, Master of the Works of Santiago Cathedral, copied from the Archives.

IN nomine Domini nostri Jesu Christi. Amen. Majestati regiæ convenit eis melius providere, qui sibi noscuntur fidele obsequium exhibere, et illis præcipue, qui Dei sanctuariis et locis indesinenter obsequium probantur impendere. Ea propter ego Fernandus Dei gratia Hispaniarum Rex ex amore Omnipotentis Dei, per quem regnant reges, et ob reverentiam sanctissimi Jacobi patroni nostri piissimi, pro munere dono, et concedo tibi magistro Matheo, qui operis præfati Apostoli primatum obtines et magisterium, in unoquoque anno in medietate mea de moneta Sancti Jacobi refectionem

---

[1] From Cean Bermudez, *Not. de los Arq. y Arquos de España,* i. 293-299.
[2] The sense of this word is given in Connelly and Higgins's *Dictionary,* as " the substitute of the chief architect of the building, who places the workmen and distributes the materials according to the arrangements of the plan."
[3] Cean Bermudez, i. 300.   [4] *Ibid.* i. 315.   [5] *Ibid.* i. 317.

duarum marcharum singulis hebdomadibus, et quod defuerit in una hebdomada suppleatur in alia, ita quod hæc refectio valeat tibi centum maravotinos per unumquemque annum. Hoc munus, hoc donum do tibi omni tempore vitæ tuæ semper habendum quatenus et operi Sancti Jacobi, et tuæ inde personæ melius sit, et qui viderint præfato operi studiosius invigilent et insistant.

Si quis vero contra hoc meum spontaneum donativum venerit, aut illud quoque modo tentaverit infringere, iram incurrat decunti pertinentis, et iram regiam, et mille aureos parti tuæ tamquam excomunicatus cogatur exolvere. Facta carta apud Sanctum Jacobum, viii. kalendas Marti, Era M. CC. VI. Regnante rege Dño Fernando Legione, Extremadura, Gallecia in Asturiis.

Ego Dñs F. Dei gratia Hispaniarum Rex hoc scriptum quod fieri jussi proprio robore confirmo.

[Signed also by various Bishops and Grandees.]

E

SEGOVIA CATHEDRAL

Memoir of the Canon of Segovia Juan Rodriguez, in which is related all that happened as to the Construction of the Cathedral from the year 1522, in which he began to exercise the government and administration of the fabric, until the year 1562, in which, through infirmity, he gave it up.—From the Archives of the Cathedral.

AFTER reciting his pious reasons for his undertaking, he continues his Memoir as follows; entering first of all into various particulars in reference to the subscriptions for the work and so forth, he then goes on:—

" We commence, in the name of God, to give an account of the form and order which prevailed in the work of the said church and cloister, Chapter-house, libraries, tower, sacristy, and place for relics,[1] and all the other necessary offices, which until this time have been paid for, and now belong to the said holy church, free from all interest or tax.

" Commencing at the beginning, which was in the said year of 1520, when the Chapter was driven out of the other church by reason of the alterations already mentioned, they had the divine offices in the Church of Sta. Clara, which the monks of the order of Sta. Clara had left, who at present reside in the monastery of San

---

[1] *Sagrario.*—This, I think, sometimes means the chapel, commonly called the *Parroquia*, or Chapel of the Cathedral Parish.

Antonio el Real; and beginning by having the divine office on the floor of the church on some benches or logs of wood, which were placed for it from the door of the church as far as the rooms of the keepers of the wardrobe of the convent which were there, afterwards they made a tribune on some pieces of timber or posts for the Coro, in order to have the holy office; and afterwards they put the altars right with Retablos and images, which they brought from the old church; and they put right the old cloister, which had some high battlements; and they overcame difficulties and put everything in order to be able to make use of it, and set right the chapel where the Crucifix and Sacrament were, and where the chaplains said their office. Then, likewise, was made a hall of the old corridors, in which the Chapter was held, where it was for some years, until that one was made below close to the chapel of the Crucifix. And then the tower was raised, and there they placed some of the bells of the other old church, and others they made new in the town of Olmedo; and they got a new clock from Medina del Campo, and put the whole in the old tower.

" Then, in consequence of the narrowness of the church, they took some houses in which lived the wardrobe-keepers, and pulled them down, and made a wall of lime and stone in front, and placed there the Coro of the old church, and repaired it in the said place where the divine office was said, and placed the iron screens of the two Coros; the whole of which was done between the said year of 1520 and June 8th, 1522, when, by the consent and resolution of the Lord Bishop D. Diego de Rivera, and of the Dean and Chapter of the said church, it was agreed to commence the new work of the said church, to the glory of God, and in honour of the Virgin Mary and the glorious San Frutos and All Saints, taking for master of the said work Juan Gil de Hontañon, and for his clerk of the works (aparejador) Garcia de Cubillas.

" Thursday, the 8th of June, 1522, the Bishop ordered a general procession with the Dean and Chapter, and clergy, and all the religious orders. Solemn mass was said in the Plaza of San Miguel, before the doors of the said Church of Sta. Clara, and there was a sermon, and absolution, and general pardon to all who had erred; and they demolished the other church, and gave absolution for all the faults and sacrileges which might be committed in it, as is the case in all general pardon of sins. From there the Bishop, Dean and Chapter, clergy and religious, went in procession to the part where was the foundation of the principal wall of the foot of the holy church, and in that place where the principal door was to be, which is now called ' del Pardon; and the Master of the works and the officials being there with stone and mortar, the Lord Bishop placed the foundation in the middle where the said door had to come, which is called ' del Pardon.' Giving first his benediction on the commencement of the work, he put a piece of silver with his face on it, and others of metal with certain letters, and upon them placed the stone and mortar. The workmen then raised the building.

" All this solemnity, as I have told, began to the glory of God our Lord, the Virgin Mary, and All Saints, for the promotion of the said work. This was settled and arranged between the Lord Bishop, the Dean and Chapter, to be executed in masonry of a rough description, by reason of the great poverty of the said church. And I then, feeling this, conferred on this matter with the said Juan Gil de Hontañon and Garcia de Cubillas, and it seemed to them to be a great pity to execute the work in such a way in so celebrated a city. And the Lord Bishop, the Dean and Chapter, having considered this, thought it well to give leave, confiding in the providence of our Lord, that it should be done as I had petitioned, for which many thanks be given to our Lord."

" The building being commenced, as I have said, on Thursday, July 8th, 1522, was carried on according to the plan first of all given, beginning from the principal door at the foot of the church, which is called ' del Pardon,' corresponding to the principal nave, and going on in order, taking the chapel and the chapels in the walls, of which there are five on either side, ten in all, where at present the private masses and endowments which the said church has are said.

" After the same manner the principal pillars in the said church were built, which divide, and on which is raised the principal nave, and on either side one, in all five collateral naves; the principal, of 115 to 120 feet in height, and 54 in width, from line to line; the collaterals, 80 feet in height each one of them, and 38 in width, and the chapels between the buttresses, of which there are ten, 50 feet of height, and 26 in width, as, thanks to God, they have all been made and finished to perfection, as may be seen.

" The building, so far erected, reached only to the two principal pillars of the Crossing, which are twelve feet in width, because they are the two upon which the Cimborio will have to be built, and the other two pillars will embellish the work which has to be done presently, when the Capilla mayor and the Crossing are erected. The other round pillars of the body of the said church are ten feet in thickness, and are ten in all, and upon them were built the main nave and its collaterals.

" Likewise I may mention that these principal pillars, for fear there should be any misfortune or bursting in the work, were all compacted throughout their body, with shaped stones, in pieces of the same thickness as those which are in the face of the work; so that there is not the least thing omitted which could give strength.

" Likewise the walls were made, three extending past the said three principal pillars, which were made for the Cimborio and Crossing, where the high altar was placed, and the Blessed Sacrament kept, and the conventual masses said; and on one side, towards the Alumzára, a little sacristy was made, or a vestry for the ministers of the high altar, where they kept their boxes for the things necessary for the altar and choir.

" Likewise the walls were built, where the stalls of the Coro are placed for the divine offices, ornamented and made up with such additional seats as were required, in order that they might occupy the width of the principal nave; and at the sides they made offices with their furniture for holding the singing and reading books for the divine offices of the said church, with doors at the sides for going out by at the sermon-time.

" Likewise they made high galleries on either side of the Coro, in which they placed the organs, finished and adorned, as, at present appears, for the service of our Lord.

" Likewise the cloister was founded, which was that which stood in the old church, which Juan Campero, master of masonry, undertook by contract for the sum of 4000 ducats, according to the contract with which he took it; and in the said buildings it was impossible to foresee, at the first, every necessary thing, because time and the work itself showed many things which at first were not known; and so, beginning to feel the said cloister would be low, by agreement with the said John Campero, they gave him 400 ducats, in order that he should raise it a yard, which gave him grace enough; and 70,000 maravedis, in order that he should do the door of the said cloister, which was not in his contract; and likewise he made a condition that he should not be obliged to go more than five feet below the ground.

" In the same manner they made many other adornments in the said cloister beyond what was in the contract with the said Juan Campero, such as making many things of granite, and others of carpentry, which were to have been of common masonry; which was all of much cost, so that the expenses mounted beyond the contract of the said Juan Campero another 4000 ducats, which was in all 8000, a little more or less, as appears by the account-book which the said Juan Campero kept.

" *Item.*—To the glory of God and the honour of His Blessed Mother the building of the tower was commenced, which is at the lower end of the said church, and which is a very solemn edifice. Its bulk without the walls is thirty-three feet, and it is square. The walls are four from base to summit, and each one ten feet thick; and one of them which goes from the church is fifteen feet at the bottom.

" *Item.*—This tower is more lofty than that of the cathedral at Seville, measured by a line, more than once brought from thence. It is wider than that of Toledo by one-third part, as will be seen by those who like to measure it. This measures, as I say, 33 feet inside, and that of Toledo 22 feet. I say this in order that the goodness of this tower may be known. Outside the chapel and above it is another very good chapel for the service of the church, in which necessary things can be kept; and over this chapel, and in the said tower, is another chamber, where is placed the man who attends to the bells, with all his family, and with all the offices necessary for his living; and above this, in the said tower, is another chamber, which is where the bells are hung in their frames in their order. And above this chamber, at the four sides or corners of the said tower, there are four pillars, from which rise four flying buttresses, which support another building, after the fashion of a censer with its windows. The clock is here, etc." " I hold this building of the tower to be noble and important, just as I hold it to be certain that it would be difficult to build it now for 50,000 ducats."

" Likewise there are three principal chambers which abut against one wall of the tower, and go as far as the Calle Mayor of Barrionuevo, which measure 80 feet or more. One of them below is all made with a vault of good mason's work for the workmen's tools, timber, scaffolding, ropes, and other instruments required for the prosecution of the works; and when the said church is finished it will be kept for precious things of various kinds of which the church has need, for *autos*, etc., which take place in such churches, so as not to have to make them anew each time. This chamber has a very good door for entrance, and sufficient lights to enable them to keep everything that is required to be put there.

" Over this room, on the level of the cloister, is the cloister Chapter-room, which is 53 feet long, a little more or less, and 33 wide, with very good windows, and glazing, and wooden ceiling made with fretwork, admirably executed by the hands of good workmen; quite an important room. It is of the height proper for a good room. There is no other painting in it than an inscription all round. The pavement is of white and black stone, the black from Aillon, and the white Otero de Herreros. The seats are temporary; but a large quantity of walnut has been bought for them. The doors of the Chapter-room are all of walnut, made by very good workmen, and with frames of black elm.

" Before entering into the Chapter-house there is a staircase which has three landings for going to the library, with its steps of hard stone, and its breast-wall with the four Evangelists placed against the columns; and in the four windows which light the staircase are the four principal doctors of the Church; and below the said staircase is a room in a vacant space, whose windows look into the Calle de Barrionuevo, which is for the Secretary of the church to keep all the writings, and books, and bills of the said church, and is placed close to the Chapter-house, of which the said Secretary keeps the keys.   This room is of the width of the stair-case, and its size from the wall of the Chapter-house is 27 feet, which are what remain of the 80 over and above the 53 which the Chapter-house measures.   The third part, and last in order of the above-mentioned rooms, which is called the library, is the same width and length.   It has four windows, two towards the street, and two towards the cloister, and in them medallions of SS. Peter and Paul, John Baptist, and John the Evangelist.

" And in order to answer satisfactorily any complaints of the Señores of the city, we may make a comparison with the Church of Salamanca, which is the same kind as this church, and commenced by the same Master, though this church is 100 feet broader than Salamanca, which was begun by the same Master a long time before that of Segovia was commenced anew.   The said work at Salamanca had all the ground on which it was built, so that the site cost nothing, whereas at Segovia the whole site required was bought, and redeemed of rents which were heavy," etc. etc.

F

LIST OF SUBJECTS CARVED ON THE SCREENS ROUND THE CORO OF TOLEDO CATHEDRAL

THESE screens extend across the west end of the Coro and along its northern and southern sides.   The central subject over the western doorway, and two subjects on either side of it, have been destroyed in order to make space for a more modern sculpture.   The side screens appear to have been cut off abruptly at the eastern end, so that possibly some subjects may have been removed from this part.   The subjects are arranged as follows: Nos. 1 to 9, counting from the north-west angle of the screen to the western doorway; Nos. 12 to 19, from the central doorway to the south-west angle of the screen; Nos. 20 to 40 along the southern screen, going from west to east; and Nos. 41 to 61 along the northern screen, going from east to west.   Some of the subjects are doubtful, and some unintelligible to me; and I have marked all such in this list with a note of interrogation. The whole of the subjects illustrate the earlier passages in the Old Testament in chronological order.

1. Chaos.

   GOD looking at a broken ark, and fragments of rock on the ground.

2. Creation of the firmament.

   GOD standing with the sea behind, and supporting an arc over His head.

3. Creation of fowls and fishes.

   Central figure of GOD, birds flying above, fishes and birds swimming below.

4. The creation of sun, moon, and stars.

   GOD with His hands extended. In the two upper corners (dexter side) the sun and four stars; (sinister side) the moon and four other stars. There are clouds round the feet of GOD.

5. God reverenced by angels.

   A standing figure of much majesty, with four angels on either side, some kneeling, some standing.[1]

6. Fall of Lucifer.[2]

   In the centre GOD, and on either side, above, angels; and below, figures falling headlong.

7. The Creation of Adam.

   GOD moulding a figure into the shape of a man.

   Nos. 8 and 9, the central subject over the doorway into the Coro, and 10 and 11 are destroyed.

   Nos. 12 and 13 are transposed.

13. GOD meeting Adam and Eve, and showing them the tree in the garden.

12. GOD meeting Adam and Eve in the garden after the Fall.

    They hold leaves in their hands.

14. The expulsion of Adam and Eve.

    On the left a tree, in front of it a battlemented tower or gate, before which is an angel. Adam and Eve going away.

15. Adam tilling the ground, Eve with a child in her arms looking at him.

16. Cain killing Abel (?), or Adam finding the dead body of Abel. (?)

    A man half supporting a dead body of a younger man.

17. Adam digging a grave for Abel.

    A man digging in the ground.

[1] This subject occurs in the well-known illustrations of Queen Mary's Psalter, 2 B. VII., at the British Museum library. It is described as " Here GOD reposes on His throne with His angels."

[2] This subject occurs in the *Biblia Pauperum*, with the following inscription:—" Legitur in Apocalypsi xii° Cap° et in iii° Ysaya xiiii Cap° quod lucifer cecidit per superbiam de celo cum omnibus suis adherentibus."

18. God meeting Cain.

19. Two figures in a niche at the angle of the western and southern screens, both looking up as if in prayer.

" Then began men to call upon the name of the Lord."

South side.

20.   (?)
A figure speaking to a boy; behind, and half-concealed among trees, another figure of a man naked.[1]

21.   (?)
A man with an axe which he has let fall. He has been cutting branches from a tree, and lifts up his hands in prayer: behind him stands a woman.

22.   (?)
A man with a long axe resting from his labour; a woman stands behind him, and they both look towards a young man who speaks to them.

23.   (?)
The end of a building. On the left of it an angel and a young man who looks out from it to the right, where are trees, and below them the mouth of a whale swallowing a man.

24. The burial of Methuselah. (?)
Five figures surrounding a tomb in which they bury a sixth.

25. Noah finds grace in the sight of the Lord. (?)
Two figures in supplication, apparently, before the third.

26. Noah and one of his sons before the ark.
Noah turns his head towards God, who speaks from a cloud and desires him to go into the ark.

27. The ark on the waters.
On one side of the roof a dove, and on the other one with a twig of a tree. The ark has three tiers of openings: beasts look out of the lowest, men and women from the next, and birds from the highest.

28. The ark resting on the land, and the drunkenness of Noah.
Above Noah prays by a tree. Below, Ham lifts up the garment of Noah, who is lying on the ground, and Shem and Japheth, kneeling, cover their faces with their hands.

29. Probably the promise to Abraham that he should be the father of many nations. (?)
On the left, two figures conversing; on the right, three tiers of figures. Dead bodies below, two seated figures above them, and one seated figure above again.

30. Lot and the Angels.
Lot kneels before two angels.

31. Abraham's sacrifice.
Isaac bound and lying on the ground. Abraham behind him looks back to an angel, who speaks and points to the ram in a thicket.

[1] [This will be the death of Cain.—G. G. K.]

32. Abraham and Isaac.

> Abraham binding the ram, Isaac standing looking on, with his hands in prayer.

33. Rebekah and Jacob.

> Rebekah speaking to Jacob, who shows her that his arms have no hair on them.

34. Isaac blessing Jacob.

> Isaac sits up in bed, turns his face away from Jacob, and feels his arms. The expression of blindness is extremely well conveyed.

35. Esau's distress.

> Isaac supports himself on one arm on his couch; with the other he gesticulates to Esau, who stands before him with his hand before his face, and evidently in grief.

36. Jacob's dream. (?)

> A man seated before a tree with his hand up to his face.

37. Jacob wrestling with the Angel.

38. Joseph sold to the Ishmaelites.

39. Joseph's brethren return to Jacob with his coat.

40. Joseph's brethren bowing down before him.

> This is the last subject on the south side of the Coro. It is possible that it may have been returned on the eastern side of the columns at this point, so as to allow of two more subjects being introduced on either side; but if so, these subjects have been destroyed. The first six subjects on the screen on the north side, Nos. 41 to 46, are all very similar —a king seated, with generally many persons in various attitudes around him; possibly these subjects, with the four which may have been destroyed, represented the ten plagues of Egypt. I cannot discover any other explanation for them.

47. The institution of the Passover.

> Figures marking the lintels and side posts of a house.

48. The institution of the Passover.

> The sacrifice of the lamb, several figures standing round an altar.

49. The smiting of the first-born of the Egyptians. (?)

> Two subjects, one above the other; in each a dead body laid out, and people looking on.

50. The passage of the Red Sea.

> The people are walking on the water.

51. The drowning of the Egyptians.

52. Moses stretching his hand out over the water.

> Moses stoops down and touches the water with his hand.

53. Exodus xvi. 10-12. "The glory of the Lord in the cloud." God speaking to a crowd of kneeling figures.

54 Exodus xvii. 45-6.   Moses at the rock in Horeb. (?)
God (with a cruciform nimbus) speaking out of the clouds to Moses, who speaks to a group seated before him (probably the elders of Israel, v. 6).

55. Jethro, Zipporah, Gershom, and Eliezer coming to Moses. (?) Exodus xviii.
Moses kneeling on the right, three figures seated on the left, and another speaking from out of foliage above.   I can think of no other subject which this sculpture can represent.

56. (?)   The people giving their ear-rings to Aaron to make the molten calf.   Exodus xxxii. 24.
Three figures on either side of one who stands in the centre.   They seem to be throwing things into the flames, in the midst of which is a serpent.

57. Moses' hands stayed up.   Exodus xvii. 12. (?)
Three figures, two holding a book (apparently) under the hands of the fourth, who appears to be much fatigued.   There are flames in the foreground, in the midst of which is a small head.

58. Exodus xix. 10. (?)   The people washing their clothes at Moses' order.
A central figure pointing to a sort of well in the centre.

59. Massacre of the worshippers of the molten calf.

60. Exodus xxiv. 29.
Moses holds the two tables of the Law, and is surrounded by other figures all touching the tables.

61. Exodus xxiv. 32, 33.
The two tables held by two figures above a draped altar; four figures kneeling before them.

With this subject the series concludes.

I have thought it quite worth while to give this short account of the work because it is rather rare to find so large a number of Old Testament subjects treated in this way.   On the whole, too, I think that this is the most important work of the age in Spain.   The sculptured works of this period (the fourteenth century) are comparatively rare.   The most important of those which I have mentioned in this book are the north doorway of Toledo, which has a series of subjects in all of which the Blessed Virgin appears; at Burgos the three western doors, which have—(1) the birth of the Blessed Virgin, (2) the Assumption, and (3) the Coronation; in the south door, our Lord with the evangelists, saints, and prophets; and in the north door, the Last Judgment.   At Leon, the three western doors, which have—(1) subjects from our Lord's life, introducing the Blessed Virgin, (2) the Last Judgment, and (3) the Coronation of the Blessed Virgin Mary; the south transept, on one door our Lord, the evangelists and apostles, and on another the death of the Blessed Virgin Mary; the north transept, our Lord surrounded by saints. Avila cathedral has, over its north door, our Lord in the centre, the Betrayal, Last Supper, and Coronation of the Blessed Virgin Mary; and the Resurrection of the Dead in the archivolt; and various other smaller works. I know no other example of the introduction of Old Testament subjects.

In all these examples the character of the sculpture is very similar; the architectural framing of niches and canopies is of the best kind of Middle Pointed; and the draperies, faces, and pose of the figures are very much the same as one sees in work of the first half of the fourteenth century at Bourges and elsewhere in France. The subjects round the Coro at Toledo are superior to the others in the facility which the regularity of the openings gave for the free treatment of the sculptures, and in the variety of treatment which the subjects naturally involve. But on the other hand, the artistic skill of the sculptors who were employed at Leon cathedral seems to me to have been greater than that of the sculptors of any other Spanish work of the same age. And though the character, mode of design, and manner of execution are all extremely French, I do not know why we should have any doubt about the ability of Spaniards to execute such work, when we consider how exceedingly skilful they were in the succeeding age, when they perhaps excelled any other sculptors of the same period.

The French work to which this Spanish sculpture has most similarity, appears to me to be that of the three western doors of Bourges cathedral. In some respects, indeed, there is so much likeness between the two that one can hardly avoid supposing that the sculptor at Leon had himself been at Bourges. And it is interesting therefore to observe that one of the most remarkable series of sculptures illustrating the early portion of the Old Testament is that which is carved in the spandrels of the arcade which is carried all round the lower part of the jambs of the Bourges doorways. I have, in the earlier part of this work, observed that there is evidence of the same men having wrought at Burgos, Leon, Avila, and Toledo.

G

AGREEMENT BETWEEN JAYME FABRE AND THE SUB-
PRIOR AND BRETHREN OF THE CONVENT OF SAN
DOMINGO, AT PALMA IN MALLORCA

Sit omnibus notum, quod ego magister Jacobus Fabre lapicida,
civis Majoricarum, præsenti stipulatione convenio vobis fratri Petro
Alegre, gerenti Vices-Prioris conventus fratrum Prædicatorum Majoricarum antedicti et Notarij infra scripti stipulantis, vice et nomine
dicti conventus; quod quando Prior dictæ domus fratrum Prædicatorum Majoricarum, vel ejus locum tenens, voluerit, et requisiverit
me, quod redeam ad hanc civitatem Majoricarum ex Barchinona,
quo iturus sum in præsenti, causa faciendi illuc aliqua opera, vel
ea dirigendi cum licencia vestra, et fratrum dictæ domus, ad præces
Illustrissimi Domini Regis Aragonum, et venerabilis Domini Barchinonensis Episcopi: ego illico recepta monitione vel requisitione
vestra vel Prioris dictæ domus, seu ejus locum tenentis, omnibus
operibus et negotiis postpositis, redeam ad hanc civitatem Majoricarum, salvo justo impedimento et quod vobis et fratribus vestri
conventus faciam, et consumabo opera vestri monasterij, et alia
opera faciam prout pactus sum, et facere teneor, ut continetur in
quodam publico instrumento, facto inter me et venerabilem Fr.
Arnaldum Burgeti, dudum Priorem dictæ domus; quod instrumen-
tum sit validum, et nihil pro prædictis ille videatur innovatum, aut
mutatum.   Quod si per me steterit quod non redeam, cum citatus
fuero, et non compleverim prædicta cum ea complere possim,
tenear dare, et per validam, et solemnem stipulationem dare pro-
mitto operi vestri dicti monasterij in manu et posse Notarij infrascripti, vice et nomine dicti operis stipulantis, pro pena, et nomine
penæ, quinquaginta libras regalium Majoricensium monetæ perpetæ
minutorum, quæ pro damnis, et interesse computtantur, qua pena
soluta, vel non, nihilominus rata maneant hæc prædicta, et cetera
contenta in instrumento inter me et dictum fratrem Arnaldum
Burgeti facto, et pro prædictis attendendis, et non contraveniendis,
obligo vobis, et vestro conventui supradicto, et nomine infrascripti
stipulantis, vice et nomine ejusdem monasterij me, et omnia bona
mea, ubique habita, et habenda.   Ad hæc ego Maymonus Peris civis
Majoricarum," etc. etc. "Actum est hoc Majoricis octavo idus Junii,
anno Domini millessimo trecentessimo septimo decimo sig ✠ num
Magistri Jacobi Fabre," etc. etc.

H

REPORTS OF ARCHITECTS ON THE PLAN FOR THE COMPLETION OF THE CATHEDRAL AT GERONA— A.D. 1417.

Junta of Twelve Architects, upon the mode which ought to be followed in the construction of the Cathedral of Gerona, with the Reports of each of them as they appear in the archives of the said Church.

I

In nomine Sanctæ ac individuæ Trinitatis, Patris, et Filii, et Spiritus Sancti. Amen.

ETSI mansiunculas et domos profanas mundanorum usibus dicatas fideles Domini erigunt et fabricant opere polimento, quanto magis ipsi fideles verique zelatores fidei orthodoxæ circa templi Domini fabricam construendam devotius accelerare deberent? Numquid prisci patres pro archa Domini tabernaculum opere deaurato mirifice fabricaverunt? Hodie namque archa illa verissima, et sanctissimum illud Mamuá in templo Domini a catholicis præservantur. Dignum quin imo et congruum potest et debet a quolibet reputari ut domus illa quam orationis veritas nominavit, in qua etiam illud sacrum Christi fidelibus pignus datum reconditur et tenetur, artificioso éx politis lapidibus opere construatur. Hæc enim domus rite noscitur pastori verissime dedicata, in illa nempe populus Domini et oves ejus Paschuæ cibum dulzoris assumunt. Sane in domo ista latices sacrosancti noxas perimunt, culpas diluunt et veternas cuilibet occurrenti. Heu igitur, quam dolendum sacrum Domini templum ecclesiam Sedis clarissimæ Gerundensis imperfectum opere minorari! Idcirco cunctis pateat, quod reverendus in Christo Pater et dominus dominus Dalmacius, Dei gratia episcopus Gerundensis, ipsius ecclesiæ tunc electus, et honorabile capitulum ecclesiæ Gerundensis prædictæ præmissa omnia pio sidere aspectantes, considerantesque a quantis citra temporibus fabrica dictæ Sedis cessavit ex diversorum controversia juxta opiniones varias artificum subsequentes, nonnulli enim asserebant opus dictæ fabricæ sub navi una debere congruentius consummari, affirmantes illud fore nobilius, quam si sub tribus navibus opus hujusmodi subsequatur. Alii autem a contrario asserebant dictum opus sub prosecutione trium navium continuari debere, dicentesque, quod firmius et proportionabilius esset capiti jamque cœpto, quam si cum navi una ipsa fabrica prosequatur, quoniam opus navis unius multum reddunt debile distantia parietum, ac etiam testudinis altitudo; et quod terræmotus, tonitrua, ventosque vagantes timebit apetentes etiam circa directionem operis dictæ fabricæ consummandæ solertius vacare, ac de opinione prædictorum veridica informari : et adeo ut controversia et opiniones hujusmodi clarius tollerentur, convocaverunt artifices peritissimos, lapiscidas de diversis partibus regni hujus, et etiam aliunde ad hanc civitatem Gerundæ, quorum nomina inferius annotantur, indeque habitis collationibus plurimis, tam coram dictis reverendo domino Episcopo, tunc electo, et honorabili capitulo dictæ ecclesiæ Gerundensis, quam alias inter ipsos artifices opere ·præmisso subjecto primitus oculis cujuslibet eorundem cernentium opus, quod cœptum fuerat, et qualiter hucusque fuerat; prosecutum in illo, et formatis super hujusmodi opere prosequendo articulis infrascriptis.

II

Inquiry [1]

In the name of God our Lord, and the Virgin our Lady Saint Mary, the " Maestros " Superintendents and masons summoned for the direction of the works of the cathedral of Gerona, must be asked the following questions:—

1. If the work of one nave of the said cathedral church, commenced of old, could be continued, with the certainty of remaining secure and without risk.

2. Supposing that it is not possible to continue the said work of one nave with safety, or that it will not be lasting, whether the work of three naves, continued on, would be congruous, sufficient, and such as would deserve to be prosecuted; or, on the contrary, if it ought to be given up or changed; and in that case unto what height it would be right to continue what is begun, and to specify the whole, in such sort as to prevent mistake?

3. What form or continuation of the said works will be the most compatible and the best proportioned to the Chevet of the said church which is already begun, made, and finished?

The " maestros " and masons, before being asked these questions, must take their oath; and after having given their declarations, the Lord Bishop of Gerona and the honourable Chapter shall elect two of the said masters, in order that they may form a plan or design, by which the work will have to be continued. All which the secretary of the Chapter will put in due form in a public writing,

---

[1] This interrogatory, and the declarations of the twelve architects, are in the Catalan idiom in the original, and are translated into Castilian by Fr. José de la Canal, *Esp. Sag.* xiv. 227-244. I have thought it best to give an English translation.

III

Successive dicti artifices, lapiscidæ sigillatim, ad partem medio a se corporaliter præstito juramento deposuerunt, et suam intentionem dixerunt in et super opere prelibato diebus, mensibus et annis inferius designatis et sub forma sequenti. Die jovis vicessima tertia mensis Januarii anno nativitatis Domini millesimo cccc. sexto decimo magistri et lapiscidæ sequentes juraverunt et deposuerunt apud civitatem Gerundæ infrascripti, præsentibus et interrogantibus venerabilibus viris dominis Arnaldo de Gurbo, et Joanne de Pontonibus canonicis, et Petro de Boscho præsbitero de capitulo dictæ ecclesiæ Gerundensis ad hoc per dictos reverendum dominum electum in Episcopum et capitulum Gerundense deputatis super articulis præinsertis et contentis in eisdem ut sequitur.

IV

Paschasius de Xulbe *lapiscida et magister operis sive fabricæ ecclesiæ sedis Dertusensis super primo dictorum articulorum sibi lecto medio juramento interrogatus, dixit :*—

1. That according to his knowledge and belief it is certain that the work of one nave of the cathedral of Gerona already commenced is secure, good, and firm; and that the foundations or bases of the old work already made are also so, and that the rest will be so if they are constructed in the same manner, and that they will be sufficient to sustain the vault of the said work of one nave.

2. Supposing that the work of one nave is not carried out, it is certain that the one of three naves, already commenced in the said church, is good and firm. But in the event of the plan of three naves being adopted, he says, that it would be necessary that the vault which is over the Coro, towards the altar of the same church, should be pulled down, and that it should be unroofed, in order that it may be raised eight palms—a little more or less—above what it is now, so that it may correspond to its third in its measurements.

3. That the plan of three naves is more compatible and better proportioned to the Chevet of the church than that of one nave.

Interrogatus.—Whether, in joining the lower voussoirs on the capital of the pillar over the pulpit, which corresponds to the other of the Coro, in case the work of three naves is carried out, there will be any risk of causing a settlement in the said pillar?—I answer, that there will be none, and that it can be done with safety.

II   X

V

JOANNES DE XULBE *lapiscida, filius dicti Paschasij de Xulbe, regens pro dicto patre suo fabricam prædictam, sive opus dictæ Ecclesiæ Dertusensis, simili juramento à se corporaliter præscripto, interrogatus super prædictis articulis deposuit ut infra.   Et primo super primo articulo interrogatus, dixit:—*

1. That the work of the nave already commenced can be continued, and that it will be good, firm, and without danger; but that the arches must be made to the tierce point, and that the principal arch must be shored up.   That the first abutments of the old work, situated on the south, are good and firm, and that, making the others like them, they will be so also, and sufficient to sustain the vault which has to be executed in the said church.

2. That if the plan of one nave is not to be followed, it is possible to continue that of three; and that it will be more beautiful, stronger, and better than the other.   But that the three naves ought to be carried on according to those in the choir of the church; and then it will be more beautiful and admirable.   And that the new vault which is contiguous to the Chevet ought to be taken down, because it is bastard, and because it does not correspond with the said Chevet.

3. That the work of three naves in the form which has just been explained is the most compatible and the best proportioned to the Chevet of the church.

Interrogatus.—Whether in joining the lower voussoirs of the arch above the capital of the pillar which is above the pulpit, corresponding to the other of the choir, in case the work of three naves is carried out, there will be any risk of causing a settlement in the said pillar?—I say no, provided that the arches are well shored, so that they can have no thrust.

VI

PETRUS DE VALLFOGONA, *lapiscida et magister fabricæ Ecclesiæ Terraconensis juramento prædicto medio super dictis articulis interrogatus deposuit. Et primo super primo articulo interrogatus dixit:—*

1. That the work of the said church, already commenced, of one nave can be continued, and that it will be good, safe, firm, and without risk.   That the abutments and foundations of the old work are so, and that those which have to be made will be so if constructed in the same way, and that they are sufficient to support

the vault which such a work ought to have. But that the abutments made towards the campanile require to be strengthened more than those constructed on the south side.

2. That if the plan of one nave is not carried out, that of three is congruous and worthy to be continued, provided that the second bay of vaulting, as far as the capitals and lowest voussoirs inclusive, is taken down; yet if above the principal arch a discharging arch is erected, it will not be necessary to move the lower voussoirs or the capitals, and it would be possible to raise the Crossing of that vault all its width as much as is required; and it could have a light in the gable, which could have a clear opening of fifteen or sixteen palms, which would be a notable work. He says further: that the lower voussoirs which are in the northern and southern angles ought to be altered, and that they ought to be reconstructed in accordance with the plan of three naves.

3. That without comparison the plan of three naves, in the form which has just been explained, is more compatible and more proportioned to the Chevet of the church than the plan of one nave.

Interrogatus.—Whether, in case the plan of three naves is carried out, there will be any danger in opening a hole in the pillar over the pulpit corresponding to the other of the Coro at the time of joining the voussoirs above the capital?—He said, that there would not; and that it could be done with safety.

VII

Postmodum die veneris vicessima quarta dictorum mensis et anni in manu et posse mei ejusdem Bernardi de Solerio, notarii subscripti, præsentibus et interrogantibus dictis dominis Arnaldo de Gurbo, Joanne de Pontonibus, et Petro de Boscho, magistri et lapiscidæ sequentes super prædictis, medio simili juramento, deposuerunt ut sequitur.

VIII

GUILLERMUS DE LA MOTA, *lapiscida, socius magistri in opere fabricæ Ecclesiæ Terraconæ super prædictis articulis, medio juramento, ut supra interrogatus deposuit. Et primo super primo articulo interrogatus, dixit :—*

1. That he considers that the plan of the church commenced with one nave could.be well executed, and that the Crossing will be firm; but that it is observed in old works, that bulky buildings, as that of one nave would be, sink with earthquakes or with great

hurricanes, and for these causes he fears that the work of one nave might not be permanent.

2. That the plan of three naves is good, congruous, and one that deserves to be followed, provided that the second Crossing may be new to the lowest voussoirs; and that its principals be demolished as far as the capitals, and that horizontal courses of stones be carried up to the height of fourteen or fifteen palms. That the springers which are towards the north and the south ought also to be taken down, and that they ought to be reconstructed in proper proportion to the plan of three naves.

3. That without comparison the plan of three naves is more compatible and more proportioned to the Chevet of the church than that of one nave.

Interrogatus.—If there will be danger in opening a hole in the pillar near the pulpit, to place the springers?—He said that there would not be any risk.

IX

Bartolomæus Gual., *lapiscida et magister operis sedis Barchinonensis super prædictis articulis, ut supra dicitur, interrogatus, medio juramento prædicto deposuit. Et primo super primo articulo interrogatus dixit :*—

1. That the bases and abutments of the old work of one nave are sufficiently strong, making a wall over the capitals between the abutments, which may rise a " cana " [1] from the windows, and that from that wall a vault may spring, which will abut against each of the abutments, and in this way they would remain safe. No doubt the vault may remain firm over one nave, so that it may resist earthquakes, violent winds, and other mishaps which may occur.

2. That the plan of three naves is good, congruous, and such as deserves to be carried out; but that the new vault of the second arch, the last done, ought to be taken down to the springing, and ought to be raised until there is room in that place for a circle (" una O ") of fourteen palms of opening: and in that way there will be beautiful and notable work, and it will not be necessary to undo the whole to the springing line.

3. That the plan of three naves is beyond comparison much better proportioned and more compatible to the Chevet of the church than that of one nave.

Interrogatus.—Whether there will be any risk in making an opening in the pillars in order to join the springers of the arches?

[1] " Cana," a measure of two ells Flemish.

—He said that there would not be; but he counsels that, when the said arch is taken out, the foot of the arch voussoir in the pillar which has to be altered should be larger than the other, because that has not so much weight on it.

X

ANTONIUS CANET, *lapiscida, magister sive sculptor imaginum civitatis Barchinonæ, magisterque fabricæ sedis Urgellensis super prædictis articulis ut prædicitur, interrogatus medio dicto juramento deposuit Et primo super primo articulo interrogatus, dixit :*—

1. That according to his knowledge and conscience the plan of one nave, already commenced, can be continued with the certainty that it will be good, firm, and secure: and that the abutments which the said work has are good and firm for the support of the vault, and all that is necessary in order to carry on the said work.

2. That the work already begun of three naves is good and well proportioned, but that it is not so noble as that of one nave; and that if the work of three naves is continued it would be necessary that the vault of the second bay of the middle nave should be taken down to the capitals; and that the capitals as well should be taken down eight or ten courses of stone, and so that the first pillar may be joined, which was constructed in the head of the grand nave, con·tiguous to the Chevet of the church, and that the opening shall not be made so low in the pillar, and the springing of the arch stones may be introduced in it better. And though it is true that in this way the (triforium) gallery may be lost, it is worth more to lose it than the bright effect of light in the temple, which could be secured by a round window in the said grand nave. But that, if the second nave is followed out as it was commenced, it will be most gloomy. For which reason he is sure that if the plan of three naves is to be good, it is necessary for it to be carried out working in the way he has described.

3. That the plan of one nave would be much more compatible and better proportioned to the Chevet of the church as it is already commenced and completed, than that of three naves, because the said Chevet was commenced low; and that the plan of one nave will be executed with a third at least of the cost of three naves. That if the plan of one nave is followed, the galleries, which are beautiful, will not be lost, and the church will be beyond comparison much more light.

XI

GUILLERMUS ABIELL, *lapiscida et magister operum seu fabricarum ecclesiarum Beatæ Mariæ de Pinu et Beatæ Mariæ de Monte Carmelo, et de Monte Sion, et Sancti Jacobi Barchinonæ, et hospitalis Sanctæ Crucis, civitatis ejusdem, sic etiam super prædictis, dicto juramento medio, interrogatus, dixit :—*

1. That according to his understanding and good conscience the work already commenced of one nave can be continued, and will be good, firm, and secure; and that the foundations which it has, the rest being made in the same way, are good and firm to support the work of one nave without danger.

2. That the plan of three naves is good, beautiful, and more secure than the other, wherefore it deserves to be continued. But that the vault of the second bay of the middle nave ought to be taken down to the springers, and be raised afterwards by its third, so that a fine round window may be had there, and to make an upper vault above the principal: and in this way the plan of three naves will be very beautiful.

3. That without any doubt the plan of three naves is more compatible and adequate to the choir of the church as it is now, than that of one nave, because that of one nave would be so wide that it would have great deformity when compared with the Chevet of the church.

XII

ARNALDUS DE VALLERAS, *lapiscida et magister operis sedis Minorisæ super dictis articulis, prout alii, interrogatus deposuit medio dicto juramento ut sequitur. Et primo super primo articulo interrogatus dixit :—*

1. That the work of one nave, already commenced, can very well be continued, and will be good, firm, secure, and without risk; and that the foundations which the said work has, and the rest which may be made like them, are good, and sufficient to sustain the work of a single nave; and that, though they might not be so strong, they would be firm and secure. He says further, that the work of the Church of Manresa is now being constructed, which is higher than this, which has not such great or strong foundations, and is not of so strong a stone. It is true, he says, that the Manresa stone is lighter, and combines better with the mortar than that of Gerona; and that, if he could have to construct the

latter church, he would make the vault· of other stone which was lighter, and which combined better with the mortar, but that the vaulting ribs, the lower part of the walls, the abutments, and the rest of such work could be executed in Gerona stone.

2. That the plan of three naves is good, congruous, and deserves to be carried out, provided that the vault of the second arch of the middle nave is taken down to the springers, and that they also are taken down, so that the work may be raised by its dimensions; so that it will be possible to have over the principal of the first arch a round window of twenty palms opening, with which it will look very well and not be disfigured.

3. That the plan of three naves in the manner which has been described is, without comparison, more fitting and better proportioned to the existing Chevet of this church than that of one nave; because that of one nave would make the choir appear to be so small and mis-shapen, that it would always demand that it should be raised or made larger.

Interrogatus.—Whether there would be any danger in opening a hole in the pillars in order to insert the abutments?—He said that there would not; and that if he, the deponent, should do the work, he would commence first by opening a hole in the pillars in order to join the abutments, since in that way they could not settle or give way, as certainly and without doubt might happen. That he was ready to come and continue this work in the manner which he had described; obtaining the licence of the city of Manresa, with which he had contracted to construct the church there.

XIII

ANTONIUS ANTIGONI, *magister major operis ecclesiæ villæ Castilionis Impuriarum super prædictis interrogatus, dicto juramento medio deposuit. Et primo super primo articulo interrogatus dixit :—*

1. That the plan of one nave, formerly commenced, could be continued well and firmly without any risk; and the foundations that it has, and the rest which have to be made like them, are sufficient to sustain with all firmness the said work of one nave.

Interrogatus.—Whether the work of one nave, in case it were made, would run any risk of falling with hurricanes and earthquakes?— He said that there was no cause for fear.

2. That the work of three naves continued of late is not congruous, nor of such sort as that its plan could be followed, because in no way could it be constructed with the same dimensions. But it is true that if the vault of the bay last done is taken down to the

springers, and raised afterwards fourteen or fifteen palms in its measurements, the plan of three naves would be more tolerable, though it could never be called beautiful or very complete.

3. That he has no doubt that the work of one nave would be for all time without comparison the most beautiful, more compatible and better proportioned to the Chevet of the church than that of three naves, since it will be always clear that the latter was not done carefully and with good taste.

Interrogatus.—Whether in case the work of three naves is carried out, there will be any risk in opening a hole in the pillars in order to join the abutments?—He said that it could be done, but not without danger.

XIV

GUILLERMÚS SAGRERA, *magister operis sive fabricæ ecclesiæ Sancti Joannis Perpigniani ut supra interrogatus dicto juramento medio deposuit. Et primo super primo articulo interrogatus dixit :—*

1. That the plan of one nave, formerly commenced, can be continued, and that it will be good, firm, and secure; and that the foundations which it has, with the rest which must be made in the same way, are sufficient to sustain it.

Interrogatus.—Whether if the one nave is adopted there will be risk by reason of earthquakes and violent winds?—He said that with the earthquakes which he has seen, and the winds which naturally prevail, there would be no danger that the said work should fall or become decayed.

2. That the work of three naves lately commenced is not congruous, and does not deserve to be carried on; and in case it is continued, in the first place the vault of the second bay ought to be taken down from the springers to the capitals; in the second, also, the other pillars which were made afterwards ought to be taken down, in order that they may be raised fifteen palms or thereabouts; and that with all this the work will not be completed well, but on the contrary will be *mesquin* and miserable. That the gallery, which would be lost, could not remain there; that it would not be possible to place the series of windows due to the work between the chapels higher than they would be in a single nave, owing to the thrust or pressure of the arches, which would be towards the gallery, corresponding to the new pillars of the enclosure of the choir, and would come against the void of the gallery, wherefore the work would not have the firmness it ought to have. The deponent concludes, saying, that for these and other reasons the said work of three naves would not be good or advantageous.

3. That the plan of one nave would be beyond comparison more compatible and more proportioned to the Chevet of the church already built, commenced, and completed, than would one of three naves; and he says it is the fact that the said choir of the church was made and completed with the intention that the remainder of the work should be made and carried out with a single nave.

XV

JOANNES DE GUINGUAMPS, *lapiscida, habitator civitatis Narbonæ super prædictis articulis, sicut alii prædicti interrogatus medio dicto juramento deposuit ut sequitur. Et primo super primo articulo interrogatus dixit :—*

1. That the work already commenced of one nave could very well be made and continued; and that when it is done it will be very good, firm, and secure, without any dispute; and that the foundations which are already made in the old work, and the others which will be made in the same way, are good, and have sufficient strength to maintain the work of a single nave.

2. That the plan of three naves latterly continued is not congruous or sufficient, and should not in any way be made or followed, because it never will have reasonable conformity with the Chevet.

3. That the plan of a single nave is beyond comparison more fit and proportioned to the choir of the said church, than would be that of three naves, for several reasons. 1st. That the deponent knows that the plan of a single nave with the said choir would be more reasonable, more brilliant, better proportioned, and less costly. 2nd. Because, if the work is carried on with one nave, there would not be the deformity of difference that disgusts. And though some may say that the plan of a single nave would make the choir look low and small, the more on that account would no deformity be produced, rather it would be more beautiful; and the reason is, that in the space which would be left between the top of the choir and the centre of the great vault, there would be so large a space that it would be possible to have there three rose windows: the first and principal in the middle, and another small one on each side: and these three roses would do away with all deformity, would give a grand light to the church, and would endow the work with great perfection.

Interrogatus.—Whether, if the plan of three naves is adopted, it would be dangerous to open the pillars in order to join in them the springers corresponding to it?—He said that he would not do it or consent to it on any account, because great danger, great wrong, and great damage would result, since in no part could the work be brought to perfection, and such a fissure could not be made without great risk.

XVI

Postmodum die Lunæ, quæ fuit vicesima octava mensis Septembris, anno jam dicto a Nativitate Domini millessimo cccc. sexto decimo, ad instantiam dicti domini Petri de Boscho operarii hoc anno dictæ ecclesiæ Gerundensis, super ipsius regimine operis una et in solidum cum honorabili viro domino Francisco Sacalani canonico dictæ ecclesiæ electi et deputati apud domos Thesaurariæ dictæ ecclesiæ Gerundensis coram dictis reverendo in Christo patre et domino domino Dalmacio Dei gratia episcopo et honorabili capitulo ejusdem ecclesiæ Gerundensis ad tactum cimbali, ut moris est, ibidem convocatis et congregatis; ubi fuerunt præsentes dictus reverendus dominus dominus Dalmacius, episcopus, et honorabiles viri Dalmacius de Roseto, decretorum doctor, archidiaconus de Silva in dicta ecclesia Gerundensi, Arnaldus de Gurbo, Joannes de Pontonibus, Guillermus de Brongarolis, sacrista secundus, Joannes de Boscho Thesaurarius, Joannes Gabriel Pavia, Petrus de Boscho prædictus, Guillermus Marinerii, Petrus Sala, Franciscus Mathei, et Bartholomeus Vives, presbiteri capitulares et de capitulo ante dicto, capitulum ejusdem ecclesiæ Gerundensis facientes, representantes et more solito celebrantes: dicti articuli et dictæ depositiones, et dicta a dictis artificibus super eisdem in scriptis redacta et continuata in dicto capitulo publice, alta et intelligibilli voce de verbo ad verbum lecta fuerunt, et publicata per me eundem Bernardum de Solerio, notarium, supra et infra scriptum. Et eis sic lectis et publicatis, illico dicti reverendus dominus episcopus et honorabile capitulum super concludendo et determinando per quem modum juxta opiniones, depositiones et dicta dictorum artificum melius pulchrius et efficacius dictum opus præfatæ ecclesiæ Gerundensis sub prosecutione videlicet unius aut trium navium prosequatur et consumetur, retinuerunt sibi deliberationem et ad hujusmodi fuerunt pro testibus presentes et evocati discreti viri Franciscus Tabernerii et Petrus Puig presbiteri benefficiati in dicta ecclesia Gerundensi.

XVII

Deinde vero die Lunæ octava mensis Martii anno a Nativitate Domini millessimo cccc. decimo septimo alius artifex lapiscida infrascriptus juravit et deposuit in dicta civitate Gerundæ in posse mei Bernardi de Solerio notarii supra et infra scripti, præsentibus et interrogantibus venerabilibus viris dominis Arnoldo de Gurbo, canonico, et Guillermo Marinierii presbitero de capitulo dictæ ecclesiæ Gerundensis, ad hoc per dictos reverendum dominum Dalmacium episcopum et honorabile capitulum Gerundense, specialiter deputatis super articulis præinsertis, et contentis in eisdem ut sequitur.

XVIII

GUILLERMUS BOFFIY, *magister operis sedis dictæ ecclesiæ Gerundensis simili juramento a se corporaliter præstito super primo articulo dictorum articulorum interrogatus, dixit et deposuit :—*

1. That the work of the nave of the church of Gerona, already begun, could be made and continued very well; and that if it is continued it will be firm and secure without any doubt, and that the foundations, and others which may be made like them, are and will be good and firm enough to sustain the said work of one nave. And that it is true that the said foundations or abutments, even if they were not so strong, would be sufficient to maintain the said work of one nave, since they have a third more of breadth than is required: wherefore they are very strong, and offer no kind of risk.

2. That the work of three naves for the said church does not merit to be continued when compared with that of one nave, because great deformity and great cost will follow from it, and it would never be so good as that of one nave.

3. That the work of one nave is, without comparison, the most conformable to the choir of the church already commenced and made, and that the plan of three naves would not be so. And that, if the plan of one nave is carried out, it would have such grand advantages, and such grand lights, that it would be a most beautiful and notable work.

XIX

Post prædicta autem omnia sic habita et secuta, videlicet die Lunæ, intitulata quinta decima dicti mensis Martii, anno jam dicto a Nativitate Domini millesimo cccc. decimo septimo, mane videlicet, post missam sub honore beatæ Mariæ Virginis gloriosæ in dicta Gerundensi ecclesia solemniter celebratam, dictis reverendo in Christo patre et domino domino Dalmacio episcopo, et honorabilibus viris capitulo dictæ ecclesiæ Gerundensis, hac de causa ad trinum tactum cimbali, ut moris est, de mandato dicti domini episcopi apud domos prædictas Thesaurariæ dictæ ecclesiæ Gerundensis simul convocatis et congregatis: ubi convenerunt, et fuerunt præsentes dictus reverendus dominus Dalmacius episcopus, et honorabiles viri

Dalmacius de Raseto, decretorum doctor, archidiaconus de Silva, Arnaldus de Gurbo, Joannes de Pontonibus, canonici, Guillermus de Burgarolis, sarista secundus, Joannes de Boscho, Thesaurarius, Joannes Gabriel Pavia, Petrus de Boscho, Guillermus Marinerii, Petrus Sala, Bacallarii in decretis, Franciscus Mathei et Bartholomeus Vives licentiatus in decretis, presbiteri capitulares et de capitulo ante dicto, ipsi reverendus dominus episcopus et honorabiles viri et capitulum prænotati, sicut præmititur capitulariter convocati et congregati, et capitulum dictæ ecclesiæ Gerundensis facientes, representantes, et more solito celebrantes, visis et recognitis per eosdem, ut dixerunt, prædictorum artificum et lapiscidarum depositionibus ante dictis in unum concordes deliberaverunt, *sub Navi una prossequi magnum opus antiquum Gerundensis ecclesiæ,* prælibatis rationibus quæ sequuntur: tum quia ex dictis præmissorum artificum clare constat, quod si opus trium navium supradictum opere continuetur jam cœpto, expedit omnino quod opus expeditum supra chorum usque ad capitellos ex ejus deformitate penitus diruatur et de novo juxta mensuras cœpti capitis reformetur: tum quia constat ex dictis ipsorum clare, eorum uno dempto, nemine discrepante, quod hujusmodi opus magnum sub navi una jam cœptum est firmum, stabile et securum si prosequatur tali modo et ordine, ut est cœptum, et quod terræmotus, tonitrua nec turbinem ventorum timebit: tum quia ex opinione multorum artificum prædictorum constat, dictum opus navis unius fore solemnius, notabilius et proportionabilius capiti dictæ ecclesiæ jam incepto, quam sit opus trium navium supradictum: tum quia etiam multo majori claritate fulgebit quod est lætius et jucundum: tum quia vitabuntur expensæ, nam ad prosequendum alterum operum prædictorum modo quo stare videntur opus navis unius multo minori prætio, quam opus trium navium, et in breviori tempore poterit consumari.

Et sic rationum intuitu præmisarum dictus reverendus dominus episcopus et honorabile capitulum supradictæ ecclesiæ Gerundensis voluerunt, cupierunt, et intenderunt, ut dictum est, opus magnum unius navis prædictum, quantum cum Deo poterunt prosequi et deduci totaliter ac effectum. Et talis fuerunt intentionis domini episcopus et capitulum ante dicti præsente me eodem Bernardo de Solerio, notario supra et infra scripto et præsentibus venerabilibus viris, etc. etc. etc.

I

CONTRACT OF GUILLERMO SAGRERA FOR THE EXCHANGE AT PALMA

Contract entered into at Palma in Mallorca, March 11, 1426, by which the Architect Guillermo Sagrera bound himself to construct or to continue the Construction of the Exchange of that City, according to Plans which he presented, and to the Conditions expressed.

RECITES the names of the contracting parties for the erection of the fabric of the Exchange which is being built in the Place called " del Boters," outside the walls of the city.

(The following conditions were written in the " Lemosin " or Mallorcan idiom.)

Firstly.—That the said Guillermo Sagrera promises and agrees in good faith with the said honourable members of the Building Council (Fabriqueros), that, God helping, he will complete the building of the said Exchange, to the covering of its vaults, in the first twelve years from the date of the contract: the said Exchange to be eight " canas [1] of Monpeller " in height, reckoning from the pavement to the keystone.

Item.—That the said twelve years being passed, the said Guillermo Sagrera will be obliged in the three succeeding years to make and finish all the towers, turrets, and other works which pertain to the said Exchange above the roof.

Item.—That the said Guillermo must and is bound to do all the said work at his own cost and charge, as well what may be necessary by reason of his art, as for wooden scaffolding and centering; and also for paying for all the stone, lime, gravel, and all the instruments and tools necessary for the work; and in the same manner for all the workmen, officials, and others working in the said Exchange and outside it; and lastly all the other things necessary for its completion.

Item.—That the said Guillermo is obliged to continue and complete the said work of the Exchange in the form which was begun, and according to the designs given and put into the hands of the honourable Council of the Fabric by the said Guillermo.

Item.—That the said Guillermo binds himself to build from the base and to complete all the pillars and keystones of the said Exchange in Santañi stone, fluted and according to the said design, and to floor it with the same stone, and to lay the terrace with the mixture of burnt clay and fresh lime which they call " Trespoll."

[1] A " cana " equals two yards and three inches Spanish measure.

Item.—That the said Guillermo binds himself to make the pendents of the said Exchange of Solleric stone.

Item.—That the said Guillermo binds himself to make on the outside part of the said Exchange, and above the gable of the doorway which looks towards the Royal castle of the said city of Mallorca, a solemn tabernacle with the figure of the modest Virgin our Lady Saint Mary.

Item.—That the said Guillermo binds himself to make on the other three fronts of the same Exchange, that is on the outside of each one of them, a figure of an angel, each one with his tabernacle over him; and that each of the said angels have on one side the Royal scutcheon, and on the other that of the said city of Mallorca, in the form and manner which may be pleasing to the said honourable Council of the Fabric.

Item.—That the said Guillermo binds himself to make in each one of the four corners of the said Exchange on the outside a grand statue, each one in his tabernacle, similar to the angels: that is, in the corner which looks towards the Pi Gate, that of San Nicolas; in that which looks towards the church of San Juan, that of S. John the Baptist; in that which looks towards the Arsenal, that of Sta Catalina; and in that which looks towards the said Royal castle, that of Sta. Clara; in the form and manner which may please the said honourable Council of the Fabric.

Item.—That the said Guillermo binds himself to make in one of the four turrets of the corners of the said Exchange a room where a clock can be placed.

Item.—That the said Guillermo binds himself to cover the abutments or buttresses with sharp-pointed stone weatherings, and in the top of each of the said weatherings there must be a great knop on which a flower-pot can stand; and that the balustrade which surrounds all the top of the Exchange shall be pierced with openings. And all the things which are at present within the said Exchange shall belong to the said Guillermo; and it is further declared that the aforenamed will not have to make gates nor iron screens in the said Exchange.

Item.—That the said honourable Council of the Fabric are to give and pay to the said Guillermo, on account of all the things before said and specified, 22,000 pounds of Mallorcan money, in instalments, in the form and manner following: To wit, That the said honourable Guardians and those who succeed them in the office of Guardians of the Merchants' Affairs shall be obliged to pay each year to the said Guillermo the sum for which they may have alienated the right of dues on the merchandise imposed by the said Mercantile College upon all the stuffs and merchandise entering and sailing from the island of

Mallorca, reserving to the said honourable Guardians in each year 150*l.* of the said money of Mallorca for the expenses and business of the College; and the said price of the said dues, the 150*l.* already referred to being deducted, is to be reserved for the said Guillermo every year in payment and satisfaction of the said 22,000*l.*; and this for such time and until the above-mentioned is wholly and completely paid and satisfied to the whole extent already mentioned. Declaring however and agreeing in which, the said Guillermo shall be bound to spend each year out of his own stock on the said work of the Exchange 500*l.* of the said money beyond that which he shall receive of the said price of the dues of merchandise.

Etc. etc.

Signed March 11th, 1426, by Guillermo Sagrera, Francesco Anglada, and Juan Terriola, and by others.[1]

[1] Cean Bermudez, *Arq. de España*, i. 276-279.

INDEX

INDEX

THE

Salamanca, i. 94
  Cathedral (*New*), i. 94, 95, 103 *et seq.*, 129 *n.*, 130 *n.*; (*Old*), i. 94, 95 *et seq.*, 115, 128 *nn.*, 129 *nn.*; ii. 30, 228, 231-233
  Plaza Mayor, i. 110
  San Cristobal, i. 130 *n.*
  San Emilian, i. 110 *n.*, 130 *n.*
  San Julian, i. 130 *n.*
  San Marcos, i. 110 *et seq.*, 130 *n.*
  San Martin, i. 112, 130 *n.*
  San Matteo, i. 112, 130 *n.*
  San Miguel, i. 110 *n.*, 130 *n.*
  San Nicolas, i. 110 *n.*, 130 *n.*
  San Pedro, i. 110 *n.*, 130 *n.*
  Santa Eulalia, i. 130 *n.*
  Santa Maria de los Caballeros, i. 110 *n.*, 130 *n.*
  Walls of, i. 94, 110, 128 *n.*
Salas, Church at, ii. 162, 164
Salórzano, Martin de, ii. 297
San Amat, Juan de, ii. 267
San Isidoro, Legend of, i. 156
  Body of, brought from Seville to Leon, i. 158, 159
San Juan, Pedro de, ii. 93 *n.*, 297
San Martin, Bridge of, Toledo, i. 301, 320, 322 *et seq.*, 344 *n.*
Sanchez, Bonifacio, ii. 297
Sanchez, Martin, i. 46, 47; ii. 297
Sanchez, Pedro, ii. 297
Sancii, ii. 110
Sandoval, Cistercian Church of, ii. 228, 260 *n.*
Sangüesa, ii. 174 *n.*
  San Salvador, ii. 174 *n.*
  Santa Maria la Real, ii. 174 *n.*, 175 *n.*
  Santiago, ii. 174 *n.*
Santa Celay, Miguel de, ii. 297
Santa Eulalia enshrined in Barcelona Cathedral, ii. 57 *n.*, 58, 60
Santa Fé, Sperandeo de, ii. 194 *n.*
Santa Maria, Bishop Pablo de, Story of, i. 63
Santiañes de Pravia, Church at, ii. 225, 250 *n.*
Santiago, i. 158, 177, 182, 188 *et seq.*, 212 *nn.*
  Cathedral, i. 189 *et seq.*, 212 *nn.*; ii. 108, 228
  Plaza de los Plateros, i. 202
  Plaza de San Martin, i. 198, 199
  Plaza Mayor, i. 198
  Puerta Santa, i. 199
  San Benedict, i. 218 *n.*
  San Felix, i. 218 *n.*
  San Jerónimo, i. 198, 218 *n.*
  San Martin, i. 198

Santa Maria de Sar, i. 219 *n.*
Santa Maria Salomé, i. 218 *n.*
Santa Susanna, i. 218 *n.*
Santo Domingo, i. 218 *n.*
Scenery around, i. 188, 189
Santiago, Comendidoras de, i. 355 *n.*
Santillana, Juan de, i. 48; ii. 297
Saravia, Rodrigo de, i. 106; ii. 298, 301
Sculpture in Spain, ii. 248
Segarra, Raymundo de, ii. 131
Segorbe, Church at, ii. 19 *n.*
Segovia, i. 256
  Alcazar, i. 257, 263, 266, 273, 274, 276 *n.*
  Cathedral, i. 228, 257 *et seq.*; ii. 240-243
  El Parral, i. 257, 262, 263, 276 *n.*; ii. 242
  Plasterwork in, i. 273
  Plaza de la Constitucion, i. 257
  San Andrés, i. 272, 276 *n.*
  San Clemente, i. 277 *n.*
  San Esteban, i. 245, 266, 268, 276 *n.*
  San Facundo, i. 272, 276 *n.*
  San Juan, i. 273, 276 *n.*
  San Lorenzo, i. 273, 277 *n.*
  San Martin, i. 271, 276 *n.*
  San Miguel, i. 273, 277 *n.*
  San Millan, i. 257, 266 *et seq.*, 276 *n.*
  San Nicolas, i. 272
  San Quirse, i. 272, 276 *n.*
  San Roman, i. 272, 276 *n.*
  Santa Trinidad, i. 272
  Templars' Church, i. 257, 260, 262, 270, 276 *n.*, 306
Segre, ii. 128, 130
Seminario Conciliar of Salamanca, i. 109, 130 *n.*
Serra, Pere, ii. 153 *n.*
Sigüenza, i. 286
  Cathedral of, i. 286 *et seq.*, 294 *n.*; ii. 233, 234
  N. S. de las Huertas, i. 295 *n.*
  N. S. del Campo Santo Vejo, i. 295 *n.*
  San Vicente, i. 295 *n.*
  Santiago, i. 295 *n.*
Siloe, Diego de, i. 30; ii. 298
Siloe, Gil de, i. 23, 46, 49, 84; ii. 275, 298
Simancas, Don Manuel, i. 355 *n.*
Solado, Alfonso Fernandez, i. 355 *n.*
Solivez, Francesch, ii. 148 *n.*
Soria, i. 295 *n.*
  San Juan de Duero, i. 298 *n.*
  Santo Tomé, i. 298 *n.*

THE TEMPLE PRESS, PRINTERS, LETCHWORTH

Lightning Source UK Ltd.
Milton Keynes UK
UKOW04f0611081217
314098UK00001B/2/P